D0913226

The Truman Doctrine
and the
Origins of McCarthyism

The Truman Doctrine and the Origins of McCarthyism

Foreign Policy, Domestic Politics,
and Internal Security
1946-1948

E 70

Richard M. Freeland

Schocken Books · New York

For my mother and father,
Margaret Child Freeland
and
Harry Middleton Freeland

Thus we debase
The nature of our seats, and make the rabble
Call our cares fears; which will in time break ope
The locks o' the senate, and bring in the crows
To peck the eagles.

Coriolanus, III, 1

Contents

Acknowledgments

ONE OF THE PLEASURES of writing this book was discovering
how rich are the collections of materials available to a student
of recent American history, and how ready the keepers of these
materials to assist the researches of an obscure scholar. I
visited several collections of documents: the Harry S. Truman
Library, the Library of Congress, the Clements Library at the
University of Michigan, the State Department Historical Office, Clemson University Library, and the Firestone Library at
Princeton University. At all of these institutions I found the
administrators and archivists helpfully attentive, and more
than once I was directed by a librarian to a valuable source
that otherwise I would have missed. I am particularly grateful to the people of the Harry S. Truman Library, whose fi
nancial support made possible two visits to their valuable collection. I also found useful the recollections of individuals
who participated in the events of which I was writing, and
most of the men whom I approached were quite ready to talk
at length. For their patience and assistance I want to thank
Clark Clifford, Jennings Randolph, James Reston, and Steven
Spingarn.

I am indebted to the gentlemen who presided over the
graduate program in American Civilization at the University
of Pennsylvania between 1965 and 1968, particularly Anthony
N. B. Garvan and Murrey G. Murphey, for their readiness to
subsidize me during three years of work on my doctoral dissertation. I also recognize an abiding debt to Gabriel Kolko,
my thesis adviser at Pennsylvania, whose perceptions about
modern American foreign policy prodded my thoughts and
whose personal commitment to scholarship inspired my efforts. Francis L. Broderick, Allen Guttman, and William Ken-
dall read the book at different moments in its development,
and I am grateful for their thoughtful responses.

Angus Cameron of Alfred A. Knopf, Inc., is the man most responsible for encouraging me to expand my doctoral dissertation into the present volume. Were it not for his readiness to take seriously the thoughts of a fledgling historian, I might never have written this book. And, during the writing, his criticism and memories were immensely helpful. Elizabeth Long was the well-placed friend-in-need who initially urged my manuscript upon her colleagues at Knopf. This book is the result of a scheme she and I hatched late one night in a White Tower in New Haven. Bette Alexander, Jean Walker, and Judy Pomerantz, all of Knopf, have been extremely helpful in getting me through various parts of the process of publication.

I want particularly to mention four good friends whose assistance and support were indispensable. Bruce Kuklick and I, as fellow graduate students at Pennsylvania, collaborated to help each other's work and protect each other's egos. Bruce has read and discussed the manuscript with me at every stage of its development and has been a steady source of ideas and encouragement. I have probably adopted more of his thoughts on foreign policy than I would care to admit. Edward F. Greene, a lawyer and amateur historian, read two complete versions of the manuscript with exceptional perception and understanding. Ed consistently forced me to rethink ill-conceived arguments and consider questions I hadn't formulated for myself. He is a gifted teacher whose talents, I hope, will not be entirely consumed by corporate transactions. Stephen L. Skillman, also a lawyer, critiqued line-by-line two complete drafts of the book. His was such a monumental editorial effort that I was sometimes embarrassed by the fear that the book was not worthy of it. Steve is responsible for dozens of improvements in the text and several important refinements of the argument. Finally, Ken Waltzer, whom I met during the last year of my work on the book, vastly increased my understanding of the domestic politics of the period of which I was writing. It was Ken and his wife, Sandy, who time after time took me in, fed me, and generally sustained me during the often lonely year required to produce this final draft.

The Truman Doctrine
and the
Origins of McCarthyism

Introduction

THIS BOOK had its origins in my curiosity about certain aspects of the world in which I grew up—the United States in the 1950's. These were years when fear of communism dominated much of American life, thought, and official policy. Even those of us then too young to understand their immense significance were affected by the televised drama of the Army-McCarthy hearings and the huge sections of our classroom maps blocked out in menacing scarlet. For me, as for most Americans, the peril of communism was a fixed and unquestioned condition of the 1950's. By the mid-1960's, however, the continuing preoccupation of the country with this issue began to seem odd, and I started searching for explanations. I found only difficult questions. It was commonly understood, for example, that in the 1950's the United States had attained a position of international economic and military power unmatched by any nation in modern history; how then did the idea take hold that any gain by communist forces, in whatever country, however remote and tiny, was a direct threat to American interests, to be opposed by the full force of American power? It was also evident that in the 1950's the United States had experienced levels of prosperity unknown in previous decades; why then did the specter of internal communist subversion assume an ominous reality for large numbers of American citizens? These puzzles deepened my curiosity, and reinforced the sense—now generally accepted and fully consistent with respect for the dangers of U.S.-Soviet conflict and domestic communist activity—that the anti-communist emotions of the 1950's were excessive. The origins of these excesses, for which Senator

Joseph McCarthy of Wisconsin provided a symbol and a name, are the subject of this book.

Much has been written about McCarthyism. In looking for its causes, most authors have concentrated on cycles of repression in American history, traditional political and social conflicts between classes and regions, or deep-rooted fears and obsessions of the American psyche. The present study does not challenge such approaches to the problem; indeed, I doubt that we can develop a full explanation of America's postwar anticommunism without them. What has been neglected in these studies, however—and what this book attempts to provide—is a close look at the immediate events that brought the fears and hostilities associated with McCarthyism to the surface of American life. By neglecting this examination, most students of this subject have tended, explicitly or implicitly, to regard McCarthyism as inevitable and thus to avoid the effort to discover ways in which political leaders could have prevented it—or might prevent its recurrence. The present study attempts to permit the reader to make judgments on these neglected questions.

It is not difficult to identify the events that provided Senator McCarthy with the emotional material he needed, by triggering widespread belief that communism was an immediate threat to the United States. The most important were the Soviet Union's explosion of an atomic bomb in 1949, the conquest of China in the same year by the armies of Mao Tse-tung and the subsequent outbreak of the Korean War, and the decision of a Federal Court in 1950 that Alger Hiss had been a Communist and had given classified documents to the Soviets.[1] The intrinsic significance of these events was great, but the public reaction to them lacked perspective. The Soviet atomic explosion and the Communist victory in China had been anticipated by American officials and did not create any immediate danger to the United States. Alger Hiss was a relatively unimportant figure who passed no important secrets to the Soviets. What needs to be explained, then, is the strength of the American reaction to these events: How can one account for the existence of a public mood in which developments like these caused many Americans to believe their country to be in imminent peril from communism?

This book argues that the emotional and political forces and the patterns of belief—what in aggregate might be called the "Cold War consensus"—that were to provide the essential energies of postwar anti-communism were quite fully developed by early 1948, well before any of the cited events occurred. These emotions were aroused and these patterns of belief developed, it is argued, as the result of a deliberate and highly organized effort by the Truman administration in 1947-8 to mobilize support for the program of economic assistance to Europe called the European Recovery Program, or Marshall Plan. In the absence of this Cold War consensus, it seems likely that the events that triggered McCarthyism would have been accepted with relative calm. Thus it is the campaign for foreign aid that must be analyzed if the inevitability of McCarthyism is to be assessed.

The stakes in the public debate on the Marshall Plan were immense. World War II had just ended; the United States had completed a costly military effort made necessary by America's strategic and economic interests in international developments, particularly in Europe. American armies were everywhere triumphant, but the postwar world seemed to be developing hazards as great for American interests—as perceived by the Administration in Washington—as had existed in 1939. Europe, the major foreign market for American goods, was failing to recover from the war and could not finance the high levels of imports from the United States that had been established under wartime aid programs. The American economy, having been lifted out of the depression by the war, was producing at an unprecedented rate and supporting levels of employment and income unknown in modern American history. American officials worried that unless the United States extended aid to Europe to permit transatlantic trade to continue while postwar recovery was being completed, American exports would decline, unemployment would rise, and the economy might slip back into its disastrous pre-war condition. Such a development would mean not only an immediate economic catastrophe for the country (and political catastrophe for the Truman administration), but would shatter plans that American officials had developed during the war to reorder postwar international commerce along lines conducive to international political stability and American trade. Moreover, unless the United States provided economic assistance, Europe would remain in economic conditions so distressed as to make internal political stability impossible in several major countries. With strong Communist parties in France and Italy, and Soviet armies massed across east central Europe while American armies were being hastily demobilized, the specter of continued economic disarray suggested the possibility of communist ascendency in major capitals of Europe. American officials could imagine such a development leading to a Soviet-dominated world.

The Truman administration was convinced that a program of economic aid could dispel these dangers and secure American economic and strategic interests in Europe. The effort would be large, but small in comparison to the cost of the war. And the consequences of not aiding Europe were unthinkable to American policymakers.

Yet the domestic political situation rendered it altogether possible that Congress would refuse to support aid to Europe. From the end of the war in 1945, through 1946 and into 1947, all indications were that American opinion was moving steadily away from interest in international affairs and support for the large federal budgets and interventionist economic techniques that a major aid program would entail. Both houses of the Congress elected in 1946 were controlled by the Republican Party, which was firmly opposed to the foreign economic policies of the Democratic administration and anxious to cut budgets and limit international commitments. These developments appeared to represent a repetition of the pattern that had emerged after the First World War, when, according to the familiar story, the American people had lost interest in world problems and had prevented the American government from playing the postwar role projected by President Wilson. In Washington as well as in European capitals it was widely believed that this pattern represented a fixed tendency of American opinion, and there was pessimism on both sides of the Atlantic about the likelihood of the United States sponsoring the type of aid program that the immediate situation required. Indeed, it seemed doubtful that the United States would accept the dominant position in postwar international politics that Roosevelt—like Wilson—had sought and that events had offered.

The pessimists were wrong, of course. The Marshall Plan was overwhelmingly approved by Congress in 1948, and it is widely credited with preserving traditional democracy in western Europe. Between 1949 and 1952, moreover, the Truman administration was able progressively to expand the international commitments and influence of the United States. Observers of the Truman presidency have tended to regard the development of America's international role as Truman's most important and remarkable achievement. The comment of Anthony Eden, British foreign minister under Churchill, and later Prime Minister, is typical: "In the United States [during the postwar period] were statesmen of wisdom, authority and courage who wrought a revolutionary change in their country's traditional policies. There was to be no withdrawal into isolationism as after the first World War." Dean Acheson, Under Secretary of State to George Marshall and Secretary of State from 1949 to 1952, has used similar terms to describe these developments. President Truman, he told a meeting of diplomats in 1950, "had been able to bring about a complete revolution in American foreign policy." [2]

The main battle of this "revolution" occurred during the public debate on the Marshall Plan, Truman's first major postwar proposal implying long-term commitments to international leadership. Between March 1947, when, in the Truman Doctrine speech, the President first publicly indicated his readiness to support massive aid to Europe, and March 1948, when the Marshall Plan was approved, the attitudes of the people of the United States underwent dramatic changes on almost every major question of international policy.

Prior to March 1947 the prevailing attitudes of the country toward international affairs were controlled by opinions formed during the war—optimism about the postwar period, belief that great-powers cooperation and particularly U.S.-Soviet cooperation could be preserved, confidence that the U.N. would be the dominant force in shaping postwar international developments; by March 1948 Americans had lost all hope of U.S.-Soviet cooperation, had even come to fear that war between the U.S.S.R. and the United States was possible in the near future, and had accepted as the basis of American policy unilateral, anti-Soviet programs that had little to do with the United Nations. In March 1947 public reaction against war and armaments had placed the Defense Department on the defensive, and Congress was considering the Defense budget only to reduce it; in March 1948 leaders in the Senate invited the Administration to strengthen the Armed Forces, and the Pentagon took the first steps toward arming the United States for its role in the Cold War. Prior to March 1947 the President was inclined to fear left-wing criticism of a foreign policy based upon opposition to the U.S.S.R., and had restrained American foreign policy for this reason; by early 1948 the Administration was confident that such criticisms had been neutralized, and no thought was given to modifying American policy to appease them. During the election campaign of 1946 the Administration had felt so constrained by opposition to new international programs, foreign aid, and a hard line toward the U.S.S.R. that public discussion of all these issues was suppressed. By the start of the 1948 campaign public acceptance of the Administration's position on all these matters was so general that it was not considered likely to be an issue in the campaign. Thus, during the year of public debate on the Administration's foreign aid program, a country that had seemed to be losing interest in international affairs was brought to see itself as the dominant and responsible force in the non-communist world; and a Congress that had seemed firmly opposed to foreign aid was persuaded to accept long-term commitments to international economic assistance without precedent in American history.

The procedure through which the Truman administration effected this remarkable transformation of public opinion contained two basic elements: the articulation of an interpretive framework within which international events could be explained so as to imply American policies of the kind to which the Administration was committed, and the cultivation of the broadest possible acceptance of this interpretive framework by the voting population of the country. In the Truman Doctrine speech the Administration committed itself to an interpretive framework based upon an ideological view of international affairs—the global assault of the "totalitarian" forces against the forces of "freedom"—calculated to command immediately the maximum public support. Though the public reaction to this speech was mixed and skeptical, in the year between its delivery and Congressional vote on the European Recovery Program, President Truman and his advisers successfully imbedded the world view of the Truman Doctrine in the national consciousness and effectively cast public discussion of international issues in these same terms. The Administration did this through a broad range of initiatives that fell into two general categories: propaganda activities and police activities.

By far the most important propaganda technique of the Truman administration was the consistent interpretation of major international events primarily in the terminology of the Truman Doctrine. The collapse of the brave hopes for the postwar world nourished by President Roosevelt, the pattern of events in eastern Europe, the failure of great-powers negotiations over Germany—all of these frustrating and disappointing developments were represented to the American people as the products of Soviet betrayal and aggression. The most important instance of this device, for the purposes of this study, was the attribution of the economic problems of western Europe to Soviet obstructionism and communist subversion, a view that distorted these problems and obscured the positive reasons for the Administration's advocacy of aid programs. At critical moments in the Congressional debate on foreign aid— an initial program of assistance to Greece and Turkey, the Interim Aid Program and European Recovery Program itself—

this device was combined with the techniques of crisis politics so that each of these debates occurred under the compelling influence of an international emergency that seemed to dramatize Soviet expansionism and to validate the world view of the Truman Doctrine. To support this propaganda offensive the Administration sponsored numerous speaking tours by its officials, encouraged supportive writing in the press, and released various diplomatic documents that appeared to demonstrate the hostile and imperialistic policies of the Soviet government. At the same time, a wide-ranging and highly publicized campaign against communist agents at work in the United States dramatized the issue on the home front. The Justice Department was the force behind three major programs that created the impression of widespread subversive activity: the Federal Employee Loyalty Program, the Attorney General's list, and a drive to deport subversive aliens. Simultaneously, the House Un-American Activities Committee conducted a series of spectacular investigations, with the support and assistance of the Truman administration, that kept the issue and danger of communism consistently before the public eye. Finally, the Justice Department sponsored a great patriotic campaign, built around the Freedom Train, in which the Truman Doctrine was raised to the level of the Declaration of Independence and the Constitution.

Police support for the progaganda offensive of the Truman administration took a number of forms. At the most general and informal level, the consistent identification by public officials of support for Cold War foreign policy with loyalty and patriotism, and the explicit labeling by the President among others of opponents of Cold War foreign policy as subversives and communists, tended to create very effective constraints upon political activities of a dissident nature. This type of restraint was not relied upon solely: the dragnet campaign against disloyal federal employees, triggering similar programs in other public bureaucracies at every level of government throughout the country, placed very explicit legal and economic constraints on enormous numbers of people. The tendency of these programs to confuse the issues of loyalty and security deepened the impact of the informal constraints arising from public denunciations of dissenters as disloyal. The Attorney General's list provided the Administration with a tool by which dissident organizations could be discredited without appeal on the basis of an obscure administrative determination. Activist aliens, several of whom were involved in propaganda activities in opposition to Cold War foreign policy, were arrested and held without bail. At the same time, new controls on the dissemination of public information were developed. Newsmen covering American military affairs were subjected to loyalty investigations similar to those given federal employees. Reporters considered hostile to the Administration were denied passports. Foreign visitors were prevented from engaging in public-speaking activities without the approval of the government.

The campaign for Cold War foreign policy was a spectacular success when viewed from the limited perspective of the effort to win acceptance of large-scale foreign aid. But the ideological rhetoric and propagandistic machinations of this campaign had consequences which were not entirely foreseen or desired by the Administration and became a major problem for both domestic politics and foreign policy. The campaign failed to mobilize public or Congressional support for the economic and commercial objectives that had provided much of the original impetus to the Marshall Plan; this ultimately limited the success of the aid program, for Congress refused to support legislation enabling the U.S. to adopt the commercial policies that the Marshall Plan had been designed to make possible. Moreover, the campaign implanted the idea in the public mind that the United States was imminently threatened by a massive, ideologically based assault upon everything Americans valued. This exaggerated representation of the dangers of international and domestic communism created the emotional and conceptual context within which Americans reacted to the Soviet explosion of the atomic bomb, the fall of China, the outbreak of the Korean War, and the conviction of Alger Hiss. These events, in turn, seemed to provide solid bases for the fears that the propaganda of the Truman administration had elicited. Ironically, these developments also discredited the Administration as the champion of anti-communism. Alert political opponents of the Truman administration, most notably Senator McCarthy, then were able to turn the propaganda of the campaign for foreign aid against its authors, and in the process stir the country to the heights of emotion that those who experienced the 1950's so vividly remember.

The following pages develop in detail the arguments outlined in this introduction. The book follows a simple design. The first chapter, discussing events from 1943–46, provides the general framework of interpretation of American foreign policy upon which all subsequent discussions of this subject rely. It also establishes the political and emotional conditions in the United States at the beginning of the debate on foreign aid. The next six chapters consider in detail the year between the Truman Doctrine speech and the Congressional vote on E.R.P. Chapters II, IV, and VI discuss chronologically the three key points in the debate on foreign aid. Chapters III, V, and VII relate the debate on foreign aid to developments in the area of internal security. The final chapter shows how these two themes became thoroughly intertwined in 1949 and 1950. It should be clear that although the book involves extensive discussions of international affairs, it is not a diplomatic history. It is a history of the domestic politics associated with a major foreign policy. International developments, for example U.S.-Soviet relations, are therefore discussed only as they were perceived and articulated by various groups in the U.S. The book makes no serious attempt at the kind of analysis of Soviet intentions and policies that would be required in a diplomatic history.

I
Origins of the
Foreign Aid Program

1. The Prospect of an American World Order

During World War II, American leaders developed plans to reorder international political and economic affairs. These plans portended serious difficulties in American relations with Britain and the Soviet Union and were of doubtful acceptability to the American people.

DURING THE FIRST TWO YEARS of its military involvement in World War II, the American government had to be concerned almost exclusively with repelling the extension of German and Japanese power in Europe and the Pacific. By early 1943, however, the offensive operations of the Axis powers had been halted in both theaters, and by the end of the year the military initiative had passed irreversibly to the Allies. Thereafter, the Americans and their British and Soviet associates could look forward to victory and a peace of their own devising.

By 1943 it was already evident that the postwar world would be vastly different from the one that had existed in 1939. Every traditional center of military and economic power in Europe would be enfeebled by ravaged populations and shattered economies. Among these countries, only the Soviet Union would emerge from the war more powerful than it had entered it: the war's end would find the Red Army positioned across east central Europe, farther west than Soviet power had ever reached, and without serious rival on the European mainland. Yet the Soviet Union, too, would have endured great losses, and behind the lines of political influence established by the Red Army would be a wounded and underdeveloped nation. In Asia, where Japanese conquests had isolated colonies from colonial proprietors, the stabilizing pre-war pattern of empire would be severely, perhaps irreparably, disrupted, and the forces of latent nationalism released; in the postwar period Asia would be a scene of vast and unpredictable social and political disorder. Three continents—Europe, Asia, and Africa—would have been turned into battlefields in the course of the war, causing devastation on an unimaginable scale. The task of reconstruction would be global.

The United States, like the Soviet Union, could expect its power to be increased at the end of the war. American arms would have been decisive in defeating the Axis in both Europe and Asia, which would assure the American government of a major voice in shaping the peace in both areas. Equally important—and unlike the Soviet Union—the postwar American economy, alone of the major industrialized economies of the world, would have been protected from the fire of war. Indeed, stimulated by the requirements of the Allied war effort, the American economy would have achieved unprecedented levels of production, and amidst the global devastation that the war's end would bring, it would be the only major source of money and material required by allies and enemies to rebuild. Its arms decisive in winning the war, its economy essential for reconstruction, the government of the United States could expect confidently to survive the war as the preeminent power of the globe. Faced with holding this position during a period in which pre-war patterns of international politics would have been irreparably shattered, the American government could contemplate a postwar opportunity to establish a new world order according to its own lights.

President Roosevelt and his chief advisers were acutely aware of this situation, and the need to take proper advantage of it was never far from their thoughts. Frances Perkins, Roosevelt's Secretary of Labor, has written that during cabinet meetings it was obvious that Roosevelt "never lost sight of the peace throughout the war years and at every point in the war his concern was how each victory could be woven into a pattern of permanent peace and world organization." For the President, as for his advisers, the feeling that careful planning for the postwar period was essential was intensified by the memory of Woodrow Wilson's doomed efforts to shape a new world order after World War I. Robert Sherwood recalls that Roosevelt "could never forget Wilson's mistakes" in pursuing his postwar objectives, and that "the tragedy of Wilson was always somewhere within the rim of his consciousness." Machinery for postwar planning was established early. In his memoirs, Secretary of State Hull refers to the formation of a committee on peace and reconstruction in September 1939 in order to demonstrate "how early we realized the necessity for postwar planning and the equal need for the United States to take her full share in the peace and after." After 1943 the planning activities initiated so early were intensified, not only in the State Department but also in the War, Treasury, and Commerce Departments.[1]

In developing plans for the postwar period, the officials responsible for American foreign policy sought a formula that would prevent a second recurrence of the terrible cycle, made familiar in their own lives, by which the settlement of one major war served only to create the conditions for another. The failure of Wilson's efforts to eliminate the causes of international conflict overshadowed all their thoughts on this matter. The program he had taken to Versailles had implied a drastic reordering of the political and economic bases of international relations. In place of military alliances, spheres of influence, and balances of power, international politics were to have been organized on the basis of a world community of nations in which the sovereignty of all nations was to be recognized and disputes were to be settled peacefully through an international organization. To undergird this system, Wilson had proposed to ban the nationalistic financial and commercial practices that had played such an important role in causing World War I, and to establish a new economic order in which all nations would have equal access to the markets of the world as well as to the sources of supply. Called multilateralism (because it would put an end to bilateral agreements that discriminated against the commerce of third nations), Wilson's economic system required that tariffs and other politically imposed trade barriers be reduced to a minimum and that remaining barriers apply equally to all nations. Although Wilson's political ideas had been institutionalized in the League of Nations, his economic principles had never been adopted. Indeed, the interwar years had brought a resurgence among the major trading nations of economic nationalism, bilateralism, and high-tariff policies.

With remarkable unanimity, the men around President Roosevelt—Secretary of State Hull, Secretary of War Stimson, Treasury Secretary Morgenthau, Commerce Secretary Wallace, their top assistants—shared the belief that the economic policies followed by the major trading nations after World War I had led directly to the global depression of the 1930's, and then to the Second World War. They had all observed how American tariff policies had contributed to the difficulties experienced by Europe, particularly Germany, in recovering from World War I, and how the development by Germany and Japan of exclusive, state-controlled commercial systems had led to the deterioration of diplomatic relations between the United States and both countries. It was easy for them to believe that the establishment of political stability and lasting peace in the postwar period required, above all else, the reconstruction of the world economy along multilateral lines. Hull has described the basis of this view:

> Unhampered trade dovetailed with peace, high tariffs, trade barriers and unfair economic competition with war. . . . I reasoned that, if we could get a freer flow of trade—freer in the sense of few discriminations and obstructions—so that one country would not be deadly jealous of another and the living standards of all countries might rise . . . we might have a reasonable chance of establishing a lasting peace.

Free to plan for a postwar world in which American power would be irresistible, the leaders of the American government turned to economic multilateralism as the foundation of the new world order they would attempt to construct.[2]

Despite its origins in Wilsonian idealism and the desire of America's wartime leaders to build a stable and peaceful world, the tenets of multilateralism were intimately related to American global interests, both economic and political. To understand the economic significance of multilateralism, one need only recall the increase in productive capacity achieved by the American economy during the war. Between 1940 and 1944 the industrial output of the United States rose by 90 per cent, agricultural production by 20 per cent, and the total national production of goods and services by 60 per cent. These developments brought unprecedented levels of employment and income to the American people. These conditions occurred immediately after the most devastating economic depression in the nation's history. Roosevelt's advisers were haunted by the fear that the end of the war would bring a slackening of demand, production surpluses, and unemployment, thus initiating a downward spiral toward yet another economic disaster. By inducing other countries to lower tariffs and eliminate discriminatory trading arrangements, multilateralism would open the markets of the world to America's expanded economy. "Let us admit right off," stated the Assistant Secretary of State for Economic Affairs, Will Clayton, "that our objective has as its background the needs and interests of the people of the United States. We need markets—big markets—in which to buy and sell." Indeed, it was believed doubtful that the American economy could survive unchanged if such markets were not obtained. Dean Acheson argued before a Congressional committee that "You could probably fix it so that everything produced here would be consumed here, but that would completely change our constitution, our relations to property, human liberty, our very conception of law." Without multilateralism, in the view of these officials, the United States faced economic depression and the demise of capitalism. With it, as Hull pointed out, America's superior technical skill and productive capacity would assure it a "supreme position in world finance, commerce and industry." [3]

Though events would ultimately force the United States to consider the economic implications of multilateralism in a much broader framework, those responsible for postwar planning tended to view this issue primarily in the context of Anglo-American relations. There was good reason for this. Britain was not only one of the world's largest international traders, but also the dominant member of the single most important commercial system in the world, the Commonwealth trading bloc (or sterling bloc). This was a network of commercial arrangements or "Imperial preferences" among the nations of the Commonwealth that enabled them to trade with each other on terms far more favorable than those available to other countries. Prior to the war the sterling bloc and North America had accounted for about one half of the world's trade. Agreement between the U.S. and Britain could largely determine the future of international commercial practices. The elimination of Imperial preference by the Commonwealth trading bloc was the single most important commercial objective of the American program for the implementation of multilateralism.[4]

Although those responsible for directing American foreign policy were committed to reconstructing postwar international trade on a multilateral basis, established American commercial policies posed an obstacle to the realization of this goal. Hull's efforts to liberalize American trade policies during the 1930's notwithstanding, the United States maintained a formidable range of constraints upon foreign competition with American industry. American tariffs, though reduced from the levels set in 1930, remained high and would pose, after the war, significant and in many cases prohibitive obstacles to imports. Agricultural policies adopted during the depression to protect the farm economy restricted agricultural imports through a system of quotas, embargoes, and special import fees.[5] These policies were bound to present major issues in American negotiations with other governments concerning multilateralism: Great Britain had sponsored the Commonwealth trading bloc in retaliation against the high-tariff policies of the United States and was unlikely to dismantle its commercial system without reciprocal American concessions. This situation confronted the champions of multilateralism within Roosevelt's administration with a difficult political reality, for while American industry generally was highly competitive—it was on this basis that Hull could predict American commercial supremacy in a multilateral world—multilateralism would not benefit equally all sectors of the American economy. If fully applied, it would undoubtedly damage some domestic producers. Such a policy would be difficult to sell to any Congress, and particularly one controlled by the Republican Party (Roosevelt could not discount the possibility of Republican Congressional victories in 1944 and 1946), which had traditionally opposed Hull's efforts to reduce American tariffs.

America's political interest in the establishment of multilateralism followed directly from the reasoning that caused American officials to give this theory such a high place in American policy: the belief that economic conditions determined political conditions—or, as Hull put it, that "the political line-up followed the economic line-up." [6] This conviction led American officials to assume, by a logic never fully elaborated, that democratic political institutions would necessarily develop in countries that adopted the commercial policies espoused by the Americans. This result was desirable not only because it would create a Wilsonian political context congenial to the United States, but also because, by eliminating totalitarianism, it would promote world peace. Other expected political consequences of multilateralism are easier to understand. In the immediate postwar world the United States would possess the only fully functional industrial economy. In this circumstance, American technical skill and productive capacity would make American trade supremely competitive. Other countries could prevent the United States from winning significant parts of their markets only by adopting policies that discriminated against American imports, a device that would be prohibited in a multilateral system. To the extent that a country's economy became dependent upon imports of goods and capital from the United States, its politics necessarily would be oriented toward the United States. International political power would flow from international commercial supremacy. By promoting democracy, ensuring world peace, and placing the United States in a dominant political position, multilateralism would protect the victories of the American armies. The effectiveness of American economic policy in this political context was rendered particularly important by the expectation, frequently voiced by President Roosevelt, that the United States would not maintain armies overseas in the postwar period. In the minds of those responsible for American foreign policy, there was no contradiction between realistic assessments of the political consequences of multilateralism and the establishment of a liberal international order along Wilsonian lines. In their view, America embodied Wilsonian principles and the extension of American influence implied their extension.[7]

Just as the commercial implications of multilateralism were viewed mainly as a problem of Anglo-American relations, the political implications of multilateralism presented problems primarily in the framework of U.S.-Soviet relations. It was obvious that the victories of the Red Army would place the Soviet Union in a position to attempt to assert a sphere of exclusive political and economic influence over much of eastern Europe after the cessation of hostilities. This could mean the imposition of totalitarian, communist regimes upon many areas of eastern Europe, and the history of hostile relations between the Soviet government and the Western powers strongly suggested that the U.S.S.R. would be inclined to follow this non-Wilsonian course. From the American point of view such an eventuality was politically undesirable because it would divide postwar Europe into spheres of influence, Soviet and American, thus creating a basis for geopolitical tension instead of Wilsonian harmony. It would also promote totalitarianism. For both these reasons, exclusive Soviet domination of eastern Europe would threaten American hopes to establish conditions for a protracted peace. Such a development would also disrupt traditional patterns of trade between eastern and western Europe, upon the redevelopment of which western Europe's economic recovery depended. Finally, of course, exclusive Soviet domination of eastern Europe might close this area to American commercial penetration and political influence. Soviet acceptance of multilateralism would serve American purposes by preventing all these developments.

The problem inherent in the political implications of multilateralism was that the Soviet leaders had purposes of their own and viewed the consequences of multilateralism from an entirely different perspective than the Americans. To them, the connections between American-style capitalism and democracy and world peace were not obvious. Also, the redevelopment of traditional patterns of trade between eastern and western Europe meant to the Soviets that eastern Europe would continue to be the underdeveloped supplier of the powerful west European industrial economies, a result not to be cherished by a regime whose base of power lay in the east. Finally, of course, the establishment in eastern Europe of democratic regimes with American-oriented economies was likely to be seen by the Soviets not as the elimination of spheres of influence but as the creation of a global sphere of American influence. In this context, the American desire to convince the Soviet government to adopt multilateral commercial policies posed a direct threat to Soviet security. Neither President Roosevelt nor his advisers fully understood what significant barriers to their postwar plans were raised by these Soviet perspectives, but they did understand that American hopes for preventing complete economic and political control of eastern Europe by the U.S.S.R. would be advanced by convincing the Soviet government that its postwar security did not require this step. The establishment of a solid basis of U.S.-Soviet cooperation during the war thus became a key component of the postwar plans of the American government.[8]

The Roosevelt administration also faced problems at home with respect to its postwar political objectives, just as it did with respect to its economic plans. Although its postwar plans called for the maintenance of U.S.-Soviet cooperation, it was not at all certain that the American people would support such a course. To many people in the United States the Soviet leadership did not represent a proper government but the center of an international conspiracy dedicated primarily to the destruction of the values they most cherished. Indeed, the United States had withheld diplomatic recognition from the Soviet government until 1933, only eight years before the war transformed the two countries into allies. Roosevelt had aroused strong public opposition by his proposal to extend Lend Lease to the Soviet Union following the German invasion of that country even though, at that point, maintaining the eastern front was essential to the defense of the west.[9] Even after the United States and the U.S.S.R. became allies, many Americans believed that it, not Germany, was the true enemy of the United States in Europe. If the Administration's plans for the postwar world were to be realized, these traditional attitudes would have to be overcome.

2. Planning for Reconstruction: the Strategy of Deferment

The establishment of a multilateral world order depended upon the full economic recovery of the major trading nations. American leaders understood this, but deferred serious efforts to plan for reconstruction. This decision reflected domestic political considerations and the Administration's belief that a strategy of deferment would maximize American leverage on the postwar policies of Britain and the Soviet Union.

IT WAS OBVIOUS to the members of Roosevelt's administration that postwar economic reconstruction of the major trading nations was a precondition for the establishment of a postwar world order along Wilsonian lines. Until economic recovery had been achieved, there could be no hope of political stability and no prospect for the institution of multilateralism, for only healthy economies could survive in an international commercial order that minimized political restrictions on economic competition. Moreover, in the words of Secretary of War Stimson, President Roosevelt and his advisers were "thoroughly alive" to the fact that recovery could not be achieved without programs of economic aid from the United States to war-devastated countries. Though it is clear that the scope of the problem of postwar reconstruction was badly underestimated by the American government during the war, top-level officials within the Administration repeatedly expressed their concern with this matter. As early as November 1943 Treasury Secretary Morgenthau discussed Britain's postwar situation with British leaders and concluded that some kind of special assistance would have to be extended to the United Kingdom, and Harry Hopkins expressed the same conviction in 1944. President Roosevelt told his Secretary of State that "the real nub of the problem is to prevent Britain from going into complete bankruptcy at the end of the war." At the Quebec Conference in September 1944, Churchill urged the President to promise to assist Britain with postwar financial problems, and Roosevelt informally agreed that Lend Lease aid would be made available for this purpose. What was true for Britain applied in varying degrees to the other countries of Europe. The Soviets in particular made no secret of the depth of their economic ruin or their eagerness for assistance in meeting the problems of reconstruction. When Stalin spoke of the destruction the Germans had brought to the U.S.S.R., he shed his controlled demeanor and, according to witnesses, expressed himself in highly emotional terms. In discussions of postwar issues he always placed reparations at the top of his list of concerns and at Yalta urged the Allies to accept a figure of ten billion dollars as the Soviet Union's just claim upon German resources. James Byrnes, Roosevelt's Director of War Mobilization and Truman's Secretary of State, has written that reparations were the U.S.S.R.'s "chief interest." Concern with postwar reconstruction led the Soviets to be extremely responsive to any American hint that postwar aid would be made available.

A clear consciousness of the immensity of the reconstruction problem was demonstrated by the officials actually developing American plans for the postwar period. In the words of the chief planner within the Treasury Department, where primary responsibility for considering postwar financial matters was lodged, "it would be ill-advised, if not dangerous, to leave ourselves at the end of the war unprepared for the stupendous task of world-wide economic reconstruction." Accordingly, a plan was developed for an international bank (eventually to be called the International Bank for Reconstruction and Development, or World Bank) with resources of ten billion dollars to finance postwar reconstruction.[10] In spite of such ambitious plans, it was clear that if the Roosevelt administration were to respond—through the Bank or some other mechanism—to the postwar economic needs of war-devasted countries, the money would have to come from Congress. And winning Congressional approval of expenditures for reconstruction presented difficulties.

From the earliest stages of World War II, the American government was concerned about the dangers of a resurgent isolationism among the American people after the immediate difficulties of waging war had been surmounted. These leaders could never forget what had become of Woodrow Wilson's international program when American opinion turned inward following World War I; nor could they ignore the fact that bitter opposition to "intervention" in international affairs had hindered Roosevelt's diplomacy until the Japanese attacked Pearl Harbor. President Roosevelt expressed his consciousness and fear of this tendency in American opinion when he resisted Churchill's efforts to incorporate in the Atlantic Charter a commitment to the creation of an "effective international organization" after the war; he told Churchill that he could not agree to this because of the "suspicion and hostility" that such a statement on his part would arouse in the United States. Both Hull and Stimson shared the President's fear of postwar isolationism and frequently discussed the subject during the war. Navy Secretary Forrestal expressed a related concern that there would be a postwar reaction that would lead to overhasty disarmament. President Truman reports in his memoirs that his readiness to support F.D.R. for a fourth term in 1944 derived from his fear of a postwar reaction that would affect both domestic and foreign problems, and indicates that after he inherited the presidency he devoted the little time available to him for private thought to considering the possibility and consequences of postwar isolationism.[11] The profound fear, mounting almost to an obsession, of America's key wartime leaders with a revived isolationism after the war was the crucial determinant of their attitude toward preparing the American people for the difficulties and exactions of postwar reconstruction.

The first task, as President Roosevelt viewed the situation, was to build strong, broad-based, and bipartisan support for American foreign policy in Congress and the general population. This strategy was consistent with the haunting lessons of the recent past, for it had been the introduction of strong partisan feeling into matters of foreign policy that had created difficulties for the American government both immediately after World War I and prior to World War II. Yet the development of a bipartisan foreign policy presented a difficult problem, for there were real and fundamental differences among major blocs of American opinion; it might be possible to unite these divergent groups behind a military program made necessary by enemy attack, but it would be difficult for Roosevelt, whose New Deal approach to social and economic problems was in growing disrepute at the outset of the war, to maintain bipartisanship when discussion turned to issues of America's role in the postwar world. Ample evidence of this fact was provided by the relatively conservative wartime Congress, which was controlled by Republicans from 1942 to 1944 and could be controlled by a Republican–Southern Democrat coalition between 1944 and 1946. A consistent theme of wartime debates on such issues as American involvement in U.N.R.R.A. (the United Nations Relief and Rehabilitation Agency, a temporary international agency set up during the war to handle problems of postwar relief) and Lend Lease was the fear that the Congress might be enacting legislation that would enable Roosevelt to use American resources for programs of postwar reconstruction that Congress could not control. Congressional pressure forced the scope of U.N.R.R.A.'s authorized activities to be limited to relief, with specific prohibitions upon initiatives in the field of reconstruction. In 1945 Congress adopted an amendment to the Lend Lease program that specifically forbade any use of these funds for postwar reconstruction.[12]

Faced during the war with suspicion about how he might proceed during reconstruction, President Roosevelt suppressed his sense of the importance of postwar aid and avoided public discussion of American policies for the immediate postwar period. Roosevelt was convinced, according to his close confidant Sumner Welles, "that if he spoke to the American people, under the circumstances which then existed, of postwar problems, they might be distracted from the cardinal objective of victory and controversy might develop which would jeopardize national unity." Accordingly, he took no concrete steps to make good the offer of aid he made to Churchill at Quebec and, in general, did nothing to expand America's capacity to extend postwar economic assistance beyond what could be accomplished under Lend Lease and military authority in connection with occupied territories. The single exception to this was a request to Congress, submitted in January 1945 and approved the following July, to expand by one billion dollars the resources of the Export-Import Bank, a federally operated lending institution able to make loans to foreign borrowers in order to provide markets for American exports. The impact of Roosevelt's attitude upon American planning for the postwar period was clearly perceptible in the development of the Treasury Department's plans for the World Bank. Initially conceived as an ambitious scheme to finance postwar reconstruction, under the influence of domestic politics the Bank was increasingly neglected and reduced in scope until, in the end, it was rendered incapable of responding fully to the demands of postwar recovery.[13]

Roosevelt's conviction that domestic political conditions militated against detailed planning and preparation for postwar reconstruction was reinforced by his administration's assessment of the diplomatic dimensions of the reconstruction issue. The American government was fully aware of the leverage it commanded as a result of its economic position, and of the political usefulness of this leverage in winning the cooperation of its wartime allies with its postwar purposes. This was made clear by its handling of Anglo-American negotiations regarding Lend Lease. Though the British government was broadly sympathetic with the American desire to reconstruct postwar world trade along multilateral lines, on such crucial questions as the timing and extent of Britain's adoption of multilateral practices the Americans were less than confident that their own predilections coincided with those of their British colleagues. During initial negotiations between British and American officials concerning the Lend Lease agreement, John Maynard Keynes, the chief British negotiator, aroused American fears by suggesting that Britain's postwar economic difficulties would be so severe as to require the British government to engage in bilateral commercial agreements and other forms of discrimination against American commerce. In response, the American negotiators included in their draft of the Lend Lease agreement a provision banning any form of discrimination by Britain in the postwar period. This action led to a prolonged delay in completing the agreement: the British refused to accept an ironclad commitment to the elimination of Imperial preference and objected to being asked to make such a commitment in the absence of a similar American declaration with regard to tariff policies. In the course of these extended discussions, Dean Acheson, the Assistant Secretary of State for Economic Affairs, indicated to Roosevelt that one element in British resistance was uncertainty about the extent to which the State Department's view of the "importance and urgency" of the provision regarding commercial policy was shared by the President. Roosevelt responded, in Acheson's words, "most emphatically that he did [share the Department's view] and that I should say so." Acheson developed two alternative strategies for handling the negotiations. The U.S. could either continue its efforts to win British acceptance of its commercial policy in the framework of the Lend Lease agreement or abandon these efforts on the understanding that the issue would be taken up later. British intransigence dictated the second alternative, which was implemented with a revised draft agreement and a cable from Roosevelt to Churchill indicating that Britain need feel no more committed to eliminating Imperial preference than the U.S. to abolishing tariffs. The Americans had little reason to be apprehensive about this retreat, for they were aware that it was only a momentary gesture to coalition politics. As Roosevelt said, "I hope the British will accept [the inclusion of American commercial policy in the Lend Lease agreement] because [deferring the issue] leaves them in a much more difficult future situation." [14]

Indeed, this last point was one that the Americans were in a position to predict with reasonable certainty, owing to the manner in which the repayment provisions for Lend Lease aid were handled. It was American policy not to require repayment until British gold and dollar reserves rose to a specified level, and then to insist upon it. This practice gave the Americans control over the level of Britain's financial reserves, and had the effect of assuring Britain's continuing financial dependence upon the United States. In this way, the Americans could be sure that as soon as the war ended the British government would be constrained to seek American assistance for reconstruction. When Britain did so, the issue of commercial policy could again be raised, this time in circumstances in which the British would be unable to be difficult.[15] Thus the strategy of deferring detailed planning for postwar reconstruction, made necessary by domestic political pressures, promised to strengthen the American position in postwar U.S.-British commercial negotiations.

While in its relations with Great Britain the United States relied upon the economic leverage it would inherit at the end of the war mainly to obtain commercial concessions, postwar problems with the Soviet Union involved profound political as well as economic issues. As the Allied armies began converging on Germany from east and west in 1944, the seriousness of these problems became increasingly apparent. On both fronts the liberating governments quickly took steps to assert full control of conquered territory and to encourage the emergence of political elements friendly to themselves. Following the reconquest of Italy, for example, the British and Americans established occupational authorities from which the Soviets were effectively excluded, despite agreements among the Allies to cooperate in these matters. The liberation of France was carried out with an acute consciousness by both the British and Americans of promoting the interests of French political groups favorable to themselves. Similarly, in country after country of eastern Europe—Finland, Rumania, Bulgaria, Poland—Soviet authorities moved in behind the triumphant Red Army to establish complete control of the occupation and to shape local political situations along pro-Soviet lines. By late 1944 Europe had been effectively divided into Anglo-American and Soviet spheres of influence, in which political affairs were conducted with a minimum of attention to the principles of Allied cooperation. Recognizing this, Churchill went to Moscow in late 1944 and completed an agreement with Stalin that accepted the legitimacy of these spheres of influence. The Americans, as aware as Churchill of these developments, made no effective objection to Soviet activities in eastern Europe even though Soviet policy directly threatened their plans for the postwar period. Temporarily, Roosevelt accepted the Churchill-Stalin agreement. This attitude remained the prevailing theme of American policy toward the U.S.S.R. through the end of the war, despite the steady extension of Soviet control over eastern Europe in 1945 and the increase in U.S.-Soviet tension that accompanied it.[16]

American actions with regard to the developing political situation in Europe in 1944 and 1945 can be explained only in terms of a decision to postpone efforts to influence Soviet policy in eastern Europe until the proper moment. This decision was part of the overall strategy of deferment that shaped many of America's wartime policies toward Great Britain. In the context of U.S.-Soviet relations this strategy involved a number of considerations. There were, first of all, the requirements of coalition warfare. Throughout most of the war the Soviet Union carried the brunt of the battle against Germany, engaging the

majority of German divisions and providing the Americans and
British time to prepare their massive cross-channel invasion of
June 1944; the possibility of a separate peace between the
U.S.S.R. and Germany, ruinous to American plans, could
never be forgotten. Moreover, Roosevelt was counting upon
the Soviets to come to the assistance of the United States in
the Pacific once the war with Germany was settled, a factor
that continued to influence American policy until Japan surrendered. These military considerations caused Roosevelt to be
conciliatory in all his dealings with the Soviet government during the war, despite warning signals that the U.S.S.R. was
planning to follow an independent course in eastern Europe.
In addition, Roosevelt had a keen sense of America's inability
to prevent the Soviets from doing whatever they wanted to do
in eastern Europe during the war.[17]

This last consideration was not expected to obtain indefinitely, however. Indeed, the Americans anticipated that
Soviet need for financial assistance for reconstruction would
provide the United States with considerable leverage on the
U.S.S.R. after the cessation of hostilities. President Roosevelt
stated in 1943 that he was relying upon the promise of postwar
aid to help persuade the Soviets to be moderate in asserting political influence in eastern Europe. Averell Harriman, the American ambassador to the Soviet Union, agreed "that economic
assistance is one of the most effective weapons at our
disposal . . . to avoid the development of a sphere of influence
of the Soviet Union over eastern Europe and the Balkans."
Stimson expressed the same view: "They can't get along without our help and industries," he argued.[18] The approach that
such considerations dictated was clearly evident in U.S.-Soviet
negotiations during the war. At the Moscow Conference of
Foreign Ministers in October 1943, Secretary Hull expressed
to the Soviets his anxiousness that they endorse multilateral
commercial objectives, and also suggested that American
economic assistance might be made available to them. The
Soviets showed scant interest in multilateralism; indeed, on
several occasions they expressed opposition to it. As one
high-level American official explained, the U.S.S.R. believed

that "the real object of the advanced industrial countries in advocating freer trade was to hold the markets for manufactured goods in less developed countries and check their industrialization." In contrast, the Soviets were highly responsive to American offers of economic assistance. Within four months after the Moscow Conference, they formally submitted a request for a one-billion-dollar loan. In response, Roosevelt dispatched a personal message to Stalin urging Soviet cooperation with American commercial objectives. This marked the pattern of U.S.-Soviet negotiations over postwar assistance throughout the war, and no agreement was reached.[19]

The marked deterioration of U.S.-Soviet relations in 1945, as the U.S.S.R. progressively tightened its political control over eastern Europe, rendered the Americans even less eager to consider the issue of postwar assistance outside the context of a total political settlement. American policy in this connection was reaffirmed early in 1945 when the Soviet government submitted to Washington a request for a 6-billion-dollar loan to expedite the process of postwar reconstruction. In transmitting the Soviet request, Harriman expressed his "very strong and earnest opinion that the question of the credit be tied into our overall diplomatic relations with the Soviet Union and that at the appropriate time the Russians be given to understand that our willingness to cooperate with them on reconstruction problems will depend upon their behavior in international matters." Harriman's approach won wide agreement among American policymakers and was, in fact, the policy of the Administration. Referring to financial assistance to the U.S.S.R., Roosevelt stated that it was necessary to hold back "until we get what we want." Prior to Yalta, the American government had decided not to give serious consideration to Soviet requests for financial assistance outside the framework of a general settlement involving economic and political issues in eastern Europe and until what Harriman referred to as "the appropriate time." In early 1945 this meant after American reliance upon Soviet participation in the Pacific war had been liquidated. It also was beginning to mean after the U.S. was in possession of the atomic bomb—then in the final stages of development—which was expected to supplement economic power by providing the U.S. with bargaining strength. Thus, a number of considerations argued in favor of a continuation of the strategy of deferment. This approach was reaffirmed by the Roosevelt administration shortly before the President's death and continued by the Truman administration until the end of the war.[20]

Related considerations pervaded U.S.-Soviet discussion of German reparations, for the obvious reason that such payments were at least a partial Soviet alternative to an American loan. The Americans, however, by virtue of Anglo-American control of Germany's industrial heartland, could influence the reparations issue almost as decisively as dollar credits, and for this reason early accord on reparations approximating the ten billion dollars that Stalin requested at Yalta was not to be expected. In fact, the Americans did all they could to slow the organization of the reparations commission established at Yalta, and adopted stalling tactics when the commission finally began to meet; by July 1945 the commission had made no progress toward a settlement. At Potsdam the United States consistently refused even to discuss setting a fixed figure for reparations payments and entertained the question only in terms of percentages of German production. In the end, not surprisingly, the Potsdam "compromise" on reparations permitted each side to do as it pleased in its zone, although the Americans agreed to ship limited amounts of capital equipment from the Ruhr to the Soviet zone. In its quest for reparations, as for financial assistance, the Soviet government found that it would have to satisfy American concerns about the political and economic future of eastern Europe before it would receive significant help with the problems of reconstruction.[21] By deferring discussion of postwar reconstruction, the U.S. strengthened its position vis-à-vis the U.S.S.R., just as it increased its leverage on Britain by the same device.

Although tactical considerations related to domestic politics as well as American relations with Britain and the U.S.S.R. induced the Roosevelt and Truman administrations to defer efforts to meet the problem of reconstruction, the problem itself grew increasingly evident. A report on this subject ordered by President Roosevelt in January 1945 and submitted to President Truman in April indicated a "critical" food situation and "desperate" economic conditions in Europe. A report by Assistant Secretary of War McCloy at the end of April found the same thing: "There is a complete economic, social and political collapse in central Europe." One State Department report predicted that shortages of food, cotton, wool, and coal would create a "critical situation" and the possibility of "internal chaos" in Europe at the close of hostilities. In the context of deteriorating U.S.-Soviet relations in 1945, the economic situation in Europe took on increasingly ominous political meaning. As early as April, Harriman drew the attention of the State Department to the efforts of Communist parties in western Europe to exploit distressed economic conditions and undermine the Western governments, and he concluded that American efforts to cooperate with the Soviets concerning postwar Europe had outlived their usefulness. "Unless we and the British now adopt an independent line," he wrote, "the people in our areas of responsibility will suffer and the chances of Soviet domination of Europe will be enhanced." By now Harriman and his assistant, George Kennan, doubted that American aid could be used effectively to modify Soviet policies in eastern Europe. Harriman suggested that the U.S. adopt a policy of "taking care of our western allies and other areas under our responsibility first, allocating to Russia what may be left." Secretary of War Stimson shared Harriman's concern regarding the political implications of economic conditions in western Europe. In May he wrote Truman that "it is vital to keep these countries from being driven to revolution or communism by famine." Unlike Harriman, however, Stimson was not yet convinced that the U.S. should adopt an "independent line" on these matters, for he regarded the reunification of Germany and the reopening of traditional commercial relationships between eastern and western Europe as essential to European recovery. Neither could be achieved without a U.S.-Soviet agreement, and Stimson concluded that "We must find some way of persuading the Russians to play ball." [22]

By the summer of 1945, in fact, the time had come to test the strategy of deferment. The war was over and American power was at its zenith. American military supremacy had been established through the successful detonations over Hiroshima and Nagasaki of the most destructive weapon ever devised. The American economy was operating at the highest levels in its history while every other industrial economy in the world was in ruins. Immediately after the Japanese surrender, without any consultation with Britain or the U.S.S.R., Truman abruptly terminated all Lend Lease shipments to both allies, thus cutting off both from supplies upon which they had come to depend. The American government was fully aware of the position in which this placed its allies, for a mistaken and rapidly rescinded order to terminate Lend Lease three months earlier had elicited from both Britain and the Soviet Union loud complaints and elaborate explanations of their need for American assistance. Although Truman's action was consistent with Congressional restrictions on Lend Lease aid, it also had the clear and predictable effect of enhancing the American bargaining position in negotiations about postwar issues. And, indeed, both Britain and the U.S.S.R. responded to the termination of Lend Lease precisely according to the scenario implicit in the strategy of deferment. Suddenly finding itself in what Prime Minister Attlee called a "serious financial position," the British government immediately dispatched Keynes on a mission to Washington in search of new financial assistance. The Soviets, too, rapidly submitted a new request for a loan to the American government. In effect, the termination of Lend Lease initiated the phase of inter-allied diplomatic negotiations toward which much of the Administration's wartime policy regarding reconstruction had been directed. These negotiations would determine whether their need for American economic assistance would persuade the British to accept the American commercial program and the Soviets to satisfy American concerns with respect to eastern Europe.[23]

During these same months, however, another aspect of the strategy of deferment was attracting wide concern. In his May memo on the problems of postwar reconstruction, Stimson called the President's attention to the problem of mobilizing American resources for this task. He now regarded public unreadiness to support large programs of postwar aid as a "chief danger" to the country and felt that "a great effort of education" would be required to win public support for necessary programs. In July Assistant Secretary of State MacLeish expressed concern regarding the "long delayed information program" on economic conditions in Europe. In September Commerce Secretary Wallace proposed a program to educate the country on the necessity of providing assistance to war-devastated countries. President Truman made it clear as early as May that "we are committed to the rehabilitation of Europe and there was to be no abandonment this time," but the task of winning the support of the American people to this view had yet to be faced.[24]

3. Planning a Wilsonian World: The Strategies of Co-optation and Propaganda

During the war the American government promoted diplomatic support for its postwar purposes by involving its allies in planning new international institutions. These initiatives led to a series of agreements to create the international political and economic agencies that a Wilsonian world order would require. The Administration also sought to co-opt the two major domestic political parties by involving their leaders in planning the new international agencies and by conducting a propaganda campaign aimed at the American people.

POSTWAR ECONOMIC RECONSTRUCTION was only part of the problem to be faced by the American government in constructing a Wilsonian world. Of equal importance was the

need to create a whole new set of political and economic institutions to provide structure and authority in the new international order. And this issue, unlike reconstruction, received
detailed attention during the war. Indeed, while Roosevelt's
wartime deferment of the reconstruction issue served only to
deflect attention from difficult and divisive problems, the
President and his advisers looked upon the need to create new
international institutions as an opportunity to begin the political task of building a Wilsonian world. They promoted negotiations over these matters energetically.

By early 1943 the State Department's Division of Commercial Policy had developed a comprehensive proposal for
the establishment of a multilateral commercial order. The plan
involved winning the agreement of as many nations as possible
to a convention governing the use of tariffs, discrimination,
quantitative restrictions, and other constraints upon the flow of
trade. When implemented, the convention would embody Cordell Hull's long-nourished dream of a single international
charter for world commerce. Because the Americans thought it
desirable to initiate negotiations on this plan while the spirit of
wartime cooperation prevailed, and because they viewed commercial issues primarily as problems of Anglo-American relations, in early 1943 the State Department urged Britain to
begin discussions with American commercial experts. The ensuing talks found the two countries in general agreement concerning the desirability of a multilateral commercial convention, which came to be called the General Agreement on Tariffs
and Trade (G.A.T.T.). More specifically, the negotiators concurred on the desirability of eliminating discrimination in international trade as well as achieving broad reductions in tariff
levels. At the insistence of the British, who were apprehensive
about a postwar American depression and doubted that multilateralism could be established unless this was prevented, the
negotiators also agreed that governments adhering to multilateralism should undertake to maintain high levels of employment. Finally, both sides felt that an international organization
should be established to interpret the proposed G.A.T.T.,
develop world trade policy, and settle disputes, a line of

thought that led eventually to a proposal for an International Trade Organization (I.T.O.). By December 1945 the two sides had found sufficient common ground on a multilateral commercial order to publish a set of "Proposals for Consideration by an International Conference on Trade and Employment."[25] The "Proposals" provided the immediate impetus for a series of international conferences in 1946–8 to develop both the G.A.T.T. and a charter for the I.T.O.

Concurrently with Anglo-American commercial talks leading to the "Proposals" of December 1945, financial experts from the two countries discussed such problems as maintenance of stable exchange rates and provision of capital for economic recovery, both essential to the establishment of a multilateral commercial system. Here, too, a broad area of agreement was established. To deal with the problem of exchange rates, the Anglo-American planners proposed the creation of an International Monetary Fund, which would be a repository of reserve currencies to be made available to participating countries to overcome short-term balance-of-payments deficits. The I.M.F. would provide a financial cushion that would make it unnecessary to alter exchange rates in response to payments problems except in circumstances of serious, long-term economic dislocation. This would minimize the destabilizing and restricting influence on international trade traditionally caused by fluctuating exchange rates. These negotiations also considered the American plan for a World Bank to finance reconstruction. The British were skeptical about this proposal, since power on the proposed Bank's board was to be allocated in such a way as to assure the United States the dominant voice. This British attitude reinforced other factors that were impeding the Bank's development, particularly the political mood in the United States and Roosevelt's strategy of deferment regarding reconstruction. The Bank emerged from the Anglo-American talks as a conservative lending institution capable only of making "hard" loans defensible as business propositions—hardly a proper mandate to meet the financial needs of countries whose economies were ruined by war. Plans for the I.M.F. and the World

Bank were submitted to an international conference at Bretton Woods, New Hampshire, during the summer of 1944. Their ratification provided the first solid step toward obtaining the consent of a large number of countries to the postwar commercial policies to which the American government was committed.[26]

By the end of the war, extensive Anglo-American discussions on the economic aspects of multilateralism had produced a significant area of agreement on a number of major issues. To this extent, the strategy of co-optation was proving itself in practice, though the critical issue of the transition from wartime conditions to multilateralism had yet to be faced. As we have seen, this matter was intimately related to the problem of postwar reconstruction, concerning which detailed planning had been deferred. John Maynard Keynes, the chief British negotiator on financial matters, made this point to the House of Lords in presenting the Bretton Woods proposals: "provision for [reconstruction]," he stated, "belongs to another chapter of international cooperation, upon which we shall embark unless you discourage us unduly about this one." He assured his listeners that Britain had accepted no obligation to adopt multilateral practices until the problems of reconstruction had been resolved.[27]

While in wartime dealings with the Soviet Union the Americans both officially "minimized" developments in eastern Europe that worried them greatly and developed a strategy for taking action with respect to these problems at the proper time, they also took positive steps to assure that this strategy would have the maximum opportunity for success. This was done by involving the U.S.S.R. in the development of an international security organization. Roosevelt believed that such joint planning activities would build a cooperative relationship between the American and Soviet governments, assure the U.S.S.R. of security and acceptability in the international arena, and place moral pressures on the Soviets to live by the principles of the organization they would help create.[28] It is interesting to note that American efforts to involve the Soviet Union in planning a Wilsonian world were concentrated in the political rather than the economic sphere. This may be attributable to a belief that the Soviets would not be a major factor in postwar world commerce, but the American tendency to relate economic and political issues should not have allowed the dichotomy; perhaps the Soviets' unfavorable response to American proposals regarding multilateralism suggested deferring discussion of that issue and attempting to build a relationship with them in another area.

The strategy of co-opting the Soviets into American efforts to build a new world order unfolded in a series of international conferences during the war. One distinctive feature of this strategy was the avoidance of detailed discussion of difficult postwar issues—such as the future of specific countries in eastern Europe—and the concentration upon winning from the U.S.S.R. vague and general commitments to Wilsonian principles and postwar cooperation. This aspect of American strategy began with the partially successful effort in 1941 to win a public endorsement of the Atlantic Charter from the Soviet government. At the Foreign Ministers' Conference in Moscow in October 1943, Hull presented to his associates a proposed "Declaration of Four Nations," which committed the Allies (including the Chinese) to the establishment of a general international organization and to the principle of working cooperatively to prosecute the war and establish peace. Two provisions of Hull's proposed declaration bound the powers to act together in matters relating to the occupation of enemy territory and not to use their armed forces within the territories of other states except after mutual agreement. Soviet Foreign Minister Molotov insisted that these two provisions be stricken. Hull did not object.[29]

In the interval between the Conference of Moscow and the one at Yalta in February 1945, much that Hull had hoped to prevent by his "Declaration" had occurred. By this time, the intention of the Soviet government to dominate much of eastern Europe after the war was clear and the President had been warned by his ambassador to the Soviet Union that vague declarations of general principle had been and would continue to be ineffective in influencing Soviet policy. Nevertheless, the

President, still following the strategy of deferment, did not pose
at Yalta a significant challenge to Soviet policy regarding any of
the specific situations then developing in eastern Europe. Instead, the American delegation urged upon the conference a
"Declaration on Liberated Territories," reminiscent of Hull's
"Declaration" at Moscow, in which the powers declared themselves generally agreed to work toward the reestablishment of
democracy in the liberated territories of Europe. Roosevelt
even insisted upon excising from a State Department draft of
this Declaration language that he felt challenged too strongly
Soviet policies in eastern Europe.[30]

The strategy of wartime cooperation with the Soviets
produced detailed negotiations only in the context of the proposed United Nations Organization. The first international
conference devoted to this matter was held in Washington, at
Dumbarton Oaks, in August 1944. Skeptics within the Administration argued against developing an international organization to enforce a peace whose outlines could not yet be perceived. The division of Europe into Anglo-American and
Soviet spheres of influence during 1944 encouraged such
"realists" as Harriman, Forrestal, and Stimson to urge that
priority be given to opposing Soviet policies in eastern Europe,
not developing a new international organization. Roosevelt
and Hull, however, were determined to launch the U.N.
project while the opportunity and impetus existed and President Truman pursued this same course during 1945, despite
the rapid deterioration of U.S.-Soviet relations. Thus, in an
atmosphere of deepening tension as the war moved toward a
conclusion, the American government made strenuous efforts
to resolve a range of disagreements with the Soviets about the
structure of the new organization. In April 1945 the U.S.
went ahead with the second and final international conference
on the U.N. at San Francisco, at which the charter was signed
and the new world order officially, elaborately, and irrele-
vantly inaugurated.[31]

Although U.S.-Soviet and Anglo-American wartime planning activities promised to create the most favorable possible
diplomatic climate within which to face postwar problems, the

success of the Administration in achieving its goals ultimately depended upon domestic political factors. As the strategy of deferment about reconstruction implied, the Americans' real leverage upon the postwar policies of their allies would not derive from diplomatic good will but from their ability to extend or withhold financial assistance. And there was little reason to assume that the American people and their representatives in Congress would endorse expenditures for postwar purposes involving economic assistance to the communist government of the Soviet Union or the modification of such revered commercial practices as high tariffs and quantitative restrictions on agricultural imports. Accordingly, establishing a basis of public and Congressional support for these policies was an essential part of the Administration's wartime efforts to create a postwar atmosphere congenial to the accomplishment of its long-term purposes.

Undoubtedly the most extensive efforts made by the Roosevelt administration to develop public support for its postwar program involved its campaign to convince the American people that the Soviet government was an appropriate and trustworthy ally of the United States and that U.S.-Soviet cooperation, in the framework of the U.N., was the proper basis upon which to organize the peace. Public resistance to this line of policy was expected to be doubly intense; the American people harbored both a long history of opposition to long-term international commitments and an equally venerable heritage of disregard for the Soviet state. To overcome these attitudes the President attempted to build a favorable public image of Stalin's U.S.S.R. and of the relationship that the U.S. and Soviet governments were developing. Throughout the war, Roosevelt spoke of the U.S.S.R. only to praise it. The length to which he was prepared to go in service of this policy was demonstrated early in the war when he publicly stated that the Soviet government's policies with respect to freedom of religion were essentially similar to those of the U.S.; at the same time, he attempted to persuade Stalin to make a public statement supporting religious freedom. Such efforts to disguise differences with the Soviets were char-

acteristic of the Administration's wartime information policies. The troubling disputes over the second front, the anxie-
ties that Soviet policies in eastern Europe were arousing in
American officials, the numerous other incidents that were producing friction in the alliance were never reflected in Roosevelt's public utterances. Aware, according to one colleague,
that "pro-Soviet sentiment in America was superficial and . . .
had to be artificially fed," the President and his Secretary of
State, in every public statement on the subject, stressed the
unity of purpose of the Allies and promised that this would
be sustained after the war. To complement this campaign, the
Administration restrained its subordinate officials, some of
whom did not believe in U.S.-Soviet cooperation and doubted
the wisdom of the information policy, from speaking out on the
problems that were developing within the alliance.[32]

The strategy of co-optation was intimately related to
these propaganda activities, for the joint public pronouncements by the wartime allies after Moscow and Yalta and the
international conferences at Bretton Woods, Dumbarton Oaks,
and San Francisco all lent an aspect of credibility to the pronouncements of the American government with respect to
great-powers cooperation. In reporting on these conferences
with its allies, the Administration repeatedly interpreted events
in terms of its information policies. Thus, after the Moscow
conference, despite the crippling amendments that Molotov
had attached to the "Declaration of Four Nations," Hull returned to the U.S. to promise his countrymen that "as the provisions of the Four Nation declaration are carried into effect,
there will no longer be need for spheres of influence, for alliances, for balances of power, or any other of the special arrangements through which, in the unhappy past, the nations
strove to safeguard their security or to promote their interests."
Similarly, the public was given no official indication of the
political developments that during 1944 were reducing Europe
to Soviet and Anglo-American spheres of influence. Public
attention was focused instead upon the Dumbarton Oaks conference, which was drafting the charter of the United Nations.
It is one of the minor ironies of the war that President Roose-

velt expressed his "extreme satisfaction" with the work of this conference on October 9, 1944, the same day that Churchill arrived in Moscow to divide the Balkans into Soviet and Anglo-American spheres of influence. After Yalta, despite the inconclusiveness of the agreements reached there, Roosevelt echoed the sentiments expressed by Hull after Moscow and reported to the country that the negotiations "spell the end of the system of unilateral action and exclusive alliances and spheres of influence and balances of power and all the other expedients which have been tried for centuries—and failed." The public was hardly given reason to adopt the view, taken by Harriman, Stimson, and Leahy, that the Yalta agreements provided no real restraint upon Soviet efforts to consolidate their control of eastern Europe.[33]

The Truman administration continued the information policies established by Roosevelt. The new President excluded the press from his first conference with Stalin, at Potsdam in July 1945, in order to avoid public airing of disputes. Following the conference—which had been so frustrating and unproductive that Truman left it determined to deny the U.S.S.R. any share in the occupation of Japan—the President and his advisers worked diligently to compose an announcement that would maintain the public's belief in U.S.-Soviet cooperation. Truman's Secretary of State, James Byrnes, has written that he and the President refrained from telling the truth about U.S.-Soviet relations after Potsdam in order to maintain friendly relations with the U.S.S.R., undoubtedly because the Pacific war was still in progress and the Americans had yet to bring to bear the negotiating tools upon which they relied to influence the Soviet Union. Truman also ignored the concern expressed by a number of top officials—including Stimson, Acheson, and King, as well as John Foster Dulles—about the impact upon public opinion of the San Francisco Conference. Acheson, whose responsibility for liaison between the State Department and the Congress placed him in the middle of the campaign for approval of the charter, has written that "its presentation to the American people as almost holy writ and with the evangelical fervor of a major advertising campaign seemed to me to

raise hopes which could lead only to bitter disappointment."
Throughout 1945 Truman and Byrnes continued to exclude the
press from international conferences and, following the policy
of their predecessors, restrained those within the Administration who sought to speak openly about the difficulties of
U.S.-Soviet relations.[34]

The success of the public-information activities sponsored by the American government during World War II
was impressive. As the war unfolded public belief in U.S.-
Soviet cooperation grew steadily. At the time of the Yalta
Conference, 55 per cent of those polled by the American
Institute for Public Opinion (A.I.P.O.) believed that U.S.-
Soviet cooperation would continue to work after the war;
throughout 1945 a majority of those expressing an opinion on
this subject continued to be optimistic. Moreover, there was a
parallel increase in popular sentiment supporting American involvement in the U.N. In 1937 only 26 per cent of those polled
by A.I.P.O. believed the U.S. should join a world organization;
by 1942 the figure had risen to 39 per cent, and at the time of
the San Francisco Conference it was 81 per cent. Equally significant, of the 81 per cent supporting the U.N. in 1945, 83 per
cent regarded American involvement as "very important." [35]

To the problem of laying a basis of support for its postwar
policies in Congress, the Administration applied the same
strategy it had employed in dealing with the British and Soviet
governments. Key members of both parties of Congress were
consulted at every stage in the planning of the U.N., sat upon
the State Department committees that worked on this project,
and were included in the American delegation to the international conferences at which the new organization was given
shape. The deference Roosevelt paid to the principle of bipartisan foreign policy proved to be one of his most successful
political inventions. As the public statements of the senior
Republican on the Senate Foreign Relations Committee,
Arthur Vandenberg, attest, those who were directly included
in Roosevelt's efforts to co-opt the Congress did develop a
strong personal attachment to the policies they felt instrumental in designing and had become passionate advocates of

those policies by the time the Congressional test arrived. Such support, combined with the successful propaganda campaign for the U.N., decimated potential opposition to the new international organization. When the U.N. legislation was submitted to Congress in 1945, it passed easily with bipartisan majorities. In this manner Roosevelt and Truman avoided the fate of Woodrow Wilson.[36]

The wartime history of the Administration's campaign for its commercial program was much less a success story than was its effort on behalf of the U.N. In official propaganda, multilateralism was praised as a sound basis for lasting peace as well as a new opportunity for American business. Unfortunately, the difficulties implicit in multilateralism—like the problems of the U.S.-Soviet alliance—were withheld from public view. For example, the fact that removal of barriers to American exports would depend upon modification of American import policies was not acknowledged. Hull admitted in late 1944 that public and Congressional support for a reduction of import restrictions was highly uncertain, and an A.I.P.O. poll taken in 1945 indicated that a majority of Americans with an opinion on this subject favored high tariffs. Moreover, the Administration was not successful in building political support for the domestic economic policies that Anglo-American commercial negotiators had agreed were essential to a multilateral regime. When the Truman administration proposed full-employment legislation in 1945—a program that committed the United States to the employment policies upon which American and British negotiators had concurred—the bill was drastically altered by Congress and the full-employment provisions stricken. Even the successful campaign for Congressional approval of the Bretton Woods institutions did not indicate significant support for the Administration's economic policies. Congressional response to even the highly idealized version of multilateralism articulated by the Administration in presenting these proposals was cool, and Administration spokesmen felt it necessary to add weight to the case for approval by making the unwarranted claim that adoption assured the success of postwar reconstruction. In the end, most support for Bretton Woods derived from the connection the Administration succeeded in establishing between these proposals and international cooperation and peace. The proposals passed Congress on the wings of a general exuberance arising from the end of the war in Europe and the beginning of the San Francisco Conference. Approval hardly involved a mandate for multilateralism.[37]

The Administration was aware of the lack of support for its commercial program and went to considerable lengths to avoid any public controversy over the implications of its policies for American tariff practices. In discussions with Britain on the proposed G.A.T.T., for example, American negotiators insisted that an exception be made in the provisions regarding commodity controls that would permit the American farm program to remain intact. Even more significantly, in 1945, as the time for the negotiation of the G.A.T.T. was approaching, the Administration decided to negotiate reductions in the American tariff on the basis of existing reciprocal-trade legislation, which authorized reductions only on the basis of commodity-by-commodity negotiations, rather than taking the risk of asking Congress for authority to make a "horizontal cut" or an across-the-board reduction in the American tariff. Since one of the basic principles of multilateralism involved a general reduction in tariff levels, this declaration marked a major retreat from its own principles by the Administration. Such actions raised significant doubts in Britain about the willingness of the U.S. to act on the basis of its professed policies, and stiffened opposition in that country to concessions on Imperial preference.[38]

As the war drew to an end in the summer of 1945, it was clear that the complementary strategies of co-optation and propaganda had been only partially successful. The major success had been in the area of developing public support in America for the United Nations and continued U.S.-Soviet cooperation, but American efforts to co-opt the Soviets by involving them in planning the U.N. and winning from them public endorsements of Wilsonian principles appeared to be having no effect on the evolution of political arrangements in eastern

Europe. The campaign for multilateralism had failed to establish solid public support for this essential component of the Administration's program. Moreover, American equivocation on the application of multilateral principles to its own import policies cast a dark shadow over the general Anglo-American agreements that had been reached in the areas of financial and commercial policy. In terms of postwar objectives—as opposed to coalition politics—the strategies of co-optation and propaganda had not been notably successful. Thus, immense significance devolved upon negotiations over the deferred issue of economic reconstruction.

4. American Diplomacy and the Reconstruction Issue in 1946

*During 1945–6 the American government
succeeded in trading financial aid to Britain
and the western European countries for
cooperation with American commercial policy,
but failed to induce the Soviets to alter their
policies toward eastern Europe to obtain similar
assistance. This failure marked the end
of American hopes of establishing a Wilsonian
order on a global basis and the beginning of
explicit efforts to organize an American-oriented,
anti-Soviet bloc of western European states.*

DISPATCHED BY THE BRITISH GOVERNMENT immediately following the termination of Lend Lease, Keynes arrived in Washington in August 1945 with a request for a grant from the United States for six billion dollars to help Britain rebuild. He learned very quickly that the British had no chance of obtaining a grant and that even a loan would be made available only at the price of very considerable concessions by Britain in accordance with American multilateral objectives. By this time, responsibility for all economic affairs in the State Department had been centralized under the control of Assistant

Secretary Will Clayton, a millionaire and former international trader in cotton, and a more aggressive and thoroughgoing advocate of commercial expansion along multilateral lines than Cordell Hull. As vice-chairman of the American delegation that negotiated with the Keynes mission, Clayton was openly anxious to use America's economic leverage to accelerate what he felt to be the inadequate pace of acceptance by Britain of America's commercial program. In this attitude he was supported by influential elements of the American business community and Congress.

Faced with an American delegation that not only refused to consider a grant but insisted upon concessions, the British considered terminating the negotiations. In the end, however, Britain's financial needs were controlling. Keynes remained and negotiated a low-interest loan of 3.75 billion dollars. In return, the British accepted a number of significant obligations in the field of financial policy. Most importantly, they agreed that one year following Congressional approval of the loan all sterling earned in current transactions by residents of the Commonwealth trading bloc or residents of other areas, except the U.S., would be freely convertible. This meant that the British government would recognize an obligation to convert sterling earnings into other currencies, particularly dollars, at the request of the holder, thus freeing the holder from the necessity to spend his earnings in the sterling area. The British also agreed to make sterling earned by Americans in current transactions freely convertible as of the effective date of the agreement and, after the same date, to eschew discrimination against Americans in the use of quantitative controls on imports. These obligations amounted to substantial commitments to adopt multilateral policies in the face of highly uncertain economic circumstances in Britain. As Clayton put it, "we loaded the . . . negotiations with all the conditions that the traffic would bear." Given their hopes for a large grant, the British were hardly elated, and felt that advantage had been taken of their distress. Even the generally hardnosed Stimson regarded the terms as "somewhat cold-blooded," and Forrestal thought the commercial obligations rendered the loan of dubious value to Britain. Still, the negotiations had to be regarded as a major success for the Americans and a vindication of the reliance they placed upon deferring the reconstruction issue to achieve their diplomatic purposes.[39]

Indeed, the Anglo-American negotiations of late 1945 appeared to have established a pattern for linking the development of multilateralism to the problems of postwar reconstruction. Within a month after the Keynes mission departed from Washington, a French economic mission arrived in the American capital with similar purposes. Led by Léon Blum and Jean Monnet, the French delegation brought with it Monnet's comprehensive program for the reconstruction of the French economy. Credits totaling four billion dollars to cover anticipated deficits between 1946 and 1950 were requested. Again the Americans made it clear that assistance would not be made available without concessions, and the French, like the British, proved ready to cooperate. Though the French were less successful negotiators than the British (owing in large part to political considerations that will be discussed shortly), they did obtain an Export-Import Bank credit of 650 million dollars to meet immediate needs. In return, they agreed to participate in the development of a multilateral commercial order and made a number of specific tariff concessions.[40]

This progress toward the implementation of the American commercial program was being made at a time when increasing attention was being focused upon one of the major sources of the American commitment to multilateralism, the need to open foreign markets to absorb the outpourings of America's expanded economy. "The prevalent fear toward the war's end," according to the Council of Economic Advisors, "was that a drastic reduction in public outlays plus the rapid demobilization of our armed forces, would lead to heavy unemployment and business dislocation for a substantial period of time." By early 1946 industrial production had declined 30 per cent from the May 1945 level, and unemployment had increased from .5 million on V.E. Day to about 2.7 million in February 1946. There were estimates that unemployment would reach 8 million. The economic crisis did not develop, however, and by the second quarter of 1946 the decline had halted and what was later recognized as a period of economic expansion had begun. To the economists around the President at this time, the causes of these developments and their relative importance were not clear, but there was a strong belief that continuing high levels of exports during 1946 were very important. According to the President's economic report of January 1947, which summarized events in 1946, "intense demand of foreign countries for goods available only, or chiefly, in the United States has been one of the factors sustaining a high level of employment, production and purchasing power in the U.S. as government expenditures declined." Pointing out that American exports were running at a level of 15 billion dollars, as opposed to 4 billion dollars before the war, the President stated that "their importance to the American economy is evidenced by the fact that they exceed in volume such important elements of the national product as expenditures on durable goods, the net change in business inventories, total expenditures by state and local governments, and even private construction." It was clear that the Administration was looking forward to the maintenance of high levels of exports in its economic planning. "Foreign demand for U.S. goods will probably continue to be high in 1947," the President's report stated, and this "would be a factor cushioning the effects of any dip in domestic production and employment." The major consumers of American exports were the countries of Europe.[41]

The belief that continuing high levels of foreign demand would produce continuing high levels of American exports assumed, of course, the capacity of foreign buyers to command the dollar resources necessary to make purchases in American markets. Such resources were available from a number of sources: export sales to the dollar area, liquidation of gold and dollar reserves, and American economic assistance. One significant measure of the extent to which economic recovery had progressed was the proportion of foreign purchases in the American market financed by dollar earnings, as opposed to both economic aid and liquidation of reserves. In late 1946

Paul Nitze, one of Clayton's assistants, calculated that of the 15 billion dollars in total annual American exports, less than 7 billion dollars was being financed by dollar earnings of America's trading partners. The major portions of the 8.2 billion dollar export surplus, approximately 5 billion dollars, was being paid for through various forms of economic assistance, and the remaining 3 billion dollars by foreign liquidations of gold and dollar reserves. For the time being, therefore, American economic planners were constrained to view production, employment, and income levels in the domestic economy as substantially dependent upon foreign economic assistance. As the gold and dollar reserves of America's trading partners became increasingly exhausted, this factor would become even more important. Thus, the issue of American financial assistance to European reconstruction, a vital factor in the long-term effort to promote multilateralism, had to be regarded as equally important to the short-term health of the American economy.[42]

While the strategy of linking cooperation with America's postwar goals to American willingness to finance economic reconstruction was proving effective in the context of negotiations between the U.S. and the governments of Britain and France in late 1945 and early 1946, it did not produce similar success in the context of U.S.-Soviet diplomacy. At the London Conference of Foreign Ministers in September 1945, during discussions regarding Rumania, Secretary of State Byrnes directly challenged Soviet policies in eastern Europe for the first time. He stated that the U.S. was not satisfied with the government that the Soviets had established in Rumania and that this government would have to be broadened to include representatives of additional political groups. The Soviets responded with calm intransigence. They reminded the Americans that they had not interfered with British activities in Greece, and suggested that they be allowed similar latitude in their sphere of influence. Extended debate produced no modification of the Soviet stance. The Americans had obviously miscalculated the strength of their bargaining position. Secretary Byrnes has described the impact of this debate upon the

American delegation: "It was a gloomy Sunday . . . we talked over this interview and the problems it raised for a long time. It seemed that the Soviet Union was determined to dominate Europe. We could see no solution to our problems . . ." [43]

The London debate concerning Rumania was indicative of the results of U.S.-Soviet diplomacy on the broad issue of the political future of eastern Europe. The Soviets were not to be moved. The attitudes underlying the Soviet position can only be guessed at, but undoubtedly the most important was an inflexible determination to maintain hegemony over the countries along the U.S.S.R.'s western borders. The Soviets considered meaningless the American argument that the governments of eastern Europe could be both democratic and friendly to the U.S.S.R., and they were not prepared to accept the incursions of Western influence into this region that American economic and political policies implied. Beyond this, the Soviets expected that America's need to export would force the extension of credits to the U.S.S.R. without Soviet concessions, a view that deprived the U.S. of one of its key negotiating points. Why the bomb did not influence Soviet policy is as unclear as the basis of the American belief that it would do so. In any case, following the showdown over Rumania, American and Soviet diplomats engaged in countless diplomatic exchanges at a series of conferences, but without result. It did not take long for Byrnes to conclude that the Soviets viewed protracted negotiations in the context of the anticipated economic crisis in the U.S. and the withdrawal of American troops from Europe, two contingencies that would decisively enhance the Soviet bargaining position. By early 1946, therefore, the Secretary of State abandoned the idea that there was advantage to be gained from continued negotiations with the U.S.S.R. After this date their continuation was a matter of form and necessary housekeeping. The long-postponed American diplomatic offensive had ended in total failure. [44]

Byrnes's conclusions regarding Soviet negotiating strategy led him, in early 1946, to adopt what he liked to call a "firm" approach to U.S.-Soviet relations. His decision marked the moment when America officially adopted the policy of containment that would characterize American diplomacy toward the Soviet Union for years to come. In essence, it meant that the U.S. would no longer rely upon negotiating its differences with the U.S.S.R. but would simply oppose in the strongest possible way any extension of Soviet influence. The new approach was first employed to resolve a situation that developed in Iran in March when the Soviets failed to withdraw their troops from that country by the date specified in a wartime treaty. Rather than attempt to deal with this problem at the conference table, the American government dispatched to the Soviets what President Truman has called a "blunt message." The U.S.S.R. withdrew its troops. Byrnes concluded that firmness was indeed the appropriate method by which to deal with the U.S.S.R. When, later in the year, he became convinced that the U.S.S.R. was attempting to pressure Turkey into accepting Soviet bases on the Dardanelles and excluding non–Black Sea powers from control of the straits, Byrnes employed "firmness" again. He communicated the American attitude by sending American warships into the eastern Mediterranean and ordering the largest aircraft carrier in the fleet to pay calls at the ports of Piraeus and Thessalonika. In relation to western Europe, the new policy meant that the U.S. would now adopt the "independent line" that Harriman had urged upon the State Department in April 1945 and would concentrate its energies upon consolidating its political position in the West by "taking care of our western allies." It was an appropriate symbol of this development that Export-Import Bank funds that had been set aside since mid-1945 to finance a loan to the U.S.S.R. were reallocated in early 1946 and by May of that year had been almost totally expended, mainly in loans to western Europe. Indeed, American policy toward these countries, as well as Germany, clearly registered the shift in U.S.-Soviet relations.[45]

In all their negotiations with the Soviets over Germany following the cessation of hostilities, the Americans had assumed that the reunification of that country on American terms was vital to the reconstruction of the German economy and that German recovery was essential to the rehabilitation of western Europe. By reason of its connection to the issue of European reconstruction, German unification and recovery were important components of the broad American effort to achieve political stability in western Europe and incorporate that region in a global multilateral system. The consequence of the prolonged U.S.-Soviet impasse over reparations, mentioned above, was a complete lack of progress toward unification. In fact, communication and trade among the four occupation zones had become increasingly restricted, and economic conditions within each had remained precarious. As the only reason for permitting this situation to continue was the hope that the U.S. and the Soviets could negotiate an agreement, Byrnes's decision to abandon negotiations as the basis of American diplomacy portended immediate consequences for Germany. Early in 1946, the U.S. initiated a series of steps pointing toward the unification of the three western zones. In March the U.S. suspended shipments of reparations from the western to the eastern zone, thus abandoning the Potsdam reparations "compromise." In May the Americans invited the other powers to initiate immediate planning for the unification of the zones, a formal gesture to continued four-power cooperation without prospect of winning Soviet acceptance. Only the British accepted, and in July the two powers began planning a formal merger of their zones. In December a final agreement establishing "Bizonia" was signed. By the end of 1946 America was committed to the full reconstruction of the western zones as the industrial center of a reconstructed, non-communist western Europe.[46]

American attitudes toward political developments in all western Europe during 1946 evolved along lines parallel to those manifested in German policy. American efforts to assist European reconstruction were increasingly seen not only as means to eliminate the depressed economic conditions that tended to serve the interests of the communists, but also as political tools to undermine the influence of the Communist Party and move western European governments toward strong pro-American and anti-Soviet positions. In France, for example, the Communist Party was the strongest single political organization. The French coalition government contained Communist ministers. Moreover, France was attempting to follow a neutral policy in 1946, envisaging a reconstructed Europe "between East and West," an independent political force outside either an American or a Soviet political bloc. The French refusal to join their zone of Germany to Bizonia was a manifestation of this policy. The U.S. placed its immense economic power in the field against all these tendencies.

The response of the American government to the French economic mission of February 1946 was indicative of the American attitude. The French brought a plan calling for credits totaling 4 billion dollars over a period of four years and increased allocations of coal from the Anglo-American-controlled Ruhr. The Americans were unenthusiastic: they wanted the French to incorporate their occupation zone into Bizonia and to eliminate the Communists from the government. Until these objectives were achieved, France could not expect large-scale aid. There were reports that this situation was made clear to the French representatives. In any case, France received a minimal credit of 650 million dollars and no satisfaction with regard to Ruhr coal. The French government charged that its successful efforts to increase French coal production in 1946 resulted only in reductions of coal allocations from the Anglo-American zone of Germany. While the coolness of the U.S. to French economic requests indicated that there were serious policy differences between the two governments, the fact that the French received any loan at all reflected the American belief that a minimal grant was required to protect the political interests of the non-communist parties in France. Jefferson Caffery, American Ambassador to France, sent a number of telegrams to the State Department during the Blum mission urging that a loan be granted. Not to do so, Caffery argued, would so disappoint French hopes as to undermine the non-communist parties and produce a political disaster. The deliberations in the National Advisory Council took clear account of Caffery's messages. The loan was announced two weeks before a French election in which the Communists were less successful than had been expected. The American loan was widely credited as having been the crucial factor in the elections.[47]

The Truman administration's intention of using economic assistance to promote the political interests of pro-American elements was apparent in American dealings with other western European countries in 1946. The minutes of the National Advisory Council—which contained representatives of the executive departments concerned with foreign economic policy and was responsible for making recommendations to the President on economic assistance—indicate the consistent consideration of this factor. When the Italian Prime Minister visited Washington in search of economic aid, he was informed that his requests would be more attentively received if he would eliminate the Communists from his government. The Greek government, which, with British support, was engaged in a civil war with Communist-led guerrillas, was assured of American economic support by Secretary of State Byrnes. The tendency of all these activities was summarized in a lengthy memo on U.S.-Soviet relations drafted by presidential assistant Clark Clifford during the summer of 1946 on the basis of discussions with the highest-ranking Administration officials responsible for American foreign policy. Clifford took as his definition of Soviet aims and attitudes a cable that the chargé in Moscow, George Kennan, had sent to the State Department in February 1946. Genuine agreement between the U.S. and the Soviet Union was rendered impossible by the Soviets' paranoia and isolationism, Clifford and Kennan asserted, and any effort at cooperation that the Soviets might manifest must be interpreted as a deception to gain time, build strength, and prepare for further assertions of its claim to world domination. Nevertheless, the U.S.S.R. was seen as weak and not prepared for immediate war with the United States. Short of war, it would do everything possible to oppose and subvert governments friendly to the United States. Although Clifford expressed the need for a global policy of resistance to Communist advances, he stressed the point that the U.S.S.R.'s greatest fear was the development of an anti-Soviet western bloc in Europe, which would completely frustrate its long-range goals. Accordingly, the U.S. should move at once to develop such a bloc, dividing Europe into two spheres of influence between which cooperation would be impossible but war would not be inevitable. Clifford stressed the point that American economic assistance was the ideal tool by which to consolidate the Western bloc.[48]

Clifford's final point suggested one of the basic decisions of the Administration in the field of foreign policy in 1946. Economic aid, not arms, would be the basis of America's power in the immediate post-hostilities period. This decision reflected the belief that the Soviet Union did not want war with the U.S., that Congress and the public would not support massive rearmament, and that economic aid was the most effective way of promoting America's broad interests—economic as well as political—in Europe. Moreover, reports coming into the State Department from France and Italy repeatedly indicated that the Communists—who had adopted a policy of cooperating with established authority—would not attempt coups or revolutions in western Europe. On the basis of these various considerations, postwar rearmament was deferred indefinitely. For the next two years defense budgets were held to a minimum, and the energies of the defense establishment were devoted to the problems of reorganization.[49]

The American diplomatic offensive beginning in August 1945 and continuing through 1946 defined in practice the significance of postwar reconstruction to American foreign policy. Result rewarded strategy in the area of economic policy, where the United States was able to trade financial and material resources for concessions to its commercial program. Strategy was disappointed, however, on the overarching political issue of restricting the westward extension of the Soviet empire. From the perspective determined by political developments, economic aid ceased to be a means for establishing a Wilsonian world order and became openly a tool for consolidating America's geopolitical position at the onset of what was to become the Cold War. By adopting the position that the U.S. should use its economic power to construct an anti-Soviet bloc, the Administration violated the most basic tenet of multilateralism, that bilateral economic agreements to promote political purposes should be banned because they led to international conflict. Indeed, multilateral commercial ideas, advertised during the war as the basis of a Wilsonian world, now became an important adjunct to the construction of an American sphere of influence. If the U.S. could bind the countries of Europe into a commercial system in which the U.S. would be supreme, this would be a highly effective means of consolidating the Western bloc on a long-term basis. American efforts to promote multilateral commercial agreements were thus deprived of the noble aspirations expressed by the wartime planners and necessarily became a tool in the kind of international power struggle they were intended to prevent.

5. Deferring the Reconstruction Issue—Again

In 1946 the American government clearly understood the need for new programs of economic assistance to promote European reconstruction. But domestic political considerations caused Truman to defer the attempt to win Congressional support for large-scale foreign aid until after the 1946 elections.

ONE OF THE CONSEQUENCES attributable to the inattention given the reconstruction issue during World War II was a profound lack of realism among American officials concerning the problems of postwar recovery. Far from anticipating the fact that economic reconstruction itself would be the greatest challenge of the postwar period, wartime planners projected a rapid transition to conditions that would permit full implementation of multilateralism. This kind of thinking was slow to die. It was reflected in American insistence that the British accept full convertibility of sterling one year after the effective date of the proposed loan; it was also implicit in American refusal to pay more than 50 per cent of the costs of Bizonal Germany.

Yet the economic information received by the American government through its contacts with European officials worked hard against the grain of official complacency. Stimson has written that it was "wholly clear" by July 1945 that "not only Britain but all Europe would need large scale American help." Also writing of mid-1945, President Truman has stated that "it was already becoming apparent that we would be called upon to give aid, on a large scale, to many of the war-devastated areas . . . [it was] plain that help was badly needed and that it would have to come from us." The steady stream of aid-seeking economic missions to the United States from the impoverished nations of Europe—not only Britain and France, but also Italy, Greece, and the smaller countries—provided the Americans with constant reminders of European dependency upon American assistance. The records of the National Advisory Council, which considered and passed upon all allocations of loans through the Export-Import Bank, indicate an acute consciousness of the inadequacy of the American response to European needs. The economic situation in Italy was described as "desperate" and the 150 million dollars made available to that country was seen as adequate to finance its deficit for only a few months. In late 1946 the Americans were projecting an Italian deficit of half a billion dollars in 1947. The situation in France was equally demanding. Clayton told the N.A.C. that a "decision against a substantial loan [to France] would be a catastrophe," yet to finance an anticipated French deficit of two billion dollars the U.S. extended a credit of only 650 million dollars. During 1946 France was forced to liquidate gold and dollar reserves in large quantities. The situation elsewhere, particularly Greece, bespoke large unmet needs. Such developments as inflation in the United States and the faltering of the British export drive in late 1946 even raised doubts about the adequacy of the loan to Britain.

This evidence of the status of European recovery was, of course, fragmentary, and in late 1946 the State Department was just beginning to assemble a total picture of the status of European recovery. Early suggestions of the vast scope of the problem, however, emanated from various quarters. One State Department report in late 1946 indicated that "the devastated countries of Europe will all face in 1947 and to a lesser extent in 1948 balance of payments problems aggravated by trade difficulties . . . substantial financial assistance will be required to maintain the current rate of recovery and to get ahead with the problem of reconstruction." The one attempt to develop a specific estimate of the scope of Europe's needs in 1946 was Nitze's estimate of the American export surplus, which involved mainly trade between the U.S. and Europe. Nitze's figures led him to conclude that an American aid program of approximately 5 billion dollars annually for five years would be required to permit the countries of Europe to continue taking American exports at 1946 levels. Few top officials in 1946 would have endorsed Nitze's proposal of an aid program fully capable of financing Europe's trade deficit, but there is no question that the Administration's top economic officials were aware that American lending activities were barely keeping pace with the economic problems of Europe, and were not solving them. The minutes of the National Advisory Council for 1946 are filled with references to the fact that European needs were far greater than American capacity to help. By mid-1946 the lending authority of the Export-Import Bank was exhausted, despite the reallocation to Europe of the one billion dollars previously earmarked for the Soviet loan. Yet, as Dean Acheson has written of late 1946, "the needs for relief, instead of declining, seemed due to rise." In a moment of despondency, the N.A.C. debated making loan commitments in excess of the lending authority of the Export-Import Bank.[50]

There existed in 1946 a number of financial mechanisms through which economic aid could be channeled to war-devastated countries. There were, first of all, the international institutions—U.N.R.R.A. and the World Bank—that had been established during the war to meet the needs of postwar reconstruction. The evolution of the international political situation in 1945–6 had had the effect, however, of cooling the enthusiasm of American officials for addressing the problem of reconstruction through international agencies. As economic assistance developed into the basic tool of American foreign policy in the Cold War, the American government became progressively more anxious to have complete control over its deployment. Thus, in 1946, the U.S. withdrew from U.N.R.R.A., having concluded, as Byrnes wrote, "that any new appropriations by Congress for foreign relief should be allocated by the United States." [51] The World Bank, scheduled to begin operations in early 1947, was so designed that it could grant only "hard" loans to borrowers capable of servicing their debts, a limitation that made it impossible for that institution to respond to the pressing needs of the most distressed countries, whose wrecked economies could not provide the necessary assurances. Conceivably the U.S. could have proposed a modification of the Bank's charter to meet the unfolding problems of reconstruction, but such a move was hardly consistent with a policy of unilateral control of economic assistance, and it seems never to have been considered. In practice, programs of economic assistance to Europe would have to come through one of the two devices available to the American government for unilateral assistance: the Export-Import Bank or special Congressional appropriations. The Truman administration took initiatives in both areas. In September 1945 the President informed Congress that he intended to submit a request for expanding the Bank's authority. In January 1946 the Administration submitted to Congress its proposal for a loan of 3.75 billion dollars to Great Britain. In the Congressional response to these proposals lies the story of the Administration's dilemma with regard to postwar reconstruction in 1946.

As the Administration's first postwar request to meet the special needs of economic recovery in Europe, the British loan was infused with a special significance. The loan's importance was increased by its absolute indispensability to the long-range American commercial program into which immense resources of official time and energy had been invested. It was indicative of the significance of this proposal that the Administration planned and carried out a prodigious campaign to develop public and Congressional support for it. The State Department planned speaking tours for a number of high-ranking officials. Clayton personally enlisted the support and participation of Byrnes, Wallace, Ickes, and Acheson. Clayton himself made several major addresses around the country, as well as numerous radio appearances and informal talks. During March and April, when Senate hearings were in progress, this campaign resulted in hundreds of speeches by major officials on behalf of the loan, with appearances by prominent figures carefully coordinated with key points in the hearing process. At the same time, Clayton mobilized assistance within the business community by sending hundreds of letters to influential leaders. He also contacted numerous organizations, including the Chamber of Commerce, the National Foreign Trade Council, and the American Farm Bureau, to enlist support. Finally, the appearance of top-level Administration officials at the hearings was carefully orchestrated and reinforced by a sustained personal campaign by Clayton among Congressmen and Senators. In the course of his efforts, Clayton sponsored a series of dinners at which he was able to urge approval of the loan personally upon every member of the House. Throughout this campaign, the basic argument advanced on behalf of the loan was that it would guarantee the adherence by Great Britain to America's multilateral program and, specifically, that it would open the Commonwealth trading bloc to American exports. This approach won broad support within the business community and among the nation's newspapers. The Administration anticipated a rapid progress for the loan through Congress, with approval coming in March or April.[52]

The expectation proved illusory. The loan encountered serious difficulty in Congress. The center of the opposition in the Senate was a group of midwestern Republican conservatives with reputations for both isolationism and economizing: Gurney of South Dakota, Brooks of Illinois, Reed of Kansas, Willis of Idaho, Ferguson of Michigan, Wherry of Nebraska, and, most important, Taft of Ohio. Taft, the spokesman for this group, made it clear that he was going to make an issue of the loan proposal and that his opposition would focus upon the economic internationalism to which the State Department was committed. He indicated that he would support a reduced bill to finance British relief, but would not endorse a program intended to subsidize what he considered to be the delusion of fully convertible, multilateral trade. Although the Senate Banking and Currency Committee reported the loan bill over Taft's objections, the outcome of floor debate appeared increasingly uncertain. Press polls indicated growing opposition to the loan in the Senate, and the House was expected to pose an even more difficult obstacle. As debate dragged on through the spring, hopes for early approval disappeared and the prospects for passage declined steadily.

To understand Congressional debate on the British loan, it is necessary to look beyond Congress itself, for the men around Taft, who represented the center of the opposition, had been in Congress in 1945 and had opposed Bretton Woods on the same grounds that they now opposed the loan. The Congressional vote on Bretton Woods had not really involved an endorsement of the Administration's commercial policies, but had been testimony to a vague belief in internationalism generated by the defeat of Germany and the opening of the San Francisco conference on the U.N. In that atmosphere, many Congressmen and Senators who were basically indifferent or even skeptical about Bretton Woods had been persuaded to support the Administration, and the determined oppositionists had been isolated and rendered ineffective. As the minority for which Taft spoke was equally determined in 1946, it was clear that broad popular support for the loan would again be required to assure its passage. This was especially significant because 1946 was an election year, the first since the war and the first since the death of Franklin Roosevelt. In this setting, skeptics were hardly likely to support the Administration in the absence of a clear popular mandate. Growing Congressional opposition to the loan in the spring of 1946 registered a lack of public support for the Administration's proposal. Indeed, polls taken during this period consistently recorded majorities in opposition to the loan.

Public opposition to the British loan emanated from a variety of sources. The Anglophobia of several ethnic groups appeared to be important. The socialism of the Labour government and Britain's efforts to revive the Empire also provided lightning rods for oppositionist sentiment. The main lines of objection to the loan, however, involved something more than a congeries of anti-British attitudes; they suggested configurations of opinion that directly reflected the patterns, successes, and failures of the wartime information programs of the Roosevelt and Truman administrations. For example, one of the major arguments against the loan was that it was a betrayal of the United Nations. When, in the midst of the debate on the loan, Churchill proposed an anti-Soviet Anglo-American alliance in his famous "iron curtain" speech, most Americans disapproved. The impressive successes of the American government to build public support for the U.N. have already been described. Similarly, the British loan was criticized as a revival of the old bilateralism against which so much of the Administration's rhetoric had inveighed and which the U.N. was specifically intended to replace. It is remarkable testimony to the effectiveness of the Administration's efforts to promote belief in this concept that Senator Vandenberg took the position in December 1945 that the U.S. should not extend aid to Britain if it were not prepared also to aid the Soviet Union, for such a step would make U.S.-Soviet cooperation impossible and doom the U.N. A second objection to the loan was that Britain's financial needs could be met at a much lower cost. This view suggested another aspect of the Administration's wartime propaganda: the suppression of discussion of the requirements of postwar reconstruction. In fact, Britain's needs would require much greater financial assistance than the loan offered.

The success of these arguments in eliciting opposition to the British loan suggests some of the most important consequences of the Administration's wartime propaganda. Intending to prevent a revival of isolationism, the Administration had succeeded in committing the public to a sanitized internationalism that was irrelevant to the conditions of 1946.

Based on a belief in the U.N. as a panacea that would end conflict and solve all problems of the postwar period, the internationalism of the American people in 1946 was not significantly different from isolationism. In fact, high levels of support for American involvement in the U.N. did not preclude a turning inward of public interests, evidence of which was to be found throughout American society. Unions striking for higher wages, lobbyists demanding an end to price control, the general public insisting upon a reduction in taxes and demobilization, all suggested a country weary of international conflict and anxious to return to business as usual. Repeatedly President Truman tried to stand against these demands with pleas for international responsibility, and repeatedly he was spurned. Public-opinion polls revealed that during 1945–6 fewer Americans considered international problems primary than during the late 1930's, when isolationism had been a major constraint upon American diplomacy. Such respected figures as Herbert Hoover and Bernard Baruch took the position that careful consideration of domestic needs should precede any program of aid to Europe.

The country was also manifesting reduced support for the kind of activist, high-budget federal operation associated with Franklin Roosevelt. This was perhaps inevitable after the war, but it also reflected the Administration's failure to prepare the public for the problems that would have to be faced in the postwar period. The Republicans, sensing the strength of this sentiment, emphasized in the early stages of the 1946 campaign the need to reduce the scope of federal activities, and they promised a tax cut as a symbol of their commitment to this goal. Early political reports of resurgent Republicanism suggested the effectiveness of this appeal. All of this worked strongly against public support for the British loan, which would divert resources from pressing domestic needs in order to promote an experimental international program labeled by one Senator as a "worldwide W.P.A." [53]

Against these currents of opinion the representations of Clayton and his colleagues on behalf of multilateral trade made little headway. In part this reflected overuse of the arguments for multilateralism during previous legislative campaigns, particularly the one for the Bretton Woods proposals. More importantly, however, the ineffectiveness of these arguments reflected the Administration's failure to build public support for its commercial program. A March 1946 poll, for example, asked respondents who had demonstrated that they were informed about the loan what they considered to be the best argument in its favor; only 16 per cent pointed to the fact that it would promote American business and world trade. A series of confidential surveys made available to Clayton during the first half of 1946 reported that most support for the loan had little to do with multilateralism. One 1946 sampling concluded that the basic public attitude toward foreign trade was disinterest.[54] By mid-1946 it appeared that the absence of support for multilateralism in the public and Congress might well cause the defeat of the loan.

In this situation, a whole alternative line of argument for the loan presented itself to the Administration. Congressional leaders in both House and Senate began urging the Administration to stress the significance of the loan in the context of deteriorating U.S.-Soviet relations, and to combine this with strong public statements exposing the defunct status of the wartime alliance. These leaders argued that this was the only way to save the loan. Such suggestions reinforced a school of thought that had gathered support within the Administration. Several men close to the President believed that unwarranted public optimism about the U.N. and U.S.-Soviet relations had became the single most significant constraint upon American diplomacy. Navy Secretary Forrestal was the first to reach this conclusion; his concern over public pressure for demobilization had led him to urge a reversal of Roosevelt's public information policies as early as October 1945. At first Byrnes had opposed this view, but by January 1946, his negotiations with the Soviets having proved fruitless, he agreed with Forrestal. Thus, as Congressional debate on the loan proceeded inconclusively in mid-1946, pressures mounted on the Administration to undertake a dramatic reorientation of American attitude toward U.S.-Soviet relations.[55]

These pressures placed President Truman and the political leadership of the Democratic Party in a difficult position. The loan was critical to American economic policy and had to be passed. At the same time, the 1946 elections were pending, and an anti-Soviet turn by the Truman administration could only aggravate the electoral difficulties already portended by the absence of Roosevelt, the normal pattern of off-year elections, and the evident indications of a postwar turn toward conservatism. Support for the U.S.-Soviet alliance remained strong in the U.S. in 1946, particularly among traditionally Democratic segments of the population. From his earliest moments in the presidency, Truman had been under fire for turning away from his predecessor's policies on both foreign and domestic issues. Criticism was particularly strong among the liberals, to whom Truman was the Midwest conservative who had been placed on the ticket in 1944 in place of Henry Wallace, the liberals' true spokesman. In May 1946 a national alliance of three influential liberal organizations was established, in part to lobby for the continuation of U.S.-Soviet cooperation. Truman was convinced that the viewpoint represented by this group commanded broad support. The President's defiant stand against a series of strikes in 1945–6 had also undermined his position with labor, another center of support for the U.S.-Soviet alliance. Opposition to Truman in 1946 was sufficiently strong among liberal and labor groups to produce consistent discussion of a third party for 1948. Under these circumstances, despite his commitment to a foreign policy that precluded U.S.-Soviet cooperation, the suggestion that he alter his public information policy and take an anti-Soviet line must have seemed to a politician like Truman less a real alternative than an invitation to suicide. When Clark Clifford submitted his memo on U.S.-Soviet relations in September 1946, Truman told him it was too "hot" to be circulated and locked it away in his office safe.[56]

Under these circumstances, the Truman administration equivocated on the issue of its public stance regarding U.S.-Soviet relations. Beginning in January 1946 the President did alter his policy of shielding the public from U.S.-

Soviet disputes as they developed. For example, when the Soviets failed to withdraw their troops from Iran in March 1946, Secretary Byrnes went to the U.N. in person and with great fanfare presented the case against the Soviet action. When the U.S. decided to take a "firm" stand in response to the Soviet pressures on Turkey in August 1946, a strong statement of American policy was released immediately to the press. Byrnes also altered his attitude toward press coverage of his conferences with Soviet Foreign Minister Molotov and began to insist upon complete press access to these meetings. The basic strategy of this shift in public-information policy in 1946 is obvious from these developments; the Administration drew aside the cloak of propaganda and censorship that had previously veiled U.S.-Soviet relations and permitted the public to view events as they developed. Such a policy, however, stopped well short of enunciating a strong anti-Soviet position as the basis of American diplomacy, and this the President consistently refused to do in 1946. Though Byrnes, Forrestal, and Kennan made speeches that began to suggest the depth of the break between the U.S.S.R. and the U.S., Truman did not do so. Indeed, prior to the elections both he and the Secretary of State delivered major addresses that seemed to anticipate continued U.S.-Soviet cooperation. Consistent with this general approach, the Administration rejected the suggestion that it urge approval of the British loan on the basis of an anti-Soviet appeal, though, according to one subsequent report, Secretary Byrnes did make one trip to Capitol Hill during House debate "to make the House of Representatives' flesh creep with anti-Soviet horror tales." [57]

The British loan was finally approved by Congress in July. The argument that proved decisive was the anti-Soviet one, even though the Administration did not launch an anti-Soviet campaign on behalf of the measure. Several key Congressional leaders, particularly Vandenberg in the Senate and McCormack in the House, took the initiative in this matter, and their arguments provided the margin of victory. Despite the final vote, Congressional action was in many ways a defeat for the Administration. It was certainly a defeat for the commercial policies of the State Department, as Clayton readily recognized. Indeed, the State Department was so impressed by the lack of support for its economic policies that it decided to suppress until after the election information concerning the tariff reductions it was planning to propose at the international conference on the G.A.T.T., scheduled to convene in Geneva in early 1947. The loan debate was also a defeat for the Administration's broad efforts to respond to the problem of European reconstruction in 1946. Its unwillingness to undertake a major reorientation of public opinion with regard to the one issue—U.S.-Soviet relations—on which support for economic aid could be crystallized obviously precluded any major initiative in this field. In the face of the Congressional mood, the Administration withdrew its proposal for an expansion of the resources of the Export-Import Bank, although the National Advisory Council had reported that the expansion involved a "minimum figure" to meet only "the most urgent foreign needs." The Administration also rejected a variety of proposals that it ask Congress for special appropriations on behalf of a number of countries in particularly acute difficulty, including France, Italy, and Greece. One high-level economic official in the State Department has summarized the Administration's attitude toward reconstruction at this time: "throughout 1946, Washington was not in a mood to encourage any initiative among its representatives on measures to aid Europe. The fear of Congress was very great and there was no chance that any measure that would make it necessary to seek additional funds from Congress would be approved by the State Department." [58] In short, the issue of reconstruction was again deferred. Europe would have to wait upon the outcome of the American election.

II
The Truman Doctrine

1. Winter 1946–7

*In the months immediately following the 1946
elections all major factors inclining the Truman
administration toward sponsorship of foreign
aid—the economic and political situation
in Europe, the requirements of the domestic
economy, the progress of international
negotiations over multilateralism—indicated
that the need for American economic assistance
to Europe was reaching the crisis stage. But
the elections showed that domestic political
opposition to such assistance was greater than
ever, and placed Congress under the control of
the Republican Party, which had traditionally
opposed the Administration's commercial program.*

THE PROGRESS OF ECONOMIC RECOVERY in Europe during 1946
had been uneven. Though there were numerous indications
that full reconstruction was not in sight, both Britain and
France, the countries Clayton described as the "key to the
European situation," had mounted effective campaigns to increase production for export that provided increased earnings
of the dollars required to finance essential needs. Such hopeful
signs had permitted the men responsible for American foreign
policy to believe they had time to defer the program of economic aid they knew to be inevitable and await more congenial domestic political circumstances.

Events during the winter of 1946–7 changed this situation abruptly. In December it was reported that Britain's production drive was faltering, and the Attlee government was
prompted the following month to issue a white paper on the
economy, calling the situation "extremely serious." At the end of

January Britain was subjected to an unusually severe and protracted winter storm that brought the entire economy to a standstill. The earlier downturn was transformed into a major disaster. Simultaneously, other difficulties began to appear. A number of Commonwealth countries, to which Britain had incurred immense indebtedness to finance the war, suddenly began asserting claims for dollars on the British Treasury. Price inflation in the United States diminished the real value of both Britain's dollar reserves and the 1946 loan. The result of these combined developments was a rapid acceleration in Britain's loss of dollar reserves, an event registered on the American side of the Atlantic by an increase in the rate of British drawings on the loan. During the first quarter of 1947, withdrawals nearly equaled the total for 1946; it was becoming clear that the credit would be exhausted much more rapidly than had been anticipated. The British loudly proclaimed their distress in an Economic Survey for 1947, issued in February. In response, *The New York Times* editorialized that "the emergency in Britain has . . . projected before our imagination the picture of a world without British power." Walter Lippmann, the most perceptive political journalist in the United States, wrote that the report "states the hard facts that will compel us in the fairly near future to take extraordinary measures." [1]

The Americans were always somewhat slower to respond to the problems of the rest of Europe than of Britain—undoubtedly because of Britain's greater significance to America's commercial program—but on the continent, too, the winter of 1946–7 produced a series of disturbing signals that could not go unnoticed. In September 1946 a Temporary Subcommittee on Economic Reconstruction of War Devastated Areas, a study group containing American representation formed the previous June by the Economic and Social Council of the U.N., reported serious shortages of food, housing, domestic equipment, tools, clothes, footware, and raw materials throughout Europe. Manpower shortages were impeding economic recovery. The report found that in every country of western Europe except Sweden industrial production remained considerably below pre-war levels, and that most countries could expect grain crops in

1946 no better than 60 per cent of pre-war volume. Coal production was operating at 72 per cent of pre-war output. The
severe winter that paralyzed Britain affected the continent
also. In January the U.N. reported that Austria, Greece, Hungary, Italy, Poland, and Yugoslavia needed assistance merely
to prevent mass starvation, not to speak of economic recovery.
The French continued to liquidate gold and dollar reserves
with no signs of a letup. Belgium and the Netherlands, whose
gold reserves had held steady in 1946, began to report major
liquidations in early 1947. These conditions were constantly
impressed upon American officials by European diplomats and
visiting heads of state. The State Department was in the
process of combining its reports on individual countries into a
total sense of the problem of European reconstruction. In early
March Clayton—possibly using the figures developed by Paul
Nitze in late 1946—proposed that Congress be asked immediately to appropriate five billion dollars to initiate a program of
grants and loans for reconstruction. In the same month the
National Advisory Council took note of the inadequacy of
existing financial resources to meet the needs of recovery.[2]

The rapid expansion in American awareness of economic
conditions in Europe forced the Truman administration to
consider a range of immediate economic and political possibilities that, taken together, could defeat American plans for
the postwar world. Because the economic crisis was centered
in Britain, the implications for American economic policy
were particularly ominous. The Economic Survey for 1947
made clear that Britain's payments imbalance was so severe
that the government would have to maintain rigid controls on
dollar imports for the indefinite future. There were also reports
that, in order to increase its dollar resources, Britain was considering the imposition of controls on exports to continental
Europe and the redirection of this trade to the dollar area.
Because of Britain's central position in international commerce,
such policies would have far-reaching implications. A reduction in Britain's exports to continental Europe would increase
the necessity for those countries to maintain controls on dollar
imports in order that critical supplies made unavailable from

British producers could be purchased in the United States. Restrictions on dollar imports by Britain and the countries of continental Europe would limit the capacity of Latin American countries to export to Europe and thus reduce the dollars available to them to finance purchases in the American market. From the American perspective, these possibilities portended a general reduction in the level of American exports at a time when the Administration believed high levels of exports to be a critical factor in preventing a domestic depression. Extensive foreign aid was required to keep trade flowing, but in early 1947 the existing economic-assistance programs were drawing to an end with no replacement in sight. According to the Council of Economic Advisors, widespread awareness in early 1947 that there was no obvious prospect of maintaining current levels of exports led to "renewed declarations that a business slump was imminent." [3]

The implications of Europe's plight for America's long-range economic objectives were serious. The minimization of politically imposed controls on international trade was the central purpose of America's multilateral program. Yet the immediate future seemed to promise an increase of such controls. Moreover, there were reports in the British press that the Economic Survey for 1947 had understated Britain's problems in order to avoid panic and that Britain would be forced to default on commitments to adopt multilateral practices, particularly the convertibility requirement of the 1946 loan.

These prospects could not have appeared at a worse time for the United States. The long-awaited international conference to develop the General Agreement on Tariffs and Trade was scheduled to convene in Geneva in April 1947. The chief prize to be won at this meeting was agreement by Britain to renounce import policies that discriminated in favor of the members of the Commonwealth trading bloc. The importance the Americans attached to the outcome of this conference was indicated by the President in a speech on March 6: "We have proposed negotiations directed towards the reduction of tariffs, here and abroad, towards the elimination of other restrictive measures and the abandonment of discrimina-

tion. . . . The success of this program is essential to the establishment of the International Trade Organization, to the
effective operation of the International Bank and Monetary
Fund, and to the strengthening of the whole United Nations
structure. . . . The negotiations at Geneva must not fail." The
United States fully understood what developments in British
commercial policy suggested, that multilateralism could not be
achieved in the absence of economic recovery. This was a
constant theme of Clayton's public statements. It had been a
major conclusion of the September 1946 report of the U.N.
Temporary Subcommittee. It had been articulated in the report of the preliminary international conference that had made
the arrangements for the Geneva meeting. It is not surprising,
therefore, that Clayton, while preparing himself for the Geneva
conference, produced the first top-level proposal for immediate
action to provide economic assistance to Europe. His memo
specifically indicated that American aid should be used as a
means of requiring recipient countries to adopt multilateral
policies.[4]

The economic conditions that developed in Europe during the winter of 1946–7 seriously undermined the political
stability of western European countries and American efforts
to organize this region into an anti-Soviet bloc. The collapsing
British economy was one of the main props of western Europe
in early 1947. British industrial exports were playing a vital
role in reconstruction of the continent. If Britain were to
forcibly restrict exports to the rest of Europe and thereby
further reduce supplies of essential goods in countries where
almost all materials were in short supply, the political consequences were certain to be in the direction of instability and
polarization. The American government could not ignore the
possibility that these circumstances would strengthen the
Communist Party in France and Italy and might well bring
communists into power in either country through elections or
a forcible coup. Moreover, Britain was providing direct financial support to several important countries of Europe. It was
paying half the bill for the occupation of Bizonal Germany,
itself an economically depressed area with a dollar deficit

exceeded in Europe only by those of Britain and France. Britain was providing dollar aid to Turkey and Greece, and in the latter country it was maintaining seventy thousand troops and bearing much of the cost of a full-scale civil war between the monarchist government and Communist-led guerrillas.

The Economic Survey for 1947 drew attention to Britain's overseas expenditures in Germany, Greece, and elsewhere, which, taken together, roughly equaled Britain's dollar deficit. It was well known that Chancellor of the Exchequer Hugh Dalton, among others, was pressing the government to liquidate some of these commitments. The political consequences of such a move by Britain seemed ominous. Greece and Turkey could conceivably be absorbed into the Soviet sphere of influence that surrounded both of them. Such a development would endanger western European access to the oil resources of the Middle East, upon which American planners were depending for programs of European recovery. Harriman and Forrestal were particularly obsessed with the need to maintain access to Mid East oil, and Clifford's 1946 memo had seen this as one of the major areas of conflict between the U.S.S.R. and the U.S. As early as November 1946 a cabinet-level committee of the American government had considered the possibility of termination of British aid to Greece and Turkey and had decided that, should this occur, the United States would step into the breach.[5]

The appreciation by top-level American officials of the significance of the reconstruction problem was hardly a new development during the winter of 1946–7. But domestic political considerations had consistently frustrated efforts to give reconstruction the attention and priority it deserved. Most recently, in the face of adverse political developments in early 1946, the Truman administration had deferred an effective response to the issue until after the Congressional elections. Neither the campaign nor the election, however, produced any comfort for the champions of a vigorous American response to the problem of economic recovery. The Republicans based their campaign upon the same conservative sentiment that had posed a problem for the Administration in its efforts to mobilize support for the British loan. They promised a tax cut, a reduction in the scope of federal activities, a return to business as usual. Their political instincts proved correct. They won an overwhelming victory, gaining fifty-six seats in the House, thirteen in the Senate, and obtaining decisive majorities in both. The elections produced the famous Senate "class of 1946," dominated by members of the most conservative wing of the Republican Party: John Bricker of Ohio, William Jenner of Indiana, William Knowland of California, George Malone of Nevada, Joseph McCarthy of Wisconsin, Arthur Watkins of Utah, John Williams of Delaware.

The results of the elections could not have provided less reason for optimism that bold departures in American foreign policy would soon be forthcoming. The distinctive feature of American foreign policy as it had been developed by the Truman administration in 1945-6 was that it was based not upon the negotiation of treaties or the use of armed forces but on the extension of economic assistance. While executive initiative had been established and accepted with respect to functions traditionally associated with diplomacy, the Administration's strategy had the unprecedented effect of centering foreign policy in an aspect of federal activity—appropriations —where initiative traditionally rested with the legislative branch, particularly the House. This revolutionary development implied difficulties of many kinds, including the requirement that the State Department operate in somewhat uncharted waters, the relative lack of expertise in the area of foreign policy of the House of Representatives, and the low status of the House Committee on Foreign Affairs. These problems were enormously aggravated, of course, by the assumption of control of the Congress by the Republicans. This party had based its campaign upon limiting federal expenditures and reducing taxes; it would be difficult for it now to support vast new programs of economic assistance. Republicans had attacked innovative, New Deal–style government; a massive foreign-aid program would inevitably carry the American government into types of activities and commitments without precedent in American history. The G.O.P. had accused the Administration of failing to deal effectively with the problem of inflation; by placing increased demands upon American supplies, foreign aid would exert upward pressure on prices. Perhaps most significant, the Republicans had never shown much support for the foreign economic policies that the foreign-aid program would be intended to promote. Twenty-eight of thirty-six Republican Senators had opposed the Bretton Woods proposals. Twenty-five of thirty-four voting Republican Senators had opposed the last extension of the Trade Agreements Act. One hundred twenty-two of one hundred eighty-three voting Republican Representatives had opposed the British loan. Moreover, the critical committee chairmanships were now in the hands of Republicans. The House Appropriations Committee had become the fief of John Taber, an uncompromising economizer, enemy of the New Deal, and critic of the State Department. Senate Appropriations was under Styles Bridges, also a fundamentalist on federal activities. House Foreign Affairs was chaired by Charles Eaton, a former minister from New Jersey, without much standing in the House or close ties to the State Department. Senate Banking and Currency fell to Eugene Millikin, an intransigent opponent of Reciprocal Trade Agreements, Bretton Woods, and the whole economic program of Hull and Clayton. The only hope for the Administration lay with Arthur Vandenberg, the late-blooming internationalist, who had participated in the planning for the U.N. and appeared to enjoy the opportunity to strike statesmanlike poses.[6]

One of the major issues raised by the Republicans in their successful campaign involved the leadership of President Truman. Employing the campaign slogan "Had Enough?", the Republicans had berated the Administration for ineptitude in handling the country's problems, a charge made credible to many voters by the unbroken series of strikes and the inflationary conditions in the economy. Of particular significance for American foreign policy was the President's handling of an incident arising out of a speech delivered in September 1946 by Commerce Secretary Wallace, the most prominent spokesman for the liberal wing of the Demo-

cratic Party and the only major New Deal figure to have been
retained by the Truman administration. Wallace's speech urged
the Administration to pursue a policy of cooperation with the
U.S.S.R. and acknowledged that country's right to a sphere of
political influence in eastern Europe. At a news conference,
President Truman stated that he had read the speech and fully
approved it. Coming at a time when Secretary Byrnes was engaged in international negotiations with the announced purpose of preventing the Soviets from asserting political control
over eastern Europe, the President's comment caused considerable confusion. Foreign governments had to be reassured that
the President's remarks implied no change in American foreign policy. Republicans were able to charge that the President was betraying eastern Europe in a cynical bid for the
support of the Democratic left. Truman first tried to deny that
he meant what he said. When the furor failed to subside,
he asked Wallace to leave the cabinet. The episode did more
to portray Truman as a bungler in high office and a traitor to
the tradition of Franklin Roosevelt than all the oratory of his
critics on both the left and right. Even more significantly, the
incident left the impression that the President did not understand the most basic elements of American foreign policy.

The combined effect of his own mistakes and the Republican campaign was to diminish public confidence in Truman
almost to the vanishing point. Indicative of this was his failure
to make a single campaign appearance in support of Democratic candidates, despite previous statements that he would
participate actively in the election. Instead, the party sponsored
broadcasts of recordings by Franklin Roosevelt. Walter Lippmann called Truman's decline in standing a "grave problem
for the nation" and asked: "How are the affairs of the country
to be conducted by a president who not only has lost the support of his party but is not in command of his own administration . . . is not performing and gives no evidence of ability
to perform, the functions of commander in chief?" Significant
numbers of Americans seemed to share this view. One poll,
which had reported 87 per cent of the electorate approving

Truman's leadership shortly after he took office, found his support fallen to 32 per cent by November 1946.[7]

There were numerous pronouncements at this time about the necessity of maintaining bipartisanship in foreign policy, but it was difficult to find a single high-level official who believed that this would occur. The President, who felt that the "Republican leadership was still suffering from the after effects of isolationism," that the Eightieth Congress was "reactionary controlled," and that politics was politics, did not believe in it. Senator Vandenberg, who thought that the Democrats were "natural born oppositionists" and "will revert to type," did not believe in it. Political journalists reported that it was unlikely. The opening weeks of the Eightieth Congress seemed fully to justify pessimism about bipartisan support for new departures in foreign aid. By early February Congress had reduced the already harassed Defense Department to new agonies of despair by summarily striking six billion dollars from a proposed Defense budget. Senator Hugh Butler, a newly elected Republican from Nebraska, wrote Clayton to assert that the election was a public repudiation of the Reciprocal Trade Agreements Program, and the Jenkins Resolution, which prohibited further tariff agreements prior to full investigation by the tariff commission, was introduced in the House, reportedly with the support of the Republican leadership. The newly elected Speaker, Joseph Martin of Massachusetts, distressed Administration officials and European diplomats by declaring in his maiden address that "there is danger that war-stricken nations may be led to rely too much on the United States and try too little to help themselves . . . we must avoid the danger of so depleting and weakening ourselves as to be dragged down with them." [8]

These developments constrained the State Department to assume a defensive posture at exactly the moment that its officers felt the international situation required bold and aggressive action. The dilemma was posed with particular sharpness in the field of commercial policy. Clayton was about to leave for Geneva to negotiate the G.A.T.T. His entire authority to reduce tariffs in these negotiations derived from the Reciprocal Trade Agreements Act. Yet that program was now under attack in Congress, apparently with the support of the majority leadership. Understandably distressed, Clayton and Acheson sought the assistance of Vandenberg and Millikin, but were able to win postponement of a full-scale attack on Reciprocal Trade only by agreeing to sponsor an executive order restricting the President's authority to reduce tariffs. Republican hostility to the Trade Agreements program made it more imperative than ever that the U.S. win a dramatic victory for American business at the Geneva Conference. Indeed, the head of the State Department's Commercial Policy Division felt it necessary to guarantee that the British would agree to eliminate Imperial preference at Geneva. As we have seen, the economic situation in Britain was driving that country's commercial policy in precisely the opposite direction, and the new restrictions upon the authority of the American executive to reduce tariffs was likely to reinforce this tendency by reminding the British that they could not count on the Americans to accept the multilateral principles they were sponsoring. At the moment that it was most imperative for the Department to achieve a success, the prospects were uniquely poor.[9]

As Clayton pointed out in his memo of March 5, large-scale economic assistance could provide an effective tool by which to win acceptance of multilateral principles by European countries and was, in fact, the indispensable component of the Administration's entire foreign policy. But the prevailing political atmosphere had engendered in the State Department what one official described as a mood of "utter despair about the possibility of foreign aid." Thus, despite its growing awareness of the problems of postwar recovery in Europe, members of the Truman administration continued, in early 1947, to be fearful of speaking openly about the imperatives that lay ahead for American foreign policy. For example, in his address of March 6 on foreign economic policy, the President made no reference to proposals in the field of foreign aid. According to Joseph Jones, a State Department information officer who later wrote an invaluable history of the origins of the Marshall Plan, such proposals "were too radical even to consider mentioning in the political atmosphere that prevailed when the speech was conceived and drafted." Early drafts of a speech prepared for delivery by Secretary of State Marshall at Princeton in late February contained strong and clear references to the need to appropriate vast sums to meet the goals of reconstruction, but these were all excised or reduced to vague banalities by the time the speech was given. Perhaps the mood is best expressed in a memo written by Jones in late February:

> While we progress rapidly towards this [economic crisis], the front pages of today's papers are filled with accounts of the compromises which the President and Mr. Clayton and Mr. Martin of the Export-Import Bank are obliged to make with Congress on trade pacts, foreign relief, and foreign loans. . . . I think we must admit the conclusion that Congress and the people of this country are not sufficiently aware of the character and dimensions of the crisis that impends, and of the measures that must be taken in terms of relief, loans, gifts, constructive development programs and liberal trade policies—all these on a scale hitherto unimagined—if disaster is to be avoided. . . . The State Department knows. Congress and the people do not know. We thus face a situation similar to that prevailing prior to Pearl Harbor: a powerlessness on the part of the government to act because of Congressional or public unawareness of the danger or cost of inaction.[10]

2. Breakthrough on Foreign Aid

*Great Britain's decision to terminate financial
aid to the beleaguered Greek government
presented the Administration with an
opportunity to ask Congress for new programs
of aid to Europe. The request came in the
form of a declaration of global resistance to
communism, the famous Truman Doctrine speech.*

ON FEBRUARY 21 AND 24 the British Ambassador in Washington delivered to the State Department notes stating that his government would not be able to continue financial assistance to Greece and Turkey after the end of the British fiscal year, March 31, 1947. The notes referred to Anglo-American agreements that the Soviet Union ought to be prevented from acquiring a dominant position in either of these countries and implied that the further implementation of this policy would have to be an American responsibility. As we have seen, the Americans fully appreciated the implications of a British withdrawal from Greece and Turkey and had decided several months previously how they would respond to such a move. The fact that George Marshall, Chief of Staff of the American Army during the war, had replaced James Byrnes as Secretary of State in January 1947 had not affected American policy in this area. Indeed, Marshall's lack of a partisan political past made it easier for the Administration to face a problem it had been avoiding for months, that of requesting funds from Congress to provide financial assistance to Europe.

From the political perspective of the State Department, the situation created by the British action had positive and negative features. Given the fact that the issue of economic aid would have to be faced soon in any event, there were clear advantages in facing it first in the context of Greece. This was the only country of Europe actively threatened by a Communist uprising. If Congress had any willingness at all to extend foreign aid, it would probably respond to this situation, and a favorable result here would establish the principle of financial assistance for future application. On the other hand, it would be impossible to discuss the need to aid Greece without reference to the general problems of Europe. The primary significance of both Greece and Turkey had to be measured in terms of the implications of events there for the rest of Europe and the Middle East. Moreover, the crises in Greece and Turkey were really a manifestation of the crisis in Britain, since it was the withdrawal of British aid that had created the present situation, and Britain's problems were only a part of the general problems of Europe. Administration officials displayed an acute awareness of the broad aspects of the situation created by the British decision. As the State Department worked on its specific response to the situation in Greece and Turkey, it initiated the broad planning for European reconstruction that would culminate in the Marshall Plan. President Truman, in discussing Greece and Turkey with the cabinet, made it clear that American aid to those countries "would be only the beginning." But to state publicly that American aid would be required not only for Greece and Turkey but for all Europe would be to suggest commitments so immense and far-reaching that Congress might refuse to respond. Out of these conflicting considerations, the State Department developed a compromise: it would attempt to establish the principle of aid without revealing the full financial implications of the principle. This decision was made by Dean Acheson, Acting Secretary in the absence of Marshall, who was attending a conference in Moscow. Acheson explained his strategy this way: "If FDR were alive . . . he would make a statement of global policy but confine his request for money right now to Greece and Turkey." [11]

The history of the steps by which the decision to ask Congress for money to assist Greece and Turkey as part of a global policy was transformed into the Greco-Turkish Aid Program and the Truman Doctrine has been told in Jones's account. For the purposes of this study it is necessary only to note that Acheson's decision corresponded well with the thinking of the President and his chief adviser, Clark Clifford. Clifford's memo of September 1946 had suggested that it was necessary for the United States to enunciate a global policy of resistance to Soviet expansion. In a comment that probably refers to Clifford's proposal, Truman has said that he had wanted to make a statement like the Truman Doctrine speech for months prior to its actual delivery. The main constraint upon him had been a desire not to alienate the left wing of the Democratic Party before the 1946 elections. By February 1947, of course, that constraint had been removed. Moreover, though the election was a disaster for the Democrats, the returns suggested that the Wallaceite left had less popular support than the President had supposed. Almost all the candidates endorsed by the Political Action Committee of the C.I.O. (C.I.O.-P.A.C.), the core political organization of the liberal-labor alliance, had been defeated.[12] In the context of this political situation and the pressing nature of the problem of reconstruction, the President decided to make the statement that he had hitherto avoided. His speech before a joint session of Congress at noon on March 12, 1947 was broadcast nationally by radio.

> The gravity of the situation which confronts the world today necessitates my appearance before a joint session of Congress. The foreign policy and national security of this country are involved. One aspect of the present situation . . . concerns Greece and Turkey. . . .
> When forces of liberation entered Greece they found that the retreating Germans had destroyed virtually all the railways, roads, port facilities, communications, and merchant marine. More than a thousand villages had been burned. Eighty-five per cent of the children were tubercular. Livestock, poultry, and draft animals had almost disappeared. Inflation had wiped out practically all savings. As a result of these tragic conditions, a militant minority, exploiting human want and misery, was able to create political chaos which, until now, has made economic recovery impossible. . . .
> The very existence of the Greek state is today

threatened by the terrorist activities of several thousand armed men, led by Communists. . . . Greece must have assistance if it is to become a self-supporting and self-respecting democracy. The United States must supply that assistance. . . . There is no other country to which democratic Greece can turn. No other nation is willing and able to provide the necessary support for a democratic Greek government. . . .

Greece's neighbor, Turkey, also deserves our attention. . . . Since the war Turkey has sought financial assistance from Great Britain and the United States for the purpose of effecting that modernization necessary for the maintenance of its national integrity. That integrity is essential to the preservation of order in the Middle East. . . . As in the case of Greece, if Turkey is to have the assistance it needs, the United States must supply it. We are the only country able to provide that help.

I am fully aware of the broad implications involved if the United States extends assistance to Greece and Turkey. . . . The peoples of a number of countries of the world have recently had totalitarian regimes forced upon them against their will. The Government of the United States has made frequent protests against coercion and intimidation, in violation of the Yalta agreement, in Poland, Rumania, and Bulgaria. I must also state that in a number of other countries there have been similar developments.

At the present moment in world history nearly every nation must choose between alternative ways of life. The choice is often not a free one. One way of life is based upon the will of the majority, and is distinguished by free institutions, representative government, free elections, guarantees of individual liberty, freedom of speech and religion, and freedom from political oppression. The second way of life is based upon the will of a minority forcibly imposed upon the majority. It relies upon terror and oppression, a controlled press and radio, fixed elections, and the suppression of personal freedoms.

I believe that it must be the policy of the

United States to support free peoples who are resisting attempted subjugation by armed minorities or by outside pressures. . . . I believe that our help should be primarily through economic and financial aid which is essential to economic stability and orderly political processes. . . .

It is necessary only to glance at a map to realize that the survival and integrity of the Greek nation are of grave importance in a much wider situation. If Greece should fall under the control of an armed minority, the effect upon its neighbor, Turkey, would be immediate and serious. Confusion and disorder might well spread throughout the entire Middle East. Moreover, the disappearance of Greece as an independent state would have a profound effect upon those countries in Europe whose peoples are struggling against great difficulties to maintain their freedoms and independence while they repair the damages of war. . . . Collapse of free institutions and loss of independence would be disastrous not only for them but for the world. . . . Should we fail to aid Greece and Turkey in this fateful hour, the effect will be far-reaching to the West as well as to the East. . . .[13]

Two themes of American policy found expression in the President's statement. The first of these, anti-communist and anti-Soviet, was expressed in the references to "several thousand armed men, led by Communists" who were challenging the authority of the Greek government, to the difficulties being encountered by Turkey "for the maintenance of its national integrity," in the broad statement that "a number of countries of the world have recently had totalitarian regimes forced upon them against their will," and in the specific references to violations of the Yalta agreement in Poland, Rumania, and Bulgaria. The second theme referred to America's world economic responsibilities, particularly those concerning the problem of postwar reconstruction. It was expressed in the emphasis on Greece's economic situation, particularly its devastation during the war and its current condition of "human want and misery," in the reference to European countries endeavoring to "repair the ravages of war," and most importantly in the assertion that "our help should be primarily through economic and financial aid." In its discussion of these two themes the speech made reference to two matters concerning which the proclamation of new American policies had been deferred for a considerable period of time. In conjoining them the President adopted the position taken by Forrestal and Byrnes early in 1946 that popular support for extensive foreign aid could be achieved only in the framework of an exposition of the expansionist nature of Soviet policy and the announcement of a policy of resistance to it.

The aid program proposed in the speech was extremely modest. The President asked for a total of 400 million dollars for both Greece and Turkey. The 250 million dollars for Greece was divided between economic and military aid. The money for Turkey was entirely for military aid. That a presidential statement of the scope, significance, and rhetorical force of the Truman Doctrine was employed for the primary purpose of assuring Congressional passage of such a limited program is a measure of the Administration's respect for the political resistance of Congress and the country to new commitments in the field of foreign aid. In terms of this primary purpose, the speech was, of course, a complete success. The President had turned debate on two modest proposals into a vote of confidence on his administration's foreign policy and a test of American willingness to resist a threat defined to endanger the basic security and values of American society. In so doing, as Arthur Vandenberg complainingly pointed out, the President had presented Congress with a *fait accompli*. Congressman Francis Case of South Dakota, who presided over the House during much of the debate on Greco-Turkish aid, objected in writing to the President's heavy-handed tactics: "The situation was regarded as an accomplished fact. You had spoken to the world. At least 75 members, I judge, would have voted against final passage, myself included, had it not been that we thought it would be like pulling the rug out from under you and Secretary of State Marshall in the positions you had taken at Moscow and would of necessity take until settlement is reached of many problems. . . ." The Greco-Turkish Aid Program was approved by overwhelming bipartisan majorities in both houses, a victory that was testimony to the tactical power of the Truman Doctrine speech. The log-jam on foreign aid was broken.[14]

3. The Truman Doctrine as an Instrument of Propaganda

The crisis of March 1947 related more to American than Greek politics, and the rhetoric of the Truman Doctrine was based more upon the Administration's need to win political support for Greco-Turkish aid than a desire to portray accurately American foreign policy.

THE TRUMAN DOCTRINE speech was an official pronouncement of unusual historical significance. Although rapidly composed in the absence of the Secretary of State, it was to become the seminal declaration of American foreign policy in the postwar period. For many years it would be employed by American politicians on every level to define the nature of America's purposes in the Cold War. In a more limited sense, it inaugurated the long-deferred campaign to win public and Congressional support for a comprehensive American response to the economic needs of postwar Europe. Although the Marshall Plan itself, which would constitute the bulk of the American program for European reconstruction, was not proposed publicly until June 1947, the Truman Doctrine speech, and the manner in which it was used to assure Congressional passage of aid to Greece and Turkey, established a pattern of procedure that the Truman administration would employ at every major point in Congressional consideration of the foreign-aid program. The speech had its roots in the frustration that American policymakers had experienced during 1945–6.

In his memo of March 5, 1947 proposing that Congress be asked for five billion dollars for foreign aid, Assistant Secretary Clayton stated that "the United States will not take world leadership effectively unless the people of the United States are shocked into doing so." He proposed an exposé of the communist threat as the proper means of achieving this. Senator Vandenberg expressed a similar view when he was told that the Administration intended to ask Congress for money to aid Greece and Turkey. He told the President he would have "to scare the hell out of the country" in order to win approval of the program. The Truman Doctrine speech was admirably designed to achieve the purposes suggested by Vandenberg and Clayton. There were two basic elements of this design: the first involved the atmosphere of crisis in which the proposals were put forward; the second involved the rhetoric by which the speech defined the world situation.[15]

Although, prior to the President's speech, the American press had printed numerous indications of increasing American involvement in Greece, and despite two meetings between the President and Congressional leaders to discuss the situations in Greece and Turkey, nothing had prepared the great number of Congressmen and Senators for the urgent message to which they listened on March 12. In the wake of the speech the question was raised as to why this major step had been taken so hastily that the Congress could not be prepared or consulted prior to the full commitment of American resources. To this a simple answer was offered: there had been no time. The Administration stated that the British withdrawal from Greece had been unexpected and had left Greece in such a desperate state that if immediate assistance were not forthcoming, the Greek government would surely fall. Both of these assertions need to be examined.[16]

During the war the British had assumed responsibility for the liberation and occupation of Greece. With the accession of the Labour Party in 1945, however, the British government, aware of its domestic economic difficulties and politically embarrassed by its patronage of a rightist Greek regime, made initial efforts to turn Greece into an area of Anglo-American cooperation. The first fruit of this policy was an Export-Import Bank loan to Greece in January 1946, but this aid did not begin to satisfy Greek requirements, and the need to attract additional American credits was a major theme of Anglo-Greek discussions later in 1946. America's interest in Greece was increased after August 1946 when the Soviet Union initiated its efforts to wrest partial control of the Dardanelles from Turkey, and the Administration decided to defend Turkey against such pressures. The American navy began to make appearances at ports in the eastern Mediterranean. America's activities in this region resulted in increased contact between the United States and both England and Greece. In this new set of relationships, the United States assumed the dominant voice in countering Soviet moves directed against Greece and Turkey. America's financial involvement deepened accordingly. By September 1946 Byrnes assured British Foreign Minister Ernest Bevin that if the U.K. continued military aid to Greece, the United States would supply economic aid. In October the United States promised to send a mission to Greece to determine that country's economic requirements. Meanwhile, in September, the United Kingdom began to liquidate its commitment to Greece by announcing the partial withdrawal of British troops from that country, even though the military situation showed no signs of improvement.[17]

At the urging of the United Kingdom, Prime Minister Tsaldaris of Greece visited Washington in December 1946 to plead for additional American assistance. He met with a number of top American officials, including President Truman, Secretary Byrnes, Under Secretary Acheson, and Senator Vandenberg. By his own subsequent account, Tsaldaris received assurances during these meetings, particularly from Byrnes, that the United States recognized Greece's need for immediate economic assistance and was determined to make aid available. The Administration urged the Export-Import Bank to consider approving a loan to Greece, but this request was denied owing to the inability of Greece to service such a credit. After this decision it was evident that the only means of channeling aid to Greece was a Congressional appropriation. By December 1946, therefore, the Administration was aware of the need to ask Congress for the funds that had been promised to Greece; such a request comprised one half of the appropriation for Greece proposed in the Greco-Turkish aid bill.[18]

The second half of the Greek-assistance portion of the Greco-Turkish proposal was for financial and material assistance to the Greek army to replace British funds, which were to be discontinued on March 31. It was, of course, the British notes of February 21 and 24, announcing the termination of British support for the Greek armies, that had supplied the immediate rationale for requesting an appropriation for Greece. Throughout the period during which Greco-Turkish aid was under consideration, the Administration maintained that it had had no forewarning of the British decision. There is reason to doubt this, however. To be sure, Byrnes has reported that when Bevin told him in December 1946 that the British were anxious to withdraw their troops, he did not name a specific date for this action. This account coincides with Bevin's own later boast that the prompt American response to the British indicated not prior consultation but his own shrewd perception that political conditions in the U.S. assured a desirable initiative by the Truman administration. There is no reason to disbelieve these accounts on the limited point involving prior Anglo-American discussion of the timing of the British withdrawal. It is clear, however, that several highly placed American officials had concluded that British withdrawal was imminent by late 1946. Secretary Acheson acknowledged during the hearings that the United States had been aware for some time that Britain was considering the termination of aid to the Greek armed forces as a way of relieving pressure on the British economy. In fact, it was only after American urging—following the straits crisis of August 1946—that the British agreed to extend their commitment to Greece until March 31, 1947. In September 1946 Byrnes indicated that he was already committed to the idea that the United States had to assist both Greece and Turkey to whatever extent was required. His views provided the background for the meeting of the State–War–Navy Coordinating Committee in November, at which the possibility of the termination of British aid to the armed forces of both Greece and Turkey was considered. Both Clark Clifford and

Constantine Tsaldaris have indicated that the British had made it clear by November 1946 that their withdrawal was imminent. Acheson is on record as having been convinced by December that Congress should be asked to appropriate funds immediately to meet the situation that would be created by the withdrawal of British troops from Greece. Byrnes has reported that he believed withdrawal to be imminent at the time he left office in January 1947.[19]

Enough information of this tendency was known in Congress in March 1947 to produce considerable cynicism about the unexpectedness of the "crisis," and anger at the possibility that the Administration had allowed it to occur as a way of railroading Congress. The Administration outflanked any effort to turn such attitudes into opposition to the Greco-Turkish aid proposals by asserting that if assistance to Greece were not immediately approved the position of the Greek government would quickly become untenable. In his speech, the President stated, ". . . the situation is an urgent one, requiring immediate action"; and again, ". . . should we fail to aid Greece and Turkey in this fateful hour, the effect will be far-reaching to the West as well as to the East. We must take immediate and resolute action." In his opening presentation on the first day of the hearings, Acting Secretary Acheson stated: "The cessation of outside aid to Greece means immediate crisis. Unless help is forthcoming from some other quarter, Greece's economy will quickly collapse." Acheson placed a time limit on Greece's ability to survive without American aid. "Essential imports for civilians and for the army under the circumstances can continue for only a few weeks. Two weeks ago the dollar resources available to Greece were only $14,000,000, enough for one month's imports." Later, in response to questioning, the Acting Secretary repeated his statement: ". . . if we do not extend aid of the type required here the total foreign moneys which Greece has will enable it to buy what it needs from the outside for about one month." [20]

Subsequent events were to prove that the crisis was very much less acute than had been indicated by Administration officials. The Greco-Turkish aid bill was signed into law on May 22, 1947, two months after Acheson had given the Greek economy the capacity to survive for one month. Four days later the United States informed Greece of the approval of the aid program and then waited three weeks to receive a formal reply from Greece. During June and July the State Department moved to organize a permanent committee to expedite aid to Greece and Turkey but during this time no American aid was actually delivered. As late as August 1947 retransfers from British sources still accounted for much the largest portion of military assistance received by the Greeks. In August a small amount of American military aid procured under the new program was delivered to Greece—but it should be remembered that the crisis defined by Acting Secretary Acheson had referred to economic aid, not military requirements. The first economic aid to reach Greece under the Greco-Turkish Aid Program did so in October 1947, eight months after the "crisis" of the previous March.[21]

Considering together the long development of the American commitment to Greece and the long period that elapsed after the aid had been approved before any of it arrived there, it is difficult not to conclude that the crisis of March 1947 had its origins in American politics rather than developments in Greece. It has been argued that what Greece really needed in March 1947 was reassurance, and that the mere commitment of American support was sufficient to produce a substantial improvement in the situation of the Greek government. Though this may be true, it basically concedes the point it is offered to rebut. The question must be asked: Why did the Greek government require reassurance at this moment? The answer is not to be found in increased military successes of the guerrillas or in the condition of the Greek economy, though both the military and economic situations were extremely difficult in early 1947. The basis of anxiety was the conviction that the British were rapidly liquidating their support and skepticism about the willingness of the Americans to assume Britain's role. Moreover, by irrevocably and publicly joining this latter issue not only in terms of Greece but in terms of the entire world, the Truman Doctrine speech played a major role in creating the crisis of March 1947, by expanding the dimensions and significance of the issue before Congress. This becomes evident when one considers how serious the crisis would have seemed if the Administration had asked only for a short-term emergency program of assistance to Greece rather than a broad commitment to resist communist expansion. When an interim program was suggested to Clayton during the hearings, his response indicated that the crisis was to be found not in economic or military developments in Europe but in political events in Washington: "Any partial action . . . would raise a very grave doubt in the minds of the Greeks and the Turkish people and the other people in the world who are watching this matter and would throw doubt in the minds of people where we want to restore hope and some optimism." [22] The technique of the Truman Doctrine was to invert reality by imputing the urgency of a political crisis in the United States to the movement of events in the international sphere, particularly in Greece, thereby affecting an alteration of the domestic political situation, which, in turn, significantly influenced the international situation. Once Congress had shown itself willing to support the President's proposals, the situations that the proposals had been designed to meet lost much of their urgency. Indeed, the mere passage of the Greco-Turkish Aid Program was the decisive American victory in the first stage of the Cold War. It indicated the failure of the Soviet Union's efforts to promote American withdrawal from Europe and thereby marked the end of the initial struggle against communism in western Europe that had begun with the liberation.

The rhetoric of the Truman Doctrine, no less than the crisis of which it was a part, had its immediate origins in the domestic political forces impinging upon the Truman administration in early 1947. The program of aid to Greece and Turkey was the first Administration proposal for unilateral financial aid following the debate on the British loan during the first half of 1946. The latter proposal, it will be recalled, had encountered strong opposition in Congress, particularly from a group of Senate Republicans who were able to mobilize

opposition among colleagues inclined toward both government economies and isolationism. The threat to the loan posed
by this opposition had been neutralized only by the injection
of the anti-Soviet issue into the debate by several Congressional leaders who were aware that numerous Senators and
Congressmen who would not endorse the commercial internationalism of Will Clayton and Cordell Hull would respond
to an anti-communist appeal.

After the 1946 elections it was even more important to
propose foreign aid on a political basis that would be acceptable to minds not readily inclined toward expanded international commitments, since the new Republican majority was
well stocked with men of this mentality, and since few Republicans would follow the Democratic administration on an issue
as politically controversial as foreign aid in the absence of
strong public support. In a post-election assessment of the
prospects for foreign aid in the Eightieth Congress, James
Reston of *The New York Times* pointed out that the Republicans had traditionally been even more passionately anti-communist than the Democrats and suggested that this could provide the basis for an appeal by the Administration for aid to
Europe. The potential value of anti-communism in this respect
was being persuasively demonstrated at the time that the Truman Doctrine speech was being drafted. In February 1947, as
its final gesture to internationally organized relief, the Administration had submitted to Congress a proposal for three hundred and fifty million dollars in post-U.N.R.R.A. aid for Italy,
Austria, Greece, Hungary, and Poland. Congress was unre-
sponsive to this proposal, mainly on the ground that some of
the aid was going to countries in the Soviet sphere of influence. (The strength of this opposition was fully revealed by a
House vote on April 30 that reduced the amount from three
hundred and fifty to two hundred million dollars.) [23] The
moral of this episode—that foreign aid proposals, deprived of
the anti-communist rationale, would have difficulty in the
Eightieth Congress—could not have been lost upon the men
drafting the President's message on the Greco-Turkish Aid
Program.

The Administration received a particularly impressive illustration of the politics of foreign aid when the President assembled Congressional leaders to discuss with himself, Secretary Marshall, and Under Secretary Acheson the situation created by the British notes. This meeting was probably the most significant occasion in the entire campaign to win approval of Greco-Turkish aid: if the Republican leadership, particularly Arthur Vandenberg, refused to support the Administration, there was little chance of a successful appeal to Congress. As it developed, the meeting was nearly a disaster, for the explanations of the decision to aid Greece and Turkey offered by the President and Secretary of State failed to elicit support from the legislators. Secretary Marshall, according to Jones's account, left the impression that the program was broadly humanitarian and also supportive of the British position in the Middle East. The ineffectiveness of such arguments would have been predictable to anyone who had watched the domestic political scene closely during the preceding year, since the first was bound to collide with pressing domestic needs and the second with the anti-British feeling that had been expressed during the debate on the British loan. Acheson, who had been in charge of Congressional liaison for the State Department during the campaign for the loan, sensed the trouble and asked for the floor. "Never have I spoken with such a pressing sense that the issue was up to me alone," he has written. Despite the tension, he struck precisely the right note. He referred to Soviet pressure on the straits, in Greece and in Iran, which if successful "might open three continents to Soviet penetration. Like apples in a barrel infected by the rotten one, the corruption of Greece would infect Iran and all the east. It would also carry the infection to Africa through Asia Minor and Egypt and to Europe through France and Italy." This was the kind of talk the Senators and Congressmen understood and knew their constituents would understand. A long, impressive silence followed Acheson's statement. It was broken finally by Senator Vandenberg, who made it clear that Acheson's political judgment had been astute: "If you will say that to the Congress and the country," he told the President, "I will support you and I believe that most of its members will do the same." [24]

The success of Acheson's presentation at this meeting, which immediately preceded the drafting of the Truman Doctrine speech by State Department writers under his direction, was probably the single most important determinant of the rhetorical content of the President's message, though Acheson's assessment of the proper theme for the speech was generally shared by other officials who participated in its composition. There was, nevertheless, a certain tension evident in the drafting process, between the immediate requirement of winning support for a particular proposal and the broader purpose, always implicit in the campaign for aid to Greece and Turkey, of opening the way for future programs responsive to the broad needs of European reconstruction. The problems of Greece and Turkey were in many ways unique in Europe. Turkey was economically sound but under Soviet pressure as a result of its strategic position athwart the Dardanelles. Greece was involved in a full-scale civil war, and its most pressing needs were of a military nature, though economic dislocation was general in Greece, in part the cause, in part the result of the military conflict. No other country of Europe had either of these problems to any significant degree. Everywhere else, the problems were almost exclusively economic. In Britain there was no communist threat whatever. The strong Communist parties in France and Italy were cooperating with existing governments and promoting reconstruction. The dilemma of the drafting of the President's speech, then, involved composing a statement that had the political impact and appeal of Acheson's presentation to the legislators yet would establish a precedent for future aid programs to such countries as Britain.[25]

The successive State Department drafts of the speech reflected a desire to keep the issue of economic reconstruction at the center of attention. The draft of March 6, for example, which was the first one sent to the White House, began with a lengthy statement defining the Greek situation in terms of that country's traditional poverty and economic devastation during the war and speaking of the civil war as the result of economic dislocations. The draft then proceeded to the broad declaration of anti-Soviet policy that was retained in the final speech and followed this with a discussion of the general economic disruptions wrought by the war. The effect of this arrangement was to place the general declaration of policy entirely within a framework of the economic requirements of postwar reconstruction. Mention of the Communist-led guerrillas in Greece was cursory and included in a long essay on the afflictions of Greece near the end of the speech. Turkey, whose difficulties were entirely the consequence of its military position with respect to the Soviet Union, was mentioned only briefly at the end of the speech. The President, who had witnessed Acheson's performance before the legislators and tended, according to Jones, to view the speech mainly in terms of its immediate political reception, disapproved of this economic emphasis; Truman was later to write that the State Department draft sounded like an "investment prospectus." With the assistance of Clark Clifford the speech was edited and rearranged so that much of the economic material was removed and the statement about Communist-led guerrilla activity in Greece was retained in full and placed at the beginning of the speech. The discussion of Turkey was moved to the beginning. A peroration was added. The effect of these changes was to increase the attention given the emergency and military elements of the policy, upon the dangers from "armed minorities" or "outside pressures," and obscure the more general problem, emphasized in the State Department drafts, of the dangers to free institutions presented by the economic dislocations of the war.[26]

Four days before the President delivered the speech, an attempt was made to include in it some clear statements of America's substantive interests in extending aid to Greece and Turkey. The inspiration of this effort is unknown, but the agent was Clifford, who approached Acheson with three suggestions. Two of these related to American economic interests. The most important was the classic argument of the Hull-Clayton internationalists: that the present economic condition of the world portended increasing establishment of state-controlled economic systems and that should this trend continue unchecked, with its inevitable result of political controls over all international commerce, the general level of trade and of American exports would be so reduced as to compel the United States to adopt similar policies, eventually threatening both capitalism and democracy in America. Clifford also suggested that the speech contain a specific reference to Mid East oil and the necessity of maintaining access to these resources. Acheson objected to the inclusion of both points, mainly on the ground that they distracted attention from the essential, political content of the speech. He also pointed out that the first suggestion might prove embarrassing at a later date, since Britain had instituted state control of certain elements of the economy, and the U.S. might wish to extend further aid to it. Though there is no record of this, it is difficult to imagine that Acheson's objection to this proposal did not reflect his awareness that it was part of the same canon of multilateralism that had proved so politically impotent during debate on the British loan. Clifford's third suggestion was that a specific reference to the strategic importance of the Middle East be included. Jones has related one reason for Acheson's objection to this: "The American people were not accustomed to thinking . . . in strategic-military terms in time of peace, and too much emphasis upon supplying military aid to Turkey might have been alarming to the point of defeating the proposal." [27] Clifford provided no advocacy for these three suggestions, and Acheson's view prevailed.

The net effect of the drafting process of the Truman Doctrine speech was to cut away and deflect references that distracted attention from the broad ideological and political appeal upon which, the President and Acheson were convinced, rested the best hopes for Congressional approval of the aid proposal. The speech that emerged from these deliberations constituted, as the passages quoted previously indicate, an almost exclusively ideological appeal for support of a limited aid program. The heart of the speech was the President's assertion that the basic principles of America's political doctrine were being challenged in a worldwide campaign of totalitarian aggression composed of communist subversion and Soviet expansion. It was to this threat, the President suggested, that the U.S. had to respond, rather than to the problem of postwar economic reconstruction. Americans had to respond, moreover, because it was proper to defend "free peoples," not to protect specific economic and strategic interests that were not mentioned in the speech. The President's statement contained no reference to the necessity of maintaining a balance of power in opposition to the Soviet Union. It did not suggest that the United States might be more inclined to intervene in Europe than in Asia or more ready to provide assistance to countries with which it had commercial relations than countries with which it had none. In short, it was barren of discussion, except in the most oblique terms, of those considerations of substantive self-interest that were basically responsible for the decision to go to the aid of Greece and Turkey.

This fact was immediately noted by observers intimately familiar with American foreign policy. Secretary of State Marshall, in Paris en route to Moscow, was "somewhat startled to see the extent to which the anti-Communist element of the speech was stressed" and wired Truman to indicate that the speech "was overstating the case a bit." The President replied that "from all his contacts with the Senate, it was clear that this was the only way in which the measure could be passed." James Byrnes, who three months previously had been replaced by Marshall, called the speech "nervous, because . . . some . . . of the reasons given for the assistance seemed to imply . . . that we would oppose the efforts of communists in any country to gain control of the government. . . . that was not and should never be the position of our government. . . . However in a government like ours different reasons may inspire different individuals in the Congress and the executive branch . . . to reach the same conclusion." George Kennan, about to be named head of the State Department's policy-planning staff, also objected to the "sweeping nature of the commitments which [the speech] implied." Kennan observed that "it placed our aid to Greece in the framework of a universal policy rather than in that of a specific decision addressed to a specific set of circumstances. . . . It seemed to me highly uncertain that we would invariably find it in our interests or within our means to extend assistance to countries [provided only that they face] the threat of 'subjugation by armed minorities or outside pressures.'" Bernard Baruch's response was to the point: the speech "was tantamount to a declaration of . . . an ideological or religious war." [28]

It should be understood that treatment of the Truman Doctrine speech as an instrument of propaganda is not intended to imply that it involved a total distortion of American foreign policy. Although there is good reason to doubt Soviet support for the Greek guerrillas in 1947, there is no reason to believe that those responsible for American foreign policy had any uncertainties on this issue at the time. There is no question that these men were uniformly convinced that the U.S.S.R. was committed to an expansionist policy not only in the Balkans but also in western Europe, and that only American intervention could prevent their success. Nor should it be doubted that they deeply abhorred communism as synonymous with Soviet imperialism, were sure no people would willingly choose it except in the most distressed circumstances, and were anxious to prevent—within the limits of American interests and capabilities—the extension of communist influence. To the extent that the Truman Doctrine represented this world view, it was an accurate reflection of American policy. The elements of propaganda were introduced by the handling of the entire affair in an atmosphere of intense crisis, by depicting the problems of Europe as the result of Soviet betrayal and communist subversion, and by representing American policies vis-à-vis communism as based upon philosophical scruples rather than considerations of practical self-interest. These points were not minor but fundamental. The Administration's reliance upon them was the clearest possible indication of its belief that the American people would not support a foreign policy based upon a candid explanation of their government's intentions.

4. A First Try to Escape the Truman Doctrine

High State Department officials attempted to use the hearings on Greco-Turkish aid to reassert the basic lines of political and economic policy that had been obscured by the Truman Doctrine speech, but then were compelled to abandon this intention and reaffirm the Truman Doctrine when aroused Congressmen began to press them as to the real nature of American policy.

THE PRIMARY MISSION of the Truman Doctrine speech was not to provide a correct statement of American foreign policy but —as Byrnes recognized and Truman acknowledged—to assure Congressional approval of the Greco-Turkish Aid Program. In these terms, as has already been indicated, the speech was a complete success, for its mere delivery made Congressional rejection of the aid program impossible. The speech did have a secondary and immensely significant mission, however, which was to open the way for future programs of economic aid in support of European reconstruction. In this context the criticisms of Byrnes and Kennan were highly relevant, for it was not at all obvious that the speech had provided a political or rhetorical basis upon which a broad program of economic assistance could be delivered.

In this connection, the speech contained difficulties of two basic kinds. The first of these involved its definition of the kind of problem that the U.S. faced and the kind of response that was appropriate. The use of Greece and Turkey as precedents tended to focus attention upon the military threat represented by the Red Army and revolutionary guerrillas. Early State Department drafts of the speech revealed a desire to draw attention to economic issues, but the final version altered this emphasis to the point that economic considerations were entirely obscured. Though a few highly informed journalists—among them Walter Lippmann, Marquis Childs, and James Reston—responded to the speech in terms of its bearing on the broad problems of European reconstruction, most comment in the press and in Congress centered upon the suggestion of a Soviet military threat to Europe. This led to a submergence of the critical economic issues in a flood of images of massed Soviet troops preparing to sweep to the British channel. The Department's concern with this development was articulated in a letter from Jones to Lippmann in early May: "In my opinion one of the chief meanings of the Truman Doctrine speech of March 12 has been largely ignored, namely that the United States is prepared to use its economic resources to help remedy the conditions of economic anarchy in which communism breeds. There has been too much concentration on the military aspects of that program which are, in fact, quite unusual."

The second basic problem with the Truman Doctrine speech was that it implied a global commitment to combat communism rather than a concentrated effort to build the strength of areas of particular significance to the United States. The Administration was quite aware of the fact that it did not have the resources to defeat communism everywhere and it was equally clear—as its whole strategy during World War II had implied—that American interests were preeminently concentrated in Europe. As Navy Secretary Forrestal wrote in response to an inquiry about the Administration's policy: "It is clear that America can't save the whole world but she can provide, by supporting certain nuclei of stability, such as western Europe, the hope for the rest of the world." [29] If the Administration was to succeed in such a program, it had to refine the meaning of the Truman Doctrine to permit a concentration of effort. Once the Truman Doctrine had accomplished its primary purpose of assuring Congressional approval of Greco-Turkish aid (which is to say, immediately after it was delivered), the Administration turned its attention to the two problems posed by its intended use as a precedent for future aid to Europe. Only in these terms is it possible to understand the surprising testimony of high-level Administration officials during Congressional hearings on Greco-Turkish aid.

The Administration's desire to shift the focus of discussion from Soviet aggression and communist subversion to economic reconstruction was obvious in Under Secretary Acheson's opening testimony to the House Foreign Affairs Committee:

> The cessation of outside aid to Greece means immediate crisis. Unless help is forthcoming from some other quarter, Greece's economy will quickly collapse, very possibly carrying away with it the authority of the government and its power to maintain order.
>
> Essential imports for civilians and for the army under the circumstances can continue for only a few weeks. Two weeks ago the dollar resources available to Greece were only $14,000,000, enough for one month's imports of food and other essentials from the United States and other countries. If imports should cease, the price of such goods as are available would very rapidly reach astronomical figures. This is inflation. Its result would be paralysis of the government and of economic life. It would also very probably mean the end of Greek freedom and independence.
>
> The armed bands in the north, under communist leadership, are already fighting, Greek against Greek. In the event of economic collapse and government paralysis, these bands would undoubtedly increase in strength until they took over Greece. . . .
>
> The situation in Turkey is substantially different, but Turkey also needs our help. . . . Today the Turkish economy is no longer able to carry the full load required for its national defense and at the same time proceed with that economic development which is necessary to keep the country in sound economic condition. With some help from the United States, and further assistance which Turkey may be able to negotiate with the United Nations financial organs, Turkey should be in a position to

continue the development of her own resources and
increase her productivity, while at the same time
maintaining her national defenses at a level necessary to maintain her freedom and independence.[30]

These statements by the Acting Secretary defined an
official State Department position that both Acheson and Clayton attempted to follow in their testimony during the hearings.
Their interpretation of the Balkan crisis surprised members of
the Senate and House Committees, and numerous attempts
were made to wring from them acknowledgment of the anti-
Soviet, anti-communist elements of the President's speech.
The following exchanges are indicative:

MR. PEPPER: . . . Is it fair to say that it [the President's policy]
  does represent, however, a joining of the issue with the
  spread of Russian influence and communism in this part of
  the world at this particular time, and perhaps in other parts
  of the world when that issue is made?
MR. ACHESON: No, I think it is more accurate to say, as I said
  this morning, that this is an attempt, in these two countries,
  to see to it that their constitutional systems shall not be
  overthrown by coercion of any sort, or pressures of any sort.
MR. PEPPER: Mr. Secretary, is it not generally assumed that
  this is really for the purpose of keeping Greece from going
  communistic, keeping Greece from getting to be a com-
  munistically controlled and dominated state?
MR. ACHESON: I cannot answer for what is generally assumed,
  Senator.
MR. PEPPER: Is that not the real purpose of it?
MR. ACHESON: No. The real purpose of it is what I have said,
  that there is an armed minority in the country which is
  taking advantage of economic disintegration there to force,
  by force, a different regime upon Greece.

*   *   *

MR. SMITH: This morning, Mr. Secretary, I received a most
  interesting letter from a constituent. He asked me a question

that I cannot answer, and I am going to ask you if you can answer it. He said, I want to know if this bill is a blow at Russia, a blow at communism, or against armed guerillas in northern Greece.

MR. ACHESON: Well, I think we have discussed various aspects of that before. This bill is not a blow at anyone unless it is a blow at the forms of disintegration and pressure which come upon Greece from the disintegration of its economy. . . .[31]

Once they had adjusted themselves to the State Department's position, members of the Committees began to see the implications of the reasoning to which they were listening. Congressman Mundt treated Clayton to the following explication of the Department's logic:

> . . . We recognize we are creating a pattern now, for the future, that we are writing a precedent with conformity to what the newspapers call the Truman foreign policy which is to aid free men in their resistance to communism everywhere. However, if we simply approach the Turkish situation as an economic problem, without letting the people and the world realize that we are doing it because a unique set of facts are imposing themselves upon Turkey from the outside, then I think we have a very dangerous and expensive precedent. If we limit it to your position here this morning, the railroads, the army, and the economic internal programs which Turkey certainly needs, you could say everything you said about Turkey thus far about each of the following: about Iraq, Iran, Norway, Sweden, Belgium, and Denmark. You could go on to name fifteen other countries.[32]

The misgivings expressed by Congressman Mundt were widely felt among the members of the Committees. Several members sought definite assurances that the proposals were not the first step in a large program of reconstruction assistance.

MR. MANSFIELD: . . . Now, is it possible that other countries, like Hungary, Syria, Lebanon, Palestine, Italy, France, and Austria, may be participants in a program such as the one we are now contemplating in the future?

MR. ACHESON: I do not recall the countries that you mentioned. Some of them would be participants in the $350,000,000 relief bill.

MR. MANSFIELD: That is true, but what I am trying to get at is, is this going to be the sort of policy by which Greece and Turkey are only to be the lead-off countries, and, if so, just how far do we expect to be able to go in undertaking problems of this kind?

MR. ACHESON: Well, I have tried to cover that, Mr. Mansfield. The Department of State and the government has no secret plans up its sleeve which it has not disclosed to you. You are really asking me for the "unknowable."

MR. MANSFIELD: I know there are no secret plans, but I am trying to consider the implications of this very far-reaching legislation.

MR. ACHESON: I think you should be very clear about this—that whatever may be necessary to be done in the future is in the hands of Congress. We are not asking for any blanket authority now.

Representative Smith put the question concisely to Clayton:

MR. SMITH: I think it is understood, is it not, that other countries are going to make similar requests for aid and the Department has the matter under consideration at the present time.

MR. CLAYTON: Not that I know of.[33]

Under the pressure of this kind of questioning, the witnesses were led to deny that the Administration's involvement in Greece was caused by the problem of postwar reconstruction:

MR. JAVITS: Mr. Secretary, from what you have said to us about Greece it is fair to characterize the United States' undertaking as the economic reconstruction of Greece, is it not?

MR. CLAYTON: No sir.

MR. JAVITS: Is it fair to characterize it as being at least the principal advisor in the economic reconstruction of Greece?

MR. CLAYTON: I think a better characterization would be that Greece has certain critical, urgent needs for financial economic assistance, that this program is expected to meet those needs and to put Greece in a position where she can develop her permanent plans for reconstruction and development with the aid of the International Bank.

Acheson echoed this view in the following statement to the Senate Committee:

> The proposals now before the Congress deal with the emergency aspects of the problem. In the longer range the United Nations may be able to take over various parts of the economic and financial problem in Greece and Turkey.[34]

The testimony of the State Department witnesses followed a circular orbit which ended by arriving back at the Truman Doctrine. To focus attention upon the economic aspects of the President's proposals, they had denied that the major thrust of the program was anti-Soviet or anti-communist; having achieved this aim, they were asked for assurances that the United States was not accepting a general responsibility for reconstruction; to provide such assurances, the witnesses drew attention to the emergency aspects of the situations in Greece and Turkey; in so doing, they focused attention upon the Soviet and communist threats in those two areas. The following dialogue between Clayton and Senator George reveals this pattern:

MR. GEORGE: . . . What I am getting at is, is this simply one angle of a big problem that we are asked to go into now?

MR. CLAYTON: No sir; I do not think that it would be wise to draw any conclusions of that kind at the moment, that this is just the first step in a great, big program of relief or for other purposes which have not been disclosed to the Congress. I do not think it would be wise to assume that. These are the only two critical, really critical, situations that I know of at the moment.

MR. GEORGE: They are critical because there is a great power in Europe now that is engaged in a program of expansion. I think we might as well be frank about it. . . .[35]

The Administration's efforts to draw attention to the issue of economic reconstruction during hearings on the Greco-Turkish aid bill were far from successful. Rather than leading to Congressional acceptance of a definition of American policy on which programs of assistance to European recovery could be based, their efforts had led to a line of questioning that caused the most authoritative officials of the government to deny that there was any thought of a broad program of assistance to Europe.

Administration witnesses also failed in their efforts to draw back from the global implications of the Truman Doctrine to a more limited definition of American purposes that would permit concentration of aid in particular areas, specifically Europe. Acheson made a forceful attempt in this direction, however, as the following exchange indicates:

MR. MUNDT: Is this program which we have before us to be considered in the light of its being the first step in a consistent and complete American policy so designed as to stop the expansion of communism. . . .

MR. ACHESON: I think the President made this point very clear, Mr. Mundt. We are dealing with two situations which were presented to us at the moment. The President stated why those situations are ones which call for our assistance . . . We do not think that the President at any time stated this policy is a crusade against any ideology.[36]

Acheson's attempt to modify the sweeping, global implications of the Truman Doctrine invited interrogation by Congressmen on an issue of far-reaching significance: China.[37] This country, like Greece, was in the grip of a full-scale civil war. In China, even more than in Greece, the conflict pitted a Communist army and political organization against a government—the Nationalist regime of Chiang Kai-shek—supported by the United States. China, moreover, was a country of considerable significance to the United States. Its subjugation by the Japanese in the 1930's was one of the major causes of the U.S.-Japanese conflict that led directly to World War II. On Chinese soil American men had fought and died during the war. In China, and in Chiang, President Roosevelt had found and publicly advertised a symbol for a new Asia in the postwar period. Many Americans had been ready to respond to this idea, for the American people had a long history of special interest in China. Despite all this, the American government was very close, in early 1947, to writing off China as a lost cause. American efforts to bolster the Nationalist regime had proved consistently unsuccessful. Almost unanimously, American officials, military and civilian, assigned to China became convinced that the government of Chiang Kai-shek was hopelessly corrupt, entirely inefficient, and wholly lacking in popular support.

Official assessments of the situation in China after the war produced the conclusion that Chiang's armies could not defeat the Communists without an unlimited American military commitment. As American public opinion, demobilization, and the urgent need for American resources elsewhere rendered such a policy unthinkable, there seemed only one possible line along which to proceed—the unification of all China under a coalition headed by Chiang but including the Communists. The Americans hoped that such an arrangement could be effected, and if Chiang could take advantage of it by reforming his organization and building popular support, he could unite the Chinese people behind his leadership, build strength, and eventually isolate the Communists and deny them power. In 1945–6, American efforts were directed toward the goal of a Nationalist-Communist coalition. Patrick J. Hurley, a special emissary to China appointed by President

Roosevelt, made the initial attempt to mediate between the two parties. Frustrated over conflicts with regular Foreign Service officers, Hurley resigned in late 1945 and President Truman sent General Marshall to China to replace him. Marshall's extensive efforts to find a mutually acceptable basis for a coalition proved fruitless, largely, Marshall became convinced, because Chiang would make no meaningful concessions. By the end of 1946 Marshall had terminated his mission, returned to the U.S. to assume his new post as Secretary of State, and, thoroughly pessimistic about the future of China, recommended the suspension of aid to Chiang. In effect the Americans had made a tactical withdrawal from China. The question of whether this would later be redefined as a final retreat had been left undecided.

There was in the United States an extremely committed and very vocal body of support for the Nationalist Chinese. It had spokesmen in important positions in American business— for example, Henry Luce, the publisher of *Time* and *Life*— and American government, particularly Congress and more particularly among the Republican members. Frequently referred to as the China lobby, this loosely knit group had a history of success in mobilizing American support for Chiang. The President believed that their support for the Nationalists had made Marshall's attempts to negotiate a compromise settlement extremely difficult. Members of the China lobby were deeply disturbed by Marshall's decision to suspend aid to China in late 1946, and the new Secretary of State had been subjected to criticism by Republicans in Congress for his action. The Republican victory in the 1946 elections portended an increase in such criticism. Vandenberg stated in January that China was an area where bipartisanship had not traditionally applied, and he made clear his belief that far from suspending aid to Chiang, the time had come to "firmly sustain" the Chinese leader. Other Republican spokesmen, such as John Foster Dulles and Styles Bridges, also attempted to build interest in the Chinese issue by making statements urging American support for Chiang.[38] These men considered the situation in China as urgent as the situation anywhere else in the world;

indeed, they considered it far more urgent than the situation anywhere else. The rhetoric of the Truman Doctrine quite obviously suggested a policy toward China quite different from the policy that the Truman administration appeared to be following. This was not lost upon Chiang Kai-shek's champions in the United States.

When Acting Secretary Acheson was questioned about the meaning of the Truman Doctrine during hearings on Greco-Turkish aid, the discussion readily turned to America's China policy. This provided a moment of truth for the Administration in its attempts to draw back from the Truman Doctrine and defend American policy in the realistic terms in which it had been conceived. A frank statement of America's China policy would have required Acheson not only to risk alienation of Nationalist China's Congressional friends but to repudiate the Truman Doctrine itself. The Acting Secretary was evidently not prepared to run these risks. When Congressman Walter Judd, who had made the affairs of China a matter of special concern to himself, stated that he was unable to understand the Truman Doctrine because the U.S. had been encouraging Chiang to cooperate with the Chinese Communists while taking the opposite position in Greece, Acheson answered by stating that the United States was giving substantial aid to the Chinese government and was not encouraging it to cooperate with the Communists. He argued that the threat of a Communist takeover in China was not imminent. This line of questioning was continued by Congressman Fulton.

MR. FULTON: Mr. Secretary, you gave as one reason for the difference in the State Department's policy between Greece and China that China's government was not facing defeat.

MR. ACHESON: I did not attempt to say there is a difference in policy.

MR. FULTON: May I restate the question please? Of course, that leaves the inference that if there were a defeat there would be a change in policy. May I have your comment on that?

MR. ACHESON: I would like to reiterate that I have not said at any time that there is a difference in policy. I was trying to straighten out the actual conditions which I thought were different in the two countries.

MR. FULTON: Could I comment on that: in answer to a question of Dr. Judd, as to the possibility of the policy being different in Greece and different in China, you said that China's government was not facing defeat, and that was one of the reasons for the present policy. Now if China's government were facing defeat as an alternative what is your comment then?

MR. ACHESON: My comment would be that China would be much worse off than it is now.

MR. FULTON: I refer to the attitude of the State Department.

MR. ACHESON: I cannot possibly comment, Mr. Fulton. You are asking me about a hypothetical situation. I would hope that the Chinese government would never be in that position, and I see no reason why it should be.

MR. FULTON: Suppose that Russia adopts the same policy of aid to Greece. Could you give me a yes or no answer with no details as to whether the State Department has considered a plan of action in such event?

MR. ACHESON: No.[39]

The refusal of Administration witnesses, under the pressure of direct questioning, to sustain their evident wish to draw back from the literal implications of the Truman Doctrine was indicative of the hearings generally. These lengthy discussions provided only one brief reference to American economic interests in Europe and no discussion whatever of the conceptions of geopolitics that had led the Administration to commit itself to developing a western European bloc. The Administration's complete reliance upon the techniques of propaganda during consideration of Greco-Turkish aid raised serious questions about the extent to which it had succeeded in establishing a precedent for large-scale economic assistance to western Europe. In the end, all it proved was that the American people and the American Congress remained susceptible to sensational appeals to their deep-rooted fears and prejudices about the Soviet Union and international communism. This had always been the hidden insurance in Roosevelt's wartime propaganda on behalf of the U.S.-Soviet alliance. The former President had believed that "pro Soviet sentiment in America was superficial" and that "if the . . . necessity arose, the American people would accept the inevitable without much comment." [40] The necessity had arisen. Public opinion polls, which continued in early 1947 to indicate as many Americans believing as disbelieving in U.S.-Soviet cooperation, showed a dramatic and unbroken decline toward general disbelief in the months following the President's speech. How easily the American people would "accept the inevitable" remained to be seen.

III
Foreign Aid
and Internal Security

1. The President Announces
a Domestic Truman Doctrine

*Immediately after the Truman Doctrine speech,
the President announced a plan to protect the
American government from subversives. His
action seemed part of the global battle against
communism that was the new basis of American
foreign policy.*

ON MARCH 21, 1947, nine days after the Truman Doctrine
speech, President Truman issued an executive order establishing a new program to rid the government of disloyal employees and protect it from future infiltration by subversive
individuals. Called the Federal Employee Loyalty Program,
the President's plan involved an unprecedentedly broad program of background investigations and screening procedures
for all incumbent and prospective federal employees. On its
face, the President's action seemed a fitting sequel to the Truman Doctrine speech, for it reinforced the idea, essential to
that statement, that the global communist movement was at
work and did constitute a present menace to American security. Like the speech, the new program made clear that the
President was determined to combat international communism,
at home as well as abroad. Beyond such obvious and headline-
evoking considerations, however, the President's action raised
a number of questions to which clear answers were not apparent.

Federal employees had always been subject to investigations and security clearances, but the government had maintained a long tradition of avoiding inquiry into the political beliefs and associations of individuals on the grounds that such practice was improper in a free society and susceptible to misuse for partisan purposes. Only under the emergency conditions of World War II had the question of "loyalty" been admitted into the scope of background investigations, and even then these inquiries had been conducted on a much more limited scale than was called for by the new order. Observers of President Truman's action wondered if the postwar threat to American society was so great as to require not only departure from long-established peacetime tradition in the field of employee investigations but also the provision of protective measures more stringent than those employed during the war itself. This question, of course, could not be answered without reference to the international situation, and few doubted the existence of the communist movement or the need for the United States to combat it. But the connection between the threat to Greece and the internal threat to the United States was not obvious, though the timing of the President's action seemed to suggest a relationship between the need for new measures in both areas. These issues were the cause of much speculation in the spring of 1947, but the origins and purposes of the loyalty program and its relationship to the Truman Doctrine remained obscure. No one realized that the President's action was part of a major battle in a postwar political war over internal security that would become a major influence on the formation of American foreign policy and affect almost every aspect of life in the United States.

2. The Battle Over Employee Loyalty

The Federal Employee Loyalty Program was the product of political considerations rather than the requirements of security. These political considerations were inextricably connected with the Administration's difficulties in the field of foreign policy, for the Truman administration could not hope to base its foreign policy upon opposition to communism without creating irresistible pressures for an attack on domestic communists.

THE HISTORICAL BACKGROUND of the Federal Employee Loyalty Program can be quickly told. The activities of communists and their supporters within the United States became a matter of concern to American political leaders shortly after the Russian revolution, and in the two and a half decades prior to the end of World War II interest in the subject ebbed and flowed as domestic and international events rendered it less or more significant. Between 1919 and 1935 Congress initiated four investigations of communist and other subversive activities, three by committees of Congress and one by the Justice Department. In general these investigations concentrated on the problem of subversive propaganda, were limited and superficial, and produced few useful or concrete results. During the 1930's, however, concern over alien and subversive propaganda grew steadily, probably as a result of continuing economic problems at home, the rise of totalitarianism in Europe, and the increasing likelihood that the United States would be drawn into the maelstrom of political currents that appeared to be moving Europe toward another war. By 1938 anxiety over international developments prompted Congress to require American-based agents of foreign entities to register with the federal government and moved the House to establish yet another committee to investigate alien and sub-

versive activities. In May of that year a special committee was
created to investigate what the enabling legislation referred
to as "un-American activities" and the chairmanship was given
to Martin Dies of Texas, a spokesman for popular concern
about alien propaganda. At the outset there was no reason to
believe that the new committee would not enjoy a brief life in
the sunshine of publicity and controversy, as had its predecessors, and then join them in oblivion. But Dies's energetic and
well-publicized investigations of communist and fascist activities struck a responsive chord in a public increasingly distressed by events abroad, and by the end of the committee's
first year overwhelming majorities of recorded popular opinion
favored its continuation. Congress complied. This proved a
persistent pattern, and between 1938 and 1941 the Dies committee established itself as a perennial and unusually visible
fixture of the American political scene. Though the committee
suffered a partial eclipse during the war, it had banked enough
political support to win repeated renewals of its mandate, and
in 1945 it was made a permanent committee of the House and
renamed the House Un-American Activities Committee
(H.U.A.C.). From 1938 onward, therefore, American politics
gave prominent place to a highly vocal source of concern with
the problem of alien and subversive influences in American
life.[1]

Traditionally, Congressional inquiries into subversive
activities were dominated by representatives of the right wing
of the American political spectrum, and this had the effect
of focusing such efforts upon subversive tendencies on the
left. The Dies committee proved a supreme example of this
tradition; despite its origins in a time when the main problem
appeared to lie with fascist organizations of various types, the
committee consistently displayed primary interest in the problem of domestic communism. It quickly became apparent,
moreover, that the political bias of the committee opened to it
a whole area of activity and influence that had not been apparent in its mandate, for to certain conservative elements in
American politics the embodiment of leftist subversion in the
United States was not so much the American Communist

Party as the New Deal administration of Franklin Roosevelt. This attitude was most tenaciously held in two sectors of American political life, the conservative wing of the Republican Party, supported mainly but not exclusively by the Midwest and the Southern Democrats. Each persuasion had a vocal representative on the Dies committee—Dies himself was a Texas Democrat, and J. Parnell Thomas was a Republican from New Jersey—and both quickly made clear their intentions of exposing the connection between the New Deal and the communists. It thus developed that the special investigating committee became a fertile source not only of public discussion of communism but bitter and bipartisan criticism of the Democratic administration.[2]

During its early years, the committee's attacks upon both domestic communism and the New Deal were scattered over a broad range of organizations and activities, but during the war the committee came increasingly to emphasize the alleged presence on the federal payroll of individuals of subversive inclination. For a variety of reasons, this proved a point on which the Roosevelt administration was vulnerable. Under the successive impacts of the New Deal and the war, the federal bureaucracy had undergone a rapid expansion, drawing into the government large numbers of individuals with a maximum of haste and a minimum of careful screening. Because the federal government, particularly a liberal, Democratic government, drew heavily upon men who were likely to have been not only politically active on the outside but active in the liberal, social reformist, anti-fascist activities of the 'thirties and early 'forties, the expansion of the bureaucracy inevitably brought into the public service individuals of political tendencies certain to arouse the suspicions of men like Dies and Thomas. This would have been the case even if many of the major social reform and anti-fascist movements were not connected—as they were—with the American Communist Party, which was then building bridges to all segments of American liberal opinion. The added ingredient of communist affiliation and sympathy that could be imputed to many New Dealers through their organizational associations provided the

Dies committee with an irresistible target. Between 1941 and 1944 the committee repeatedly charged the Roosevelt administration with harboring subversives, and from time to time it identified specific individuals it considered unfit for the public service. In the end it forced the Justice Department to undertake investigations of a long list of government employees and persuaded the House, over Roosevelt's strong opposition, to prohibit payment of the salaries of several men considered suspicious. Not incidentally, the committee also helped to develop a political issue for opponents of the Roosevelt administration. During the campaign of 1944, the Republican candidate for the presidency, Thomas Dewey, attempted to exploit the idea of Roosevelt's close alliance with the communists, which the Dies committee had done so much to implant in the American consciousness.[3]

Throughout the war the general issue of the relationship between the New Deal and communism and the specific issue of subversive federal employees were of marginal political importance. The country was basically united behind the President and increasingly supportive of his policy of cooperation with the Soviet Union. In 1945 and 1946, however, with the war ending and U.S.-Soviet tension developing, two startling events focused public attention on the problem of federal employees with communist affiliations or sympathies. In June 1945 the F.B.I. raided the offices of a small magazine specializing in Asian affairs, *Amerasia,* and discovered a large number of classified State Department documents that apparently had been passed to the magazine's editors by government officials. In February 1946 the Canadian government announced that it had discovered a ring of Soviet spies operating within its bureaucracy, and press reports suggested that the espionage network extended to the United States. These disturbing developments plucked the issue of subversive employees from the fringes of political debate and made it a matter of major national concern. A public-opinion poll showed wide support for measures to keep communists from public office. A subcommittee of the House Civil Service Committee, chaired by J. M. Combs, held hearings on the issue during the spring of 1946 and recommended that the Administration sponsor an investigation of the entire matter and take steps to improve its methods of screening federal employees. The minority report, written by a Republican from Kansas, Edward Rees, argued that the committee had not gone far enough and stated explicitly that "an immediate and thorough housecleaning of all those of doubtful loyalty is what is needed." During the election campaign of 1946 the Republican Party made a major issue of the Administration's alleged laxity regarding subversive employees, and there were predictions that a Republican victory would bring just the "housecleaning" that Rees had called for.[4]

The attitude of the Truman administration toward this entire issue during 1946 has never been defined with clarity. There were press reports immediately following Truman's accession to the presidency that he would be far more cooperative with the efforts of H.U.A.C. and others on the issue of subversive activities than Roosevelt had been, but there were no actions by the executive during his first months in office to sustain this prophecy. The President's inaction with regard to subversion among federal employees was not attributable to a lack of basis for official concern, for he and high officials of his administration received several warnings of subversive activity at top levels of the federal bureaucracy. In 1945, for example, Whittaker Chambers, the former editor of *Time* magazine who would later distinguish himself by exposing Alger Hiss's communist affiliations and activities, informed the F.B.I. that individuals associated with the Communist Party occupied responsible positions within the federal government. His comments elaborated on information he had given the State Department and F.B.I. in 1939 and 1943. In late 1945 Elizabeth Bentley, who would later attain notoriety for publicly naming several high federal officials as communists and espionage agents, told her story to the F.B.I. The allegations of Bentley and Chambers prompted F.B.I. Director J. Edgar Hoover to send a memo to the President warning of Communist espionage activities. Among those named by Bentley and Chambers was Harry Dexter White, the chief Treasury Department planner in the field of financial policy and the architect of the International Monetary Fund and the World Bank. The allegations regarding White came at a time when he was being considered for the presidency of the I.M.F. and occasioned scrutiny by the President's closest advisers as well as the President himself. In this case, as in the others raised by Bentley and Chambers, the official conclusion was that the allegations were not sufficient to justify action. White was duly appointed to the I.M.F. and nothing was done with regard to the other cases. Unquestionably, however, these cases, combined with the *Amerasia* discovery and the Canadian spy disclosures, provided a basis for official concern about the problem of official subversion and espionage.[5]

Truman's Attorney General, Tom Clark of Texas, became convinced that bold action was required with regard to the problem of disloyalty in official places. Almost as soon as the Combs subcommittee completed its hearings, Clark began lobbying within the Administration for the appointment of the presidential commission to investigate employee loyalty recommended in the subcommittee's report. There is reason to believe that Clark raised this matter before the cabinet as early as mid-July 1946, and it is clear that he pressed the issue in calls to the White House during August and September. Clark's advocacy of a new initiative in this area was consistent with the concern over internal security he had manifested since his appointment as Attorney General. Shortly after he took office in 1945, for example, he urged President Truman to order the repatriation of "alien enemies" who adhered to foreign governments or their principles, and moved to expand the investigatory authority of the F.B.I. There is also reason to believe that in urging new action with regard to employee loyalty Clark was reflecting the views, if not following the advice, of F.B.I. Director Hoover. The records of the loyalty program indicate that the Attorney General consistently sought and generally accepted Hoover's advice on questions of internal security. Prior to his appointment to the Attorney Generalship, Clark had been Assistant Attorney General in charge of the Criminal Division, where he had been responsible for matters related to internal security and had worked closely with Director Hoover.[6]

President Truman did not follow Clark's advice that he appoint a commission to investigate the problem of employee loyalty. Despite the information he had received through the F.B.I. and despite the public concern prompted by the *Amerasia* and Canadian spy disclosures, prior to the 1946 elections the President took no action beyond quietly instructing Hoover to give top priority to the matter of subversive employees. Then, immediately after the elections, with their portent of a Republican "housecleaning" of the federal bureaucracy, the President issued an executive order establishing the President's Temporary Commission on Employee Loyalty (which would produce the new program implemented in March 1947) to look into the entire matter. This sequence of events has caused numerous observers to conclude that the President was reluctant to initiate a new program of investigations of federal employees and was forced to take action to protect his administration against a broad attack by the victorious Republicans.[7]

This interpretation is persuasive, for there is considerable evidence to support the view that the establishment of the loyalty program in March 1947 did not derive from a substantive determination that the problem of internal security required broad new investigative action with regard to federal employees. This evidence can be developed through the consideration of three questions: (1) Were existing loyalty/security procedures flawed by inadequacies that endangered national security? (2) In drafting the new loyalty program, did the President's Temporary Commission concern itself significantly with the problems of security? (3) Were the recommendations of the President's Commission likely to improve security within the government?

During World War II, the government adopted the criterion of "loyalty" as a qualification for federal employment. Three procedures were established to protect the government against hiring or continuing the employment of "disloyal" persons: the Civil Service Commission was instructed to conduct background investigations of all applicants for federal

jobs; the Federal Bureau of Investigation was ordered to provide, upon requests of concerned departments or agencies,
background checks of incumbent employees; powers of summary dismissal were granted to the heads of security-sensitive
departments. These mechanisms were all in effect when the
President established the Temporary Commission on Employee
Loyalty. The only official critique of these security provisions
prior to the appointment of the Temporary Commission was
the report of the Combs subcommittee. This report discovered
in the existing system only one weakness that could possibly
have been considered a present danger to federal security: it
noted that the Civil Service Commission had been forced by
limited appropriations to adopt inadequate procedures in conducting background investigations of applicants. This, of
course, was a matter subject to correction only by Congress.
The other criticisms of the subcommittee were directed at
procedural and technical inconsistencies and shortcomings in
the existing loyalty and security system, and the basis of the
subcommittee's recommendation for a full investigation of this
matter was not the discovery of a threat to American security,
but the view that uniform standards and procedures ought to
be employed throughout the federal bureaucracy. The subcommittee's criticisms affirmed by implication that however inadequate or uneven the existing system might have been, no
danger to federal security arising from structural flaws in it
could be demonstrated. There is thus no reason to doubt that
existing provisions were sufficiently protective of the national
security at least to allow the President's Temporary Commission time to consider with some care the extent to which disloyal employees constituted a problem of security for the
federal government.[8]

The executive order establishing the President's Temporary Commission charged it with determining "whether
existing security procedures in the executive branch of the
government furnish adequate protection against the employment or continuance in employment of disloyal or subversive
persons." This requirement was probably disingenuous: although no serious danger to government security was known

to exist, the Commission was provided with a mandate of less than two months, was forced to rush its deliberations, and found it difficult in this period even to devise a new program. From the first, in fact, the Commission interpreted its terms of reference as requiring the establishment of a new loyalty program and it chose to consider only the technical problems of establishing a fair and uniform system of procedures. This attitude governed the deliberations of the Commission from its first meetings in early December 1946 until mid-January 1947.

As the Commission's work progressed it became clear that there were significant differences of opinion among Commission and staff members as to the seriousness of the problem of employee loyalty and the scope of the program required to remedy it. By mid-January, two weeks before the report was due for submission to the President, the drafting process was arrested by this disagreement. The Commission made an effort to resolve the issue by inquiring, at last, into the nature of the problem of employee loyalty. Information was sought from the F.D.I. concerning the number of names in the Bureau's subversive files, the percentage of those names that involved persons in the employ of the federal government, and the nature of evidence required to place an individual's name in these files. Answers to these questions were not forthcoming. After two unsuccessful attempts to obtain information from the F.B.I., the Commission heard Attorney General Clark, who ended debate by stating that "the gravity of the problem should [not] be weighed in the light of numbers, but rather from the viewpoint of the serious threat which even one disloyal person constitutes to the security of the United States." Thereafter the Commission busied itself with the technical problems of writing its report. It had produced no substantive justification for the establishment of a new loyalty program or even the continuation in peacetime of those measures promulgated during the war. What little information it had gathered on employee loyalty as a security problem was conjectural, superficial, and contradictory. In submitting its recommendations the Commission was forced to admit: "While the Commission believes that the employment of disloyal or subversive persons presents more than a speculative threat to our system of government, it is unable, based on the facts presented to it, to state with any degree of certainty how far-reaching that threat is." [9]

The program established by the President's loyalty order made few substantive changes in existing security mechanisms. That part dealing with the investigation of applicants for federal employment merely renewed provisions that had been established during the war. Existing summary dismissal provisions were retained. The major innovation of the new order was the requirement that all incumbent employees be investigated; the wartime measure had required investigation only upon request of the employing agency. Was this innovation likely to improve national security? It is doubtful that this was expected. Purges of government employees by this means had been attempted on two previous occasions. The first occurred in 1942 when the Attorney General's Interdepartmental Committee on Employee Loyalty investigated several thousand suspected employees; its report stated that "the futility and harmful character of a broad personal inquiry have been too amply demonstrated." Congress had expressed dissatisfaction with this "whitewash," however, and its response had prompted the establishment of another investigating committee, the Interdepartmental Committee on Subversive Activities, to conduct further inquiries into the problem of employee loyalty. Herbert Gaston, chairman of this committee during the war, testified before the President's Temporary Commission on Employee Loyalty on January 24, 1947. He was asked, according to the minutes, "whether there had been [during his chairmanship] any leakings of important information. Mr. Gaston stated that he did not know of any but there might have been." He was asked "whether there should be more investigations than there had been in the past. Mr. Gaston doubted that there should be more." He could not have expressed more clearly the conclusion, based upon five years' experience, that loyalty investigations of the type eventually proposed by the Temporary Commission were ineffective means of protecting the government from subversion. He told the Commission that the motivation behind espionage is usually not disloyalty and asserted that the way to protect against it was through effective counterintelligence. The report of the Temporary Commission took up this same point, stating: "Unless this entire problem is considered with proper emphasis on the counterespionage aspect of its solution, the Commission is convinced that the achievement of the basic objective may well fail." The Commission gave no attention to the government's counterespionage system, however, because its mandate did not include this subject. Nor did the Administration take steps to study this question by other means. In brief, both what the Administration did do—its extension of the system of loyalty investigations—and what it did not do—its failure to study the problem of counterintelligence—strongly suggest that in promulgating the loyalty order it was only incidentally concerned with national security. Indeed, the President's executive order itself indicated how little confidence the Administration placed in it as a security program by specifically stating that the summary-dismissal powers of the security-sensitive agencies would not be affected by the new order.[10]

While the history of the Temporary Commission on Employee Loyalty strongly supports the thesis that its appointment by the President in November 1946 represented a political rather than a substantive determination, this does not necessarily justify the widely asserted view that the results of the 1946 elections alone forced the President to take action in this area. He had great reason, of course, to fear a Republican attack on the executive bureaucracy; the campaign had made this likelihood clear enough. And, knowing the stories of Bentley and Chambers, he could be sure that a Congressional inquiry regarding employee loyalty could produce some spectacular and politically damaging headlines; indeed, there was reason to believe that members of Congress were already aware of these stories. It is also true that the President sought to make employee loyalty an area of bipartisan cooperation by appointing well-known Republicans to the top positions in the new program. Nevertheless, had his deliberations been influenced only by the prospect of a Republican assault on the federal bureaucracy, he might well have chosen to adopt a defiant stance, as Roosevelt had done, and attempt to ride out the storm.[11] He certainly understood politics well enough to know that the Republicans were not likely to abstain from attacking the Administration in this area because the President had taken action, and it could be forcefully argued that the establishment of a new loyalty program would promote public concern about subversion and thus whet rather than slake Republican thirst for new action in the field of internal security. None of these considerations require the conclusion that the results of the 1946 election were not decisive in the President's thinking about employee loyalty, but they suggest that his unhesitating post-election decision to appoint the Temporary Commission may have reflected factors other than the Republican attitude toward official subversion.

The Administration's situation with respect to foreign policy may well have been the consideration that made the initiation of the new loyalty program inevitable. During 1946 the Administration had deferred new programs of foreign economic assistance until after the elections. This decision reflected the view that neither Congress nor the country was receptive to new initiatives in the field of foreign aid. It also reflected the view that the only way to arouse broad public support for foreign aid was through a strong anti-Soviet appeal that would damage the chances of the Democrats in the 1946 elections. Indeed, throughout 1946 President Truman refrained from openly announcing his abandonment of the effort to achieve U.S.-Soviet cooperation and his commitment to a policy of "firmness" with regard to the Soviet Union, mainly, it seems, to avoid alienating the left wing of the Democratic Party. A similar consideration would have carried equal weight in the President's assessment of the political consequences of initiating a new loyalty program, for such action would be as offensive to liberals as the renunciation of Roosevelt's foreign policies. The issues of Cold War foreign policy and internal security were related in another way. The whole history of Congressional action in the field of internal security indicated that increased international tensions were likely to produce new demands for initiatives against domestic subversives. The traditional coalition of conservative Republicans and Southern Democrats had demonstrated a consistent ability to win votes in Congress in support of activities to strengthen internal security, and this coalition would undoubtedly be moved to action by any presidential announcement of an anti-Soviet foreign policy. Given all this, the President's awareness, prior to the 1946 elections, that an open declaration of the Cold War with the Soviet Union was not far away would have suggested to him also that new action in the field of internal security was inevitable, whatever the results of the elections. There is reason to believe that this was, indeed, the tendency of the President's thought. According to Jennings Randolph, the chairman of the House Civil Service Committee, the President stated in September 1946—two months before the elections—that he intended to go ahead with a new loyalty program. His failure to announce the initiative prior to November 1946, therefore, may have been more significantly related to the development of his public positions on foreign policy than to a fugitive hope that the Republicans would not gain control of the Eightieth Congress.[12]

Whatever the President thought on these issues prior to the elections, he knew after them that the situation with regard to foreign policy required new action in the field of internal security. The Republican victory greatly strengthened the need to base new programs of foreign aid on an anti-Soviet appeal. And the need to adopt an openly anti-Soviet stance greatly restricted the President's alternatives in the field of internal security. Not only would a strong anti-communist line in foreign policy provide the Republicans with a political opportunity to launch the attack upon communists in the United States and in the government that they had been promising in their campaign, but important segments of the Republican Party continued to be basically isolationist and were inclined to regard the threat of communism at home as greater than the threat abroad.[13] Both factors made it extremely unlikely that an anti-communist foreign policy would be supported by the new Congress without parallel action at home. Thus, whatever the President's attitude toward the issue of subversion by disloyal employees, and whatever his assessment of the strength and consequences of Republican pressure for new initiatives in this area in November 1946, his knowledge of the course ahead in foreign policy denied him any possibility of attempting to resist the "housecleaning" that the Republicans seemed certain to demand. The Administration's commitment to basing its foreign policy upon opposition to communism implied a domestic equivalent.

Nor was the relationship between bipartisanship in foreign policy and new programs in the field of internal security limited to these general considerations. The pressures that the President was to face in the Eightieth Congress become even more intelligible when one considers the situation that he knew would prevail in the appropriations committees, upon whose assent and cooperation any programs of foreign aid would depend. Even under Democratic leadership the Senate Appropriations Committee had been preoccupied with the problem of employee loyalty. During 1946 hearings on the State Department budget, members of the committee had criticized Secretary of State Byrnes for tolerating subversives in his department and had taken the lead, at Byrnes's suggestion, in extending to the State Department the powers of summary dismissal already possessed by the War and Navy Departments. Under Styles Bridges, the new Republican chairman, the Senate Committee would be even more contentious on this point. Bridges had been prominent in calling for an American follow-up to the disclosures of subversion in Canada and had given voice in the Senate to newspaper rumors that the State Department was preventing the Justice Department from going ahead with investigations and arrests. John Taber, the new chairman of House Appropriations, was the outstanding Congressional champion of a drive against subversives in government and often expressed a willingness to use his influence over federal expenditures to bring about this result. The need for a purge of State Department employees had been one of the major themes of Taber's floor speeches during debate in 1946 on the State Department budget. (When President Truman issued his loyalty order in March 1947, the *Christian Science Monitor* commented pointedly: "Some Congressmen threatened to use their power over the nation's purse-strings—withholding appropriations—to force possibly reluctant departments to act quickly and forcefully in weeding out the disloyal.") President Truman, considering in November 1946 the situation he would confront in the Eightieth Congress, could know that both appropriations committees would be controlled by strong advocates of stern measures in the field of employee loyalty, and that the focus of much of their suspicion, particularly in the case of John Taber, was that department which would have to be instrumental in advocating and administering new programs of foreign economic assistance.[14]

Any doubts that the President may have harbored about the strength of the Republican commitment to ridding the federal bureaucracy of subversives or the depth of the connection between an anti-Soviet foreign policy and internal security were eliminated in the opening weeks of the Eightieth Congress. In his maiden address as Speaker on January 3, Joseph Martin told his colleagues that "there is no room in the government of the United States for any who prefer the Communistic system" or any "who do not believe in the way of life which has made this the greatest country of all time." Federal employees of this stripe, Martin announced, "should be—they must be—removed." In the first weeks of the new Congress the Republicans made clear their intention of acting upon Martin's exhortation. Shortly after Martin spoke Representative Jonkman announced that he would attempt to have the House Foreign Affairs Committee investigate the State Department regarding the adequacy of its security procedures. Taber told Forrestal at the same time that he intended to go after the "communistic personnel" in the Federal Housing Authority. In February David Lilienthal, head of the Tennessee Valley Authority and recently designated by Truman to direct the Atomic Energy Commission, was closely questioned about leftist tendencies by Senators during confirmation hearings, and a strong stand by Vandenberg was required to prevent defeat of the appointment. Similar issues were raised during hearings regarding Lilienthal's replacement as head of the T.V.A., Gordon Clapp. In March Styles Bridges attempted to stop the appointment of John Carter Vincent, an expert on Chinese affairs in the State Department, to the position of career minister because he was "leftist in the extreme." The debate on the Labor Department appropriation the same month included lengthy discussions of the need to ferret out subversive employees. Two committees of the new Congress—House Judiciary and Senate Civil Service—announced intentions to consider new legislation in the area of employee loyalty. The connection between all these expressions of concern about subversives and Congressional thinking on foreign policy also received prompt expression in the Eightieth Congress. On January 23 a number of House members denounced communist activities in the recently held Polish elections, and used the occasion to urge the Administration to take a firm stand against international communism. Congressmen Dirksen, McCormack, Rankin, Bates, and Mundt warned the House that international communism was on the march and urged that strong measures be taken to halt its progress both at home and abroad. All agreed that the two problems were inseparable, although McCormack, a Democrat, avoided references to the problem of employee loyalty. Mundt and Dirksen, however, stated that the first task in combating domestic communists was to remove them from the federal payroll.[15]

Ready and waiting to take the lead in the battle against domestic communism was the House Un-American Activities Committee, now under the chairmanship of J. Parnell Thomas. In January H.U.A.C. announced an ambitious program of anti-subversive activity, beginning with an effort "to expose and ferret out the communists and communist sympathizers in the federal government" and including investigations of communist activities in unions, the movie industry, and education. H.U.A.C. also planned broad programs of public education with regard to the dangers of communist subversives and a program of counter propaganda to offset communist informational activities. Speaker Martin pledged the cooperation of House Republicans with the full sweep of H.U.A.C.'s program. But first priority was given to the issue of disloyal federal employees, and in early February one of H.U.A.C.'s members announced that hearings were about to begin on the subject. The President's post-election establishment of the Temporary Commission on Employee Loyalty did not appear to be having much of a restraining influence on the Republican Congress, and the likelihood now presented itself that at the beginning of its campaign for Cold War foreign policy the Truman administration would be publicly confronted with the embarrassing stories of Chambers and Bentley about communist penetration of the Roosevelt administration.[16]

The Truman administration responded forcefully and effectively to the developing situation. The Justice Department announced that it was convening a federal grand jury in New York City to consider the entire question of subversive employees and review charges of official subversion. Bentley and Chambers were subpoenaed by the Justice Department and thus prevented from speaking publicly on the issues before the grand jury. It is difficult to understand the action of the Justice Department except as a political move to prevent the proposed investigation of employee loyalty by H.U.A.C. The Justice Department had possessed the information upon which the call of the grand jury was based since 1945 and had taken no action, apparently because it was convinced that there was insufficient evidence to produce any convictions; and, indeed, the grand jury would not produce a single indictment for official subversion. The convening of the grand jury, however, did persuade H.U.A.C. to postpone its investigation of the federal bureaucracy, for the committee did not want to open itself to charges that its activities were prejudicing the determinations of the grand jury or interfering with the efforts of the F.B.I. to indict suspected subversives.[17]

The announcement of the new loyalty program shortly after the Truman Doctrine speech further strengthened the Administration's defenses with regard to the employee-loyalty issue. Indeed, the combination of the federal grand jury and the loyalty order gave the Administration control of the issue and prevented the Republicans from mounting any effective attack on the Administration in this field. During debate on Greco-Turkish aid numerous Senators and Congressmen, including Vandenberg and Thomas, bracketed the problems of Soviet expansion and internal security, but the loyalty order prevented this argument from being turned against the Administration's requests for new programs of foreign aid. Outflanked legislators could only grumble that the Democrats were seeing the light a little late in the day. Quite clearly, the Administration had won a battle over the issue of employee loyalty, but this did not alter the fact that in the field of internal security, as on the issue of China, the rhetorical basis of the Administration's foreign policy had placed it on the defensive. Indeed, the Administration's problems regarding China and internal security were not unrelated. At the time of his resignation as the President's special envoy to China in 1945, General Hurley had charged that his efforts had been undermined by subversives in the State Department and Bridges picked up this theme in his attack on Vincent in March 1947. In early 1947 these were only two of a number of scattered attacks upon the loyalty of State Department personnel and the whole federal bureaucracy. But, as we shall see, the significance of Hurley's and Bridges's charges was not yet fully apparent.[18]

3. Internal Security and the Campaign for Foreign Aid

In the growth of public concern over domestic communism there were significant benefits for the Truman administration related to its efforts to mobilize support for a foreign policy based on anti-communism. The Administration perceived this and adopted a policy of full cooperation with the elements in Congress anxious to focus public attention on problems of internal security.

THE BATTLE between the Democratic administration and the Republican Congress for control of the employee-loyalty issue did not preclude the existence of a significant community of interest between these two natural political enemies. The broad task that the House Un-American Activities Committee had set itself in January 1947 was to draw the attention of the American people to the problem of communist influences in many areas of American life and to launch a program of public education against communist propaganda. Activities in both areas could be highly complementary to the Administration's own efforts to mobilize support for its foreign policies. For these Administration efforts were encountering problems of "internal security" that were real, pressing, and of fundamental importance to America's international interests.

Of the many domestic political restraints upon the Administration's foreign policies at the beginning of 1947, none was more important, in the eyes of the men around the President, than continuing public optimism that the world of U.S.-Soviet cooperation that Roosevelt had promised yet would be born. First Forrestal and then Byrnes had become convinced that the only way to unify public support behind necessary international initiatives was to focus public attention on the depth and scope of the deterioration in U.S.-Soviet relations and fix the full blame for this on Soviet policies. During 1946 these two men had led a major effort of public information to dispel the illusions of the Roosevelt years. Their activities were placed under severe limits, however, by the President's unwillingness to announce an open break with the Soviets before the elections. In these circumstances, the Administration's strategy depended upon gradually drawing aside the veil of censorship and propaganda that had previously prevented the public from seeing the U.S.-Soviet alliance for the conflict-ridden expedient that it was. Byrnes reversed the policy of excluding newsmen from international negotiations and began to use his meetings with Soviet officials less for diplomacy than for the advancement of his new information program. When the occasion offered, as it did in the dispute over Iran in early 1946 or the straits crisis in August of the same year, Byrnes went directly to the public with strong statements exposing and denouncing Soviet policies.

The failure of Byrnes's strategy to have a decisive effect upon American attitudes regarding U.S.-Soviet relations during 1946 was only partly the result of the limits placed on him by domestic political considerations. Soviet diplomats were well aware of the forces of public opinion that were limiting the foreign policies of the American government, and were determined to encourage them. Thus, when the Soviets learned of Byrnes's intention to take the Iranian dispute to the U.N., they quickly agreed to meet American demands and suggested that there was no need for a public scene. When Byrnes insisted that the issue be placed on the U.N. agenda anyway, the Soviets did everything possible to prevent this. Similarly, in December 1946, when the Greek government complained at the U.N. that anti-government guerrillas were being assisted by the infiltration of supplies from the Balkan satellites, the Soviets, fearing a public reaction against obstructionist tactics, reversed a policy of opposing U.N. inquiries into the situation along the Greek borders and supported an American proposal for a special investigating commission. Again, at the Council of Foreign Ministers in December 1946, when Byrnes informed Molotov that he now regarded the differences between them as insuperable and saw no reason to continue

efforts to negotiate peace settlements, the Soviet foreign minister reacted with conciliation. He immediately surrendered
most of his objections to treaties then under consideration,
and settlements were rapidly achieved for Italy, Rumania,
Bulgaria, Hungary, and Finland. Such Soviet tactics made it
difficult for American officials to make the true state of U.S.-
Soviet relations clear, or to establish in the public mind an
image of the Soviets as the aggressive and intransigent dis-
rupters of the alliance; these tactics permitted Americans to
continue in the belief that U.S.-Soviet cooperation was possible.
Indeed, the signing of treaties for the former Axis satellites in
December 1946 produced an upsurge of popular belief in continued U.S.-Soviet cooperation. At this same time, the Soviets
were making public appeals for a disarmament conference
and suggesting that only a desire to perpetuate war could
cause the Americans to reject their initiative. The Americans
were convinced that this was a propaganda trick, but they
ruefully recognized that it was an effective one.[19]

There was much feeling within the Administration that
the Soviets were more effectively influencing American opinion
than was the American government, and the continuing high
levels of belief in U.S.-Soviet cooperation, the public pressure
for demobilization, and the persistent opposition to foreign aid
seemed to confirm this analysis. American frustration over the
success of Soviet propaganda was expressed by President
Truman as early as June 1945, when he complained that the
Soviets were disseminating "propaganda that helps our parlor
pinks" and asserted that Soviet "propaganda seems to be our
greatest foreign relations enemy." In July 1946 Attorney General Clark proposed to respond to the problem by bringing
the domestic propaganda activities of diplomatic representatives of Communist nations under the controls of the Foreign
Agents Registration Act, but the proposal was vetoed by the
State Department. Forrestal responded to the situation by
seeking an alliance between the government and the news
media. "The American case," he wrote a friend, ". . . needs
much fuller and more continuous exposition if Byrnes is to
have the continuing support essential for his conduct of our

foreign policy." This view led Forrestal to make extensive
efforts to explain American policy to leading publishers and
editors and to arrange meetings for such people with government officers. "The American press," he wrote Marshall in
proposing one such session, "should be an instrument of our
foreign policy, just as is the British press." Despite these various proposals and expressions of concern, the Administration
developed no really effective response to Soviet diplomacy and
propaganda during 1946.[20]

The diplomatic and propaganda strategies of the Soviet
Union were supported within the United States by the activities of the American Communist Party. This was not surprising, and had been anticipated by the American government. A background paper on international communism
prepared within the State Department prior to the Potsdam
Conference in July 1945 drew attention to recent criticisms by
the French Communist Jacques Duclos of the "popular front"
tactics of American Communists, and it predicted that the end
of the war would bring a turn toward more radical policies by
American Communists. Specifically, the State Department
memo anticipated a resurgence of criticism of American foreign policy, with emphasis on the desertion of Roosevelt's intentions by the Truman administration. F.B.I. Director Hoover
agreed with the State Department assessment. In late 1945
he identified renewed Communist propaganda activities as
one of the two greatest prospective dangers to American internal security in the postwar period. These predictions of
renewed Communist agitation proved accurate. In July 1945
Earl Browder, the architect of the "popular-front" strategy in
America, was denounced at a special convention of American
Communists, and the American Communist Party, which had
disbanded in 1944 in deference to the Roosevelt administration, was reconstituted. In February 1946 Browder was ex-
pelled from the Party. Thus, by the time Byrnes and Forrestal
launched their public information program in 1946 the American Communists had assumed a position from which to open
an attack upon official policy. Taking Churchill's "iron curtain"
speech—which was seen as consistent with Byrnes's policies—

as the occasion for the beginning of their counterattack, the American Communist Party turned its two major organs, *Political Affairs* and the *Daily Worker,* into the instruments of a sustained assault upon American foreign policy. During 1946 these publications carried an unrelenting flow of articles criticizing the Truman administration for deserting Roosevelt's policies, seeking world domination for American monopoly capital, leading the world toward a new war, building alliances with fascists and reactionaries, and attempting to militarize American society. At the same time the new Communist leadership stressed the importance of not confining the Party's efforts to specifically Communist agencies, but of working with and through other mass movements, such as the "Win the Peace" movement, and of building alliances to labor, the Negroes, and other progressive forces. Indeed, much of the Communist effort did not go into explicitly Communist organizations but into other groups that the Communists either supported or sponsored. In this way American Communists promoted a wide variety of causes, including U.S. Soviet friendship, American disarmament, and support for the Greek rebels.[21]

The members of the Truman administration worried that the propaganda activities of American Communists, no less than Soviet diplomatic strategies, hindered their efforts to mobilize public support for Cold War foreign policy. The problem, of course, did not arise from significant public support for American Communists but from the existence within American opinion of tendencies upon which the Communists could play, through advocacy of causes not labeled as communist. Thus, Forrestal and Clark worried about a de facto alliance between the isolationists and the Communists, and President Truman complained about isolationist propaganda "under various guises." Forrestal, with his particular concern for defense policy, also worried about an ironic compatibility of attitude toward American expenditures for arms between religious people with pacifist tendencies and the Communists. Of more importance was the existence of a broad area of agreement between American Communists and liberals, particularly the followers of Henry Wallace. After Wallace's speech of September 1946, which advocated continued U.S.-Soviet cooperation and led to his dismissal from the cabinet, Truman wrote in his diary that "the Reds, phonies and 'parlor pinks' seem to be banded together and are becoming a national danger. I am afraid they are a sabotage front for Uncle Joe Stalin." Through such informal coalitions, in the opinion of several key members of the Truman administration, the American Communists were able to exert influence far beyond that inherent in their own membership. J. Edgar Hoover believed that communist propaganda disseminated through various "fronts" constituted by far the most serious aspect of what he considered to be the very serious problem of communist influence in the United States. In early 1947 he warned the country about communist-inspired charges that American foreign policy was imperialist, anti-Soviet, and warlike. Attorney General Clark shared Hoover's concern and spoke of the necessity of combating "the rising tide of totalitarianism that [is] coming to our shores." Forrestal was convinced that the Communists had played an important role in generating the public demand for disarmament. He raised the subject of Communist propaganda in cabinet on February 7, 1947, and argued for a vigorous and centralized program of counter-propaganda. His view was supported by Harriman as well as by high-ranking military personnel, including Admiral Nimitz. Communist propaganda activities directly affected American policy toward Greece prior to the Truman Doctrine speech. Joseph Jones has reported that the task of mobilizing public support for American intervention in that country "was complicated by the fact that incessant Communist propaganda, echoed by fellow travelers and misinformed liberals, had been widely successful over a period of years in portraying E.A.M. and E.L.A.S. [the Greek rebels] as organizations of patriotic liberals resisting corruption, fascism, and monarchy." [22]

For an Administration convinced that the mobilization of broad public support for its foreign policies depended upon a dramatization of the communist threat to the U.S., the propaganda activities of American Communists posed both a problem and an opportunity. To the extent that American Communists were able to appeal to tendencies within American opinion in ways that hindered the Administration's activities in the international field, they were an effective extension and reinforcement of the troublesome diplomatic and propaganda techniques of the Soviets. In this sense they posed a real threat to what the Truman administration considered the most fundamental issue of internal security, far more important than the danger of disloyal federal employees: the problem of unifying public support behind its foreign policies. At the same time, however, the existence within the United States of an organization that could be described as an agent of the Soviet government and was actively engaged in promoting policies apparently designed to serve Soviet interests offered the Administration an opportunity to dramatize the dangers of communism, which both Soviet diplomacy and communist propaganda were obscuring. A concerted, highly publicized offensive against American Communists could not only weaken their effectiveness as propagandists but demonstrate to the American people that the Soviets were indeed a hostile and aggressive force requiring intense counteractivity by the United States. The State Department paper on international communism taken to Potsdam had favored such a campaign and expressed the view that it would have a salutary effect on U.S.-Soviet relations. Joseph Grew, the Acting Secretary of State in early 1945, had played a major role in convincing President Truman to order the F.B.I. to go ahead with the *Amerasia* case and not worry about the effect of such action on U.S.-Soviet diplomacy.[23]

Such considerations provided an important part of the context within which the Administration viewed the issue of internal security at the start of the Eightieth Congress. Although H.U.A.C. and the House Republican leadership clearly hoped to use this issue to attack the incumbent Administration, their basic intention of exposing communist activities in the United States and drawing public attention to the communist threat was potentially entirely supportive of the Administration's political needs in the area of foreign policy. Even the loyalty program, which the Administration probably would not have undertaken had it been politically avoidable, could be turned to the advantage of the Administration. The announcement of this initiative nine days after the Truman Doctrine speech both reinforced the speech's image of a world-wide communist challenge to freedom and reassured the Republicans that the Truman administration intended to pursue the communist problem in both the domestic and international spheres. Indeed, there is some reason to believe that the Administration timed the release of the loyalty order to parallel the Truman Doctrine speech. The Temporary Commission submitted its report to the President on February 20 in the expectation that it would be released on February 21 for publication on the 24th. (February 21, it will be recalled, was the day the Administration received formal notice from the British of their intention to terminate financial support to the Greek armed forces.) On the 24th it was learned by the Commission that the date of the release had been postponed indefinitely. Although the White House officially stated that the delay reflected the President's desire to review the recommendations carefully, a member of the Commission's staff learned that the delay had not been caused by any such careful appraisal of the report and, indeed, the President's executive order made only two minor changes in the Commission's language.

The pairing of major anti-communist initiatives in the foreign and domestic fields could be particularly helpful in winning public support for Cold War foreign policy in the broad areas of the Midwest, where the fear of domestic communism tended to be combined with resistance to an aggressive international policy. The Administration seemed to recognize this consideration, for it was Attorney General Clark and not a representative of the foreign policy bureaucracy who was sent into the Midwest to speak in support of aid to Greece and Turkey. At the same time, of course, the dramatic and unexpected declaration of a drive against communists at home, shortly after the Truman Doctrine speech, heightened the sense of crisis in which the matter of Greco-Turkish aid was debated by bringing the communist danger directly and immediately to the American doorstep. In sum, the Administration seemed to have decided that if it could not avoid the internal security issue, it might as well make the most of it.[24]

In Attorney General Clark the Administration had a high official well disposed to lead efforts in the field of internal security. Indeed, Clark's role in the drafting of the report of the Temporary Commission on Employee Loyalty revealed his eagerness to arouse public concern over domestic communism at almost any cost. Although the Attorney General was convinced—and stated on several occasions—that communist penetration of the government was less of a problem in 1947 than it had been previously, he went to extraordinary lengths to assure the issuance by the Temporary Commission of a report that would describe the communist threat in the most lurid terms possible. Shortly before the report was to be issued Clark brought in two special assistants who had not participated in the Commission's discussions; they drafted a report depicting the problem of communists in government as very serious, using evidence submitted to the Commission in ways that distorted and even inverted its significance, ignoring testimony—such as that of Herbert Gaston—that tended to deflate the communist threat, and, in general, employing every conceivable device to represent the dangers of subversion as much greater than there was any reason to believe they were. Clark then tried to drive this report through the Commission in a rush on the eve of its scheduled release. His actions so offended the members of the Commission that they refused to approve the draft report, insisted upon a postponement of their deadline, and instructed their staff to write a totally revised report based upon an accurate rendering of the information they had developed. Their firm action prevented the issuance of a report that would have created an even greater public furor than did the relatively restrained document finally issued by the White House.[25]

Clark's rebuff by the Temporary Commission in no way exhausted the means available to him to draw public attention to the internal communist threat. Indeed, the House Un-American Activities Committee was anxious to do just that and Clark was well situated to assist them. It ought not be surprising, therefore, that despite the political conflict between the Administration and the Republicans in Congress over the issue of employee loyalty, the Administration, through Clark, adopted a policy of energetic cooperation with H.U.A.C. in pursuing the other items on its anti-communist agenda.

H.U.A.C.'s first major project in the Eightieth Congress was an investigation of Gerhart Eisler. Eisler had been identified in October 1946 by Louis Budenz, ex-Communist and former editor of the *Daily Worker*, as the top Soviet agent in the United States. Budenz had restated this charge in testimony before the House Committee in November of that year. An appearance by Eisler was scheduled for February 6, 1947. On February 1 Chairman Thomas informed Attorney General Clark that Eisler was apparently attempting to avoid giving testimony before H.U.A.C., possibly by fleeing the country, and he requested that Eisler be placed under twenty-four-hour surveillance by the F.B.I. Clark did better. On February 4 two United States marshals, acting on a presidential warrant issued by the Attorney General, arrested Eisler and conducted him to Ellis Island, New York, where he was imprisoned. The American Civil Liberties Union subsequently wrote Clark to complain of the arrest, stating that "a checkup would have shown that he [Eisler] had no intention of avoiding appearance. He had no facilities for leaving the country and he had bought railway tickets for Washington. The conclusion appears inescapable that the arrest was made without justification in order to appease those who were representing Eisler in the press as a dangerous alien about to flee the country." The Immigration Service, an arm of the Justice Department, delivered Eisler to the House Committee on February 6 but he proved an uncooperative witness, was quickly dismissed and cited for contempt by the Committee, and returned to Ellis Island. On February 18 the House of Representatives approved the citation against Eisler; nine days later the Justice Department obtained an indictment from a grand jury.[26]

The Eisler hearing proceeded without Eisler, and it quickly became clear that a significant portion of the Committee's information had been supplied by the Administration. Documentation presented by H.U.A.C. during the hearings, so far as it can be identified from the printed records, is ample indication of this. A file made available to the Committee by the Immigration and Naturalization Service contained a transcript of a hearing involving Eisler and Immigration officials in 1941, an Immigration Service memo recording alleged attempts by Eisler to flee the country, and, finally and most spectacularly, a long statement by F.B.I. Director Hoover, dated October 16, 1946, indicating several falsifications by Eisler in his statements to Immigration authorities, exposing him as a Communist agent, and recommending his deportation. The Passport Division of the State Department contributed to H.U.A.C.'s case a file containing a passport application dated August 30, 1934, made out to Samuel Liptzen but bearing Eisler's picture, and two files from World Tourists, Inc., a Soviet travel service, which had been subpoenaed by a New York grand jury in 1939 and which helped corroborate charges of passport fraud against Eisler, and three applications to depart from the U.S. made out in Eisler's name. The Passport Division also submitted two passport applications made out by Leon Josephson, a Communist associate of Eisler's, whose handwriting had been identified as that found on the application made out in Liptzen's name. In addition, the Committee utilized a record of statements made by Eisler's wife to a U.S. legation officer concerning her husband. H.U.A.C.'s chief investigator, Robert Stripling, spent much of his time during the hearing attempting to prove facts that were evident from the documentation submitted by the Administration and most of which were plainly stated in the Hoover letter. The hearing, though conducted as an investigation, was in fact a public exposition of information well known to the Justice Department. During its course, Committee Chairman Thomas praised the Justice Department for its cooperative attitude; the Department, for its part, had found a useful means to get information about communist activities into the headlines.[27]

Growing out of the Eisler hearing was the Leon Josephson–Samuel Liptzen investigation held on March 5 and 21, 1947, which pursued the charge of passport fraud that had emerged from the Eisler hearing. Josephson refused to testify at the hearing and was cited for contempt by H.U.A.C. Again, from the records of the hearing it is evident that the Administration provided substantial documentation to the Committee. The files on Josephson that the Passport Division had submitted during the Eisler hearing played a major role in these proceedings. The Josephson investigation was supported by additional documents from the Passport Division, as well as a record of Josephson's arrest on espionage charges in Denmark in 1935, which had been obtained from the Consulate General in Copenhagen. Identification of Josephson's handwriting as that found on Eisler's application was supplied by the Examiner of Questioned Documents of the Treasury Department. The House approved the contempt citation against Josephson on April 22. As in the Eisler case, the Department of Justice provided rapid follow-up. It secured a grand-jury indictment of Josephson on April 30.[28]

In mid-March the House Committee initiated another set of hearings on the pretext of considering legislation to outlaw the Communist Party, although, in reality, as Chairman Thomas told F.B.I. Director Hoover, the sessions were intended to provide yet another occasion for public denunciation of the communists. As in the Eisler case, testimony by Hoover was the most spectacular part of the hearings. This time Hoover appeared in person and made the front page of *The New York Times* by stating that the Communist Party was "a fifth column if ever there was one" and that its "goal is the overthrow of our government," that "their allegiance is to Russia, not the United States," and that "since the President called for aid to Greece and Turkey the Communists, opposing the plan, had been mobilizing, promoting mass meetings, sending telegrams and letters to exert pressure on Congress."[29]

These hearings led to another contempt citation. Eugene Dennis, National Chairman of the American Communist Party, appeared at his own request to testify against the attacks upon his organization. H.U.A.C. insisted that he divulge his given name—Eugene Dennis was an assumed one—and he refused and withdrew from the hearing. H.U.A.C. subsequently subpoenaed him to appear on April 9, and when he failed to appear the Committee cited him for contempt. The House approved the citation on April 22 and eight days later the Justice Department obtained an indictment.[30]

The active alliance of the Administration, through the Justice Department, and H.U.A.C. was a new development in the history of the Committee, actually reversing the situation that had existed previously. During the Roosevelt administration, the Justice Department had often refused to cooperate with the Committee or had offered only grudging and minimal assistance. Members of the Roosevelt administration, and on occasion the President himself, were given to making light of H.U.A.C. in public. Now the Justice Department offered energetic support of the Committee. The disposition of contempt citations voted by H.U.A.C. offers a striking example of the altered relationship. A general survey of these contempt citations before and after the Eightieth Congress reveals the following statistics: between 1940 and the opening of the Congress in 1947, the House had approved twenty-three contempt citations voted by H.U.A.C. The first, voted on March 29, 1940, produced no indictment until June 30, 1941, fifteen months later. The second, voted on April 3, 1940, was disposed on January 30, 1941, nearly ten months later. The remainder, having been voted respectively on March 29, April 17 (seventeen were voted simultaneously on this date), June 28, August 2, and August 3, 1946, were all undisposed when the Eightieth Congress convened. On March 31, 1947, following a request from H.U.A.C. for expeditious action on pending citations, the Justice Department secured indictments in all cases (with a single exception arising from a decision of the grand jury). With regard to the three citations voted by the Committee during the first months of the Eightieth Congress, the Justice Department had required nine days to obtain an indictment in one case (Eisler) and eight days for the other two (Dennis and Josephson.)[31]

Particularly interesting in revealing the unprecedented nature of the relationship between the House Committee and the Justice Department at the beginning of the Eightieth Congress was the role that J. Edgar Hoover began to play in the Committee's hearings. The Administration harbored no more committed or respected spokesman on the issue of communist subversion than the F.B.I. Director. Even during the years of the U.S.-Soviet alliance, when the official policy of the Roosevelt administration was to avoid criticism of the Soviets and the communists, Hoover occasionally spoke publicly of the communist menace. After the war and the accession of Truman, such statements became more frequent and direct. In September 1946, in a much-remarked address to the American Legion in San Francisco, Hoover delivered a wide-ranging exposition of the activities of American Communists, whom he reported to have made "their deepest inroads upon our national life" during the preceding five years. He followed this speech with a lengthy article in *American* magazine in February 1947, expanding upon his San Francisco speech and emphasizing, as he did in every address on this subject, that the main threat of the communists was the introduction of subversive ideas into American life.[32]

There is no record of the role of Attorney General Clark and other top members of the Administration in inspiring or approving these public statements by the F.B.I. Director; indeed, considering the congruity of Hoover's San Francisco speech with the campaign tactics of the Republicans in 1946, Hoover's effort on that occasion was probably self-initiated. It is clear, however, that Clark was impressed with Hoover's effectiveness as a spokesman on the issue of communism, for in early 1947 he reversed a policy established in 1940 by Attorney General Biddle (who considered Hoover "a good cheerful soldier" but flawed by a "bias against 'reds' ") of prohibiting the Director from testifying before the House Committee. Clark now assented to a committee request that Hoover be permitted to testify at its hearings on legislation to outlaw the Communist Party. This decision, incidentally, was not congenial to Hoover, who wrote the Attorney General reminding him of Biddle's policy and suggesting that public testimony by him on the subject of communism and the Bureau's activities against it could only weaken the effectiveness of the Bureau. He pointed out that the Committee's consideration of legislation to outlaw the Communist Party was only a pretext for a general denunciation of communists. Given Clark's eagerness to focus public attention upon the communist threat, this last point was not well designed to win Hoover's case, and the Attorney General overruled the Director in this instance, one of the few times he did so on an issue related to internal security. There is no record that the President directly participated in Clark's decision, though this is possible; in June 1946 the Chairman of the House Committee wrote the President, asking him to permit F.B.I. agents to testify before H.U.A.C. and the President may have withheld his decision on this, as on the loyalty order, until after the election. In a newspaper series in early 1947, columnist Jack Wilson of the Minneapolis *Sunday Tribune* suggested presidential involvement in Clark's decision by commenting that "with the President's blessing of the Committee the appearance of the boss G-Man became routine."[33]

The record of cooperation between H.U.A.C. and the Administration during the first months of 1947 could not, of course, completely disguise the inherent hostility of their political interests. From time to time this basic conflict broke through the surface of apparent cooperation and the members of the Committee assumed their familiar role of badgering the Administration for laxity in response to the communist threat. In a floor speech on April 22 in support of H.U.A.C.'s contempt citations against Dennis and Josephson, Chairman Thomas criticized Attorney General Clark for laggardness in prosecuting American Communists. When Thomas referred the results of the Eisler investigation to Clark for possible legal action, he made public a letter urging upon Clark the "long overdue" crackdown on Soviet agents in the United States. Clark immediately released a response stating that the Justice Department "will, as it has in the past, cooperate fully with the House Committee." Clark's self-effacing response to Thomas's letter fully expressed the disposition of the Administration with regard to the efforts of the House Committee to arouse public concern over internal security in early 1947. In the Truman Doctrine speech the Administration had initiated an immeasurably significant effort to mobilize support for a major new initiative in American foreign policy. It had selected as the basis of its appeal the deeply rooted hostility and fear of the American people regarding communism, and had sought to mobilize these emotions by announcing the existence of a global assault by the communists upon the forces of freedom. The efforts of H.U.A.C. to draw public attention to the communist peril at home could only reinforce the arguments of the Administration. As Clark told the Committee in early 1948, the Justice Department and H.U.A.C. "work in neighboring vineyards," for "the program of this committee in bringing into the spotlight of publicity the activities of individuals and groups can render real service to the American people." Thus, despite the political hazard that the interest of Republicans in the internal security issue represented for the Administration, a marriage of convenience was consummated between the executive and Congress, mainly at the initiative of the former.[34] Nor was this arrangement likely to end soon, for the Truman Doctrine speech and the Greco-Turkish Aid Program were only the beginning of what would inevitably be an extended campaign to develop public support for a vast new program of foreign economic assistance.

IV
The Marshall Plan

1. Planning the Marshall Plan

During the spring of 1947 the State Department rapidly developed a proposal for broad economic assistance to postwar Europe. By June plans were sufficiently advanced for Secretary Marshall to publicly invite the countries of Europe to submit requests for aid, and a combined European proposal was ready within three months. Meanwhile, economic conditions in Europe further deteriorated, and it became clear that short-term assistance would be required during the period before Marshall Plan funds could be made available.

THE ADMINISTRATION'S DECISION to propose aid for Greece and Turkey, and the combined success of the Truman Doctrine speech and the Administration's initiatives against domestic communists in assuring Congressional approval of the request, transformed the mood of the State Department from one of "utter despair about foreign aid" to energetic anticipation of a major program of economic assistance. "Now . . . American power was released for its world tasks," Joseph Jones has recalled, "and United States foreign policy could be planned without boundary." Even before the Truman Doctrine speech, Under Secretary Acheson had set a special committee of the State–War–Navy Coordinating Committee to work assessing the broad requirements of European recovery. When Secretary Marshall returned from the Moscow Conference he assigned the newly formed Policy Planning Staff, under George Kennan, to work on this problem also. Under these circumstances, the Department moved rapidly toward basic decisions on three critical issues: How much aid would be required? When must the program go into effect? What form should the aid program take? [1]

By April the special committee of the S.W.N.C.C. had concluded that a program of fifteen to twenty billion dollars spread over a period of three to five years would be required. This estimate was supported by Assistant Secretary Clayton, who was in Europe during these spring months negotiating with economic officials of European governments at the Geneva Conference on tariffs and trade. Through conversations with his European counterparts, Clayton developed a keen sense of Europe's financial plight and was shocked by what he found. In late May he submitted to the Department a summary of his observations confessing that "it is now obvious that we grossly underestimated the destruction to the European economy by the war." He was convinced that Europe would require "as a grant, 6 or 7 billion dollars a year for three years." Clayton also concluded that Britain, France, and Italy had sufficient reserves to last only through the end of 1947. The special committee of S.W.N.C.C. concurred. But the realization that several key countries of western Europe would require help by the beginning of 1948 suggested serious difficulties. At the time of debate on Greco-Turkish aid the State Department had promised Senator Vandenberg that he would not be asked to go back to Congress for any new appropriations before the' beginning of the second session of the Eightieth Congress in January 1948. It was now obvious that money would have to be obtained well in advance of this date. [2]

The question as to the shape of the aid program was complex. The obvious choice, a set of programs, one for each country of western Europe, had little to recommend it but its simplicity. The United States had been extending aid to Europe on this basis since the end of the war and had achieved little more than the prevention of collapse. Moreover, the Americans had strong predispositions about the organization of the European economy. Aware that much of their own country's economic strength derived from its inclusion of a vast and varied area and population in a single economic system, Americans had a tendency to believe that the division of Europe into numerous small economies, all using political devices to protect inefficient industries and promote self-sufficiency, was at the heart of Europe's problems. This natural bias had been reinforced for many American officials during the war by their experience with a set of all-European economic committees— called the "E" committees—that had been established to co-ordinate such problems as the distribution of food and essential supplies and the operation of inland transportation systems during the wartime and postwar emergencies. The Americans who had worked with these committees had become convinced that the type of European economic cooperation they repre-sented could work and provide the solution to Europe's eco-nomic difficulties. Indeed, the idea that integrating the Euro-pean economy was the key to the reconstruction problem had been sufficiently accepted by late 1946 to be included as one of the basic recommendations of the U.N.'s temporary subcom-mittee on reconstruction problems. The idea also bore upon the problem of Germany. The State Department had believed throughout the war that a reconstructed German economy, fully integrated into the economy of Europe, was essential for a reconstructed Europe. By 1946 the reconstruction of both Germany and western Europe was considered vital to the consolidation of the Western bloc. But other European coun-tries, particularly France, resisted the idea of rebuilding the country that had so recently used its strength against them. The concept of an integrated recovery program offered a solu-tion to this, because it would not be reconstructing the old, autonomous Germany, but a Germany restrained by its in-clusion in a supranational economic system. Given all these considerations, it is not surprising that in early 1947, when there was great pressure to develop an effective program for European recovery in a hurry, the idea of an integrated, Europe-wide plan came rapidly to the surface. Both Clayton's memo and the report of the Policy Planning Staff in May agreed that only such a program could succeed. That this concept would have obvious political appeal to Congress was an additional and important asset.[3]

The report of the Policy Planning Staff, together with Clayton's memo, provided the basic framework of the Marshall Plan. By the end of May the State Department was concerning itself with developing a political strategy for putting the plan into effect. Before moving on to this aspect of the aid program, it is worth noticing the almost incredible rapidity with which the State Department produced the Marshall Plan. Work began formally in early March and three months later all the essential decisions had been made. Such a performance by the Department would be unusual at any time. Considering that the work was directed by two men—a Secretary of State and a Director of the Policy Planning Staff—both new to their jobs and both innocent of previous experience with the economics of European recovery, it is truly remarkable. The Department has been much praised for this achievement, and with reason. But praise of the speed and efficiency with which the Department mobilized itself in early 1947 tends to obscure the far more important point that all the basic ideas in the Marshall Plan had been developed among State Department economists well in advance of March 1947. The Administration was aware as early as mid-1945 that extensive economic aid to Europe would be required, and estimates of the scope of this need grew steadily during 1946. By October 1946 Paul Nitze had developed the method of calculating Europe's financial needs that would be used by all the Department's planners in 1947, and had recommended an aid program on the scale proposed by Clayton and the special committee of S.W.N.C.C. The idea of achieving reconstruction by integrating the European economy was widely accepted in both the State Department and among European officials by 1946. The reason that these ideas had not come to the surface prior to March 1947 was political—the issue of reconstruction had been deferred at the policy-making level—not substantive. The great achievement of the Administration in the spring of 1947 was not so much in developing the conception of the Marshall Plan as in establishing a politcal atmosphere in which long-repressed ideas could be implemented.

The American government officially announced its readiness to undertake a major program of European reconstruction in two steps. First, in a speech to the Delta Council in Cleveland, Mississippi, on May 8, Under Secretary Acheson tested the idea in a lengthy speech on the economic conditions of postwar Europe. Slightly less than a month later came Secretary of State Marshall's famous address at the Harvard College commencement, in which he announced that "the United States should do what it is able to do to assist in the return of normal economic health in the world" but that "before the United States government can proceed much further . . . there must be some agreement among the countries of Europe as to the requirements of the situation." This cryptic comment was a signal, flashed across the ocean, that Foreign Minister Bevin of Britain had been led to anticipate. When he heard it, he moved instantly to convene a meeting of European nations to draw up the plan that the American government had requested. Bevin's meeting, which took the name of the Committee for European Economic Cooperation (C.E.E.C.), met throughout the summer of 1947 in Paris. Clayton, who was dispatched to Britain to confer with Bevin immediately following Marshall's speech, maintained constant contact with these planning activities.[4]

As the C.E.E.C. was deliberating about the problem of European reconstruction, the problem itself took yet another turn for the worse. The center of the new crisis was Britain. Through the first half of 1947 Britain had been losing dollar reserves at an alarming rate. In June, during the talks between Clayton and Bevin, British officials suggested that their country might need some kind of special aid prior to the implementation of the Marshall Plan, and hinted that they might have to renege on the obligation, incurred as part of the 1946 loan agreement, to implement convertibility in July. Clayton dissuaded them from requesting relief from the convertibility requirement, but implementation of it the following month so increased the drain on British reserves that convertibility was suspended within a few weeks. In the wake of this blow, Britain was constrained to institute a severe "austerity program" that imposed new reductions on imports from the dollar area. *The New York Times* reported that the crisis in Britain was so serious that it would not be able to wait for help under the Marshall Plan. Nor was the crisis confined to Britain. France would harvest the worst wheat crop in a hundred and thirty-two years and would be forced to reduce the bread ration in November. Its dollar supplies were nearly exhausted. Germany and Italy were also in serious and immediate trouble. The C.E.E.C. suggested that several countries of Western Europe needed assistance prior to initiation of the Marshall Plan.[5]

While developments in Europe during the summer of 1947 confirmed the conclusions about the immediate need for American aid that the State Department had reached in the spring, they also highlighted even more dramatically the vastness of Europe's financial needs. A draft C.E.E.C. report, completed in early September, placed the total figure to be requested at 29.2 billion dollars, almost a third above the American estimates. Moreover, even with aid in this amount, the draft report concluded, there could be no certainty that at the end of the program the dollar deficit of western Europe would be eliminated. Neither of these conclusions was acceptable to the American government. The State Department felt that the 29.2-billion-dollar figure would never be approved by Congress, and that Congress would support no program not guaranteed to solve the economic problems of Europe. Clayton met with the representatives of the C.E.E.C. and persuaded them to make the necessary changes.[6]

In September the C.E.E.C. submitted a plan to the American government requesting twenty billion dollars in aid. The countries of Europe had met the American requirements for developing a coordinated program and the State Department now proceeded to develop a final draft of the Marshall Plan for submission to Congress. First drafts of the plan were sent to Congress in mid-December.[7]

2. The Marshall Plan and American Economic Policy

*Faced with deteriorating economic conditions
in Europe and control of Congress by forces
hostile to multilateralism, the Administration
postponed the effort to establish Hull's
commercial program. It now looked to the
Marshall Plan to foster an economic situation
in which multilateralism could be instituted,
and to the 1948 elections for a chance to
recapture Congress. In this framework the major
economic argument for foreign aid was its role
in maintaining the high levels of exports needed
to avoid a postwar depression.*

DURING THE EARLY MONTHS OF 1947, despite its growing com-
prehension of the scope of Europe's economic difficulties, the
Administration retained hope that rapid progress toward the
establishment of multilateral commercial practices could be
made. President Truman's speech at Baylor on March 6 and
Acheson's speech to the Delta Council on May 8 both drew
attention to the international conference on the G.A.T.T. in
Geneva and indicated that its success was a vital element of
American foreign policy. In testimony before a Congressional
committee prior to leaving for Geneva, the head of the State
Department's Division of Commercial Policy voiced the expectation that Britain would agree to the elimination of Imperial preference at the conference. It seems clear, moreover,
that Clayton, the head of the American delegation at Geneva,
believed that the Truman Doctrine speech, with its implication
of a broader aid program in the future, would reassure the
Europeans about the problem of reconstruction and significantly strengthen the hand of the Americans during the conference. During his testimony on the Greco-Turkish aid bill,
Clayton stated that the Administration's proposal would help
prevent the adoption of "closed" economic systems in "these

and other countries," and his opening speech to the Geneva Conference stressed the point—for which the Truman Doctrine speech was the only public evidence—that the U.S. would not pursue a policy of economic withdrawal from Europe.[8]

The full power of the challenge to America's commercial program represented by the problem of reconstruction was finally impressed upon American officials during the summer of 1947 through their contacts with European officials at Geneva and by the unmistakable evidence of the new economic crisis. Not only had the United States grossly underestimated the scope of the recovery problem, as Clayton pointed out in his memo of May 31, but the countries of Europe were being induced by economic difficulties to follow financial and commercial policies antithetical to the tenets of multilateralism. In the field of financial policy, for example, the object of American policy was to establish the currencies of the major trading nations, particularly Britain's pound sterling, as freely convertible; Britain's August decision to suspend convertibility thus struck hard at one of the major purposes of American policy. The British also appeared to be backing away from the adoption of multilateral principles in the commercial field. When Clayton met with British officials in June he was told that they might be forced to ask relief from the non-discrimination clause of the 1946 loan, though Clayton had urged against this on the ground, not unlike a threat, that it might endanger Congressional approval of additional aid. At Geneva the British insisted that their country's economic circumstances were such as to make the early elimination of Imperial preference impossible, and they refused to consider action on this point or guarantee action at a later date. Again Clayton argued that the British position would jeopardize Congressional approval of the Marshall Plan, but the British—who doubtless knew what considerations were likely to be decisive in the American Congress—remained adamant. Equally shattering to the Americans, in early August the British government adopted an "austerity program" to preserve dollar reserves based upon a government-imposed reduction of imports from the dollar area by 40 per cent. The combined impact of these British actions was devastating to the American commercial program, not only in terms of Britain itself but—because British policy had such significant influence upon world commercial policies—upon the whole effort to expand world trade along multilateral lines. On August 15 Robert Lovett, Acheson's replacement as Under Secretary of State, told the cabinet that the new British restrictions on dollar imports might well start a chain reaction in Europe that could spread to Latin America and defeat America's commercial program. Lovett's apprehension was justified shortly thereafter when both France and Italy established policies restricting imports from the dollar area, and the C.E.E.C.'s September report stated that similar actions might become necessary throughout Europe.[9]

Despite Clayton's spirited advocacy at Geneva, the United States was not really in a strong position to insist upon the rapid adoption of liberal commercial policies by Britain or anyone else. The success of American efforts in this connection had always been contingent upon the Administration's effectiveness in mobilizing public and Congressional support for reciprocal action with regard to American import policies, and the British were openly unimpressed by the Administration's record in this area. An earlier chapter noted the retreat from full multilateralism implied by the American decision, taken in 1945, not to ask Congress for authority to make a "horizontal cut" in the American tariff at Geneva but to negotiate reductions on the basis of the Reciprocal Trade Agreements program. This decision strengthened the hand of British opponents of concessions on Imperial preference and made the British government suspicious of the American program. Both these attitudes were deepened by the threat to tariff reduction foreboded by the Republican victory in the 1946 elections and by the agreement between the Administration and Republican leaders to restrict executive authority to grant tariff concessions under the Trade Agreements program. "The ascendency of Mr. Cordell Hull in American thinking is over," the *Economist* editorialized. "The high-tariff party is back. . . . The condition of an American low-tariff policy under which Britain agreed to abjure 'discriminatory practice' is unlikely to materialize." Such predictions seemed justified when, in the middle of the Geneva Conference, over the strong objections of the Administration, Congress adopted an amendment to existing wool-price-support legislation that provided for an increase in the wool tariff. Because the wool trade, and particularly American wool imports from such Commonwealth countries as Australia, was one of the areas in which American concessions were critical to the success of the negotiations, this action threatened to break up the Conference, and Clayton was constrained to return to Washington to persuade the President to veto the bill.[10]

In addition to these signs of equivocation on tariff reduction, the American government was demonstrating its readiness to grant exceptions to the strict application of multilateral principles by countries unable to compete openly in international commerce. At its conference with Latin American governments in Mexico City in 1945, for example, the U.S. agreed to the inclusion in a Latin American trade charter of allowances for bilateral commodity agreements between Latin American nations to ease the problem of transition to peacetime conditions. Similarly, in a commercial agreement with the Philippines completed shortly before the Geneva Conference, the Americans established discriminatory advantages on behalf of Filipino exports to the U.S., to ease that country's adjustment to full political and economic independence. The American argument in support of this action sounded to the British very much like their own defense of discrimination on behalf of some of the nations of the Commonwealth. At Geneva the British drew attention to all these considerations to defend their refusal to eliminate Imperial preference or make major reductions in levels of discrimination.[11]

The logic of circumstances during the summer of 1947 moved the Americans toward a revised strategy for implementing their commercial program. If it was clear that both economics and politics militated against the early adoption of multilateral commercial policies by Britain and the rest of Europe, it was equally clear that these conditions were subject to change. Both Clayton and Acheson expected the 1948 presidential election to be the crucial determinant of the future course of American commercial policy. A Democratic victory could put the Americans in a strong political position to press forward for further commercial reform in Europe, while a defeat would cancel any present successes they might achieve. Additionally, Marshall Plan aid was expected to become available early in 1948 so that, while waiting for the political situation to clarify, the Administration could confidently expect the economic conditions that were working against multilateralism to be ameliorated. Finally, America's leverage upon European economic policies would be significantly strengthened once Marshall Plan aid began to flow. These considerations appear to have led Clayton to adopt an interim strategy. The attempt to achieve immediate adoption of multilateral principles would be pressed. In this context the development of the I.T.O. Charter, which was one of the tasks before the Geneva Conference, retained major significance. Its completion—with suitable amendments to provide exceptions to full application of multilateralism during a transition period—would commit America's trading partners to eventual adoption of principles presently inapplicable. As Clayton stated, "The Marshall Plan makes the I.T.O. negotiations more important than ever before because without a sound permanent program of reciprocal multilateral trade, no emergency program could possibly have any permanent results." Meanwhile, actual implementation of multilateral practices would be sought only on a limited basis, within a regional framework of western European states, which would be encouraged to move in the direction of a customs union modeled after the Benelux federation. Progress along this line would at least accomplish the negative purpose of abolishing bilateral commercial and financial practices in Europe and thus establish limited multilateral precedents that could be generalized at a later time.

One result of the Geneva Conference, then, was a tactical remodeling of the strategy of deferment. Though the Americans and British eventually agreed on limited, mutual reductions of some tariffs and preferences, the emphasis in Clayton's interpretation of the Conference was upon the principles and procedures established rather than actual reductions in trade barriers. Not only was a method developed by which future negotiations concerning the reduction of trade barriers could take place, but a draft charter for the I.T.O. was completed, bringing that project within sight of realization. The central thrust of American commercial policy was now shifted to the Marshall Plan, into which Clayton sought to write provisions assuring that progress toward European recovery would also be progress toward multilateralism.[12]

In early August Clayton outlined for the State Department the preconditions upon which he felt the U.S. ought to insist before accepting the C.E.E.C. plan. Two of his three suggestions were directed toward compelling the countries of Europe to adopt financial and production policies that would assure rapid progress toward reconstruction. The third directly reflected his desire to use the Marshall Plan as the instrument for achieving the Administration's long-range commercial goals. It held that recipient countries should be required to reach agreement among themselves for effective, collective action in the financial and commercial fields, specifically including steps for the progressive reduction and eventual elimination of exchange controls, tariffs, and other trade barriers. It is clear that Clayton felt more strongly about this than other members of the State Department's top echelon, for his suggestion that American aid be terminated if any of his three conditions was not met prompted Lovett to remind him of the political significance of the aid program. But Clayton was able to incorporate his views into the Marshall Plan. The bilateral contracts written between the U.S. and recipient countries included language directly responsive to his long-range view of the program. Recipients were bound "to cooperate with one another and with like minded countries in all possible steps to reduce tariffs and other barriers to the expansion of trade both between themselves and with the rest of the world, in accordance with the purposes of the I.T.O." This was less of a commitment to specific action than Clayton had proposed, but its implicit grant of power to the administrator of American aid was significant. And, according to the *Washington Post,* Clayton was the Administration's first choice to head the program. Though Republican control of the Congress eventually made necessary the appointment of someone not associated with the Administration, Clayton made it clear how he intended the power of the administrator to be used: "I would think . . . that if the representatives of the U.S. in negotiating with country X with reference to the provision [to reduce barriers to trade] . . . should be of the opinion that country X was not in good faith living up to that provision, then we would be justified in withholding further aid." [13]

Because it was generally understood that one fundamental purpose of American commercial policy was the expansion of American access to world markets to facilitate continuing high levels of exports, the American decision to promote a European customs union aroused considerable confusion, for it was widely pointed out that such an arrangement would discriminate against dollar imports. In the long run, of course, the Americans hoped to resolve this apparent contradiction by extending the intra-European arrangements to include other members of the proposed I.T.O. Even in the short run, however, it is clear that the Americans did not expect the Marshall Plan to lead to a reduction of exports from America to Europe. This assurance rested upon two facts: first, in extending aid under the Marshall Plan the U.S. would bind recipient countries against increasing barriers to trade from outside Europe; second, the Marshall Plan would provide direct financing for American exports.[14]

Indeed, a consistent theme within the Administration during the development of the Marshall Plan was the need to maintain high levels of American exports. As already noted (see Chapter II), the fear of a reduction in exports as a result of the termination of American aid programs had been one of the basic economic issues before the Administration in the spring of 1947. "We had at that time," Acheson has stated, "a tremendous export surplus . . . but there was very little likelihood of the recipient nations being able to fill the dollar gap." In the course of 1947 the Administration became increasingly aware of the significance of finding some means to fill the disparity between American exports and the dollar resources of buyers. As the President's Economic Report published in January 1948 summarized the situation: "During the first half of 1947, the increase in the export surplus accounted for about half the total increase in the money value of total national production. Exports of non-agricultural commodities directly and indirectly provided employment for nearly 2.5 million workers in non-agricultural industries. In some of the durable goods manufacturing industries the employment resulting from exports approached 20 per cent of the total. It is clear from these facts that exports during the first half of the year had an important bearing upon total levels of employment and production." The report did not specify the importance of agricultural exports, but this was one of the major areas of concern to the Administration. It was anticipated that continuing surpluses would occur in production of tobacco, citrus fruits, dairy products, and cotton. In his report of January 1948 Agriculture Secretary Anderson pointed out that exports were essential for farm prosperity and that "the export demand of the years immediately ahead will depend largely on American financing." The Marshall Plan legislation required procurement by recipients of U.S. surplus commodities. The Marshall Plan also provided support for American private investment in Europe, as private investment capital was also in surplus in the U.S. Finally, the foreign aid program was considered essential not only to directly subsidize exports but to keep alive the pattern of triangular trade between Europe, Latin America, and the U.S.[15]

Under these circumstances, and given the lack of spectacular progress at Geneva, the importance of the Marshall Plan as a means of directly financing American exports became the dominant economic theme in the Administration's approach to foreign aid. Clayton expressed the point with his usual directness in his memo of May 31: "Without further prompt and substantial aid from the United States, economic, social, and political disruption will overwhelm Europe. Aside from the awful implications which this would have for the future peace and security of the world, the immediate effects on our domestic economy would be disastrous: markets for our

surplus production gone, unemployment, depression, a heavily
unbalanced budget on the background of a mountainous war
debt. *These things must not happen.*" President Truman
sounded the same theme in mid-June: "The impact upon our
domestic economy of the assistance we are now furnishing or
may furnish to foreign countries is a matter of grave concern.
. . . I believe we are generally agreed that the recovery of
production abroad is essential . . . to a world trade in which
our businessmen, farmers, and workers may benefit from substantial exports and in which their customers may be able to
pay for these goods." [16]

Testimony to the importance that maintaining American
exports at existing levels played in the development of the
Marshall Plan is the method used to calculate the amount of
aid that the U.S. would make available: in every estimate of
Europe's aid requirements compiled by American officials during the spring and summer of 1947, the only consideration was
the existing European payments-deficit in trade with the U.S.
There is no evidence that Administration economists ever projected foreign aid figures on the basis of a substantive assessment of European needs, unless one could assume what European economic conditions seemed eloquently to belie, that
existing levels of European imports were a perfect reflection of
European needs. This is not to say that there was no relationship between the maintenance of existing European import
levels and the achievement of economic recovery; there obviously was a strong connection. But it is clear that what defined the needs of "European recovery" for American purposes
was an estimate of what would be required to maintain American exports at existing levels. When the C.E.E.C. submitted a
request for 29.2 billion dollars over a four-year period, the U.S.
insisted that the figure be reduced to 20 billion dollars, though
the Europeans did not regard even the larger figure as adequate and did not believe it would succeed in eliminating their
import surplus. This reduction brought the proposal down to
the range projected by American planners in the spring of
1947. From the standpoint of the domestic economy, such a
reduction was important, since any increase in export levels

under the Marshall Plan would have exerted new inflationary pressures and opened the program to attack based upon its impact upon the most important domestic political issue of the moment. Perhaps the best summary of the significance that the Administration attached to the Marshall Plan as a means of maintaining export levels was provided by Clayton:

> If we leave these countries of western Europe to shift for themselves and say, "we are sorry; we can't help you anymore," I think conditions will quickly ensue there which will, in effect, bring about a substantial blackout of that market for our goods and for the goods of the rest of the world—for Latin America, for example. If Latin America loses its markets in western Europe, we lose ours in Latin America. . . . it is highly important that we do what we responsibly can to help these countries to get again to a position where they can stand alone, because if we do not we are going to have to make such radical changes, I am afraid, in our own economy, that it would be very difficult for a democratic, free-enterprise system to make it.

In short, Europe must not only recover, it must recover in a way that would preserve it as a market for American goods, lest the entire American economy suffer a setback that would jeopardize the free-enterprise system.[17]

3. The Marshall Plan and the Western Bloc

The Marshall Plan was a natural extension of the policies underlying the Truman Doctrine speech and was the key to American efforts to build an anti-Soviet bloc in western Europe. The proposed aid program led to the neutralization of the three major political obstacles to the Western bloc: the strength of the Communist Party in France and Italy, the domination of French and Italian Labor by the Communists, and French resistance to the reconstruction of Germany.

To POINT OUT that the economic forces compelling the United States to subsidize European recovery would have been sufficient, in themselves, to move the American government to propose the Marshall Plan is not to suggest that considerations rooted in economic relationships alone influenced the development of this program. Indeed, by 1946 foreign aid had been designated the chief instrument of American efforts to consolidate an anti-Soviet bloc of western European states behind American leadership. At first glance, the relationship of the Marshall Plan to this policy is not obvious. In announcing the program in his Harvard commencement speech, Secretary Marshall stated that American policy "is not directed against any country or doctrine but against hunger, poverty, desperation and chaos" and that "any government that is willing to assist in the task of recovery will find full cooperation . . . on the part of the United States government." Far from continuing the line of rhetoric established by the Truman Doctrine or suggesting America's intention of creating an anti-Soviet bloc, Secretary Marshall's speech clearly offered to work with the U.S.S.R. and eastern Europe in achieving economic recovery and even suggested that American aid might be made available to these countries. In June 1947 Soviet Foreign Minister Molotov came

to Paris to meet with Bevin and Bidault, the French foreign
minister, to discuss the American proposal prior to the convention of the general meeting of European officials. Only after
Molotov broke up this conference by rejecting Marshall's offer
did Bevin and Bidault convene the C.E.E.C. conference.[18]
What, then, was the relationship of Marshall's proposal to
American political policies toward Europe?

To answer this question, it is instructive to examine
the history of the Secretary's speech. In developing their proposals for the aid program, Kennan and his staff were impressed by a political problem: the Truman Doctrine, directed
mainly to the domestic audience, had not been well received
in Europe. This should not have been surprising; not only did
the speech constitute a direct attack upon the largest political
organizations in France and Italy—which offended many Europeans—but it also foreboded a division of Europe into American and Soviet spheres of influence—which offended nearly
everyone else. The Cold War was far from accepted in March
1947; the President's speech was the first official American renunciation of U.S.-Soviet cooperation, and the illusions produced by wartime propaganda were still alive on both sides of
the Atlantic. All of this was made clear to Clayton during his
meetings with European officials at the G.A.T.T. conference in
Geneva, and in May he informed the State Department that
any American offer of aid would have to be based on some-,
thing other than opposition to the Soviet Union.

For many people in Europe and the U.S. the proper
vehicle for a recovery program was obvious. The U.N. had
recently established an Economic Committee for Europe
(E.C.E.), including representatives of all European countries,
east and west, to carry on the work of the "E" committees.
Kennan's group reasoned that the U.S. could not simply ignore
the E.C.E. or sponsor a unilateral program excluding communists without incurring widespread disfavor for causing
the division of Europe. At the same time, they were concerned
about communist obstructionism, and sensitive to the policies
to which the American government was committed. Kennan's
report proposed a tactical solution: "it would be best . . . to

stimulate initiative in the first instance from the E.C.E. but to do so in such a way that eastern European countries would either exclude themselves by unwillingness to accept the proposed conditions or agree to abandon the exclusive orientations of their economies." Clayton's memo of late May was more blunt: "we must avoid getting into another U.N.R.R.A. The U.S. must run this show." Marshall's speech, which was a synthesis of the Clayton and Kennan memos, thus derived from two proposals agreeing that the Soviet Union and eastern Europe should be excluded from the aid program. Clayton succeeded in having all references to the E.C.E. excised from the speech, but Kennan's basic strategy was retained. Marshall's proposal was designed to appear to offer participation to the U.S.S.R. and eastern Europe, and to ensure that they could not accept without adopting the multilateral economic policies that the Soviet Union had repeatedly rejected. Should they accept, the U.S. would reverse belatedly the defeat of its efforts to affect Soviet policies in eastern Europe, thus making the Western bloc—America's second choice for postwar Europe— unnecessary, should the Communist countries reject Marshall's offer, they, not the Americans, would incur the onus of dividing Europe.[19]

Though extending aid to the U.S.S.R. on the conditions contained in Marshall's proposal was consistent with the goals of American foreign policy, the American government was bound to view with profound suspicion any profession by the Soviets of readiness to cooperate. Moreover, the State Department was convinced that it could not extend financial assistance to the U.S.S.R. or eastern Europe because any such proposal would be doomed in Congress. Under these circumstances, the Administration took steps that appear to have been designed to foreclose even the remote possibility that the Soviets would accept Marshall's offer. American aid was to be offered for the specific, limited purpose of financing economic recovery and not for economic development. The money could be used only to pay for immediate, short-term needs, such as food and fuel, not for long-term capital investment. This was likely to be objectionable to the Soviets for several reasons.

First, it assured that the focus of American aid would be western Europe, even if the Soviets came in, for eastern Europe and the U.S.S.R., the traditional food- and materials-producing centers of Europe, were not generally in need of the kind of help the Americans were offering, unlike the industrialized West. Second, the emphasis on immediate needs indicated that the Marshall Plan was designed—as both the multilateral conditions and the requirement of an integrated "European" plan implied—to reconstruct the traditional commercial relationships between eastern and western Europe, against which Soviet economic policies were set. Third, and probably most important, the American policy meant that if the Soviet Union opted to participate in the Marshall Plan, far from receiving aid, it would be asked to make contributions from its own resources of food and materials. This aspect of the American plan must be viewed in the context of the U.S.S.R.'s repeated, vain efforts to obtain financial assistance from the United States between 1943 and 1945. Was it conceivable that the Soviets would now participate in an American-sponsored program that had all the markings of an attack upon their economic policies and would require them, as part of the bargain, to foot a portion of the bill? The satisfaction Kennan derived from having conceived this final turn of the screw was evident in his wry response when Secretary Marshall asked what the U.S. would do if the Soviets accepted his offer; the Administration, Kennan said, should "simply play it straight." [20]

The prevailing assumption in Washington before and after Marshall's speech was that the Soviets would not accept the American offer. Both Clayton and his assistant, Willard Thorp, were convinced that the requirement that the Soviet government contribute to the aid program precluded that country's participation. Clayton also expressed skepticism about Soviet willingness to alter their economic policies sufficiently to meet American conditions. Kennan and Bohlen assured Marshall that the Soviets would not accept. The American Ambassador in Moscow informed Washington shortly after Marshall's speech that the Soviets were coming to Paris only for propaganda purposes and had no intention of participating in the program. Forrestal, alone among high officials, expressed the view that the Soviets would accept, but he had not been involved in developing the proposal and probably did not understand its subtleties. In no instance did American dollar estimates of the size of the aid program include figures for eastern Europe or the Soviet Union. Secretary Marshall's speech, therefore, must be regarded as a fully consistent step in the development of the Western bloc.[21]

The Marshall Plan tended toward the consolidation of the Western bloc on both the economic and political levels. The economic implications were clear from the commercial conditions being attached to the program. Bereft of the hope of establishing a global multilateral system, the Americans continued to work toward the creation of multilateral commercial arrangements over a wide geographical area, including western Europe. The compromises with immediate economic contingencies, which had resulted in the acceptance of regional multilateral trade in both Europe and Latin America, were seen as short-term, transitional arrangements that would establish the basic principle of multilateralism and set the stage for the eventual institution of multilateral trade in much of the non-communist world. During the short term, the nations of western Europe would be bound to the U.S. through their dependence upon economic assistance. The extent of influence accruing to the U.S. as a result of this aid can be sensed from the fact that the Marshall Plan gave the Americans control of 10 per cent of the Gross National Products of the sixteen recipient nations.[22] European reliance upon American aid would also establish patterns of trade and exchange between Europe and the United States, as the aid extended would be tied to American exports. As American assistance diminished in volume and importance, the process of full economic recovery would approach completion, bringing with it—according to the terms of the Marshall Plan—the prospect of modifying the exceptions that had been made on behalf of regional trade to meet the recovery crisis. At this point the patterns of trade established during the transition period would be maintained as the sinews of an ongoing system, binding the U.S. and the countries of

Europe into close economic relationships, by which political relationships, already developed, would be sustained. Thus, in both the short and long terms the economics of the Marshall Plan promised to play an essential role in the consolidation of the Western bloc.

In the spring and summer of 1947, of course, these economic considerations were speculative. The immediate western-European reality was quite different. In the two major countries of continental western Europe, France and Italy, national Communist parties were in powerful political positions, strong enough in both instances to hold important portfolios in ruling coalitions. Moreover, these Communist parties had strong influence over labor organizations in both countries, and thus would be able to influence significantly any program of reconstruction. The solidification of the Western bloc would be difficult under these circumstances, as Kennan suggested in a speech in early May. "What is the moral for us?" he asked, referring to the strength of the French Communist Party. "I think it is the same as in the case of Italy. Any assistance extended to France by us, directly or indirectly, must be anchored in some sort of undertaking which will bind at least the French government if not French labor as well, to see that there is no dirty work at the crossroads." [23] In addition to the problem of the Communist parties in France and Italy, there remained the problem of Germany. France was still resisting the merger of its zone of occupation with Bizonia, thus impeding the full integration of the German economy with that of western Europe, a development the U.S. considered crucial to the strengthening of the Western bloc. Earlier chapters have referred to American efforts to use economic leverage to ameliorate all these difficulties, efforts that had borne little fruit by early 1947. The development of America's commitment to a vast program of aid to Europe during the middle months of 1947 paralleled a series of decisive events in western Europe that largely eliminated existing impediments to the Western bloc.

It was inevitable that the enunciation of American readiness to undertake large-scale economic assistance to Europe would lead to the elimination of Communist ministers from the ruling coalitions of France and Italy. The Americans had consistently urged French and Italian leaders to take this step and had indicated that American responsiveness to their aid requests would be influenced by their policies in this connection. At the same time, large-scale American aid promised to undermine much of the basis for cooperation between the Communist and non-communist parties in France and Italy. The availability of American aid would strengthen greatly the political position of the non-communist parties—as demonstrated by the defeat of the French Communists in the May 1946 election—and diminish their need to share power with the Communists. At the same time, American aid would tend to discredit the reasoning that had led the Communists to join these coalitions. One basic motive of Communist policy had been to achieve postwar recovery without American assistance and thereby prevent any major influx of American aid with its inevitable companion, American political influence. The Communists had paid a high price in pursuit of this policy. Their cooperation with coalition governments and opposition to strikes that would impede recovery had caused an erosion of their support within the labor movement. In France, in particular, a series of wildcat strikes in 1946 in defiance of Communist policy indicated that the Party was sacrificing its political base in the name of cooperation. Given all this, it was to be expected that the news of an American initiative in the field of financial aid would initiate a period of political retrenchment in Europe. As Raymond Aron wrote two days before Acheson's Delta Council speech: "The more or less genuine news of a vast 'lend-lease of peace' plan that America is about to produce has already touched off something of an ideological battle in France." Indeed, on May 4 Prime Minister Ramadier ousted the French Communists from the government. A week later, Italian Prime Minister de Gasperi reorganized his government without the Communists. One of America's major political objectives in western Europe had been accomplished.[24]

The problem for American policy represented by Communist domination of the labor movements in France and Italy, serious prior to the spring of 1947 despite the erosion of Communist influence that had taken place, was much aggravated by the ouster of the Communists from the governments and the implied termination of the policy of cooperation. The Communists would now be free to use their position in the labor unions to obstruct efforts at reconstruction. In both France and Italy, the Communist Parties moved toward anti-government positions during the summer of 1947, and in the fall, in direct response to a call for militancy by the Soviet government, launched a series of massive strikes specifically directed against their governments' acceptance of the Marshall Plan. On one level this tactic gave the Communists an opportunity to reassert leadership of the labor movement. On another it jeopardized their position, for in both countries the labor movements contained strong non-communist elements with a basically nationalist orientation, and these groups were not likely to follow policies that appeared contrary to the clear needs of their countries. Historically, in fact, there was much greater basis for separate Communist and non-communist workers' organizations in France and Italy than for the massive Communist-dominated coalitions that had emerged after the war. Since 1945 agents of the American Federation of Labor, in cooperation with the Department of State, had been working on this potential divisiveness within the labor movements of both France and Italy with the objective of splitting off the non-communist workers into separate organizations. By 1947 this project was approaching success, but funds, which had been supplied by the A. F. of L., were running short. The situation was saved by the decision of the American government to infuse large sums into their activities via the newly organized Central Intelligence Agency. Though it is difficult to assign weights to the various factors promoting division within European labor movements, the purposes for which the American government invested its money were rapidly realized. The November strikes in France and Italy produced splits in the labor movements in both countries and led directly to the formation of strong non-communist labor organizations. Though the Communists continued to be a major influence within a large part of the labor movement, a great deal had been accomplished toward the amelioration of a problem emphasized by Kennan in his analysis of potential Communist obstruction of the Marshall Plan.[25]

French policy with regard to Germany presented a particularly important obstacle to the consolidation of the Western bloc. The Americans considered the rapid reconstruction of the German economy and its full integration into the economy of western Europe essential to any program of reconstruction. The French, however, had resisted developments in this direction by refusing to consolidate their zone of Germany with Bizonia and using their position on the four-powers control council to thwart Anglo-American efforts to increase the authorized level of German production. The French position was fatally compromised, however, by dependence upon the United States for the dollar credits and coal upon which their own program of economic reconstruction depended. During 1946 and early 1947 the French had clung to the hope that the Soviets would support their claims to the Saar and thus provide them with a solution to their coal problem outside the framework of complete cooperation with the British and Americans. At the critical moment during the Moscow Conference in early 1947, however, the Soviets failed to support the French. Thereafter the French abandoned their efforts to maintain a neutral position "between East and West." In April they signed a coal agreement with the British and Americans. By June they were prepared to participate fully in the Marshall Plan even if the Soviets refused. At London in November they agreed to take immediate steps to merge their zone of Germany with Bizonia and support the establishment of a separate, independent West German state combining the three zones.[26]

The American government was able to derive considerable satisfaction from political developments in western Europe during 1947. The Communists had been ousted from the governments of France and Italy. French elections in October showed de Gaulle's new anti-communist party capturing nearly 39 per cent of the vote, against a Communist total of about 31 per cent. Non-communist labor organizations were developing in both countries. France was firmly in the Western camp. The basis for creating a new and independent West German state integrated into the Western bloc had been established. Although the American government interpreted the formation of the Comintern on October 5 as a direct attack upon the Marshall Plan, this was not a cause for much concern; Lovett told the cabinet five days later that this challenge could be met easily with a minimum of aid. His analysis was echoed on November 7 by Secretary Marshall, who reported that the advance of communism in Europe had been stemmed and the Soviets forced to reevaluate their position. The unsuccessful efforts of the Communists to sponsor general strikes in France and Italy in November and December confirmed the Secretary's statement. The unequal battle for western Europe was over. The Cold War had been won. The Americans had achieved a decisive victory without delivering a single penny of aid. The government was confident that only Congressional action on the proposed aid program stood between it and the total success of its policy of organizing the Western bloc.[27]

The two preceding sections of this chapter have attempted to delineate the relationship of the Marshall Plan to American economic and politico-strategic policies. It should be clear from the material presented that the foreign aid program was intimately related to both. The question arises, however, as to the relative weights of these two kinds of considerations. The truest answer one can give on this issue is that the economic and strategic significance of Europe were inseparable—Europe's strategic importance derived in large part from its economic strength—and that any attempt to discuss one side of the matter without reference to the other is artificial. Keeping this in mind, however, some observations can be made. It is clear that the American government would have proposed a program of aid to Europe essentially identical to the Marshall Plan even if there had been no communist threat to western Europe. This was the implicit meaning of repeated statements of the relationship of American commercial interests to the problem of European recovery and the explicit conclusion of the Policy Planning Staff in its report of May 23. Would the communist threat alone, in the absence of strong commercial interests, have produced the Marshall Plan? Certainly the ideological issue was not decisive; in 1947 the American government was not prepared to do battle anywhere in the world to stop communism, though it was highly conscious of the great cultural loss Americans would feel if western Europe fell under control of an ideology abhorrent to most of them. The strategic importance of Europe was such, however, as to make stopping communism there essential. Had the U.S.S.R. been able to achieve domination over all Europe it would have possessed a concentration of economic and military power that the U.S. could not have matched without transforming American society into a garrison state.[28] One conclusion, then, is that either economic or politico-strategic considerations, by themselves, would have produced a proposal like the Marshall Plan.

Having said this, it is important to recall that American readiness to extend aid to a particular country of Europe was never related—except in the cases of Greece and Turkey—in any demonstrable way to the degree of danger that country faced from communists. Indeed, the U.S. repeatedly showed itself most ready to extend aid to Britain, the European country least threatened by communism. In 1946 the Administration was willing to risk a Congressional debate to get help for Britain, but not for France or Italy. Britain would receive the largest share of assistance under the Marshall Plan. Italy, the western European country with the strongest communist movement, consistently received the smallest allocations of aid among the major countries. What determined the amounts of aid given in every case was a particular country's balance of payments with the dollar area, which meant that aid was always extended in amounts necessary to permit the recipient to continue to play its role in the existing network of commercial relationships upon which the American economy depended. The proper conclusion from this is not that the U.S. was not deeply concerned with defeating the communists in western Europe, only that the threat of communism was relatively mild and that the government was always confident that if it could restore economic stability, communism would cease to be a serious problem.

4. The Politics of the Marshall Plan

In the late spring of 1947, public enthusiasm for the Truman Doctrine began to wane, jeopardizing the entire foreign aid program. Throughout the summer the Administration proved unable to find a politically viable basis for aid to Europe and permitted the issue to go unpublicized and undiscussed; in the fall, with submission of the program to the Republican-controlled Congress imminent, most Americans had never heard of the Marshall Plan and the country seemed to be in as conservative a mood as it had shown in November 1946. Enactment of the program was seriously in question.

ALTHOUGH THE FOREIGN AID PROGRAM was developed by the State Department with remarkable speed and ease, the task of engineering its approval by Congress promised to be formidable. Unquestionably, the Truman Doctrine had been an immediate political success in the United States. There had been opposition on the Wallaceite left because the speech repudiated cooperation with the Soviet Union, bypassed the U.N., and put the United States in the position of supporting rightist regimes; on the right because it implied massive intervention abroad, put new strains on the economy, and risked war with the U.S.S.R.—but such views were voiced almost exclusively by representatives of the ends of the political spectrum. The press tended to see the speech as a needed announcement of American readiness to become a great world power, and editorial comment was generally favorable. Public opinion polls indicated a sharp increase in the President's popularity. In the weeks following the speech, however, initial enthusiasm began to give way to doubts. The adverse response of many Europeans prompted renewed discussion in the United States. Reconsidered, the criticisms of both the left and the right were found to have force: what evidence, people began to ask, had been offered that Soviet policies were as the President had depicted them? The speech began to seem an overreaction, indeed, a provocation.

Henry Wallace did much to promote such questions by stumping the country during May and June to criticize the Administration's foreign policies. Wallace consistently faulted the Administration for blaming the Soviet Union for all postwar problems and attempted to show how U.S.-Soviet conflicts in Europe were at least as much the result of American as of Soviet policies. He also attempted to focus attention upon the economic aspects of foreign aid, emphasizing the extent to which economic assistance would promote American commercial interests. The press reported an enthusiastic public response to Wallace's efforts.

In the context of growing popular skepticism about its foreign policy, the Administration was inevitably reminded of many domestic political constraints upon large-scale foreign aid. Thus, at a time when official estimates of the scope of necessary aid were indicating requirements larger than the total of all foreign aid dispensed since the end of the war, the State Department was confronted with the steady erosion of the effectiveness of the Truman Doctrine as a political basis for further aid programs. Congressional approval of Greco-Turkish aid did nothing to dispel concern on this point; it came, as Walter Lippmann wrote, "after a long delay and in circumstances which were tantamount to telling [the President] not to come back too soon for much more." Even before final approval of this proposal, the Administration began to look for another approach.[29]

Secretary Acheson's speech to the Delta Council on May 8 was the Administration's first effort to redirect the public debate on foreign aid. It opened with the suggestion that the Administration's concerns had evolved away from those emphasized in the Truman Doctrine: "When Secretary Marshall returned from the recent meeting of the Council of Foreign Ministers in Moscow, he did not talk to us about ideologies or armies. He talked about food and fuel and their relation to industrial production and the relation of industrial production to the organization of Europe and the relation of the organization of Europe to the peace of the world." Having redefined the problem in economic terms, Acheson presented a lengthy analysis of the economic consequences of the war for Europe, of the problems caused by the winter of 1946–7, and of the balance-of-payments problems being experienced by European economies. Prescriptions followed. First, Acheson called for the U.S. to help the Europeans earn more dollars by expanding American imports, and he stressed the importance of the Geneva negotiations to reduce trade barriers. Second, he pointed out that the U.S. would have to undertake "further emergency financing of foreign purchases." Third, in what appeared to be another attempt to escape the sweeping implications of the Truman Doctrine, he suggested that the U.S. would have to focus its efforts in critical areas. Acheson made no serious attempt to offer a new rationale for taking these steps. He confined his discussion of American economic self-interest to a bland comment about world "peace and prosperity," and insisted that his comments were fully consistent with the Truman Doctrine. The great significance of the speech, however, was that it represented a full-dress, public effort by the State Department to do what it had attempted to do in the early drafts of the Truman Doctrine speech and in the testimony of its top officials on Greco-Turkish aid: redefine the problems of Europe in terms that would imply the policy responses to which the Administration was committed. To assure that no one missed the point, leading journalists were informed that the Truman Doctrine had been widely misunderstood, that its economic implications had been slighted in the public debate, and that Acheson's speech was a major effort to channel public discussion in the proper direction. As a result, such writers as James Reston, Walter Lippmann, and the Alsops produced feature articles explaining the consequences of the Truman Doctrine for American economic policy and particularly for programs of foreign aid. The public debate that the Administration had studiously avoided in the presentation of Greco-Turkish aid was now joined.[30]

The Congressional response was not encouraging. Senator Vandenberg was at this time in the middle of an effort to save the Administration's proposal of post-U.N.R.R.A. relief for a number of European countries. On April 30 the House had voted to cut the program from 350 million dollars proposed by the State Department to 200 million dollars, and Vandenberg was forced to extend himself to win restoration of the full amount in a Senate vote on May 14. He was thus shocked to read Reston's article in one Sunday's *Times* indicating that the Administration was considering a five-year aid program totaling 20 billion dollars. Vandenberg immediately called Reston to tell him "either you are wrong or this government is out of its mind. Any plan of that size is out of the question." The Republican leader raised such a general fuss that Acheson and Marshall felt constrained to smooth his feathers in a private session and begin anew the job accomplished so successfully at the time of the Truman Doctrine of co opting him into championing the Administration's programs.[31]

Developments with respect to American import policy, an issue Acheson had stressed equally with foreign aid, were also discouraging for the Administration. At the time Acheson delivered his speech, the House was considering the amended version of the Wool Act of 1947, providing for an increase in the American wool tariff. Clayton's efforts to persuade the House to defeat this proposal prompted a debate on the whole issue of American import policy on May 22, less than two weeks after Acheson's speech. The Democratic floor leader for the bill, Representative Cooley of North Carolina, read into the record a letter from Clayton stating that the proposal would undermine American leadership in world economic affairs and jeopardize the Geneva negotiations. Cooley believed that the Republicans were using the Wool Act as a means of repudiating the Reciprocal Trade Agreements Program, and he joined this issue directly by proposing an amendment indicating that the bill would not be enforced in contravention to any present or future international agreement to which the U.S. was or might become a party. His amendment was easily defeated, and the bill passed. In a spectacular last-ditch effort to defeat the measure, the Administration solicited strong statements from Cordell Hull, Henry Stimson, and George Marshall urging the House-Senate Conference to reject the House bill. It even prevailed upon the Conference to hold hearings so that Clayton could make a personal appeal. None of this was effective. The House-passed bill was approved in substance by the Conference and subsequently by both houses. It would be hard to imagine a more impressive indication of Congressional attitudes toward the Administration's commercial program. The action implicitly rejected one of the major elements of Acheson's speech as well as the strongly worded arguments of the Administration and three of the country's most respected statesmen. Though the President's veto permitted the Geneva Conference to continue, the episode led Clayton to despair for popular support of his commercial ideas. He told Bevin in June that he knew the U.S. required export markets, but that his fellow citizens had different views.[32]

It is not difficult to imagine the predicament of the Administration in May 1947 as the staff work on the new aid program was being completed. Analyses of the European economic situation indicated that new American aid would be required before the end of 1947. It was therefore essential to lay the entire issue before the public and the Congress without delay. Yet no reliable basis upon which to present the program was available. If the issue involved only American opinion, an elaboration of the anti-Soviet theme of the Truman Doctrine would have been a possibility, for the reaction against the tactics of the Truman Doctrine had not altered the basic attitudes of the American people on this subject. But the need to offer aid on a basis that would permit European governments to accept it precluded the anti-Soviet approach. A straightforward economic presentation combined with vague allusions to world peace and prosperity would have met the political needs of European leaders but, as Acheson's speech had demonstrated, could not be counted upon to evoke the necessary enthusiasm in the United States. Indeed, the only economic issue that was arousing public interest in 1947 was inflation, which tended to put the Administration on the defensive, as foreign aid seemed likely to increase pressures on prices.

Secretary Marshall's speech of June 5 must be seen as a carefully reasoned reaction to this set of political forces. The strategy of the speech appears to have been dictated by two complementary perceptions: first, that the Administration had exhausted its ability to mobilize domestic support for foreign aid; second, that it was impossible to mobilize both American and European support with the same approach. These considerations suggested the possibility that the evocation of strong European support expressed in the form of a public request from Europe for help might solve the domestic political problem as well by playing to the natural sympathies of the American people and obscuring the initiating role of the Democratic administration. Acheson expressed these thoughts to a group of British journalists shortly before Marshall's speech. The speech itself was directed mainly to the European audience. This explains the complete absence of any anti-Soviet implication, and even the spurious offer to include the Soviets in the program. At the same time, the Administration went out of its way to minimize the domestic exposure and impact of the speech. Marshall, who was acutely fearful of the domestic opposition his speech might arouse, particularly in the Midwest, gave strict orders to the State Department press section that the speech was to receive no publicity. President Truman called a news conference on the same day that Marshall spoke and made several headline-producing announcements that tended to blanket Marshall's speech. Moreover, the actual offer of aid was made in language so cryptic that Bevin had to be warned in advance to be looking for it. In consequence, much of the responsibility for convening the C.E.E.C. had to be assumed by the British leader. President Truman did not endorse Marshall's proposal until three weeks after the speech, when rumors of presidential non-support began to threaten the entire strategy.[33]

Secretary Marshall's speech must be considered a masterpiece in both conception and execution. The offer of aid to the U.S.S.R. completely undermined leftist and Communist opposition in Europe and permitted the European governments to respond decisively. The U.S.S.R. was placed in the position of assuming responsibility for the division of Europe. This constituted a major propaganda defeat for the Soviets and suggested that Marshall had defeated at last the Soviet propaganda strategy that the Administration had regarded as a major impediment to its foreign policy in 1945–6. In the U.S. the speech simultaneously avoided the kind of controversy that might have crystallized opposition to large-scale aid, and weakened the arguments of critics of the Truman Doctrine, particularly those advanced by Henry Wallace and his followers. By shifting responsibility for initiating and drafting the plan to Europe, the Administration played successfully to public attitudes of generosity and chauvinism, and most Americans came to view the Marshall Plan as a form of charity to a prostrate and supplicant Europe. This appearance of European initiative provided a cover behind which the Administration was able to pursue long-held commercial and political objectives that did not have strong popular support.

Despite the virtuosity of Secretary Marshall's address at Harvard, the essential domestic political fact underlying that presentation was the Administration's lack of confidence that it could command sufficient public and Congressional support to assure enactment of an adequate foreign aid program. Following the speech, the Administration took a number of steps to strengthen its domestic political position. Remembering the way Franklin Roosevelt had handled Congress, the Administration subsidized a series of summer "inspection tours" of Europe for numerous legislators; by the fall, two hundred fifteen members of Congress had made such trips and had been briefed at various European locations by American diplomatic and military personnel. To satisfy widespread concern about the domestic economic consequences of foreign aid, the President appointed three commissions of prestigious figures—chaired by Commerce Secretary Harriman, Interior Secretary Krug, and the Chairman of the Council of Economic Advisors, Edwin Nourse—to investigate various aspects of the problem and assure the country that it could afford the Marshall Plan.[34]

None of these initiatives, however, did anything immediate to develop broad-based support for the Administration's proposals, and this problem remained unattended throughout the summer of 1947. Within the State Department there were violent disagreements as to how publicity should be handled. The result was a series of uncoordinated, contradictory, and ineffective initiatives by various offices and individuals. Some officials urged that statements clarifying Marshall's address be issued, but they were overruled. When addresses were made, arrangements for press coverage were neglected. There was some transfer of information from individual officials to members of the press, but the public-relations office was not made aware of such efforts and could not ensure that crucial information received wide distribution. The debacle probably reflected the same problem that had produced Secretary Marshall's speech: the Administration was not sure how to go about mobilizing public support for the Marshall Plan and was afraid that energetic preparations on its part might crystallize opposition. Polls testing public awareness of the Marshall Plan remained steady throughout the summer, with less than half the population indicating they had even heard of it.[35]

The potential dangers of this situation were widely and repeatedly recognized. In late June Senator Vandenberg wrote a friend that "I certainly do not take it for granted that the American people are ready for any such burdens as would be involved [in the Marshall Plan]." As early as July 9 the Alsops reported that "there are signs of real trouble ahead on the home front"; they quoted a senator who accused the State Department of "failing to protect its rear" and who predicted that if the Administration were to ask for the appropriation then, it would be "turned down flat by an overwhelming majority of both Houses." Under Secretary Lovett was equally pessimistic. In late July he told Forrestal that he doubted that "this country would be willing to produce the sums necessary" to maintain Britain's position, which sums were the largest part of the Marshall Plan. Forrestal, always sensitive to currents of public mood, told the cabinet on August 15 that a new isolationism and a "let Europe go" attitude was developing in the country. This opinion was shared by Cabell Phillips, Washington correspondent for *The New York Times*, who wrote in late July that "isolationism has reappeared on the political scene" and "stands threateningly across the path of large-scale programs for the economic rehabilitation of Europe."

By the early fall observers friendly to the Marshall Plan were openly expressing their dismay at the Administration's lack of leadership. Harold Stassen, a leading member of the internationalist wing of the Republican Party, told Forrestal on September 10 that he felt the public would support the Administration but that "more leadership and more facts" needed to be given. James Reston wrote in *The New York Times* that although "officials in the State Department say their foreign policy rests primarily on the Marshall Plan and concede that it would rise or fall on the extent to which the American people understand and support it," there was "no public relations plan at the State Department to deal with it." The *Washington Post*, a supporter of the Marshall Plan, editorialized in early November that Marshall "has missed a great opportunity to arouse public interest in his magnificent concept" and stated that Marshall's willingness to leave the people "completely out of touch with the Administration's ideas . . . is nothing short of a tragedy." Sumner Welles, a former Under Secretary of State, wrote that "in the present crisis it seems incredible that the Secretary of State's daily press conference, . . . continued until the Byrnes regime, should not have been resumed by Secretary Marshall." Opponents of the Marshall Plan could not contain their pleasure. John O'Donnell, writing in the right-wing *Washington Times Herald* on

October 21, gloated about the "wash-up of the so-called Marshall Plan" and his colleague Frank Waldrop stated two days later that "from all the evidence it looks as if the celebrated Marshall Plan is out the window."[36]

5. Return to Crisis Politics

In October 1947 the Administration made public what it had known since the spring, that short-term aid to Europe would be required in advance of the Marshall Plan, and declared a new emergency to prevent starvation and communist ascendency in western Europe. This tactic worked, and Congress approved what was basically a first installment of the Marshall Plan, but the anti-communist emphasis of the Administration's appeal enabled Republicans and conservatives in Congress to amend the legislation in several ways—including an authorization of aid to China—not consistent with the Administration's policies.

THE ANALYSES OF EUROPE'S ECONOMIC NEEDS completed by the State Department during the spring of 1947 indicated that several key countries would require financial assistance by the beginning of 1948, months before the Congress would have a chance to act on the Marshall Plan. This conclusion was strongly reinforced by economic developments during the summer, particularly the adoption by Britain, France, and Italy of restrictions on imports from the dollar area and the report of the C.E.E.C. that this pattern might spread to all Europe. Failure to provide immediate aid would mean that the people of Europe would have to face another winter with no assurance of future help. The inherent grimness of this prospect was doubled, from the perspective of the American government, by its political implications, for the Communist parties were now unrepresented in the French and Italian governments and had adopted, as the formation of the Comintern in September indicated, a policy of obstructionism toward American-sponsored programs of economic recovery. The pattern of proliferating restrictions on dollar imports suggested another reason for extending assistance immediately. The international conference to complete the I.T.O. Charter would occur in Havana during the first months of 1948, before aid under the Marshall Plan could possibly be available. The possibility of an American success at Havana would be reduced considerably if the conference were held in an atmosphere of economic crisis and widespread increases in restrictions on trade. This point was brought home to the U.S. forcefully in October when the British government indicated that it would adopt new restrictions on dollar imports if special, interim assistance were not forthcoming.[37]

After the spring of 1947, there seems not to have been any doubt within the Administration that some form of interim assistance would have to be supplied to the countries of Europe with the most serious payments problems: Britain, France, Bizonal Germany, and Italy, in order of size of deficit. The gloomy political prospects for the Marshall Plan that developed during the summer of 1947, however, led to official procrastination on the issue. Administration action was also complicated by the availability of a number of means by which short-term aid could be obtained. In the case of Britain, for example, the Administration could release dollars remaining in the British loan account, which had been frozen following Britain's default on convertibility in July. This action could be accomplished by executive order with informal agreement from Congressional leaders. The U.S. could also aid Britain indirectly, by assuming total responsibility for financing the occupation of Bizonal Germany. Funds for meeting the American part of Bizonal Germany's deficit, as well as the British part if that option were taken, could be obtained as part of the Army appropriation, which would face no serious scrutiny or debate in Congress. Short-term aid to other countries of Europe could be extended through the Export-Import Bank, the Commodity Credit Corporation, or the Reconstruction Finance Corporation. These methods, like unfreezing the loan funds, could be achieved by executive order with informal agreement by Congressional leaders that the technical adjustments required would be approved by Congress at a later date. It was also possible for the countries of Europe to obtain short-term assistance from the International Monetary Fund or the World Bank, provided the governing boards of these institutions made the appropriate decisions. Finally, of course, the Administration could convene a special session of Congress and ask for an emergency appropriation, which would require full-dress hearings and debates.[38] Faced with this range of options, the Administration announced in October that it would convene a special session to ask for "Interim Aid" for France, Italy, and Austria. At the same time, it decided to meet the needs of Britain by releasing the loan funds and assuming the full costs of Bizonia. Funds to meet both American and British shares of Bizonal occupation would be obtained through a supplemental Army appropriation requested during the special session. An examination of these decisions illuminates the Administration's response to the complex of political difficulties in which the issue of foreign aid was enmeshed

Aid to Britain was an especially difficult proposition politically. Britain had received special assistance under the 1946 loan agreement and had defaulted on its obligations under that loan. Its representatives had not been forthcoming at Geneva. It was being governed by the Labour Party, which was busy nationalizing key industries, a fact that caused Harriman to despair of getting Congress to finance Britain's difficulties. Yet Britain's needs were the greatest in western Europe, and its recovery was critical to American interests, both economic and political. This was a vexing situation, which would complicate debate on the Marshall Plan. It made sense, though, to minimize Britain's role in the aid program, and the handling of its immediate needs through technical adjustments achieved this end.

The problem of aiding France and Italy was more complicated. It was clear that the whole aid program was in political danger in the fall of 1947. To request a special appropriation would be to open, possibly prematurely, the whole

Pandora's box of political difficulties that the Marshall Plan catalyzed, and risk losing the entire program through an early defeat of part of it. On the other hand, the political problems of foreign aid were not likely to be any less difficult in early 1948 than in the fall of 1947. A preliminary debate on a short-term "emergency" program—one that could be offered as relief to prevent starvation during the critical winter months in countries where the ideas of starvation and communist subversion were easily linked—would provide the Administration a chance to win a precedent-setting victory on foreign aid while denying that Congress was really making commitments concerning the long-range program. Most press reports indicated that the issues of relief and anti-communism were the two most politically viable bases upon which foreign aid could be sought. A defeat of a short-term program, though damaging, would not necessarily doom the Marshall Plan and would at least clarify the difficulties to be encountered in the final showdown. On balance, it made sense to take the step of asking for emergency aid under circumstances that minimized the risk of defeat.[39]

President Truman considered calling a special session as early as May and was reported to have decided to do so in July. His procrastination was undoubtedly political, for to commit himself to calling a special session could give impetus to opponents of the aid program. In mid-July Truman assured Republican leaders that no special session was being contemplated, and it was not until September that the Administration even suggested to Vandenberg—via a less-than-candid letter from Lovett—that "distressing news from Europe with regard to the immediate economic and financial condition of certain countries" was causing discussion within the Administration. Vandenberg's subsequent refusal to take responsibility for calling the special session probably reflected annoyance at these tactics. On October 23, however, the President announced that Europe faced another "crisis" and that emergency action was required.[40]

The forces urging the Administration toward convening a special session during the early fall of 1947 were strengthened by considerations of an entirely different nature than the politics of foreign aid; 1948 was a presidential election year of more than usual significance. For the Republicans 1948 offered what seemed their best chance of capturing the presidency since 1928. For the Democrats 1948 would determine whether the coalition developed by Franklin Roosevelt could hold together without that uniquely effective political leader. By the fall of 1947 both parties were deeply involved in presidential politics. Before the end of the year three Republicans—Taft, Stassen, and Warren—were announced candidates for that party's nomination, and there were persistent rumors in the press that Vandenberg also harbored presidential ambitions. All this had direct bearing on the foreign aid issue, since Vandenberg was the key to Administration success and Taft seemed likely to be the center of the opposition. Vandenberg was unlikely to exert himself in support of the Administration that Taft opposed unless he could be convinced that there was solid popular support for such action.

The situation was equally complex on the Democratic side. In the White House, Clark Clifford was at work on a lengthy prescription for the President's reelection. Clifford believed that Henry Wallace probably would lead a third-party movement in 1948, splitting the Democrats at a particularly awkward moment. This view was strengthened by the success of Wallace's summer speaking tour, which seemed to indicate that his candidacy would win broad political support. Although the appealing character of Secretary Marshall's proposal at Harvard momentarily confused Wallace and sputtered his attack upon the Administration, by the fall he had decided to oppose the Marshall Plan on the ground that the aid program should be administered by the U.N. This promised to be a central issue in his campaign. To meet this and other challenges, Clifford believed, Truman had to adopt a bold and aggressive course of political conduct beginning in November 1947 and lasting until the election. It is evident, therefore, that the issue of foreign aid was completely caught up in the stresses of presidential politics in the fall of 1947 and that the special session was bound to be a major forum for several key candidates of both parties.[41]

It is instructive, in this context, to consider the reelection strategy devised by Clifford, for though his memo was not actually submitted to the President until late November, it provides the best available indication of political thinking within the White House at the time that the President was developing his plans for the special session on Interim Aid. Clifford believed that the major foreign policy issues in 1948 would be U.S.-Soviet relations and the pressures on the domestic economy caused by foreign assistance programs. He thought that the strain of domestic politics would be too great to sustain a bipartisan approach to these issues. He also believed that the President should assert himself as the nation's leader in matters of foreign policy and not permit others, for example Secretary Marshall, to assume this role. Clifford, possibly recalling the effect on the President's popularity of the Truman Doctrine speech, was entirely explicit about how this leadership could be asserted with maximum political gain. "There is considerable advantage to the Administration," he wrote, "in its battle with the Kremlin . . . the nation is already united behind the President on this issue. The worse matters get, up to a fairly certain point—real danger of imminent war—the more there is a sense of crisis. In times of crisis, the American citizen tends to back up his president." [42] This formula had much to contribute to the decision regarding the best means of obtaining special economic aid for Europe. An "emergency" session of Congress to meet a new European "crisis" would provide an ideal opportunity for the President to assert his leadership, rally the country behind him, and strengthen his credentials as the protector of Europe from the depredations of the communists.

The Administration's handling of Congressional debate on Interim Aid indicated a disposition to emphasize those aspects of the issue—emergency relief and anti-communism—most likely to assure Congressional approval and strengthen the President's political position. In his opening testimony on the aid proposal, Secretary Marshall referred to the situation as an "emergency" and stated that the funds were intended "to permit the people of these countries to continue to eat, work and to survive the winter." This description of Interim Aid for France, Italy, and Austria as emergency relief was repeated by Secretaries Lovett and Harriman in their appearances before the Congress. A similar summary was contained in a special address delivered by the President to a joint session on November 17. Common to all of these statements was the assertion that in considering Interim Aid the Congress was confronting legislation different in nature from the long-term aid program. Interim Aid, it was suggested, involved making available certain commodities, particularly food and fuel, to sustain certain European countries during the coming winter; the Marshall Plan involved a sustained program of economic reconstruction. Though this distinction was expedient both because it permitted Congress to consider Interim Aid without implicitly judging the Marshall Plan and because it emphasized the emergency and humanitarian aspects of the Administration's proposal, it involved a basic distortion of the economics of foreign aid. Interim Aid, like the Marshall Plan, was intended to maintain the flow of trade between the U.S. and Europe at certain levels. The amounts of aid requested for Interim Aid would sustain this trade for the first three months of 1948, after which the Marshall Plan money would continue the operation. The only difference between the two programs was the period of time for which maintenance of trade was being sought.[43]

Though the emergency relief aspect of Interim Aid was a political asset, the key to Congressional action on the proposal was relating it to the communist challenge, and the Administration lost no opportunity to bring this issue to the fore. On October 24, one day after he announced the decision to convene a special session, the President made a radio address to the nation describing an impending crisis in France and Italy and warning that "totalitarian pressures" might become irresistible during the winter if emergency assistance were not approved. On November 10, the first day of hearings on Interim Aid, the Administration released the first report on Greco-Turkish aid; it revealed that communist pressures on the Greek government had greatly increased in recent months, requiring much of America's intended economic aid to be diverted to military uses. On the same day, the report of the Harriman Committee, appointed by President Truman during the summer of 1947, was released; it made headlines with its prediction that American failure to approve the foreign aid program would lead to communist domination of all Europe, the Middle East, and North Africa, and might ultimately force changes in the American economic and political system. On November 17 the President addressed a joint session of Congress and repeated the argument he had presented in his radio address three weeks previously.[44] (This speech seems to be a clear indication of the impact of the kind of thinking represented in Clifford's memo on the handling of the campaign for Interim Aid. In it the President asserted himself as an advocate of strong anti-communist measures by proposing the aid program, and as determined to prevent economic aid from increasing inflation by proposing price controls. The latter proposal seemed such a transparent attempt to embarrass the Republicans by making them either renege on previous opposition to price controls or accept future blame for inflation that the speech was widely criticized as an attempt to use the special session to launch a reelection campaign.)

The Administration's propaganda initiatives in support of Interim Aid were reinforced by public statements of other prominent figures. On October 15 former Secretary of State Byrnes climaxed his personal efforts to make the American citizenry aware of the Soviet danger by publishing a memoir entitled *Speaking Frankly*, which received extensive coverage in the press. In this volume (inspired, Byrnes wrote, by several friends, probably including some of the officials struggling with the politics of foreign aid), the former Secretary confessed that he had disguised the true nature of U.S.-Soviet relations during his Secretaryship, and cast the blame for all postwar difficulties on Soviet intransigence and imperialism. The book published for the first time captured German documents revealing the nature of the Nazi-Soviet pact of 1939, in which Hitler and Stalin divided Europe between themselves. Byrnes used these documents to justify the conclusion that the U.S.S.R.'s intention was "to dominate, in one way or another, all of Europe." His final chapter contained a plea for approval of the Marshall Plan. On November 29 Clayton published an article in the *Saturday Evening Post* that predicted, following the same reasoning used in the Harriman report, that failure to enact the Marshall Plan would lead to communist domination of all Europe and, ultimately, changes in the American system of government. In the atmosphere created by these statements, the Communist-led strikes that broke out in France and Italy in late November to protest the Marshall Plan took on the aspect of revolutionary insurrections.[45] This would not be the last time that a communist reaction to an American initiative would play the ironic role of confirming for many Americans the fears of communist aggression that had been used to justify the original initiative.

In the context of this outpouring of high-level concern about communism in western Europe, Congress considered Interim Aid. As Clifford's memo had predicted, the potentially inflationary impact of the program made many legislators hesitant to support the Administration. Vandenberg commented on November 18 that "If the resistance which is building up to the little short-range European relief bill . . . is any criterion, our friend Marshall is certainly going to have a helluva time when he gets around to his long-range plan . . . politics is heavy in the air." But Vandenberg had been thoroughly won over by the Administration, and he knew how to use the public mood that the Administration had created. America's self-interest in Interim Aid, he told his colleagues, "is the self-interest which knows that any world revolution would rate America as a top-prize scalp." Within a few days he was able to report the rout of the opposition in the Senate: "I shall be greatly surprised if more than a dozen Senators dare to vote against the bill." The bill passed the Senate easily, with only six "daring" to oppose it. Even Senator Taft went along, though insisting that he was unalterably opposed to the Marshall Plan itself.[46]

The Administration's problems in the House were even greater than in the Senate, for there the immediate political impact of the inflation issue was greater and in the House there was no Vandenberg to fight the Administration's battles. The first signs of trouble came when Eaton was unable to prevent the reduction of the Administration's proposal by seven million dollars in the bill reported by his Foreign Affairs committee. Attempts during floor debate to cut the authorization still further were defeated, but opponents of the aid program showed considerable strength and won a number of victories, including the imposition of limits on wheat exports under the bill. But the debate in the House, as in the Senate, was dominated too much by the issue of communism to permit more than token victories for opponents. Representative Busby of Illinois complained about this: "Never before has the Congress been so bombarded with propaganda. . . . we get it from all sides by official speakers, the press and the radio. They all say the same thing—either vote for this aid to Europe or all Europe will go communist." But other Representatives, perhaps feeling a need to justify a politically uncertain vote, adopted the Administration's rhetoric with passion and eloquence. Congressman Everett Dirksen, for example, spoke of "this red tide . . . like some vile creeping thing which is spreading its web westward and westward." The bill passed easily. As Ted Lewis wrote in his political column: "The Republican Party cannot risk, if it wants to win the election in 1948, the responsibility for commie ascendency in western Europe—a responsibility that Truman would try to pin on the opposition if stopgap aid is too little or too late." [47]

Congressional debate on Interim Aid was, in a number of significant respects, a repetition of its action on Greco-Turkish aid. Again Congress had acted in the context of an emergency defined by the Administration as a choice between immediate action and communist ascendency in Europe. Again the emergency had been largely contrived by the Administration in response to domestic political pressures. Again the Republicans in Congress had muttered resentments against the Administration's tactics, but again they had been overwhelmed by them. Again, most importantly, the real issues involved in foreign aid went undiscussed. Neither the hearings nor floor debate produced any serious discussion of the relationship of foreign aid to American economic policy or polit-ico-strategic interests. The chief casualty of this reversion to crisis politics was public understanding of the government's foreign policy. An A.I.P.O. poll, designed to measure the extent to which Americans were aware of the relationship between foreign aid and the domestic economy, asked a national cross section in November to name the best ways of avoiding a business depression; only 1 per cent responded that increasing exports or lending money to Europe so that they might buy American products would be an appropriate policy. Public consciousness of the relationship between foreign aid and communism was much more evident. A poll taken among resi-dents of Washington by the *Washington Post* indicated that the communist issue was the chief factor in forming people's opinion of the program: 65 per cent of those favoring the program and 28 per cent of those opposing it believed that the communists would come to power in western Europe if Ameri-can aid was not provided. But public concern about this possi-bility reflected the vague philosophical opposition to com-munism promoted by the Administration rather than any clear understanding of its relationship to concrete American in-terests.[48]

It was not necessary to be a purist about democratic proc-esses to be alarmed about the character of the discussion of foreign assistance that occurred during debate on Interim Aid. Serious practical objections to the terms of the discussion were already obvious. One of the most important was implied by the growing anger and confusion in Congress and the public at reports that the U.S. was actively supporting trade between the communist and non-communist worlds. If the Soviets were really planning aggression westward and if Europe were really on the verge of communist takeover, it was asked, why was the Administration permitting and even promoting trade be-tween East and West? When Britain completed a trade agree-ment with the Soviet Union in December there was a howl of protest in Congress. Continuing American trade with the Soviet Union was exposed and condemned on Capitol Hill and in the right-wing press. Senator Knowland likened such trade to sending scrap iron to Japan prior to World War II. The Commerce Department was forced to end its efforts to develop U.S.-Soviet trade relations. The ironies of these developments were profound. We have seen that the revival of East-West trade in Europe was one of the major purposes of American foreign policy. Indeed, the State Department actually favored extending American aid to eastern Europe under the Marshall Plan to promote East-West trade, though for political reasons it did not suggest this to Congress. Now, as a result of the rhetorical devices that the Administration was employing to win popular and Congressional approval for the aid program, it was forced to apologize for and take steps to curtail trade that it considered complementary to the program and economically advantageous to the United States.[49]

Undoubtedly the most serious problem generated by the anti-communist emphasis of the debate on foreign aid involved American policy toward China. During debate on Greco-Turkish aid, a number of Republicans who objected to Marshall's imposition of an embargo on arms shipments to China, and to the Administration's general attitude of resignation with respect to events in that country, had put Administration witnesses on the defensive by asking if there was any intention of applying the Truman Doctrine to China. Administration responses had been equivocal. Within the Administration, George Kennan, who had objected to the Truman Doctrine before its delivery precisely because it implied American aid to any country threatened by communism, urged in the report of the Policy Planning Staff in May that steps be taken to correct this misconception of American policy. During the summer of 1947, however, nothing was done to implement Kennan's suggestion.

Indeed, events evolved in precisely the opposite direction. Early in the summer the Chinese Nationalists attempted to exploit the Truman Doctrine by initiating a new campaign for American aid. Republicans in Congress responded warmly. Senator Vandenberg wrote Marshall to complain about the preoccupation of the Administration with Europe, and he suggested that Congress was not likely to approve any aid program that did not present a "total balance sheet." Other Republicans pressed the Administration for a reappraisal of the China policy. To diffuse these demands, the Administration lifted the arms embargo and sent General Albert Wedemeyer, the American commander in China during World War II and a champion of a strong American commitment to that country, to China on a fact-finding mission. Although the Administration appears not to have intended to imply readiness to sponsor a major new program of aid to Chiang by these actions, it could not avoid giving that impression. In any case, these attempts to appease Republican demands on China were an indication of the Administration's handling of the China problem during the summer of 1947. Its quite obvious intention was to satisfy the Republicans with minor concessions rather than to develop bipartisan support for its own policy. Vandenberg's strong advocacy of aid to China appears to have been the critical consideration moving the Administration in this direction, for it was largely to strengthen his position that the concessions were made.[50]

By the fall of 1947, whatever possibility may have once existed for developing a bipartisan policy on China had been lost. In the context of the presidential election, the Republican Party had seized on China as its issue in foreign policy. This development involved a coalition of those genuinely concerned about the future of China and those more concerned about the future of the Republican Party. Arthur Vandenberg was a strong adherent to this movement, and in his letters he consistently referred to China as the Republican contribution to American foreign policy. In October he stated that he opposed "any so-called 'Marshall Plan' which does not include China." Governor Dewey of New York, the leading prospect for the Republican nomination, was making speeches urging a "two-ocean foreign policy." Other members of the "China bloc" in Congress—led by Bridges in the Senate and Judd and Vorys in the House—could be counted upon to take similar views. At the same time, Senator Taft was stressing his opposition to the Marshall Plan. The Administration was thus faced with the possibility of opposition from legislators who tended toward isolationism and government economies, as well as the China bloc. Under these circumstances it elected to make additional concessions to the advocates of aid to China. It approved limited American military action in China of an advisory and training nature, and it indicated that a program of economic aid for Chiang was being developed. Though these decisions involved very limited amounts of money, they entailed a fundamental shift from a policy of gradually liquidating the American commitment to one of strengthening it. These concessions satisfied Vandenberg, but were not enough for Republican champions of China in the House. Judd and Vorys successfully sponsored an amendment including China in the House Interim Aid bill, and urged Vandenberg to honor their initiative on this point. Basically sympathetic to their purposes, Vandenberg agreed. The final Interim Aid bill included a small allotment for China.[51]

The inclusion of aid to China in Interim Aid, and the growing Congressional pressure to reduce commerce between East and West, indicated how wide was the gap between the rhetoric that the Administration was using to create support for foreign aid and the substantive economic and political interests the aid program was designed to serve. In both cases the rhetoric was being used to force the Administration into policies directly contrary to its real intentions. But having let the period between Secretary Marshall's speech of June 5 and the debate on Interim Aid pass without a serious effort to mobilize solid public support for its purposes, the Administration was constrained to do political battle upon the basis of its crisis rhetoric rather than its substantive policies. On these issues, as on the issue of domestic communism and employee loyalty, the limitations of that rhetoric were becoming apparent. Although there was possibly still time to correct this trend before the final debate on the Marshall Plan early in 1948, the lesson of Interim Aid was that the Truman Doctrine, only nine months previously a stroke by which the Administration had turned Congress to its will, was now being turned back on its authors.

V
The Cold War at Home

1. Focusing the Internal Security Issue: Spring 1947

As the campaign for foreign aid developed, pressures on the Administration to take vigorous steps in the field of internal security remained intense. The most important sources of these pressures were Congress and the Justice Department. While the imminent battle over the Marshall Plan denied Truman the option of resisting these demands, complying with them would support the effort for foreign aid.

CONCESSIONS WITH REGARD TO EAST-WEST TRADE and China were not the only prices the Administration paid for foreign aid in 1947. As the first months of the year had shown, the Administration's reliance upon a strong anti-communist appeal to mobilize support for foreign aid provided Congressional Republicans with an irresistible opportunity to insist upon strong initiatives in the field of internal security. This circumstance had played a major role in precipitating the battle between the Administration and Congress for control of the employee loyalty issue, which the Administration had won by proposing the loyalty program and convening a grand jury to consider evidence of subversion by federal officials. During the spring of 1947, however, Congressional Republicans made it clear that they would not easily be preempted in this area. Betraying the extent to which their interest in the employee loyalty matter was political, they refused for several months to appropriate the funds requested for the President's program, and in mid-July the House approved a substitute measure sponsored by Congressman Rees. Only the existence of the President's loyalty order provided the Administration with the leverage it needed to defeat the substitute in Senate committee and assure the establishment of a program under its own control.

Predictably, the President's victory on employee loyalty did not prevent legislators from making regular attacks upon the new program or preclude specific demands by Congress with regard to other problems of internal security. Indeed, in the months immediately following the Truman Doctrine speech the Administration was provided with strong evidence that its difficulties arising from the political relationship between internal security and Cold War foreign policy were just beginning. In May, for example, Styles Bridges won a point in his battle with the State Department regarding John Carter Vincent, the Asian expert, who according to Bridges was influencing American policy toward China in favor of the Communists; Vincent was transferred out of the Division on Far Eastern Affairs.[1] Even more striking was the success of Bridges and Taber in forcing the State Department to dismiss summarily ten employees on grounds of disloyalty. The latter incident merits a moment's discussion, since it provided the most striking possible evidence of the Administration's inability to resist the demands of Congressional Republicans in the field of internal security.

When the Senate Appropriations Committee had been considering the State Department budget in 1946, Committee members had criticized Secretary Byrnes for retaining on the payroll, particularly in the overseas information program, employees of whose loyalty the Committee was suspicious; shortly thereafter, to enhance Byrnes's ability to cope with this problem, Congress had granted powers of summary dismissal to the Secretary of State. During the following year, no State Department employees had been removed under this provision. In the spring of 1947 the Department's budget again came before the Congress, and in May Taber's House Committee voted to strike the entire proposed allocation for the overseas information program. When the Department appealed this decision to Bridges's Senate committee the following month, Secretary Marshall had just delivered his speech at Harvard College, committing the Administration to new initiatives in the field of foreign aid. Marshall's proposal bore upon the Senate committee's deliberations in several ways. First, should the committee support the House committee's decision to eliminate the information program, the State Department would be denied a tool it considered essential to combat communist propaganda in Europe against American economic aid. Such propaganda was no small problem, as indicated by the attention given European sensibilities in the framing of Marshall's proposal. Marshall repeatedly expressed concern about communist propaganda in Europe and during the summer of 1947 he delivered a major address specifically denouncing it. Second, Marshall's proposal made the establishment of cooperation between the State Department and the Congressional appropriations committees even more essential than it already was, since both committees would be in positions to exert major influence over Congressional action on the Marshall Plan. (In fact, Taber was explicitly identified by Marshall as one of those whose response to the Harvard speech he most feared.) This was the setting in which Administration representatives testified on the State Department budget before Bridges's committee. The issue of internal security was quickly raised and the State Department representatives were criticized for the Secretary's failure to make use of his power of summary dismissal. The Senators indicated that the price of this laxity would be a cut in the State Department's appropriation, undoubtedly from the information program, and the action of Taber's committee left no doubt of the potency of this threat. The State Department thus faced both the loss of a program of great importance to the success of the Marshall Plan and a serious conflict with the appropriations committees if it failed to satisfy the Senate committee as to the loyalty of its employees.

On June 23 ten officials of the Department of State were summarily discharged from their positions. Newspaper reports, based upon a State Department press release, indicated that the employees had been discharged for reasons of security. Secretary Marshall, in announcing his personal review and approval of the dismissals, stated that several of the ten employees had been involved with a foreign power. The inference was widely drawn that some of them had been Communists. The ten dismissed employees, who had been granted no hearings or statements of charges, found themselves stigmatized as disloyal and unable to find other employment. Their requests that they either be presented with formal charges and an opportunity to answer them or permitted to resign without prejudice were ignored. It was not until the prestigious law firm of Arnold, Fortas and Porter accepted the cases and subjected the State Department to months of legal harassment and adverse publicity that its officers agreed to permit all the employees to resign without prejudice. In terms of its political significance, this was decidedly not a happy ending, for the Department had shown itself either unwilling or unable to offer any basis for the dismissals and thus seemed to have been motivated only by a desire to appease the appropriations committees. The *Washington Post* likened the State Department's action to the Administration's concessions in the area of policy toward China, and expressed the view that Marshall and Lovett could have been induced "to defend so indefensible a procedure" only because they "were the victims of ruthless blackmail from the appropriations rulers on Capitol Hill." The comment was appropriate. Following the announcement of the ten dismissals, a suitable compromise was obtained on the budget for the overseas information program.[2]

The Rees bill and the cases of Vincent and the ten State Department employees left no doubt that the Congress would continue to press the Administration for more aggressive action in the field of internal security. This in itself would have provided the impetus for continued attention by the Administration to the question of subversion during the spring and summer of 1947. But the driving force behind concern with internal security was by no means limited to the political infighting between a Republican Congress and a Democratic administration. Within the Administration itself were individual and agencies as anxious as the Republicans in Congress to take strong steps in this field.

None was more distinguished in this respect than F.B.I. Director Hoover, who had long been anxious to move decisively against the forces he felt were subverting traditional American values. Given the circumstances of increasing public concern with communism, Congressional interest in this issue, and Hoover's immense personal standing among groups especially concerned with internal security, the F.B.I. Director was in a strong position. Hoover seems to have comprehended the situation fully. He indicated this in April by asserting the right to conduct a full background investigation of any incumbent federal employee on whom the preliminary check of F.B.I. files, required by the President's loyalty order, developed "derogatory information." As the loyalty order had specifically left the decision to make such an investigation to the head of the employing department or agency, and had specifically designated the Civil Service Commission as the agency responsible to make this kind of investigation when requested, Hoover's action seemed a blatant effort to expand his influence over the loyalty program and thus over the entire federal bureaucracy. In the opinion of Stephen Spingarn, a member of the staff of the Presidential Commission that developed the loyalty order, Hoover's move looked "as if the F.B.I. were subverting the Temporary Commission's report and the President's E.O. without so much as a by-your-leave to any of the interested parties outside of Justice." The issue was brought to the attention of the White House and precipitated a major showdown between the Civil Service Commission and the F.B.I. that clarified the attitudes of several important individuals in the Truman administration. Attorney General Clark strongly backed Hoover and interceded with the President in his behalf. Truman, however—in the words of a note by Clifford—felt "very strongly anti-F.B.I. and sides positively with Mitchell and Perkins [of the C.S.C.]. Wants to be sure to hold F.B.I. down, afraid of 'Gestapo.'" Although a compromise acceptable to the President was devised, Truman was not optimistic that it would stick. As he wrote in a note to Clifford, "J. Edgar will in all probability get this backward-looking Congress to give him what he wants. It's dangerous." The President's fears were well founded, for thorough investigations of incumbent employees was the most popular of all issues related to internal security among Congressional Republicans. In due course Congress cut the budget for the loyalty program proposed by the White House in a way that substantially curtailed the role of the Civil Service Commission.[3]

As this incident makes clear, the President was quite aware of the forces acting on him in the field of internal security in the spring of 1947, but his sense that the situation was "dangerous" did not lead him to take any strong steps to soothe growing public agitation over the problem. His position is not difficult to understand. Failure on his part to satisfy public and Congressional concern in this area could undermine his Administration politically and leave him vulnerable to Republican attack. At the same time, by confusing his position on communism, such action would cripple his capacity to mobilize support for the foreign aid program at a critical moment in the campaign for its approval. In short, the potential costs of a strong stand against the F.B.I. or H.U.A.C. would be very great, while the gains would be speculative and uncertain of achievement.

At the same time, as the announcement of the loyalty program and the H.U.A.C. hearings already had demonstrated, continued decisive and conspicuous action against American communists and subversives could help the Administration solve what it considered the fundamental problem of internal security, which had nothing to do with disloyal federal employees but was related to the absence of strong public support for its international policies.[4] Such a benefit was not to be spurned by an Administration faced with an extended and difficult battle for foreign aid. It was especially not to be spurned as public enthusiasm for the Truman Doctrine began to wane in the late spring, making the Administration aware of the need to rekindle the kind of public concern over the communist challenge that had contributed so decisively to passage of Greco-Turkish aid. In this setting, while planners in the

State Department were developing the Marshall Plan and girding themselves for the political battle it would precipitate, officials elsewhere in the Truman administration were preparing to move forward with new and dramatic initiatives against American communists and subversives. These plans fell into two broad categories: (1) programs of counterpropaganda and police controls intended to destroy the effectiveness of American communists and subversives as well as combat Soviet propaganda; (2) programs of education and propaganda, designed to overcome the widely held attitudes that inhibited public support of the Administration's foreign policies.

2. Policing Internal Security

Under the pressure of its effort to win support for Cold War foreign policy, the Administration developed a number of programs to police public opinion. The Attorney General's list was published as a means of discrediting dissident organizations. Deportation actions were brought against aliens considered subversive. New efforts were made to control public access to information about international events and national policy. Taken together, these actions constituted a system of constraints upon opposition to official policy comparable to those used during the two world wars of the twentieth century.

WHEN MEMBERS OF THE TRUMAN ADMINISTRATION SPOKE of the problem of communist propaganda, they always referred to the ability of the communists to appeal to broad segments of the population through apparently patriotic appeals or organizations that concealed their relationship to the communist movement. Thus, President Truman worried about a coalition of "reds, phonies and parlor pinks"; Forrestal, Clark, and Truman feared the susceptibility of the isolationists to communist appeals; Forrestal saw a de facto alliance of communists and pacifists, and J. Edgar Hoover labeled "front" organizations the most effective instruments of communist subversion. Despite general agreement on the dangers represented by this form of propaganda in 1945 and 1946, at the time of the Truman Doctrine speech the Administration had devised no effective tool to combat it; indeed, the Communists staged a major campaign against Greco-Turkish aid during the spring of 1947.[5] The Administration's efforts in the realm of counterpropaganda were limited to cooperation with the House Un-American Activities Committee, a crude instrument that the Administration could not control and one whose effectiveness was limited by its reputation for partisanship as well as bizarre and irresponsible sensationalism. The inception of public debate on the foreign aid program lent new urgency to the problem of communist propaganda, for nothing was more predictable than the political opposition that foreign aid would encounter or the intensity with which the communists would exploit and encourage these difficulties for their own purposes. In this setting the Justice Department developed one of the most effective and controversial political instruments ever devised by the American government: the Attorney General's list of subversive organizations.

The list was nothing more than a public designation by the Attorney General of organizations operating within the United States that he considered "communist," "fascist," "totalitarian," or "subversive." Compiled for the first time during the spring and summer of 1947 and made public late in the year, the list immediately demonstrated a capacity to undermine the political effectiveness of cited organizations. The day following publication, for example, the Connecticut State Youth Conference, an organization listed because it had demonstrated against American intervention in Greece during the spring of 1947, was informed that the facilities of a Hartford hotel that it had engaged for a planned convention would be unavailable. The National Council for American-Soviet Friendship, which had actively promoted U.S.-Soviet cooperation since 1943, reported that as a result of being designated "communist" it and its local affiliates "lost numerous members, officers and sponsors; lost public support; lost contributions; lost attendance at meetings; lost circulation of their publications; lost acceptance by colleges, schools and organizations of their exhibits and other material; have been denied meeting places; have been denied radio time . . . are unable to gain members and support from federal employees . . . have been seriously frustrated." The National Council also reported substantial personal and professional damage to its leadership. Other organizations had similar experiences. Though no quantified analysis of the impact of the list on cited organizations has been undertaken, existing scholarship supports the view that the list seriously impaired the functions of those groups included on it. The fact that membership in an organization on the list very quickly became the basis for disqualification for employment by numerous state and local governments and educational institutions indicates that it was accorded wide credibility, and this would seem a significant measurement of its effectiveness as counterpropaganda. When the Supreme Court considered a challenge to the list brought by three cited organizations, all the Justices agreed that it had significantly impaired the effectiveness of the organizations it named.[6]

The authority under which the Attorney General developed this list was contained in the executive order by which President Truman established the loyalty program in March 1947. The apparent purpose of the list was to provide federal officials administering the loyalty program with one criterion by which an employee's loyalty might be ascertained. In the language of the executive order, "membership in, affiliation with, or sympathetic association with any foreign or domestic organization, association, movement, group or combination of persons designated by the Attorney General as totalitarian, fascist, communist or subversive" would be one consideration in assessing an employee's loyalty. Precisely how this standard was introduced into the loyalty program is not clear from the records of the President's Temporary Commission. It is clear, however, that the Commission provided for the development of the list as the natural consequence of its acceptance of this standard of loyalty and that it considered the list only in relation to the limited purposes of the loyalty program. Passing consideration was given to the question of publication, and the Commission agreed that it opposed such action, but left the decision in each case to the Attorney General. Clark chose to publish the entire list.[7]

The official story has always maintained that publication of the Attorney General's list was never intended for any purpose other than that implied by the President's loyalty order. As Attorney General Clark wrote in 1949, "the designations made pursuant to the order are intended to relate only to the specific purposes of the order."[8] This may be true. And it may be true that the onerous consequences of the list's publication that ultimately led the Supreme Court to accord legal redress to cited organizations were nothing more than unintended by-products. There is, however, strong reason to regard this story as official fiction, and to doubt that the Attorney General's decision to publish the list represented anything other than a deliberate attempt by the Department of Justice to neutralize various political organizations that were, among other subversive things, impeding the Administration's efforts to win support for Cold War foreign policy.

The concern felt by the Attorney General in 1946 and early 1947 regarding communist propaganda activities and his eagerness to combat them have already been discussed. Clark's frustration derived from his inability to apply legal sanctions against communist activities. Neither of the federal statutes aimed at subversive organizations—the Voorhis Act and the Foreign Agents Registration Act—had proved to be an effective means of exposing communist activity. To bring communist organizations under their regulations required the government to demonstrate that American communist organizations were creatures of the Soviet government, or that they sought to overthrow the American government by unconstitutional means, attributes that, though generally assumed, could not be proven in a legally acceptable fashion. The Smith Act, aimed at subversive activity by individuals, was ineffective in punishing communists for the same reasons. Attorney General Clark was pessimistic about devising a constitutional means of subjecting communist activities to legal controls. He advised Congress against legislative efforts that would define the Communist Party in such a way as to bring it within the purview of the subversion statutes.[9] His problem, then, was to destroy the effectiveness of communist and communist-affiliated organizations without bringing legal sanctions against them. The Attorney General's list achieved this purpose.

That such a list, once published, would operate as counterpropaganda could not have been unanticipated by someone with as much experience in the field of internal security as Clark. The list he published in 1947 was not the first such engine produced by the American government. The practice of publicly citing organizations as a counterpropaganda technique had been employed by Congressional committees on a number of occasions. The Senate Judiciary Committee in 1919, the Fish Committee of the House in 1930, and the McCormack Committee of the House in 1935 had all published lists of communist organizations in order to limit their effectiveness. In more recent years, the Dies Committee (later the House Un-American Activities Committee) had employed this technique as standard practice. Both Clark and Hoover endorsed the principle of publicizing communist activities as a potent means of combating them. Thus, the concept of publicly listing subversive organizations derived from a tradition of counterpropaganda. Certainly it is difficult to discover any connection between publication of such a list and the purposes of the loyalty program. The executive order contained no requirement that the list be published, and it is hard to imagine how its intended function of assisting loyalty boards would be enhanced by such action. Indeed, the precedent with regard to the use of such lists as part of loyalty programs was to treat them as confidential; this policy had been established by the Justice Department during World War II when it developed a similar list as part of Roosevelt's loyalty program. The list published in 1947 differed from the wartime list in another important respect: while the earlier list contained only organizations to which government employees belonged, a very small percentage of the organizations cited by Attorney General

Clark in 1947 or later contained any government employees. Indeed, potential inclusion of government employees was not a consideration that Clark's department considered relevant to placing organizations on the list. Moreover, as most of the groups cited by the Attorney General were ostensibly engaged in activities entirely consistent with patriotism—though not, of course, the Administration's policies—and as a high percentage of their members had no knowledge of their subversive leadership or purpose, the list would not seem to have been a particularly valuable guide to discovering disloyalty among government employees.[10]

Although Clark has never explained his reasons for publishing the list, a sense of his view of it can be derived from various acts and statements. In his most extensive public discussion of the list, before the House Un-American Activities Committee in February 1948, Clark described it only in terms of counterpropaganda: "It is our purpose to continuously survey this field in order to prevent listed organizations from assuming an alias as well as additional organizations being used for subversive propaganda." Later he referred to listed groups as "those organizations that are engaged in propaganda activity of a subversive character." This preoccupation with counterpropaganda is revealing, for the ostensible purpose of the list was to identify organizations that were the instruments of foreign states or sought violent revolution. Clark's explanation to H.U.A.C. of his total strategy for combating communism in America further suggests that he viewed the list as a broad political instrument. "Our strategic objective," he stated, "must be to isolate subversive movements in this country from effective interference with the body politic." He listed an eight-point program to achieve this, which included: "(5) continuous study and public listing by the Attorney General of subversive organizations under the President's executive order; (6) complete elimination of subversive persons from all government positions." As this makes clear, Clark viewed the list as an anti-communist tool entirely distinct from the effort to rid the government of disloyal employees.[11]

This testimony dates from early 1948, well after the list

had been published and its effectiveness as counterpropaganda revealed, and thus proves only that Clark was ready to use the list for a purpose for which it apparently had not been intended. However, Clark's unblinking acceptance of the consequences of publication, combined with his refusal to withdraw it or to establish formal hearing procedures to protect innocent organizations once these consequences were apparent, and, indeed, his complete endorsement of these consequences, strongly support the view that the results of publication were neither unexpected nor unintended. Moreover, in April 1947, when work on the list was just beginning, Clark sought legal advice on the Justice Department's potential liability for placing organizations on it; it is doubtful that this question would have arisen had he not intended to publish it and were he not aware of its potential consequences. Moreover, as he told the House Appropriations Committee in late 1947, he was extremely cautious in developing the list and assigned a significant portion of the legal manpower in the Criminal Division to the task because of his awareness that the list represented something "a little bit contrary to our usual conception of democratic process." It is doubtful that he would have exercised such caution or made such a statement with regard to a document intended to remain confidential and to be used for internal administrative purposes.[12]

In order to assess the impact of the Attorney General's list on the public debate over Cold War foreign policy, it is necessary to understand the manner in which it was compiled. The authority of the Attorney General to assign organizations to the list was limited by no procedural requirements and qualified by no right of appeal. It was solely the result of secret determinations within the Justice Department and—until compelled by the Supreme Court in 1950—the Department consistently refused to make any public statement regarding the criteria by which its designations were made. This left the Attorney General free to apply as broad a definition to such words as "communist" or "subversive" as he saw fit. There is reason to believe that the men working on the list were inclined to define these words quite broadly. Two of

Clark's special assistants drafted a memo during the summer of 1947 setting forth the bases by which organizations should be assigned to the list. Their guiding principle was that "the proposed criteria are designed to be elastic and flexible" and their suggestions were consistent with this spirit. In general, the criteria involved the advocacy of political, economic, and social ideas that were "hostile or inimical to the American form of government" or tended to "promote the ideas and serve the interests of a foreign government" or "indicate lack of bona-fide allegiance to the government of the United States." The criteria involved no reference to specific acts. They made no reference to specific connections between domestic organizations and foreign governments. A "communist" organization was not defined as a group that took orders from the Soviet government or the American Communist Party, but one that advocated Marxist ideas, or supported the policies of the Communist Party while advocating democratic ideas, or followed policies "in accord with the governmental policy of Soviet Russia and opposed to that of the United States." The role of the criteria set forth in this memo in influencing designations to the list is not clear, though its authors consistently worked very closely with Clark in matters related to internal security. At a minimum, the memo indicates the type of thinking that existed within the Justice Department in 1947 when the list was first compiled.[13]

By such criteria, it seems fair to state, any organization that consistently opposed Cold War foreign policy would have been a serious candidate for designation, and several organizations that were active in this respect were cited. In addition to the National Council for American-Soviet Friendship, already mentioned, two Greek-American groups that had opposed the Tsaldaris government were cited on early editions of the list. The American Slav Congress, which worked actively against the Marshall Plan, was also cited. We shall probably never know, in most cases, on what evidence designations to the list were made or whether some organizations were cited solely because they opposed Cold War foreign policy. In general, the early editions of the list were considered by contemporary observers to be quite restrained, and even the *Washington Post,* which strongly opposed the list in principle, took no issue with the specific designations on the list published in 1947. So far as this writer knows, only one organization, the National Council for American-Soviet Friendship, has ever won a court ruling indicating that the Justice Department was not able to justify its designation.[14]

The major influence of the list on the debate over Cold War foreign policy, however, may not have derived from its effects on the organizations it named, onerous as these were. It must be remembered that prior to 1950 no one knew or could know on what basis groups were placed on the list. The meaning of the list was so ambiguous that the *Washington Post* could state in an editorial in late 1947 that "to be comprehensive and to avoid discrimination the Department of Justice would have to sweep into the disloyal category every organization which in any way disavows policies the government is following." In circumstances permitting such a view from such a sophisticated source, it would have been entirely reasonable—it may even have been right—to assume that active and consistent opposition to the Administration's foreign policies was sufficient to win a place on the list. Given the burdensome consequences of such a citation to the organizations and individuals affected, the mere possibility of this could not but have had a significant effect on organized dissent from the Administration's foreign policies. Unfortunately, quantitative measurements of the actual effects of the list have been few. Ralph S. Brown, author of a study of federal security programs, told a Senate subcommittee in 1956 that the only scientific study done in this area did find, on the basis of testimony by government employees, that the existence of the list made them reluctant to join organizations of which they were unsure. Since the list also became a test of employability in state and local governments, defense-related industries, and schools, and of eligibility for passports, occupancy of federally financed housing, and tax exemptions, it does not seem excessive or imprudent speculation to suggest that the Attorney General's list had a profoundly suppressing effect upon political dissent in the United States. In this sense, the impact of the list's publication was to enroll the whole country in a vast loyalty program. The President's loyalty order had had the important but limited result of creating conditions in which individuals on the government payroll would feel it necessary to keep to a straight political path; now this effect, based in part upon an appeal to patriotism, in part upon intimidation, reached out to the whole population. With specific reference to the Marshall Plan (support of which was becoming a measurement of a citizen's patriotism and opposition to communism), this conclusion would seem to apply with particular force. It was widely speculated in late 1947, for example, that the next edition of the list would include Henry Wallace's Progressive Citizen's Association, which represented the major organized opposition to the Administration's foreign policies. And in fact government employees who publicly opposed the Marshall Plan were challenged by security officials under the authority of the loyalty order.[15]

The Attorney General's list was only the most dramatic and innovative effort by the Justice Department to support the campaign for Cold War foreign policy during the summer and fall of 1947. Clark also mobilized the F.B.I. and the Bureau of Immigration and Naturalization for a full-scale program to deport aliens involved in communist activities. Like the device of issuing lists to cripple dissident organizations not subject to legal sanction, the practice of deporting aliens to rid the country of subversive ideas had a long history of sporadic usage in the annals of American security policy. The association of American radicalism with immigrants and aliens is one of the classic traditions in American politics; for example, the major radical organization in the United States in the late nineteenth century, the Industrial Workers of the World, contained a high percentage of immigrants and aliens, and this pattern also applied to the American Communist Party following its formation in 1919. In these circumstances, efforts in Congress to combat radicalism frequently took the form of amendments to the immigration laws. Numerous such proposals were directed against the I.W.W. but, for a variety of political reasons, it proved impossible to develop Congressional majorities in support of them. The nativist sentiment produced by World War I, however, proved potent enough to inspire legislation providing for the exclusion and deportation of aliens espousing revolutionary ideas or belonging to organizations that did so; that no broad deportation drive ensued was the result of the interpretation of these powers by the executive branch. The political tensions immediately preceding World War II produced legislation increasing the government's powers to expel radical aliens, but the war in Europe and the U.S.-Soviet alliance prevented any broad application of these laws to domestic communists. Thus, at the end of World War II, the Justice Department possessed broad and largely unexploited powers to deport aliens engaged in subversive activities. Meanwhile, the American Communist Party had been growing steadily, and the population of the United States had come to include thousands of aliens who participated actively in the Party's affairs. This combination of circumstances, in the context of the Administration's desire to neutralize the American Communist Party, rendered a major deportation drive almost inevitable.[16]

It came as one of the earliest clear indications of the deterioration in U.S.-Soviet relations, when the Truman administration was still publicly optimistic about continuing the wartime spirit of cooperation. Clark began to deport aliens who were considered communists by the Justice Department shortly after assuming the Attorney Generalship. By mid-1946 the program had reached sufficient proportions to elicit a complaint from the National Lawyers Guild. In February 1947 Clark reported that "we have deported 124 persons on the grounds of communism." Following the Truman Doctrine speech Clark intensified the campaign as part of the general effort to consolidate the country behind Cold War foreign policy. He instructed F.B.I. Director Hoover to prepare a list of alien communists, and initiated deportation proceedings against them whenever possible. By the end of the year he was able to report three hundred active cases. At the same time, he sponsored a study of the ethnic characteristics of American

communists and discovered that over 91 per cent were either
immigrants or the children of immigrants or married to someone in one of these two categories. In short, almost all communists were vulnerable directly or indirectly to punishment
through deportation proceedings. Perhaps inspired by this
realization, Clark ordered the preparation of legislative proposals to clear away existing impediments to prompt deportation actions. In instances where immigrant activists had
protected themselves against deportation by taking out citizenship, the Justice Department showed itself resourceful in finding means to overcome this obstacle: in June 1947, for example,
the Immigration and Naturalization Service sought revocation
of citizenship from Isadore Lipshitz, an immigrant who was
active in the Society for the Prevention of World War III, on
the ground that an adulterous affair had rendered him unfit to
be an American.[17]

In its relationship to the debate on Cold War foreign
policy, the deportation drive functioned in a manner similar
to the Attorney General's list. In the most limited sense it provided a potent means of excising from the body politic a significant number of dissident voices. In at least several instances
aliens who were active in opposition to Cold War foreign
policy and the Marshall Plan were arrested and held without
bail on Ellis Island. Gerhart Eisler was apprehended while
making a speaking tour to denounce American foreign policy
as the "renazification of Germany." John Williamson, the labor
secretary of the Communist Party, was taken into custody following his publication in the *Daily Worker* of a series of articles criticizing C.I.O. President Philip Murray for his support
of the Marshall Plan. Ferdinand Smith was picked up twenty-
four hours after he shared a speakers' platform with Henry
Wallace and while en route to a meeting of the National Maritime Union at which endorsement of the Marshall Plan was the
main item on the agenda. Attorney General Clark was completely candid that his use of the legally dubious practice of
holding these and other aliens without bail—a practice that
was disallowed by a federal court in March 1948—was intended to prevent the detained individuals from continuing

their political activities. "I ordered Mr. Eisler picked up," he stated in discussing one of the cases, "because he had been making speeches around the country that were derogatory to our way of life." [18] As with the Attorney General's list, the major impact of these arrests on the campaign for the Marshall Plan undoubtedly lay in their indirect psychological and political consequences rather than their direct silencing of subversive voices. They were a clear warning to all unnaturalized aliens (upon whom, as the report to Clark on American communists indicated, radical movements heavily depended) that active opposition to Cold War foreign policy could subject them to severe penalties. They also suggested to native Americans that opposition to the Administration's policies was an alien concept, to be associated with deportable criminals.

While Clark's Justice Department was developing the Attorney General's list and the deportation drive as ways of striking directly at those who were organizing dissent from the Administration's policies, several agencies of the government were developing programs reflecting an entirely different approach to the problem of policing internal security: the tightening of official control over information, particularly information about governmental activities. In many ways official censorship is the natural counterpart of police activity against dissidents: the former limits the basis for dissent at the source while the latter attacks those seeking to promote dissent; and the two instruments have tended to be used by the American government in tandem, most notably in time of war. Both have been justified, traditionally, as essential instruments of national security. But because both also abuse democratic concepts of civil liberty, tradition prior to 1947 had tended to limit their use to military emergencies. The problem, of course, lies in defining a situation in which national security requires extraordinary measures. The two world wars of the twentieth century were clear cases, and there was no significant opposition to the establishment of formal censorship procedures during these conflicts. But what of the circumstances prevailing in the United States in 1947, when the officials primarily responsible for the conduct of American foreign policy considered themselves engaged in international problems as significant as any war, and when the electorate was threatening their efforts to respond to this situation? It is clear from the Administration's development of such unprecedented peacetime policies as the employee loyalty program and the Attorney General's list that it was prepared in these circumstances to employ instruments that had traditionally been reserved for wartime emergencies; it is not surprising, therefore, that efforts were also made to invoke various forms of official censorship.

The impulse was most clearly articulated by high officials of the defense community who had watched public opinion force the reduction of military activities and expenditures to levels they considered imprudent. In late 1946, for example, Forrestal received a letter from Walter Lippmann pointing out that "public relations officials of both the War and Navy Departments have been out of hand for some time" with their announcements of "new and terrifying weapons" and "other stories . . . which are boastful or threatening." Lippmann was worried that such publicity would produce a "public reaction" that would make it even more difficult than it already was for the two departments to obtain adequate appropriations. Perhaps inspired by Lippmann's letter, Forrestal became very conscious of stories emanating from the military establishment, and in early 1947 he wrote Marshall complaining about testimony by certain naval officers before a Senate subcommittee on Armed Services. While claiming that the testimony had been factual, Forrestal expressed worry about "their future use, when the wave of pacifism comes, by people interested in attacking all those identified with our military forces."

Robert Patterson, the Secretary of War prior to the merger of War and Navy, seemed to feel the thrust of Lippmann's comments congenial also. In a letter to Roy Howard, publisher of the Scripps-Howard papers, in August 1947 he responded to a series of articles by Robert Ruark exposing the malpractice of a U.S. Army general in Italy: "After every war," Patterson wrote, "it has been the fashion to take snipes at the army. In other times there has been no great harm done because a long period of peace and tranquility was in prospect. This time, I fear, it is different. We stand in need of a strong army and constant criticism of the demoralizing variety may cost the country dear." [19] Forrestal's letter to Marshall and Patterson's to Howard involved quite different types of press stories, but both expressed deep official concern with the kind of information about the Armed Forces being printed in the mass media, and both betrayed an implicit desire to bring such stories under some form of control. Forrestal's belief that the press should be used as an "instrument of American foreign policy" has already been mentioned, and this belief led him, when he became Secretary of Defense in 1947, to propose various innovations in the relationship between the government and the press that seem designed to meet the kind of problem identified by himself and Patterson.

He tried various approaches. One was to prevent hostile reporters from covering military activities. In October 1947 it was reported that the Army had revoked the credentials of eleven American correspondents during the previous twelve months and denied credentials to another fifty on the grounds that they had communist connections. In early 1948 Forrestal sought to systematize this policy by requiring all newsmen applying for accreditation to the Armed Forces to pass a loyalty test. Among the proposed grounds for disqualification was membership in or close relationship to organizations cited on the Attorney General's list; apparently, newsmen were to be held to the same requirements of loyalty as government employees. Forrestal's plan, patterned after procedures developed during the war, evoked much criticism and had to be modified substantially. Another approach was to develop an ongoing structure for cooperation between the press and the Armed Forces. In March 1948 Forrestal asked the press to agree to consult with an information board, which he intended to establish within the Department of Defense, prior to publishing information in areas that he would designate vital to the national security. This suggestion, too, produced a storm of criticism from the press, and the plan was shelved. Forrestal's argument that such a procedure was essential to protect military secrets was ineffective because he could not document serious breaches of security under the existing system and because the newsmen suspected that what he had in mind involved far more than the protection of official secrets. The press immediately labeled the proposal a plan of censorship and in April the American Society of Newspaper Editors passed a resolution condemning "all forms of censorship." Given Forrestal's acknowledged attitude toward the press, it is difficult to fault the suspicions of the newsmen.[20]

In rejecting Forrestal's proposals, press officials argued that the proper place to control information was at the source, within the federal bureaucracy, not through increased controls over the press. The point was well taken by several key members of the Truman administration. Indeed, it was one that the Administration had anticipated, for the executive order creating the loyalty program provided that the disclosure of "confidential" information by a federal official could be the basis for dismissal on grounds of disloyalty. The development of this provision further illustrates the attitude of the Administration toward public opinion and the requirements of internal security in 1947. The President's loyalty order empowered the Security Advisory Board of the State–War–Navy Coordinating Committee to develop procedures to govern the handling of official information, and the Board circulated a draft set of rules in the fall of 1947. Under it official documents were divided into classifications of "top secret," "secret," "confidential," "restricted," and "unclassified." The draft rules also defined the roles of agency officials in classifying information and enforcing regulations, and detailed procedures for the handling and transmission of documents. These categories and procedures were based upon rules that had been employed for many years by the Armed Forces.[21]

In discussing these proposals, it must be recognized that the government had ample reason to consider the development of improved controls over official information essential. The *Amerasia* case had made it quite clear that existing procedures were far from perfect, and the allegations of Bentley and Chambers, being explored by a federal grand jury as the Security Advisory Board was drafting its rules, lent further support to this view. Attorney General Clark believed that improved procedures were required to combat modern espionage tactics, and during 1947 his department drafted legislation that proposed expanding the Espionage Act of 1917 to include any improper transmission of information concerning national defense. The danger of such proposals, of course, was that they could reach far beyond their purported purposes and become tools by which the Administration enforced certain modes of thought on its own public. This was clearly the case with the Attorney General's list and Forrestal's plans for cooperation between the press and the military; it was also the case with the rules for handling information developed by the Security Advisory Board. The definition of "confidential" proposed by the Board illustrates the point:

> The term confidential as used herein applies to information the unauthorized disclosure of which, although not endangering the national security, would be prejudicial to the interests or prestige of the nation or any governmental activity thereof or would cause unwarranted injury to an individual or serious administrative embarrassment or difficulty or would be of advantage to a foreign nation.[22]

It is difficult to imagine any factual disclosure that might in any way subject the government to criticism that could not have been interpreted as being within the meaning of this definition and therefore a basis for a charge of disloyalty. The application of military information controls to the entire federal government was in itself a proposal of unprecedented severity; the definition assigned to "confidential" information seemed designed to eliminate entirely the possibility of public statements by federal employees that might serve as a basis for controversy, criticism, or dissent concerning Administration policies.

By chance, a newspaperman obtained a copy of the draft rules and published a series of articles describing them —with spectacular results. The American Society of Newspaper Editors adopted a resolution condemning the attempt to apply military censorship codes to the entire government. An investigation was launched by the Executive Expenditures Committee of the House. Questioned on the matter at a news conference in November, President Truman belittled the issue by calling it a "straw man" and stated that the rules were merely preliminary and had not been considered or approved by him. As a result of pressures from Congress and the press, no attempt was made to implement the rules. The matter was dropped. The Chairman of the Security Advisory Board was dismissed. Despite these developments, however, the status of the draft rules remained unclear. Under Secretary of State Lovett authorized a statement that the rules had merely codified existing procedures, and in August 1948 Senator Homer Ferguson told the Senate that it was entirely possible that the rules were currently operating on a de facto basis. Under these circumstances, it seems likely that even without formal application of the proposed rules the willingness of federal officials to disclose information that could become the basis of public controversy was diminished. The matter was not clarified until 1951, when President Truman promulgated an executive order identical in its essentials with the proposals he had dismissed as a "straw man" in the fall of 1947.[23]

The Administration's efforts to establish greater control over the information received by the American people was not confined to Forrestal's proposals for press/government cooperation and the new provisions of the loyalty program. The State Department used its powers for similar purposes by adopting a policy of denying passports to American reporters whose overseas travels were considered "not in the interest of the United States." What this could mean became clear in early 1948 when A. B. Magil, a reporter for the *Daily Worker*, was denied permission to leave the country. The State Department refused to give reasons for the decision, but it is difficult to disagree with the view voiced by Representative Isaacson on the floor of the House that the case involved an attempt to "pre-censor" the American press "by barring its correspondents from an area of the news." The case produced so much adverse publicity that the State Department agreed to issue Magil a passport, but this did not alter the fact that the case had revealed what State Department officials referred to as the "settled policy" of the Administration. Representative Isaacson was himself denied a passport in 1948, and the Administration even discussed applying this sanction against Henry Wallace, though the idea was rejected as politically hazardous. The Justice Department and the State Department cooperated to apply a policy complementing these passport regulations to aliens visiting the United States. Communists were simply refused permission to visit the country except in extremely limited and highly controlled situations involving diplomatic personnel. Aliens granted visas to the United States were placed under a new set of regulations that shortened from a year to six months the period of time they were permitted to remain in this country. If a visitor intended to travel the visa was granted for only three months. Steps were taken to tighten surveillance of alien visitors and to prevent them from influencing public opinion in an undesirable manner. Each visiting alien was now required to agree "not to pursue any purpose not specifically authorized by immigration officials." In reporting the new rules, the *Washington Post* cited Justice Department sources as indicating that this new requirement meant, in effect, "that visitors will be required to pledge that they will refrain from any speechmaking or propaganda activities unless authorized to do so by this government." [24]

To consider the combined significance of the various restrictions placed upon public debate during the period in which the foreign aid program was before the Congress is to become aware of what must inevitably seem a coherent pattern of official behavior. The Attorney General's list, the deportation drive, the new controls on official information and on access of the press and public to it, the new controls upon alien visitors—all had a common origin in policies that had been developed during wartime emergencies to protect national security by assuring public support of the military effort. This is not to say that a central decision was ever taken by the President or the cabinet to use such techniques to support the campaign for Cold War foreign policy. Such a decision may have been taken, but it would not have been necessary to explain or understand these developments. For it is clear that there was among high officials of the Administration a shared sense of crisis arising out of the reluctance of the American people and the Eightieth Congress to support the levels of expenditure for an involvement in international affairs that the Administration considered essential to the protection of American economic and military interests. The Truman Doctrine speech, the handling of the debates on Greco-Turkish aid and Interim Aid, and the manner of the announcement of the Marshall Plan were all indicative of the Administration's awareness and fear of this situation, and of its response to it. The controls upon public debate that were developed during this same period were fully consistent with the spirit and intention of the Administration's approach to the debate on foreign aid; they are therefore explicable as the individual acts of high government officials operating within the broad framework of policy established by the President and attempting to use the powers of their offices to advance these policies. When these developments are considered together, of course, the question of whether they were all part of a centrally determined policy becomes far less important than the realization that in 1947, as much as in 1917 or 1941, the American people were being mobilized for world war.

3. Education for Security

To overcome the shortcomings of American opinion revealed by the campaign for foreign aid, the Administration designed a series of educational programs to promote internationalism, patriotism, and love of democracy.

THE MEN AROUND PRESIDENT TRUMAN could not have been more conscious of the fact that it was the tendencies of broad public opinion, rather than the activities of subversive organizations, that made necessary the tactics employed during debates on foreign aid and required new restrictions upon public discussion of national issues. Nor, aware that the debate on foreign aid was only the beginning of an extended postwar concern with international questions, did they ignore the fact that these techniques were short-term palliatives that did not reach the heart of the Administration's political difficulties in the field of foreign policy. What was really required, it was widely agreed, were sustained programs of public education to propagate a deeper commitment to the American system and a fuller understanding of America's international role that would immunize the people against subversive and dissident appeals.

Attorney General Clark was inclined to believe that public susceptibility to what he called "the rising tide of totalitarianism that is coming to our shores" derived from a letdown in patriotic sentiment or, more fundamentally, a loss of enthusiasm for American democracy. He believed that what was required was "to reawaken in the American people the loyalty we know them to have to the American way of life," and he had no doubt as to how this should be achieved. "In the final analysis," he told an audience in Boston, "our best defense against subversive elements is to make the ideal of democracy a living fact, a way of life such as to enlist the loyalty of the individual in thought, in feeling, and in behavior." He believed that the goal could best be reached through programs of public education that would eliminate inequality and prejudice in American society and promote democratic values. Clark was not alone in his analysis of the problem or his emphasis on education as the solution. A presidential commission on military training listed as the first requirement of national security a population that was strong, healthy, educated, and imbued with an understanding of democracy and sense of personal responsibility to make it work. The President's Commission on Higher Education reported that "one of America's urgent needs today is a continual commitment to the principles of democracy" and that "we cannot be so sure that the future of the democratic way of life is secure." It proposed programs that would instill "a fuller realization of democracy in every phase of living." This Commission touched on a second issue of major importance by proposing additional programs "directed explicitly for international understanding and cooperation." This was a point with which the leaders of the foreign policy bureaucracies could readily agree. As Forrestal put it: "The education of our people on world matters is one of the most vital needs of the country." The Commissioner of Education, John Studebaker, summarized the tendency of all these viewpoints succinctly: in the face of the communist challenge, he stated, the essential and pressing educational task was "to bring up young citizens who really understand and cherish American democracy, who are well-informed and skillful in thwarting the purposes of the totalitarians, and who understand and accept their responsibilities in today's rapidly shrinking and increasingly interdependent world." [25]

Such ideas did not originate with the men around President Truman in 1947. It was a common perception of President Roosevelt's wartime advisers that the fundamental popular disinclination to international involvements, combined with the expected postwar letdown in patriotic sentiment, would make it difficult for the American government to pursue the kind of foreign policies that were considered essential to American interests. Roosevelt's advisers had attempted to develop programs responsive to this problem, and the one that attracted the most attention and support was compulsory military training for all young men. Though such a program was significantly related to anticipated postwar military requirements, its value as an educational tool was considered to be of equal, if not greater, importance. In 1945, for example, Secretary of War Stimson told a committee of Congress that Universal Military Training (U.M.T.) was desirable because it could help create "the disciplined, trained and patriotic citizenry" essential to the support of the international role of the United States in the postwar world. General Marshall expressed a similar view. Forrestal indicated that this aspect of U.M.T. was even more important than the military aspect: "I want [U.M.T.]," he told a friend, "but I want it more for citizenship than for defense." Truman explained that he didn't "like to think of it as a universal military training program. I want it to be a universal training program" that could instill values such that "we will have sold our republic to the coming generations." Given this wide support for U.M.T. at the highest levels of government, it is not surprising that the postwar administration, faced with the political problems that Roosevelt's advisers had anticipated, turned to U.M.T. with enthusiasm. President Truman first proposed it to Congress in 1945, only to find that political currents were running strongly against any new military program. Unwilling to accept this verdict as final, Truman resubmitted U.M.T. in 1946 and 1947, only to meet recurrent Congressional rebuffs. Frustrated on U.M.T. and confronted with the pressing need to solve the political problems that the Administration's international policies had uncovered, the Administration sought new approaches. An appealing suggestion came from Congressman Clarence Brown of Ohio, who mentioned to Forrestal that many of the purposes of U.M.T. could be achieved through the public schools. This idea—though not necessarily as a result of Brown's suggestion—took hold within the Administration.[26]

The mission of educating young Americans for life in the Cold War fell to the Office of Education. The impact of this upon the Administration's educational policies was dramatic.

In 1946 Commissioner Studebaker's annual report had concerned itself with teacher shortages, inadequate physical facilities, and other traditional educational complaints. The 1947
report struck an entirely different note: "When historians come
to record the developments of the past year," the Commissioner
began, "they will probably set in bold italics the grave disappointment and growing anxiety of the American people with
respect to the fruits of World War II." These new international developments, Studebaker reported, basically altered
the significance and mission of public education in the United
States. Perhaps aware that the Administration was now looking to public education to perform a task once intended for a
program of military training, Studebaker took as the new role
of education the one assigned it in the report of a presidential
commission on Universal Military Training. "The single most
important educational frontier of all," he stated, involved the
need to "strengthen national security through education."
During 1947 the Office of Education developed new programs
responsive to all aspects of the official analysis of the shortcomings of American opinion at the onset of the Cold War.[27]

The most significant new thrust was designed to combat
the widely observed letdown of patriotic sentiment. Embodied
in the "Zeal for American Democracy" program, this effort was
intended, according to the Office of Education, "to vitalize
and improve education in the ideals and benefits of democracy
and to reveal the character and tactics of totalitarianism." The
main thrust of this program was to encourage the schools to
promote a "patriotic emphasis" in public education and to provide technical assistance and material to schools to carry out
this effort. The Office of Education pursued these objectives
by sponsoring several conferences for national organizations
of educators and dedicating National Education Week for
1947 to the problem of education and security. The effect of
such efforts was demonstrated when the American Federation
of Teachers chose the theme "Strengthening Education for
National and World Security" for its annual convention in
August. To provide substance to its campaign, the Office of
Education prepared a series of pamphlets and study guides

for use in schools at all levels. Among the latter was a series entitled "Growing into Democracy," which "shows how the principles of democracy may be inculcated in children through precept and experience," and a series of study guides for both secondary and college classes "as an aid to the use of 'The Strategy and Tactics of World Communism' issued by the Eightieth Congress." [28]

A second area of major emphasis in the new educational programs was the promotion of what the Office of Education called "world-mindedness." Undoubtedly a response to the realization that most adult Americans had little or no understanding of the outside world or appreciation of its importance to the United States, this program encouraged local schools to sponsor courses related to international affairs and understanding. The Office of Education distributed bibliographies dealing with the United Nations and its member states, as well as records of meetings of the General Assembly. At the same time the National Education Association, the American Federation of Teachers, and the American Council on Education sponsored programs with similar purposes. The school children of the postwar period were not to be raised according to the provincial notions of the men and women who had elected the Eightieth Congress. [29]

Unlike the Administration's efforts to win approval of foreign aid through appeals to fear and prejudice, there was in the conception of these educational programs much that was positive and reflective of the highest ethical ideas in American culture. The emphasis in the program to promote "world-mindedness" for example, was on the principles of the United Nations, not *realpolitik*. The literature published by the Office of Education to support the "Zeal for American Democracy" program did not emphasize militant patriotism or anti-communism, but egalitarianism, lack of prejudice, fairness, decency. Even Attorney General Clark, who tended to speak loudly and carry a big stick when it came to communism, emphasized the perpetuation of these positive social values in his discussions of the role of education in the Cold War. Nor did Clark and other Administration officials fail to recognize that these values implied certain substantive reforms, for example in the areas of civil rights and economic and educational opportunity.

Such ideas flowed from a response to the challenge of communism entirely distinct from the Truman Doctrine, the Attorney General's list, and the deportation drive, and represented in many ways a domestic analogy to multilateralism. For just as the wartime architects of the Administration's policies believed that the establishment of what they conceived to be an equitable international order would both strengthen the position of the United States and promote world peace, so the proponents of these educational and social ideas believed that the creation of a just social order at home would strengthen the position of the federal government and undermine efforts to promote dissidence and disharmony. To recognize this analogy, however, is to suggest a major problem, for the Wilsonian aspects of multilateralism, as distinct from its usefulness as an economic and political tool in the Cold War, were increasingly being regarded in 1947 as visionary formulations of doubtful applicability to the immediate international situation. The Office of Education's educational and social ideas also represented idealistic, long-term approaches whose immediate impact upon the campaign for foreign aid could be marginal at best. Indeed, neither the spirit of international cooperation being propagated through the campaign for "world-mindedness," nor the libertarian, democratic values encouraged by the "Zeal for American Democracy" program were really consistent with the foreign policies of the Truman administration in 1947 or the methods being used to promote them. We have already seen that the Administration felt constrained to squash the Wilsonian illusions that Roosevelt had promoted, and it was equally unlikely —at least in the short run—that the values encouraged by the Office of Education's new programs would prevail against those promoted by the immediate pressures of the campaign for Cold War foreign policy.[30]

Illustrative of the fragility of the concepts underlying these educational programs was the one attempt that was made in 1947 to merge the ideas of the "Zeal for American Democracy" program with the immediate requirements of the campaign for foreign aid. Appropriately, this project was sponsored by Attorney General Clark, who was a spokesman for the drive to achieve security through education as well as the architect of the Administration's campaign against subversion and dissent. The idea, conceived by Clark and F.B.I. Director Hoover in the spring of 1947, was to sponsor a nationwide patriotic campaign that could overcome the present national mood, combat communist propaganda, and rally the population behind the Truman administration and its policies. The centerpiece of this effort was to be the Freedom Train, a special railroad train outfitted as a museum housing such important documents from the history of American liberty as the Declaration of Independence, the Constitution, and the Emancipation Proclamation. Clark sponsored a White House Conference on the Freedom Train in May 1947, which led to the establishment of the American Heritage Foundation, a group of private citizens selected by Clark that undertook to conduct the Freedom Train program. The group projected a nationwide tour for the Freedom Train, with visits to over two hundred cities, each stop to provide the occasion for a local "rededication" program. Clark was pleased, for he felt the times required "a Paul Revere that would go around behind a modern engine" and promote an "upsurge of patriotism." Clark's view fully reflected the Administration's basic approach to the campaign for foreign aid, but such a program could not effectively promote the concepts of democracy inherent in the "Zeal for American Democracy" program, and, unavoidably, it inspired militant, patriotic rallies. The Freedom Train thus symbolized the greater political usefulness to the Administration of the ideas of international relations and democracy propagated by the campaign for foreign aid and the attack on domestic dissent than the notions about the same subjects encouraged by the Administration's long-range educational programs.[31]

The relationship of the Freedom Train to the campaign for Cold War foreign policy was intimate. The Truman Doctrine speech had made it clear that the basic appeal of the Administration for popular support of its foreign policies would be opposition to communism, which, expressed positively, took the form of fundamental patriotism and loyalty to the American system. Plans for the Freedom Train were initiated immediately following the Truman Doctrine speech as a way of promoting an "upsurge of patriotism." The train's tour would begin during the special session of Congress in which the Interim Aid program would be considered, and would continue throughout the period of formal debate on the Marshall Plan. The Truman Doctrine, included as one of the basic documents of American liberty in the train's exhibit, thus would be associated with a national patriotic campaign during the drive to obtain Congressional approval of its substantive counterpart, the Administration's foreign aid program. Perhaps not incidentally, the train's tour would also coincide with the 1948 presidential campaign; the effort to rally the country behind the Truman Doctrine was related to the need to rally the voters behind the Truman candidacy.

4. Internal Security and Interim Aid

The Administration's efforts in the field of internal security during the summer of 1947 refocused public concern on the communist threat and enhanced the Administration's image as the enemy of communism. As a result, they provided invaluable support to the fall campaign for Interim Aid and became part of the President's campaign for nomination and election.

BY THE FALL OF 1947, IT WAS CLEAR that a debate over foreign economic assistance would be accompanied by expressions of concern over domestic subversion. The relationship of Republican demand to Administration response in the area of internal security had been established during consideration of Greco-Turkish aid, and the continuing force of this relationship was demonstrated by the case of the ten dismissed State Department employees during the same summer months that the Administration was planning its campaign for the Marshall Plan. No less a figure than Arthur Vandenberg, the Administration's Republican standard-bearer on foreign aid, was emphasizing the need for a firm stand against communism at home and abroad. We must, he wrote a friend in August, "strike hard for adequate national defense for the side of peace. And strike hard against all internal subversion which threatens to destroy us from within." The point was echoed repeatedly during Congressional debate on Interim Aid. Several Congressmen chose this occasion to complain of communist sympathizers in the State Department, and one strongly questioned the wisdom of permitting a government agency so infested to administer the foreign aid program. Moreover, as Congressional attention turned from the limited program considered in the spring to the more costly and controversial subject of aid to Europe generally, it had to be expected that the demand for an attack upon American communists would become even more intense: one of the rallying points for opposition to foreign aid was that its inflationary tendencies would weaken the American economy; was such a policy, it was asked, not playing into the hands of communists in the United States, who, like those in Europe, functioned best in circumstances of economic disarray? This point found several expositors during the Congressional debate on Interim Aid. The Administration was not likely to be surprised by such arguments. It had understood the political relationship between internal security and foreign aid since the end of 1946, and during the debate on Greco-Turkish aid it had shown that it knew how to outflank the Republicans and use the necessity of doing so to advance its own campaign for foreign economic assistance.[32]

The significance of the internal security issue in the fall of 1947 was not confined to the politics of the debate on foreign aid. By this time, as we have seen, the 1948 presidential election was influencing all political activity. Clifford's political memo of late November showed the President how he could use the debate on Interim Aid to enhance his standing with the electorate, and Truman's speech to Congress on November 17 suggested that Clifford's thinking was influencing the Administration's handling of the special session. Clifford's memo did not neglect the subject of internal security. He pointed out that the Republicans could be expected to use the debate over Cold War foreign policy to press for new programs in this area, but he was confident that the Administration had "stolen their thunder" with the establishment of the loyalty program. He also observed that initiatives in the field of internal security would help the President retain control of the passionately anti-communist Catholic vote, which would be of critical importance to the Democrats in 1948. Finally, Clifford saw in this issue the means to neutralize Henry Wallace, whose successful speaking tour during the summer had convinced Clifford that Wallace would become a third-party candidate for the presidency and base his campaign on opposition to the Administration's anti-Soviet policies. Wallace's influence could be minimized, Clifford felt, by publicly linking him with the communists, which would not be hard to do, as his positions could be represented as pro-Soviet and as he was being actively promoted for the presidency by the American Communist Party. It followed from this reasoning that the greater the concern in the U.S. over domestic communism, the less danger Wallace would pose to the Administration.[33]

As the Administration prepared for the special session in the fall of 1947, it had compelling reasons—in terms of both the debate on Interim Aid and the electoral politics of 1948—to assert itself as the leader in the battle against domestic communism. It was fully prepared to do this, for during the summer of 1947 it had developed a panoply of appropriate innovations. The fall political season opened with a rash of Administration announcements of new initiatives against internal subversion. The State Department led the way. On October 8 it announced a set of security procedures by which it intended to rid itself of all security risks. Taking no chances with national security (or the appropriations committees), it defined the category "security risk" to include not only any employee associated in any way with a subversive organization but any employee associated with any individual so associated. The loyalty program, which had disappeared from the headlines of the nation's newspapers after its creation in the spring, was suddenly back in the limelight. On October 27, four days after the President made public his decision to convene the special session, Civil Service Commissioner Fleming announced that steps would be taken to accelerate loyalty investigations. On November 8, two days before hearings on Interim Aid began, the President announced his appointments to the Loyalty Review Board, established by the loyalty order as the ultimate arbiter of cases involving allegations of disloyalty. Seth Richardson, a prominent Republican attorney, was named chairman of the group. Six days later the board held a much-publicized first meeting, attended by President Truman and Attorney General Clark. On December 4, the first day of House debate on Interim Aid, the publication of the Attorney General's list placed the loyalty program once again on the front pages of the nation's papers.[34]

The Office of Education also chose this moment to draw public attention to the plans it had developed during the summer to combat subversion. Commissioner Studebaker went on the stump in behalf of the "Zeal for American Democracy" program. On November 11 he told a gathering in New York that public education had not done enough to arouse a "passionate devotion" to democracy or to combat the despotisms of nazism, fascism, and communism. Two weeks later, in St. Louis, Studebaker focused specifically upon the menace of communism and called upon American educators to "make a more determined effort to create in American youth a zeal for American Democracy in the interest of national strength and security." "STUDEBAKER MAPS WAR ON COMMUNISM" reported *The New York Times*. On November 30 the Commissioner convened a new nine-member commission on "life adjustment" to consider high-school and junior-college education in the United States. He told the commissioners that they should emphasize education in citizenship to combat communism. Under the pressure of events, the Commissioner of Education seemed to be defining patriotism in a manner not unlike that of the F.B.I. Director.[35]

The most spectacular development of all was an impressive and carefully programmed "week of rededication" in the nation's capital during the opening days of Senate debate on Interim Aid. On November 20 the Administration staged a series of mass demonstrations at which thousands of government employees took a "freedom pledge" and sang "God Bless America." The highlight of the week was the arrival in Washington on November 27 of the Freedom Train, which occasioned extensive high-level oratory. Attorney General Clark told a special luncheon gathering that "the importance of the Freedom Train is that it points up other ideologies in the world today that are attempting to destroy the freedom of religion upon which this country was founded." Speaker Martin, addressing opening ceremonies on November 27, told his auditors that "America is now spending billions to help other people achieve freedom and live in freedom. We must stand as a united people to stop the march of despotism across the world." After his visit to the exhibit on November 28, President Truman linked the train to the debate on Cold War foreign policy by commenting that the ideas of individual liberty embodied in the documents on the train were what the country was presently fighting for. In his address to the Senate initiating debate on Interim Aid, Senator Vandenberg pointed to the Freedom Train as symbolic of the legislation he was introducing.[36]

In the face of such manifest determination on the part of the Administration to combat domestic subversion, Congressional Republicans—anxious to use debate on Interim Aid to make new charges of government laxity in matters of internal security—were confronted with an impossible task. Moreover, the efforts that were made were immediately outflanked by the Department of Justice. On October 29, for example, the *Washington Times Herald* reported a member of the House Un-American Activities Committee as stating that subversives were entering the United States through Canada and that

American officials were assisting them. This charge was followed by additional admonitions from Congressional sources
that under then-current arrangements federal security officials
allowed enemy aliens to roam freely about the country.
H.U.A.C. proposed an investigation of this situation. On
December 6 the Justice Department announced a new program, to be applied immediately and most stringently to Soviet
visitors, by which aliens entering the United States would be
required to notify immigration officials each time they changed
address, and to obtain clearance before departing the country.
The following day the Department stated that it was intensify-
ing precautions against infiltration across the borders by enemy
agents.[37] These Justice Department measures were a continuation of the pattern that had been established at the outset of
the Eightieth Congress by which the Administration cooperated fully with the programs of Congress, particularly those
of the House Un-American Activities Committee, in the field
of internal security. Indeed, in the investigations conducted by
H.U.A.C. during the fall, the Justice Department once again
proved itself an assiduous and invaluable ally.

In September, H.U.A.C. conducted a hearing regarding
Hanns Eisler, brother of Gerhart, a composer and putative
propagandist of communist causes. Possible irregularities in
Hanns Eisler's visa arrangements had been mentioned to
H.U.A.C. counsel Robert Stripling by State Department officials
during the inquiry into Gerhart's immigration record. During
the September hearings H.U.A.C. made use of documents obtained from the State Department to question the propriety of
Eisler's continued residence in the United States. It also placed
in the record a large number of documents—newspaper clip-
pings, articles, and songs published by Eisler in both the
U.S.S.R. and the United States, and papers indicating Eisler's
affiliation with "communist-front" organizations—that tended
to support the claim that Eisler was involved with communist
activities. No indication of how this detailed file was compiled
appears in the record, but it seems reasonable to speculate
that the F.B.I. assisted H.U.A.C. here, as it had done openly in
the case of Gerhart Eisler the previous spring. At the end of

the hearings H.U.A.C. sent a letter to Attorney General Clark insisting that Eisler be arrested and deported. Clark received this request and complied readily, despite the fact that the hearings had been used in part to attack the Roosevelt administration. Three days after H.U.A.C. dispatched its letter to Clark, H.U.A.C. Chairman Thomas was told by the Immigration Service that a warrant had been issued for Eisler's arrest. Thomas praised the Justice Department for its "excellent cooperation." [38]

H.U.A.C.'s most spectacular project of the fall was its investigation of communist infiltration of the motion picture industry. This investigation had been projected in the eight-point program announced by Chairman Thomas at the beginning of the Eightieth Congress, and a preliminary hearing had been conducted in Hollywood in May. Between October 20 and 30 H.U.A.C. held the most intensely publicized hearings of its career. Much of the public interest stemmed from the parade of celebrities who passed before the committee's microphones during the first week to denounce the activities of communists in the film industry. More substantive material was presented the following week, when H.U.A.C. heard testimony from ten screenwriters whom it accused of being Communist operatives. As in the Eisler case, the committee made no effort to indicate the way in which it obtained the detailed and persuasive documentation placed in the record to support its charges. It was made clear, however, that the research had been done by three former officials of the F.B.I., one of whom had been an administrative assistant to Bureau Chief J. Edgar Hoover. The most definitive evidence introduced by H.U.A.C. was photostatic copies of Communist Party registration cards issued to each of the ten writers. It would seem likely that this material was supplied by the F.B.I. Committee investigator Russell, who had spent ten years with the Bureau, merely stated that the documents had been "furnished." As during the Eisler hearings, H.U.A.C. sought to implicate the Roosevelt administration in improprieties by attempting to demonstrate that the White House had pressured certain

movie producers to make pro-Soviet films during the war.
Nevertheless, when the uncooperative behavior of the writers
resulted in contempt citations, the Justice Department moved
rapidly to prosecute. Indictments were obtained within ten
days.[39]

Unquestionably, the Truman administration's activities in
the field of internal security during the fall of 1947 enabled it
to continue stealing the Republican thunder on this issue, to
use Clifford's phrase. But this was only part of their usefulness
to the Administration. All of these initiatives, it must be remembered, occurred in the framework of the Administration's campaign for Interim Aid, with its dire warnings of communist
ascendency in western Europe. Just as the dramatic announcement of the loyalty program nine days after the Truman Doctrine speech had heightened the sense of crisis in which Greco-
Turkish aid was debated, so the new initiatives in the area of
employee loyalty, Studebaker's warnings of communist subversion, the Freedom Train with its spirit of a wartime patriotic rally, and the new H.U.A.C. investigations—all served to
heighten the sense of danger caused by an emergency session
of Congress to consider the new crisis in Europe.

The Administration's method of handling the announcements of its new initiatives seemed designed to promote rather
than calm public fears of communist subversion. The published version of the Attorney General's list, for example, included ninety-one organizations, a distressingly large number
unless one looked closely enough to see that a significant percentage of them were fascist and nazi organizations dating
from the pre-war period and already disbanded. While their
inclusion may have served a purpose in investigations of incumbent employees, it also inflated the impression of immediate danger that the list was bound to promote, a result
that the Administration made no effort to avoid. All the
new developments in the area of employee loyalty were
announced with a maximum of publicity. In addition, the
newspapers suddenly and mysteriously began to obtain information concerning the federal grand jury that had been in-

vestigating the charges of official espionage made by Bentley and Chambers in executive session since June. These stories first appeared in the right-wing press in New York, Baltimore, and Washington on October 16 and 17, and indicated that the grand jury had discovered massive penetration of the federal bureaucracy by communists, that communists had achieved high levels of government responsibility, and that the grand jury would soon be handing down a number of indictments. In mid-November and again at the beginning of December more leaks from the supposedly secret hearings appeared in the press and reported similar findings. It was stated that the conspiracy within the American government would make the revelations about atomic espionage in Canada seem modest. Then, inexplicably, on December 9, as debate on Interim Aid was drawing to an end, it was reported that no indictments would be forthcoming and that the jury was going to be presented with new evidence. A conspiratorial interpretation of these developments was voiced by a former assistant to Attorney General Clark, O. John Rogge, who told *The New York Times* that the Attorney General's office was responsible for the leaks and that they were motivated by a desire to "whip up a new wave of anti-Soviet hysteria to coincide with the opening of the special session of Congress." Rogge's charges are certainly open to question, for he has never offered any evidence to support them save his personal knowledge of the workings of Clark's office, and in 1947 he was carrying on a personal campaign against the Justice Department. Still, his interpretation of the leaks was consistent with the Administration's other efforts to draw public attention to the communist danger during these months, and their recurrence over an extended period indicates that Clark did not wish to stop them. Moreover, it is indisputable that the leaks had the public effect that Rogge suggested. As Marquis Childs wrote in the *Washington Post* on November 21, "this long, drawn-out investigation— with the leaks, rumors and speculation accompanying it—has contributed immeasurably to the current atmosphere of suspicion and distrust." The events contributing to the sense of crisis in the fall of 1947 reached a zenith of a sort with a mock bombing raid on Washington staged by the National Guard one day before the opening of hearings on Interim Aid.[40]

Interim Aid was approved, but the amendments regarding East-West trade and China attached by Congress made it clear that the Administration's political tactics had certain undesirable tendencies in relation to foreign policy. Its tactics also contained unfortunate implications in the field of internal security. As early as May Archibald MacLeish voiced concern over growing "political pressures" on educators to reinforce certain modes of thought in the young. During the summer, George Kennan felt it necessary to "deplore the hysterical sort of anti-Communism which . . . is gaining currency in our country." In October President Conant of Harvard warned the country against misconceiving the nature and exaggerating the depth of the present conflict between the United States and the Soviet Union. He expressed the fear that notions of inevitable, irreconcilable conflict between the two countries might create a panicky mentality among Americans, and pointed to the loyalty program as evidence that his concern was not entirely theoretical. "There is a danger," he stated, "that we may jeopardize the morale of our government and officials—not only that, but perhaps even create the atmosphere of a witch hunt which could adversely affect our democratic institutions." Arthur Schlesinger, Jr. supported Conant's arguments in an article discussing the possibility that the present climate might evolve into a witch-hunting atmosphere. He rejected the idea being propagated by a number of leftist writers, particularly abroad, that the United States was currently seized by an anti-communist hysteria, but he expressed concern about excesses in the loyalty program. It was a time, he wrote, for responsible behavior by politicians, the press, and American liberals to prevent the atmosphere from degenerating in the manner of which Conant warned.[41]

The Administration was quick to offer assurances that there would be no witch hunts, but the behavior of the State Department in the case of the ten dismissed employees was not reassuring, and federal officials were beginning to feel that a preoccupation with security in hiring practices was essential to protect their agencies from Congressional attack. In fact, the Administration had shown no disposition to oppose Congressional demands in the field of internal security, and its policy of complete cooperation with the activities of H.U.A.C. did not entitle it to be regarded as either restrained or independent in this field. So far this policy had been helpful to the purposes of the Administration, but now H.U.A.C. was announcing its intention to consider legislation directed specifically against communists, a step the polls showed to have wide public support, although the Justice Department considered it counterproductive and unconstitutional. Nor was the growing concern over domestic communism confined to national institutions. During 1947 at least two state legislatures created committees to investigate subversive activities; a third upgraded a temporary committee dealing with the subject, and one passed a new law against organizations and individuals serving the interests of a foreign government. Movements were under way in other states to institute anti-communist investigations and draft anti-communist legislation. Three universities refused in late 1947 to permit their students to be addressed by men suspected of disloyalty. In Philadelphia a rally of Wallace's Progressive Citizen's Association was broken up by an angry crowd; in New York, a Communist Party rally was disbanded by war veterans; in Trenton, New Jersey, a group of Communists was prevented by a mob from holding a scheduled rally.[42] In the face of such indications of the public mood, the Administration's assurances that everything was under control were open to question.

Clearly there were powerful and emotional forces at work throughout the society in response to developments in the fields of foreign policy and internal security. In the fall of 1947, however, these developments did not seem part of any general pattern, and there was no conclusive reason to regard MacLeish, Kennan, Conant, and Schlesinger as the prophets to be heeded. Of greater substance and importance to the Administration was the fact that it had won the battle for Interim

Aid, strengthened its political position vis-à-vis both Wallace and the Republicans, and maintained political control of the potentially damaging issue of internal security. It was now clear, however, that this control would be severely tested by the political tensions generated during the climactic debate on the Marshall Plan and the beginning of the presidential campaign.

VI
The Battle for the European Recovery Program

1. The Alignment of Forces

Although the Marshall Plan was the essential element in the Administration's efforts to consolidate America's international position, Congressional approval of the enabling legislation submitted in late 1947 was in question.

THE LEGISLATION to institute and fund the Marshall Plan—now officially named the European Recovery Program (E.R.P.)—was submitted to Congress on December 19, 1947, the day that both Houses of Congress passed the Conference report on Interim Aid. The Administration expressed two primary objectives for the forthcoming debate. The first involved the scale of aid to be extended. The Administration felt it essential that Congress authorize the full 6.8 billion dollars that it proposed for the first fifteen months of the program. With any lesser amount, it was felt, there could be no hope of achieving the objective of European economic recovery and self-sufficiency in four years. The Administration also sought approval of a general authorization of 17 billion dollars to finance the program for its intended four-year duration. The second major issue involved the schedule for Congressional action. The Administration was anxious to have Congress approve its proposals before April 1, 1948. This objective stemmed from two considerations: Interim Aid funds could keep the flow of trade moving at requisite levels only until April 1, and, probably more important, Italy was holding national elections on April 18. To the Americans, the Italian elections offered the critical postwar political showdown between the Communists and the non-communists not only in Italy but in western Europe. As early as June 1947, Hugh Dalton, the British Chancellor of the Exchequer, commented following a conference with Clayton that "The Italian vote is now the biggest foreign factor in [American] politics." If the Communists could be beaten decisively in the country where they were strongest, the Americans felt a major point in the political Cold War would have been registered. They believed that the assurance of aid under the Marshall Plan would influence Italian voters against Communist candidates.[1]

Congressional debate on the European Recovery Program was certain to be one of the most important public debates in the United States in the postwar period. Approval was indispensable to American efforts to organize an American-oriented bloc of European states to balance the Soviet sphere of influence in eastern Europe; it was equally essential to the promotion of the multilateral commercial policies that would provide much of the internal strength and cohesion of the non-communist world as well as essential commercial outlets for America's growing economy; finally, E.R.P. was necessary to the maintenance of existing levels of trade between the North American, European, and Latin American continents, upon which high levels of income and employment in the United States were felt to depend. The entire international position of the United States and much of the country's internal stability would be jeopardized by Congressional refusal to endorse the proposals. Acutely aware of these considerations, Secretary Marshall referred to the impending debate as "the greatest decision in our history" and was reported to regard the program as so fundamental to American foreign policy that he would not be held responsible for the consequences of its rejection.[2]

Preliminary public-opinion polls indicated substantial

support for the European Recovery Program, support that directly reflected the association of foreign aid with relief for destitute Europeans and opposition to communism, which had been emphasized in the presentation of Interim Aid. Such readings were not to be taken as definitive, however. The Administration knew that its public support was vague and thin rather than solidly based and reliable, and that there were potent sources of opposition in Congress to its proposals. One weekly news magazine summarized this situation: "Opposition to [E.R.P.] is much greater than is generally realized. In many instances the nature of the opposition has not been fully revealed. Sometimes it comes from men who vaguely endorse the objectives of the program but privately raise objections." The likely sources of opposition had all become familiar in the two years since the British Loan had been submitted to Congress and particularly during the preceding ten months in the debates on Greco-Turkish aid and Interim Aid. Because Britain would be the major beneficiary of the program, the anti-British attitudes that had influenced the debate on the loan were particularly relevant. In what was probably an indication of sensitivity to this problem, the Administration attempted to withhold from Congress breakdowns of the amounts of aid to go to each country under E.R.P., but was forced by Congressional pressure to supply this information. Moreover, polls measuring public opinion on the relative importance of foreign and domestic issues indicated levels of belief in the primacy of international problems only slightly higher than those registered at the time of debate on the British Loan. The Administration's battle against postwar isolationism was far from won; indeed, debate on E.R.P. would be the critical indication of the readiness of the American people to accept a continuing role as a great power in international affairs. Not only did most Americans consider domestic issues preeminent in January 1948, but the primary domestic issue—inflation—seemed likely to affect directly public attitudes on E.R.P., since the prevailing notion was that foreign aid would place new strains upon domestic supply. This argument against E.R.P.

was being pressed on both left and right, in the pages of the *Daily Worker* and in the speeches of Republican Senators from the Midwest. A second domestic issue of major importance was tax reduction, which also seemed likely to come into direct conflict with large-scale foreign aid.[3]

Pervading discussion of all other issues in the debate on E.R.P., of course, was the partisan politics of a presidential-election year. The first primaries were only three months away when E.R.P. was submitted to Congress. Truman had already begun to campaign, and his address to the Congress during debate on Interim Aid was generally felt to have injected partisanship into the foreign aid issue. Congressional Republicans, whose party intended to cast itself as the champion of the American consumer by advocating budget cuts, tax reduction, and strong anti-inflationary measures, were not expected by the Administration to eschew partisanship in the debate on E.R.P.

The Administration was never permitted to doubt that the various sources of opposition to foreign aid would produce a determined attack upon E.R.P. During debate on Interim Aid, numerous Republicans—most prominently Senator Taft—had supported the Administration while making clear statements of opposition to the long-range program. It was clear, however, that the opposition would not attempt to defeat the program outright—a goal that would split the Republican Party and make it susceptible to charges of consigning Europe to the communists—but to develop alternative proposals behind which Republicans could unite. On the same day that the Administration submitted E.R.P. to Congress, for example, the House Foreign Affairs Committee began hearings on an alternative foreign aid program sponsored by Republican Representative Christian Herter of Massachusetts. Herter's proposals had to be taken seriously, as he was highly respected in Congress as an expert on international problems and had chaired a special committee of the House that had been investigating the problems of European recovery and foreign aid since April 1947. Moreover, it had been the House Foreign

Affairs Committee that had forced a reduction in the amount of the Interim Aid program and added to it, against the wishes of the Administration, an authorization for China. In the Senate, of course, the Administration could rely upon strong support from Arthur Vandenberg. Still, Taft was openly against E.R.P. and this foreboded a solid core of opposition from Midwestern Republican Senators. Though Taft himself, made cautious by his presidential aspirations, remained in the background, by the second week in January a Taft-oriented group of twenty Senators had organized behind Republican Whip Kenneth Wherry in opposition to the Administration's proposals. Vandenberg, like Taft a presidential hopeful, seemed certain to attempt to accommodate these Republican dissidents, and this might lead him toward concessions that the Administration would prefer not to make, as it had on the China issue during Interim Aid. Both the Senate group and the Herter proposal agreed that the Administration's program should be altered in two specific ways: by reducing the total amount to be authorized for the first year to four billion dollars, and by creating a private corporation, directed by businessmen and independent of the Democratic administration, to run it. The second point was one where Congressional concern over internal security impinged very directly upon E.R.P., for one major source of support for this suggestion was the feeling—repeatedly expressed during the debate on Interim Aid—that the State Department was subject to communist influence.[4]

Upon what appeals could the Administration rely to combat Congressional opposition to its proposals? As we have seen, in the period between March 1947 and January 1948 it had failed to develop solid public support for any of the substantive policies upon which the foreign aid program was based. The close relationship of E.R.P. to the multilateral commercial policies that the Administration was attempting to promote seemed more likely to hurt than help the program in Congress. The importance of maintaining existing levels of trade to domestic production, employment, and income seemed likely to be overshadowed by public and Congressional concern over the inflationary aspects of foreign aid. The relief aspect of the foreign aid program had always been one of the strongest sources of public support for the Administration but, as Taft's attitude indicated, this seemed less likely to be decisive in debate on a large-scale, long-term program like E.R.P. than Interim Aid and could not be relied upon to assure support for the full authorization requested by the Administration. There was, finally, the anti-communist appeal. Previous debates on foreign aid had indicated that this was the Administration's most potent argument, and early indications were that this factor alone was enough to keep the Republicans from making an open attempt to defeat the program. But previous experience had also shown that the anti-communist argument could be turned against the policies of the Administration by forcing it toward expanded commitments to China and restrictions on trade with the communist world. Moreover, to insist too strongly upon the necessity of E.R.P. to protect Europe from the Soviets without discussing American economic self-interest was to raise questions about the preferability of economic over military aid to western Europe.

While all the likely arguments for E.R.P. were flawed, there was no possibility that President Truman could compensate for their weakness through the exertion of personal influence and prestige. Indeed, in early 1948 the President's popularity ratings were as low as they had been in November 1946. Henry Wallace had declared his presidential candidacy as head of a third party in December 1947, indicating the President's vulnerability on the left. Truman's decision not to support the partition of Palestine had reduced his standing among American Jews. His civil rights message to Congress in February rapidly organized Southern Democrats against him and initiated movement toward a second split in the Democratic Party. Under attack from all sides, without strong personal standing with the electorate, Truman seemed a political goner in early 1948. The press talked matter-of-factly of the next administration and reported Democratic pressures on him not to seek nomination. A personal appeal from him would count for little in the battle for E.R.P.[5]

2. The Campaign for E.R.P.

*In speeches and testimony before Congressional
committees, Administration officials argued
that E.R.P. was essential to save western Europe
from communism and to protect American
economic interests. But these officials failed to
make a coherent case for the program on
either strategic or economic grounds, and the
public remained apathetic. As the vote in
Congress approached, a defeat for the
Administration seemed likely.*

THE ADMINISTRATION HAD BEGUN ORGANIZING its campaign for
E.R.P. during debate on Interim Aid. The Harriman, Krug, and
Nourse reports—all impressive volumes—were submitted to
the members of Congress. Speaking tours were scheduled for
a number of top Administration officials, including Marshall,
Clayton, Forrestal, and—consistent with the Administration's
understanding of the political link between foreign and internal security—Attorney General Clark. A semi-official organization of prominent businessmen and government officials, the
Committee for the Marshall Plan, was organized to lobby for
E.R.P. Charles Bohlen, a State Department Soviet expert, was
placed in charge of public relations concerning E.R.P., and
Lewis Douglas, a former Congressman turned diplomat, was
given responsibility for Congressional liaison. Machinery was
established to provide daily reports on the attitudes of Congressmen and Senators. The entire operation was set in motion
on January 5, when Bohlen delivered the first in a series of
promotional speeches. Congressional hearings began in the
Senate on January 8 and in the House on the 11th.[6]
    When the campaign for the Marshall Plan began, it
became clear—as the appointment of a Soviet expert to direct
public relations had implied—that the issue of opposing
communism was to receive primary emphasis. The Administration claimed that Soviet and communist policies were

largely responsible for the problems of Europe and hence for the necessity of the European Recovery Program. This had emerged as a dominant theme of speeches on foreign aid by Marshall and Acheson in the summer of 1947; it was the thrust of Marshall's report to the nation following the London Conference in November 1947; and it figured prominently in the presentation of Bohlen on January 5 as well as those of Marshall and Douglas in their opening statements in testifying on behalf of E.R.P.[7]

Though this interpretation of events served the political interests of the Administration in promoting foreign aid, it did little to illuminate the basic economic problems of postwar Europe. As has been indicated in earlier chapters, these problems derived almost entirely from the economic and social dislocations that had been produced by the war and from the failure of the Western governments—including the U.S.—to make adequate provision for postwar reconstruction. Communist Parties in western Europe had adopted policies of vigorous support of recovery efforts in France and Italy and had altered this stance only when forced out of the coalition governments in early 1947. The May 1947 report of the Policy Planning Staff had emphasized the point that it did "not see Communist activities as the root of the present difficulties in western Europe" but attributed these problems to the effects of the war. Though Soviet control of eastern Europe had certainly played a role, though by no means the major one, in retarding recovery in western Europe, it was far from candid to characterize Soviet policies as designed to prevent recovery in the West; rather, as we have seen, they reflected Soviet priorities regarding economic and political reconstruction in the East.

The Administration's claim that Soviet intransigence was the cause of the division of Germany, of the lack of progress in reconstructing that country, and of integrating its economy with the rest of Europe did not accord with the facts. During the war, the influence on American policy of the idea of "pastoralizing" postwar Germany and the resistance of the U.S. to efforts by the Allies to develop four-powers plans for German occupation combined to retard preparations for the economic reconstruction of Germany and promote the kind of autonomous zonal-occupation arrangements that made recovery difficult. In postwar negotiations among the Allies on Germany, the level of industrial production proposed by the U.S. was no higher than that proposed by the Soviet Union. The delay in negotiating a German settlement satisfactory to both the U.S. and the U.S.S.R. derived at least as much from American as Soviet intransigence. Moreover, the most persistent opposition to German reconstruction came from France, not the Soviet Union. As to the critical problem of integrating German production into the economy of western Europe, as late as October 1946 Thomas Blaisdell, Chief of the American Mission for Economic Affairs in London, felt it necessary to complain to Clayton that the American government's failure to develop terms for economic cooperation between the military authorities in Germany and the Mission for Economic Affairs was retarding the development of an integrated approach to the problem of European recovery.[8]

By early 1948, of course, the issue of great-powers cooperation having died, American diplomacy with the Soviet Union was concerned primarily with achieving propaganda victories. In this context, one could hardly expect clear treatments of the facts from either side, and the political fortunes of the foreign aid program were very much enhanced by stating that the problems it was intended to correct were the results of Soviet and Communist perfidy. Calling attention to the propagandistic nature of official statements on this point is worthwhile only because it helps to explain the intense bitterness that developed among the American people toward the U.S.S.R. in the postwar period. Told that the Soviets and the Communists were responsible for disappointing the always illusory American hopes for the postwar world and thus for forcing the U.S. to accept unwelcome burdens, the American people developed a thoroughly understandable hostility toward their former ally, an attitude made more bitter by their long-held distrust of the Soviet state. The value of the immediate political gains won by the Administration in fostering this public mood must be weighed against its tendency to limit possibilities for reducing East-West tensions in subsequent years.

A second basic theme in the Administration's case against communism was that failure to appropriate the funds requested under the E.R.P. would lead to communist ascendency in western Europe. Secretary Marshall provided a characteristic statement of this argument in his testimony before the Senate Foreign Relations Committee:

> So long as hunger, poverty, desperation, and resulting chaos threaten the great concentration of people in western Europe . . . there will steadily develop social unease and political confusion on every side. Left to their own resources there will be, I believe, no escape from economic distress so intense, political confusion so widespread, and hopes of the future so shattered that the historic base of western civilization . . . will take on a new form in the image of the tyranny that we fought to destroy in Germany.
> . . . Our national security will be seriously threatened. We shall live, in effect, in an armed camp, regulated and controlled. . . . Our assistance, if we determine to embark on this program of aid to western Europe, must be adequate to do the job. . . . Either undertake to meet the requirements of the problem or don't undertake it at all. . . . If we decide that the United States is unable or unwilling effectively to assist in the reconstruction of western Europe, we must accept the consequence of its collapse into the dictatorships of police states. . . . There is no doubt in my mind that the whole world hangs in the balance.

The Defense Department provided Congress with a concrete statement of what the danger of which Marshall spoke meant in terms of American expenditures for national security. If E.R.P. were approved, the U.S. could look forward to continued reductions in expenditures for arms, but if it were rejected the Defense Department would be forced to recommend an immediate increase of 25 per cent in military spending. To pro-

vide support and emphasis for its warnings regarding the
Soviet Union, the State Department made public in mid-
January a number of diplomatic documents captured from
Germany during the war. These papers concerned discussions
between the U.S.S.R. and Germany in 1939 on the subject of
dividing Europe into two spheres of influence and seemed to
confirm the assertions of American officials that the Soviet
Union was an expansionist power. This last initiative surprised
British Foreign Minister Bevin, who criticized the action
before Commons on February 4, stating that the documents
were out of context and did not tell the whole story.[9]

The danger of employing heated elucidations of the
communist menace as arguments for expeditious approval
of the Marshall Plan was that this technique had become
identified with Administration efforts to force Congressional
action on foreign aid. Although the Senate Foreign Relations
Committee treated Secretary Marshall with bland respect
during his testimony, Lewis Douglas, appearing the next day,
was warned by a friend of E.R.P., Senator George, that the
State Department had better be careful about asserting its
proposals too dogmatically. George indicated that he felt
Douglas and Marshall were using the fear of communism to
bludgeon Congress into approving the Administration's program in exactly the form proposed. "I do not think the State
Department is justified," George stated, "in presenting absolute alternatives. . . . For instance, the Secretary of State
says that we must do the whole of this or none. Now I do not
know whether, if we reduced it slightly, it would necessarily
destroy the whole program . . . that is the technique of the
propagandist that I do not think you should resort to." This
confrontation was quickly smoothed over, with mutual agreement that neither side suspected the other of dishonorable
motives. Nevertheless, it had been suggested strongly that the
Administration's manipulation of Congress on the issue of
Greco-Turkish aid had not been forgotten and that the memory would complicate consideration of E.R.P. When Marshall
and Douglas appeared before the House Foreign Affairs

Committee a few days later, their discussion of the communist menace was considerably muted. Secretary Marshall said no more than an honest analysis would permit: "The situation in Europe has not yet developed to the point where the grim progression from economic uncertainty to tyranny is probable. But without United States support of European self-help, this progression may well become inevitable." This tentative tone was also discernible in the testimony of Douglas.[10]

In addition to the resistance of Congress to efforts by the Administration to railroad approval of the Marshall Plan, there was a second reason, in some ways more basic, why State Department witnesses found it necessary to retreat from the strong anti-Soviet arguments that they had presented early in the hearings on E.R.P.: the Marshall Plan assumed a continuation of good relations between the Soviet Union and the West. As previous discussions of the recovery problem have pointed out, many of the raw materials required by western European countries to achieve their production goals could be obtained only from eastern Europe, and the recovery program developed by the C.E.E.C. depended upon a continuation and expansion of trade between this region and western Europe, a trade that the Soviet Union was in a position to control. Was it sound policy to implement a recovery program that depended upon the cooperation of a country that manifested, in the words of Secretary Marshall, only "determined opposition to a plan for European recovery" and that intended to seize western Europe by employing "economic distress . . . for political ends"? When the subject of East-West trade was under discussion, a variant assessment of U.S.-Soviet relations was employed by Administration witnesses, as is clear from the following exchange:

MR. JAVITS: Is it not also true that one of the assumptions of the Paris Plan is that within the next four or five years a much greater quantity of, for example, timber will flow from eastern Europe to western Europe?

SEC. MARSHALL: That is the hope.

MR. JAVITS: So the basic assumption in the whole E.R.P. even goes to the betterment of relations with the Soviet Union and its satellites?

SEC. MARSHALL: That is what we hope.

Characteristically, President Truman rendered the most concise statement of the Administration's paradoxical analysis of U.S.-Soviet relations. Asked at a press conference to comment on the continuation of commercial relations between the United States and the Soviet Union at a time when the two countries were engaged in an open power struggle, the President stated simply that the U.S.S.R. was a "friendly nation and had been buying from the United States right along." [11]

In the course of 1947, as it became clear to American officials that there would be no rapid progress toward the establishment of multilateral commercial relations, the emphasis of the Administration's economic case for foreign aid shifted from concern over the reordering of world trade relationships to the more immediate problem of maintaining existing levels of trade and assuring American access to important markets. This emphasis was noticeable in the campaign for E.R.P. For example, when Secretary Marshall addressed the Chamber of Commerce in Pittsburgh in mid-January, he warned that if E.R.P. were not approved, European countries would be forced to adopt restrictive trade practices, government control of European commerce would become inevitable, and commerce between the eastern and western hemispheres would be depressed: "The cumulative loss of foreign markets and sources of supply would unquestionably have a depressing influence on our domestic economy and would drive us to increased measures of government control."

One of the interesting developments during the hearings was that, as the Administration toned down the anti-communist argument on behalf of foreign aid, it tended to give increased weight to commercial considerations. Thus, in his appearance before the House Foreign Affairs Committee shortly after Senator George had reprimanded Douglas and the State Department for being too aggressive in asserting the communist issue, Marshall not only offered a much-diluted statement of the communist danger in Europe but accorded equal weight to political and economic factors: "Why should the people of the United States accept European burdens in this manner? European economic recovery, we feel sure, is essential to the preservation of basic freedom in the most critical area of the world today. European economic recovery is essential to the return of normal trade and commerce throughout the world." Marshall repeatedly ranked these two considerations as equal in his testimony before the House Committee, as did Douglas. The thrust of this testimony was strongly supported in the testimony of other cabinet officers before both House and Senate Committees. Secretary Harriman stated that "production of many industrial and agricultural products in this country . . . has been developed based upon the participation of Europe in international multilateral trade" and that "the decline of Europe would require far-reaching adjustments" that would "be costly in terms of employment and standards of living to our people." Secretary Krug stated that "the European Recovery Program is essential to our well-being and security; multilateral trade throughout the world must be restored." Secretary Anderson pointed out that "we are going to have abundance of agricultural production and we shall continue to need export outlets for some of our most important commodities." He stated that "it would not be pleasant to contemplate" a world in which Europe "provided little or no outlet for United States farm products." [12]

This emphasis upon the economic necessity for the United States to extend aid to Europe seemed to catch Congressmen and Senators by surprise. For example, Senator Vandenberg, who worked in very close association with the State Department throughout this debate, told Secretary Anderson, following his argument about the reliance of the farm economy upon exports, that "you leave me rather breathless with your presentation because I would think, fundamentally, that any exports would have some sort of an impact on domestic price levels." Vandenberg also pointed out that "the preoccupation of our colleagues is with the impact of this program on the domestic economy." And, indeed, whenever Administration witnesses drew attention to the role of E.R.P. in promoting exports, Congressional inquisitors turned to the issue of inflation. To soothe concern on this point, the Administration offered various assurances. It pointed out that procurement provisions under E.R.P. would permit domestic procurement only of items not in short supply. It argued that maintenance of high levels of exports lowered production costs and thus actually reduced prices. It estimated that the levels of exports under E.R.P. would not rise but actually decline somewhat. Despite such arguments, most Congressmen and Senators who responded to the economic argument remained skeptical. Like Vandenberg, most seemed surprised that the Administration would try to sell the program as profitable to the U.S., when so much of the public rhetoric depicted E.R.P. as an exercise in American self-sacrifice. From the speeches made about E.R.P. on the floor of the Congress, it is evident that these economic arguments did not carry much weight with the legislators.[13]

In explaining the relationship of E.R.P. to its long-range commercial policies, the Administration faced its greatest challenge. The extent of the problem was suggested by the response of Vandenberg when he learned that Clayton believed the provisions of the E.R.P. legislation "requiring the participating countries to cooperate to reduce barriers to trade not only among themselves but with other countries . . . morally committed the U.S. to a reciprocal policy of general tariff reduction, as we could not impose upon the European nations what we were not willing to do for ourselves." Though Clayton's comment was fully consistent with the whole history and design of E.R.P., Vandenberg responded with a strong rebuttal: "I do not agree with the Clayton interpretation. . . . Mr. Clayton will not help our present case by any such argument." The political judgment of Vandenberg seemed to be shared by members of the Administration, for they did not offer the promotion of multilateralism as an argument in favor of E.R.P. and did not include Clayton in the list of officials to testify in support of the legislation. In fact, had the legislation not contained specific requirements that participating countries promote multilateral commercial policies, the subject might never have been raised during the hearings. When asked by a Congressman who had noticed this provision, "if I approve this bill . . . would I be expressing my approval of the Reciprocal Trade Agreements?" Douglas answered, "Definitely not." Douglas argued that the provisions of E.R.P. with regard to the reduction of trade barriers "applies to the undertakings made by these particular countries and . . . does not expressly commit the United States to such a policy." Though this carefully worded statement was true, it was far from a candid exposition of the implications of E.R.P. for American commercial policy. The Administration fully recognized that the countries of Europe would never succeed in achieving a balance of payments in their trade with the dollar area—the stated objective of E.R.P.—unless they could increase their earnings of dollars via exports. The chief means by which this could be accomplished was a relaxation of American import restrictions. Thus, reductions in the American tariff were a critical part of the entire strategy of E.R.P. When Clayton appeared before the House Foreign Affairs Committee at the request of Representative Javits, he made this point clear by stating that the success of the European Recovery Program depended upon the establishment of the International Trade Organization. Moreover, as Clayton also made clear, the Administration saw E.R.P. as a means of achieving the multilateral commercial objectives to which it continued to be committed, which also implied acceptance of these principles by the U.S. The principles of the I.T.O., Clayton pointed out, would be implemented through the E.R.P., prior to the establishment of the proposed organization.[14]

In its development of the economic aspects of E.R.P., as of the political aspects of the program, the Administration failed to make a coherent case for its proposals. One moment, the Administration was stating that the U.S. had no selfish interests in E.R.P.; the next, it was insisting that the program was essential to the American economy. One high-ranking official went on record to the effect that the program had nothing to do with the Reciprocal Trade Agreements Program; a second indicated that trade agreements were an indispensable part of E.R.P.

Under these circumstances, it is not surprising that the Administration's campaign for E.R.P. failed to elicit a strong surge of public support. By the end of January it was evident that the public information program to promote E.R.P. was having little effect. Although the polls indicated that awareness and approval of the program were widespread, they also revealed that this support was superficial and entirely unenthusiastic. For example, the percentage of Americans approving the program fell off sharply when it was linked by pollsters with the necessity of postponing the tax cut or accepting increased inflation or food rationing. The lack of real public commitment to E.R.P. was to be explained by the fact that almost no one in America understood the fundamental importance of the program. A poll taken in February by the Gallup organization reported that 56 per cent of Americans regarded E.R.P. as essentially an act of charity, 8 per cent felt it was designed to "curb communism," and 35 per cent offered miscellaneous explanations or had no opinion. The A.I.P.O. reported in the same month that only 14 per cent of Americans could be classified as "informed" about the Marshall Plan, an astonishingly low figure even given the public's traditional apathy toward foreign affairs. During debate on the British Loan 25 per cent of the population had been classified as "informed," and 37 per cent were found to be in this category during debate on Greco-Turkish aid.[15]

The popular indifference to E.R.P. was widely recognized. At a meeting of the Senate Foreign Relations Committee on January 26, Senator Vandenberg referred to this matter and suggested that the program was too complex to be readily understood by the general public. Senator Barkley blamed the press for not giving adequate coverage to the discussion of issues during Congressional hearings. Also on January 26, the Alsops observed that the Administration had failed to arouse a sense of urgency in the population about E.R.P. and offered as an explanation the "strange anomaly" of recent American foreign policy that the Administration's major proposals had been "put forward in elaborate moral, humanitarian, and economic fancy dress with the real motives . . . largely suppressed." Walter Lippmann also blamed the Administration for failing to discuss the issues of foreign policy with the people. "There is a notion held by some in Washington," he wrote, "that the only way to win the support of Congress for the Marshall Plan is to frighten it. . . . The practitioners of this notion have been operating for nearly a year, ever since the crisis of last March during which the Truman Doctrine was improvised." Lippmann felt that the lack of public support for the program was attributable to the Administration's failure to make a strong case to the public on its behalf.[16]

As it became clear that the Administration had failed to generate a clear public mandate for E.R.P., the likelihood that the program would be altered in the manner proposed by the Herter recommendations or the Wherry group in the Senate increased. The opposition forces were given a strong boost in late January when former President Herbert Hoover, a respected elder statesman with acknowledged expertise in the area of postwar relief, publicly announced himself in favor of a program costing four billion dollars, the same figure toward which both groups were working. Ironically, the Administration's willingness to permit Americans to regard E.R.P. as charity rather than policy strengthened the appeal of Hoover's alternative, as his proposal was frankly concerned with relief rather than recovery. The Alsops wrote on January 25: "Hoover has . . . greatly increased a threat that was already quite black. . . . Altogether it is time to admit that the position [of E.R.P.] in Congress is very black indeed." Their assessment the following day was even more grim: "As of today action on E.R.P. is likely to be greatly delayed; the program will probably be festooned with unworkable restrictions and the amount appropriated is expected to be somewhere near . . . four billion dollars." Lippmann shared the Alsops's pessimism regarding the disposition of Congress. On February 9 he predicted that the Administration would win no more than a tentative, interim appropriation for E.R.P., with the question of a long-term commitment deferred until after the election. Predictions elsewhere in the Washington press were similar.[17]

The Administration recognized that it had failed to generate a public mandate for E.R.P., and there were indications that a new effort to stir public support was being considered. Lippmann reported that Marshall had been advised to "make another speech, or another two or three speeches, about the horrors and dangers of communism and to publish some more documents and some more intelligence reports." The Alsops stated that a high-level debate was going on within the Administration over how to create an adequate sense of urgency in the public regarding E.R.P.[18]

3. E.R.P. and Crisis Politics: The War Scare of 1948

In the midst of Congressional debate on E.R.P., the elected government of Czechoslovakia fell before a Communist coup and the Soviet Union strengthened its military ties to Finland. The interpretation of these events by Administration officials produced a full-scale war scare in the U.S., which decimated Congressional resistance to E.R.P. This war scare was without real foundation and represented another effort by the Administration to scare the country and Congress into supporting foreign aid.

OF THE TWO HOUSES OF CONGRESS, the Senate posed the lesser problem for the Administration in the debate on the European Recovery Program. There were several reasons for this. The Senate was considered more experienced and reliable in matters of foreign policy. It was also less likely to be influenced decisively by public opinion. Finally—and most important— the fate of E.R.P. in the Senate was in the hands of a powerful and expert champion, Arthur Vandenberg. The ability of the Republican Chairman of the Senate Foreign Relations Com-

include an authorization for aid to China in the program. In both cases, the positions taken by the House committee had very nearly defined the final shape of the Interim Aid bill. Moreover, the extended deliberations of the House committee had delayed Congressional action on Interim Aid two weeks beyond the date thought acceptable by the Administration. All of this had made Eaton pessimistic about his ability to win approval for E.R.P. from his own committee. On January 2 he predicted that action on the program might not occur until June 1, two months beyond the Administration's deadline.[21] Other observers shared Eaton's fears about the outcome of House consideration of E.R.P. Representative John McCormack predicted in December that the battle for E.R.P. would be the "most difficult" fight he had experienced in Congress. The reports of the Committee for the Marshall Plan consistently referred to the situation in the House as unpromising. Lippmann and the Alsops agreed that the House would provide the major obstacle to approval of the Administration's program.[22]

When the House committee began drafting its European Recovery bill during the first week in March, it appeared that the potential danger to the Administration's program that it represented would be realized. Although by this time Herter's proposal of an independent agency to administer E.R.P. had ceased to be an important issue, Vandenberg having supplied an effective solution to dispute on this matter, two crucial issues remained. First was the amount to be authorized—and here Herter's proposal for expenditures of 4.5 billion dollars in the first year had strong support among House Republicans. Second was the timetable for House action. On March 1 the House Committee decided to include E.R.P. in an omnibus foreign aid bill that would include all pending Administration proposals—the program of economic assistance for China that the Administration had promised during debate on Interim Aid, a new installment on Greco-Turkish aid, and a number of lesser programs. Moreover, Speaker Martin indicated that the House would insist upon extending military aid to China, rather than the economic aid program that the Administration proposed.[23] The potential effect of these decisions upon the Administration's schedule for action on E.R.P. was alarming: the inclusion of the program for Europe in a complex omnibus program would offer E.R.P.'s increasingly frustrated opponents an opportunity to mire the program in extended debate and might involve time-consuming negotiations between House and Senate; the highly controversial nature of the House's intention to insist upon military aid to China (which the Administration strongly opposed) also seemed likely to lengthen debate on the aid program indefinitely. If the proposed House procedure were retained it seemed likely that the April 1 deadline set by the Administration would not be met; gaps would appear in the foreign aid pipeline, and Marshall Plan funds would not be available in time to influence the Italian elections.

Ostensibly concerned about the latter issue—though in all probability he was equally upset by some other aspects of the House proposals—Secretary Marshall, accompanied by Lovett, went to Capitol Hill on March 8 to urge Speaker Martin to have E.R.P. considered as a single measure. The following day the House Republican leadership announced its decision to ignore Marshall's request, arguing that E.R.P. might be jeopardized in the House if it were submitted alone, but expressing the hope that passage of the omnibus bill would be achieved by April 10. Chairman Eaton, however, agreed to attempt to convince his committee to consider E.R.P. as a single measure. This came to nothing. On March 11 the House Foreign Affairs Committee voted against Eaton and insisted that E.R.P. be included in the omnibus bill. The *Washington Post* commented that this decision "foreshadowed a possible delay in the final approval of the European Recovery Program until too late to influence the Italian elections." Marquis Childs, predicting that these plans might delay approval of E.R.P. until June, called the Republican behavior so irresponsible as to require Americans to rethink their apparent intention to turn the country over to them in November. *The New York Times* reported that the House Committee's action "brought to a new low level the prospect for a bi-partisan approach to foreign policy questions in the House." The Administration, certainly, concluded that E.R.P. could not be passed in time to keep the foreign aid pipelines full, for President Truman requested that the Congress approve immediately fifty-five million dollars in additional Interim Aid to finance European recovery until Marshall Plan funds became available.[24]

The danger that Congressional approval of E.R.P. would be delayed by the actions of the House was eliminated by a dramatic alteration in the atmosphere of international politics as perceived and interpreted in Washington. The events that produced this new situation occurred two weeks prior to the critical moment in the House Foreign Affairs Committee's deliberations on E.R.P. On February 25 the non-communist government of Czechoslovakia fell from power and was replaced by a Communist regime. Shortly thereafter it was learned that the Soviet Union had invited Finland to participate in a mutual-defense treaty. These events, like previous indications of Soviet imperialism, triggered in the United States apprehensions as to the ultimate design of the U.S.S.R.'s pattern of expansion. The *Washington Post* ran a front-page map of Europe with the area under Soviet domination shaded. The caption stated: "Russia Moves Westward—Where Next?" Arrows pointed to Italy, France, Finland, and Austria. Marquis Childs reported on March 4 that the coup in Czechoslovakia had eliminated the assurance, previously widespread in Washington, that the U.S.S.R. did not want war with the United States. For a short time it appeared that the anxiety produced in America by this new manifestation of Soviet importunity would subside, as had happened on previous occasions. Then, on March 10, it was reported that the symbol of Czech democracy, Jan Masaryk, had been killed under mysterious circumstances in Prague. This catalyzed a remarkable series of events.[25]

At a news conference on March 10 Secretary Marshall was asked to express his views on the international situation. He replied with unexpected foreboding: "There are great fears as to the developments. . . . The situation is very, very serious." With specific reference to events in Czechoslovakia and the death of Jan Masaryk, Marshall stated that a "reign of terror" existed in that country. Such statements from a man not noted for his emotionalism attracted considerable attention. *The New York Times* printed the headline: "MARSHALL STIRRED BY WORLD CRISIS." On March 11 President Truman was asked at his news conference if he retained his often-expressed confidence in world peace. He answered: "It has been somewhat shaken, but I still believe that eventually we will get world peace." The *Washington Times Herald* made a headline of the comment: "TRUMAN . . . SAYS CONFIDENCE IN PEACE SHAKEN." Also on March 11, Secretary Marshall, in an address at the National Cathedral in Washington, repeated the sentiments he had expressed on the previous day: "The world is in the midst of a great crisis, influenced by propaganda, misunderstanding, anger and fear." He urged the rapid approval of the European Recovery Program.[26]

On March 13 former Secretary of State Byrnes, speaking at the Citadel in South Carolina, cited the above statements of the President and Secretary of State as evidence that a major international crisis was at hand. Byrnes told his audience that "There is nothing to justify the hope that with the complete absorption of Czechoslovakia and Finland the Soviets will be satisfied." He referred to Soviet ambitions in Greece, Turkey, Italy, and France. Turning to the Italian elections, he suggested that the Communists could not win. "If the Soviets intend to act in Italy as they have in Hungary and Czechoslovakia," he went on, "we can expect them to move whenever they reach the conclusion that the Communists cannot win. . . . They will not wait until the elections to disclose that the Communists are in the minority." Calling for rapid passage of E.R.P. and a program of national rearmament, Byrnes concluded that "it is important to think of the situation that may exist four or five weeks from now as a result of our failure to provide adequately for the national defense." His reference to the possibility of a clash between the U.S. and the Soviet Union over Italy in the next few weeks was widely reported in the press. The *Washington Times Herald* carried the headline: "BYRNES SEES WORLD CRISIS WITHIN FIVE WEEKS." The *Washing-*

ton Post also printed the story on page one and reported in its lead paragraph Byrnes's warning that world crisis might come within four or five weeks.[27]

Testifying before the Senate Foreign Relations Committee on March 15 on behalf of an extension of aid to Greece and Turkey, Marshall stated that "The hour is far more fateful than it was one year ago. . . . Totalitarian control has been tightened in . . . [the] countries of eastern Europe. . . . Other European peoples face a similar threat of being drawn against their will into the communist orbit." On the same day the *Washington Times Herald* reported that the Administration was considering a promise of military support for the western European nations and a warning to the U.S.S.R. that further expansion of communist power would produce a direct U.S.-Soviet confrontation. The headline stated: "TRUMAN WEIGHS NEW 'STOP-RUSSIA' MOVE."[28]

On March 16 the White House announced that the President would make a special statement before a joint session of Congress the following day. The headline in *The New York Times* read: "TRUMAN TO TELL CONGRESS TOMORROW OF WORLD STATUS." The *Washington Post* also ran a headline on the announcement: "TRUMAN TO ADDRESS CONGRESS TOMORROW AS CRISIS MOUNTS." The *Times Herald* printed the headline: "HILL HEARS TRUMAN TOMORROW ON CRISIS: MILITARY AID AGAINST REDS LIKELY THEME." *The New York Times*'s headline the following morning read: "TENSE CAPITAL AWAITS TRUMAN SPEECH." The *Washington Times Herald* told its readers: "TRUMAN WILL ASK VAST WAR PREPARATION." The President's address to Congress on March 17 was carried on nationwide radio. He stated that "rapid changes are taking place [in Europe] . . . which affect our foreign policy and our national security. There is an increasing threat to nations which are striving to maintain a form of government which grants freedom to its citizens." He then turned to a detailed indictment of Soviet policy, which had "destroyed the independence and democratic character of a whole series of nations in eastern and central Europe," and warned that "this ruthless course of action and the clear design to extend it to the remaining free

nations of Europe" was the essence of the current crisis. He
referred to the situations in Czechoslovakia, Finland, Greece,
and Italy, and concluded: "I believe that we have reached a
point at which the position of the United States should be
made unmistakably clear." He then urged the Congress to approve the E.R.P. rapidly, to enact a program of Universal
Military Training, and to approve a temporary renewal of Selective Service. "At no time in our history," he stated in
closing, "has unity among our people been so vital as it is at
the present time." On the evening of March 17 the President
repeated the same themes in a St. Patrick's Day address in
New York City, a speech also carried on nationwide radio.
Headlines the following morning were devoted to his state-
ments. The *Washington Post:* "TRUMAN ASKS TEMPORARY
DRAFT, UMT AND AID FOR EUROPE TO CHECK AGGRESSION BY
RUSSIA"; the *Times Herald:* "CONGRESS SPLIT ON PRESIDENT'S
DEMANDS FOR UMT, DRAFT TO STOP RED EXPANSION"; *The New
York Times:* "TRUMAN ASKS TEMPORARY DRAFT IMMEDIATELY
AND UNIVERSAL TRAINING AS THE PRICE OF PEACE." [29]

Formal efforts to increase the strength of the Armed
Forces began immediately after the President requested them.
Marshall addressed the first session of a hearing by the Senate
Armed Services Committee on Universal Military Training
within hours after the President's speech: "I wish to express
in person to you my own concern over the accelerated trend
in Europe," he stated. "In the short years since the end of
hostilities this trend has grown from a trickle into a torrent."
He referred to the Balkans, Hungary, Czechoslovakia. He interpreted the Italian election as deciding "not only whether
Italy will continue with its restoration of true democracy" but
"whether the disintegrating trend to which I have referred
may reach the shores of the Atlantic." He concluded with an
analogy to Hitler: "It is said that history never repeats itself.
Yet if these free people are one by one subjugated to police
state controls even the blind may see a deadly parallel." Marshall stressed the importance of passing E.R.P. quickly to meet
the threat. His statement prompted the headline in the *Washington Times Herald:* "MARSHALL FEARS WAR MOVE BY COM-

MIES." The next day the Senate Armed Services Committee heard the heads of the military establishment, who testified to the immediate necessity of rebuilding the Armed Forces. *The New York Times* ran the headline: "MILITARY HEADS CALL UMT, DRAFT VITAL FOR SAFETY." Also on March 18, the State Department made public dispatches from Athens reporting that three Soviet-supported International Brigades were poised in the Balkans ready to attack across the border into Greece. The themes employed by Marshall in his testimony before the Senate Armed Services Committee characterized two addresses he delivered shortly thereafter on a trip to the West Coast. On March 19, at Berkeley, he again likened the present situation to that which existed in 1939, when he had "watched the Nazi government take control of one country after another until finally Poland was invaded in a direct military operation." He urged speedy approval of E.R.P. The next day, in Los Angeles, he stressed again the parallel between the situation in Europe and German expansion under Hitler. Again he urged quick action on E.R.P. *The New York Times* reported both speeches in front-page headlines.[30]

On March 20 it was reported that the Soviet representative on the Allied Control Council in Berlin had walked out of a council meeting. This event came at the end of a stiffening of relations between the former Allies in Berlin. Two days later the White House announced that it had cancelled plans for the State Department to take over responsibility for the occupation of Germany in July. The Army would retain control. On March 21 the White House released the "United States Industrial Mobilization Plan—1947," a general blueprint for mobilizing the country's industrial resources in case of war.[31]

The Senate Armed Services Committee heard the Defense Department's proposals for an enlargement of the Armed Services on March 25. Secretary Forrestal prefaced the presentation with a statement repeating the analogy voiced by Secretary Marshall between German expansion in 1939 and current Soviet policy. Following his introduction, each of the Services presented specific programs for increases in their strengths. *The New York Times* reported: "TOP MILITARY MEN URGE U.S. TO ARM TO SHOW WE WOULD FIGHT FOR FREEDOM." The most spectacular piece of information produced by this testimony came from Navy Secretary Sullivan, who told the committee that submarines "belonging to no nation west of the 'iron curtain' have been sighted off our shores." Eschewing interpretation of this development, he nevertheless recalled, "that an early step of the Germans in 1917 and 1941 was to deploy submarines off our coasts." Although this statement was only a small piece in an immense body of testimony, it received headline attention. *The New York Times* ran it as a subhead and the *Times Herald* made its headline of the disclosure: "RUSSIAN SUBS PROWL WEST COAST WATERS." Subsequent hearings on the rearmament proposals produced a steady procession of front-page stories about current military dangers.[32]

This series of ominous disclosures, portentous interpretations, and somber warnings produced, through its harvest of spine-tingling headlines, a dramatic effect upon the political atmosphere of Washington. As early as March 13, following the first statements about the new crisis by Marshall and Truman, the *Washington Times Herald* published an article by Walter Trohan entitled "Whispers of War Grow Loud Throughout the Capital," which described the mood of anxiety that these statements had excited. James Reston, writing in *The New York Times,* described a similar atmosphere: "The mood of the capital this weekend is exceedingly somber. For the moment the sweep of great events seems to overwhelm the men trying to deal with them. . . . even the President has mentioned that awful three-letter word, war." Several days later the Alsops published an article in the *Washington Post* entitled "How War Might Come," which began with the observation that "the atmosphere in Washington is no longer a postwar atmosphere. It is, to put it bluntly, a prewar atmosphere. . . . it is now universally admitted that war within the next few months is certainly possible." On March 28, Jerry Klutz, in his *Washington Post* column on the civil service, reported that the war scare had produced rumors that the federal government was about to transfer a number of agencies out of Washington. Walter Lippmann described the atmosphere in Washington at the end of the month by stating that "The President's message, the speeches, testimony, and press conferences of Mr. Marshall, Mr. Forrestal, Mr. Royall, Mr. Sullivan and Mr. Symington have put this country in the position of preparing . . . for a war." [33]

The war scare of 1948 terminated the problem of achieving House authorization of the Administration's proposals for the European Recovery Program. On March 16 the House Republican leadership and the majority members of the House Foreign Affairs Committee, anticipating the President's speech, decided to accelerate the timetable for House action on E.R.P. Speaker Martin announced that House Foreign Affairs would report the bill by March 18 or 19, and that final House action would be forthcoming by the Administration's April 1 target date. The following day the Foreign Affairs Committee rejected Herter's proposal that aid to Europe during the first year be reduced to 4.5 billion dollars and approved the program in exactly the amount proposed by the Administration. The omnibus foreign aid bill was reported on March 19. In the report the House committee stated that it was taking swift action on E.R.P. to help "reverse the trend of communism in Europe" and expressed the hope that the measure would have an influence on the Italian elections. The spiritual leader of the bill's opponents, Herbert Hoover, also rethought his position. On March 23 he announced himself in favor of the Administration's program. The bill was never seriously threatened during a debate that consumed most of the final week of March. In that debate forty of the forty-four Congressmen who expressed opinions on E.R.P. argued that the purpose of the measure was to oppose communist aggression. There was little chance that a measure so conceived would meet serious opposition in the atmosphere that prevailed in mid-March 1948. House action approving the bill as reported came on March 31 in a remarkable session described by *Washington Post* writer Ferdinand Kuhn: "As the roll call went on in a seething and excited House shouts of 'aye' came from one Republican after another who had seldom, if ever, voted for any international legislation." [34]

In effecting the early release of the European Recovery Program from the House Foreign Affairs Committee and prompting its rapid ratification by the whole House, the war scare of 1948 brought the Administration's foreign aid program safely through what had been anticipated to be its most difficult test. The extent to which this expeditious House action depended upon the unusual mood of mid-March was made clear two months later when the appropriation bill for E.R.P. was being considered. In May the House Appropriations Committee, chaired by John Taber, the most indefatigable cutter of budgets in Congress, reported a reduced appropriation for E.R.P. On this occasion, the fear of war with the Soviet Union having subsided, the sponsors of E.R.P. were unable to obtain sufficient votes to defeat Taber's proposal. During the March crisis an attempt to cut the authorization for E.R.P. had attracted only sixty votes in the House. Taber's efforts, though supported by the House Republican leadership, were eventually frustrated by the adamant opposition of Senator Vandenberg and even Senator Taft, who together persuaded the Senate not to compromise the program initially approved by Congress. Their successful battle to save the Administration's program demonstrated to what extent E.R.P. was saved from reduction by the war scare, for it was the vote on the authorization—its implied "moral commitment" to E.R.P. and its practical effect of having set the program in motion at the authorized level—that provided Vandenberg and Taft with their chief arguments in opposing Taber.[35] Because the war scare played such a decisive role in achieving final passage of E.R.P. it is worthwhile to examine the ingredients of that hectic and bodeful interlude.

The war scare of 1948, specifically the events in Czechoslovakia and Finland that prompted it, must be viewed in the context established in the first chapter of this book. Two situations there described had formed the basic assumptions of American policy in the postwar period prior to March 1948: (1) the Soviet Union's physical devastation during the war had made it unlikely that it could sustain any major military effort and questionable that it could control a sphere of influence larger than that attained as a result of the war; (2) America possessed the ability, through air supremacy—particularly the atomic bomb—to punish the Soviet Union intolerably should it launch an attack, even though there was no force in western Europe capable of resisting the Red Army. These two factors had allowed the Americans to be confident that the U.S.S.R., whatever its ultimate ambitions might be, did not want and would not initiate war with the United States. A corollary of this assessment was that the Soviets were willing to conduct their international relations on the basis of a tacit understanding concerning spheres of influence. In practice this meant that although the Soviet Union supported the efforts of national Communist Parties to reduce American influence in western Europe—just as the U.S. attempted to strengthen the position of the non-communist parties in eastern Europe—it was clear that the U.S.S.R. would no more intervene actively on behalf of such efforts than the United States would go to war to prevent communist domination of Poland or Hungary. America's entire foreign policy, including the decision to defer rebuilding the Armed Forces until E.R.P. had been approved, was based on the assumption, successfully tested in Iran, Greece, and Turkey, that if the United States made a strong show of opposition to communist ambitions in an area within the western sphere of influence, the Soviets would concede the point.

Were events in Czechoslovakia and Finland of such a nature as to invalidate the above set of assumptions and policies? There were two possible interpretations of these events; either the Soviet Union was consolidating its position within its sphere of influence before the United States, through E.R.P., was able to institutionalize its power in the West, or the U.S.S.R. was abandoning its previous adherence to the spheres-of-influence arrangement and intended to obtain territory in the West before American aid increased the difficulty of expansion.

During and after the war the U.S.S.R. consistently had

asserted, and the United States accepted, the dominant interest of the Soviet Union in Czechoslovakia. The first indication of this situation had come in 1944 when, the eventual liberation of Czechoslovakia being a certainty, the Czech government proposed a treaty with the United States, Great Britain, and the Soviet Union. The U.S. and U.K. rejected the Czech offer, pointing to the inability of their armies to reach central Europe for some time; the Soviet Union, whose troops were on its border with Czechoslovakia, accepted. From that time, on matters ranging from the management of U.N.R.R.A. to the liberation of Prague, the United States had repeatedly recognized and deferred to the wishes of the Soviet Union in Czechoslovakia. The influence of the Soviet Union on this country became clear during the summer of 1947, when the Czech government, having accepted Secretary Marshall's offer to participate in the European Recovery Program, withdrew at the behest of the Soviet Union. As for the coup itself, the Czech Communists had held all the vital positions of power since 1945 and could have imposed communist rule at any time. Their failure to do so reflected their belief, which by early 1948 had proved unjustified, that they could come to power through parliamentary elections. The movement toward the coup had been discernible as early as January 1948 and reflected not a pattern of Soviet expansion westward but consolidation of Soviet control over an area it already dominated.[36]

The distribution of power in Finland was similar to the situation in Czechoslovakia. At the end of the war, the Soviet army had dominated Finland. The Allied Control Commission in that country had been an agency of the Soviet military authorities. In the post-occupation period, Finland had followed international policies explicitly in harmony with the wishes of the Soviet Union. Indeed, Finland's President from 1946–56, Juho Passikivi, had laid down in 1944 the "Passikivi line," by which the Finns pledged themselves to "do nothing in conflict with the wishes of the Soviet Union." The mutual-defense treaty proposed to Finland by the Soviet Union in February 1948 was lenient by Soviet standards. It pledged Finland to fight any aggressor attacking the U.S.S.R. through Finland,

but Finland was not obliged to assist the Soviets in other circumstances and Soviet help to Finland would be "subject to
mutual agreement." [37]

While it is easy to establish that there was nothing about
events in Czechoslovakia and Finland in early 1948 to support
the belief that a basic shift in Soviet policy had taken place,
other developments in Europe established a context within
which these events might have assumed special significance.
In January 1948, for example, Britain had initiated talks with
France and the Benelux countries to explore the establishment
of bilateral defensive agreements. The immediate impetus for
this seems to have been the failure of the London Conference
of November 1947 and the decision, taken by the Western
powers following it, to eschew all pretense of seeking the reunification of Germany and proceed with the establishment of
a separate West German state. The western European powers
concurred that the London decision on Germany moved the
Cold War in Europe to a new level of tension, and at Brussels
in February they agreed to the establishment of a regional
defensive alliance. American support was immediately solicited. Two other situations lent support to the notion of a significant increase in tensions in Europe. First, there had been
some reports of a potential Communist coup in Italy if the
elections seemed to be going in favor of the non-communist
parties. Intelligence of this kind had worried Secretary Forrestal as early as September 1947, to the point that he discussed with Lovett America's ability to intervene militarily to
suppress such an action and made the matter the subject of a
meeting of the National Security Council. Prior to the elections
there were reports through British intelligence channels that
a coup was being prepared with outside support. Soviet troop
movements were taking place that could be interpreted as
preparing support for a coup. A second point of concern was
Berlin. On March 5 General Clay sent a telegram to Washington that reported a marked stiffening of U.S.-Soviet relations in the German capital, evidently an early warning of the
U.S.S.R.'s subsequent boycott of the Control Council. Clay
commented that he had for some time been confident that

war between the United States and the Soviet Union would not come for several years but that he was now afraid that war "might come with dramatic suddenness." [38] All of these developments were on the minds of American officials in early 1948.

For the purposes of this study, of course, the intrinsic significance of developments in Europe in 1948 is less important than the perception of them by American officials at the time. It must be remembered that the war scare of 1948 did not occur in response to published reports from eastern Europe in February but following a series of statements and leaks from high American officials in mid-March, all of which can be traced to one of three sources: (1) the State Department, mainly through Secretary Marshall; (2) the Defense Department; (3) the White House. Interacting with all three sources, of course, was the press itself. The behavior and interaction of these four elements are what must be explained if the war scare of 1948 is to be understood.

The contribution of Secretary Marshall and the Department of State to the war scare was substantial. Marshall's press conference remarks on March 10 were the first official comments in the series of events that produced the war scare, and in the subsequent two weeks his appearances before Congressional committees and his speeches on the West Coast heightened the growing sense of immediate crisis. Two facts about these initiatives are notable: the three formal speeches that Marshall delivered in this period were all appeals for the rapid approval of the European Recovery Program, and Marshall's press conference of March 10 came one day after the House Republican leadership announced its decision to ignore his request that E.R.P. be considered as a single measure. These facts suggest the possibility that Marshall was motivated to alter his usual calm and aloof manner mainly to expedite passage of E.R.P. He undoubtedly felt frustrated by his efforts to hasten approval: his apparent attempt to intimidate the Senate Foreign Relations Committee had won a strong rebuke from one of the Committee's key members; now the House leadership was ignoring his appeal. According to Walter

Lippmann and the Alsops, as indicated above, there had been discussions within the State Department since mid-February concerning how to create the sense of urgency required to expedite passage of E.R.P. with explicit consideration given to a public statement by Marshall defining anew the communist threat to Europe. Lippmann had reported that the Department was considering the publication of more diplomatic documents; the subsequent release of materials reporting Soviet troop movements in the Balkans suggests that his information was sound.

There is no reason to believe that Marshall at any time altered his assumption that the U.S.S.R. did not want war with the United States. He had been informed in the fall of 1947 by George Kennan that if the Marshall Plan became effective, the U.S. would have to expect the Soviets to consolidate their position in Czechoslovakia. Although Kennan was out of the country in mid-March 1948, when he heard how events were being interpreted in Washington, he immediately dispatched a cable to the State Department reiterating his view. Marshall was certainly not surprised or alarmed by the decision of the western Europeans to form a military alliance, or inclined to base an interpretation of events in February on this decision, for the western European alliance was the product of a conversation between Marshall and Bevin in December 1947.

Unfortunately, there is no published record of Marshall's response to the Clay telegram or the intelligence reports about Italy, but following the Czech coup he consistently took positions indicating that he did not expect war with the Soviet Union. For example, when he was visited on March 2 by a delegation of Senators anxious to know if the coup required new efforts toward military preparedness, he replied that what was needed was swift enactment of Universal Military Training. U.M.T., which Marshall had advocated for several years as a signal to the world that the U.S. did not intend to shirk international leadership, was designed primarily to strengthen the reserves by requiring all eighteen-year-olds to undergo six months of training and accept a position in a reserve unit. As these men would not be available for active service after their training, U.M.T. was directed toward creating a pool of trained men over an extended period of time and—except for its tendency to increase voluntary enlistments in the regular forces—would not significantly increase the Army's ability to respond to an immediate emergency. It was by no means a crash program to prepare for imminent hostilities. Moreover, when he testified on behalf of U.M.T. before the Senate Armed Services Committee in mid-March, Marshall voiced the belief that if U.M.T. were approved, "the probabilities are that we will avoid trouble." On May 7 he told a high-level budgetary meeting that American policy was based upon the assumption that there would be no war. Marshall's public statements, in fact, never suggested the imminence of war, only the existence of a new international crisis. He never made clear the exact nature of this crisis, and given his assumption that the Soviets were not about to initiate war, it is difficult to understand what he meant, unless he believed that the consolidation of the Soviet position in areas it already controlled constituted a significant crisis for the West. The more likely possibility is that to Marshall the crisis of March 1948—like the crises of March and November 1947—was mainly a crisis of domestic politics, given reality by the appropriate interpretation of international events.[39]

Had Marshall's campaign for E.R.P. occurred in isolation, the crisis of March 1948 might never have developed into a full-scale war scare. For the statements, disclosures, and developments that caused an image of armed conflict to materialize in the empty space of fear created by Marshall's announcement of a new and undefined crisis all had their origins elsewhere, mainly in the Defense Department. It was the Pentagon, after all, that was responsible for proposing a rearmament program in March 1948 and for much spectacular testimony before Congress, including Sullivan's comments about hostile submarines. The Pentagon was also responsible for former Secretary Byrnes's startling speech of March 13, which suggested a showdown with the U.S.S.R. in a few weeks.

To understand the activities of the Defense Department

in March 1948 it is necessary to recall the Administration's policy of deferring efforts to rearm until the foreign aid program was approved by Congress. The resulting lack of attention to defense appropriations had brought the Armed Forces to a state of nearly total impotence by early 1948. The extent of the depletion was revealed in a Defense Department report on February 18. It indicated that troop levels were far below the numbers currently authorized and were not sufficient to implement the existing emergency war plan. The commitment of a single division at any of the numerous trouble spots of the world would require a partial mobilization. This presentation brought home sharply to Forrestal, the Secretary of Defense, the need to set plans in motion to rebuild the Armed Forces—plans that would in any case have been in order with the campaign for E.R.P. nearing conclusion. U.M.T., the Army's long-standing solution to its manpower problem, had been consistently blocked by Congress. On February 16 Chan Gurney, Chairman of the Senate Armed Services Committee, reiterated to Forrestal his committee's unwillingness to begin hearings on U.M.T. until a precise statement of the program's cost and a total military budget were produced. Forrestal reflected at this time that it would be advisable to convene the Service chiefs outside Washington for a conference to develop a comprehensive defense program.[40]

On March 2 Forrestal lunched with Marshall, following the latter's meeting with the delegation of Senators concerning the situation in Europe. Both men were impressed by the apparent readiness of the Senators to respond to Marshall's suggestion that quick action be taken on U.M.T. Talk at the lunch centered upon ways of mobilizing forces for a new campaign for this long-sought program and, according to Forrestal, consideration was given to "a joint effort by Marshall and myself to get a concurrent resolution through the House and Senate giving approval immediately to the principle of U.M.T., linking the implementation to a subsequent bill, the thought being to capitalize on the present concern of the country over the events of last week in Europe." This meeting was undoubtedly the origin of the decision to include a new appeal for U.M.T. in the President's address of March 17, but Forrestal—with recent reports of low troop levels on his mind —had an agenda of his own. The day after his lunch with Marshall, he told the Chairman of the House Armed Services Committee that he believed serious consideration should be given to a revival of Selective Service in order to bring troop levels up to authorized strength. Forrestal moved quickly to initiate his program while the crisis lasted. On the evening of March 3 he and Army Secretary Royall dined with former Sec-retary Byrnes and persuaded him to make a public plea for rearmament, including U.M.T. and Selective Service. This was the immediate origin of Byrnes's speech of March 13, for which Forrestal provided both material and publicity arrangements. In his memoirs, Byrnes does not recall any discussion of the danger of war with the Soviet Union at the dinner with For-restal and Royall; the conversation, he writes, was about the difficulty of getting Congress to approve expenditures for re-building the Armed Forces. The following day Forrestal con-tinued his campaign by calling Senator George to suggest that a group of key Senators be convened to hear a "presentation of the world situation by a member of the army staff," which would undoubtedly have been the same disturbing report of low troop levels that convinced Forrestal of the necessity of Selective Service. Forrestal also decided that the time had come to convene the meeting of Service chiefs that he had conceived two weeks previously. The conference was sched-uled for the following week in Key West, Florida.[41]

It is important to note that all of these initiatives oc-curred prior to the receipt of Clay's provocative telegram on March 5. This telegram has played a major role in most explana-tions of the war scare of 1948, mainly, it seems, because the published version of Forrestal's diary includes a copy of it along with editorial notes suggesting that it was the cause of much anxiety and furious intelligence activity in Washington. It is difficult to know the real effect of this telegram because it was immediately pressed into service by Forrestal to support the campaign for rearmament that he had already launched. It is equally difficult, for the same reasons, to interpret the ac-

tivation of the Armed Forces' intelligence services that Clay's
telegram apparently caused, particularly their combined estimate, issued in mid-March, that war was not probable within
sixty days. Both developments were so thoroughly self-serving
in terms of the interests of the defense community and so
thoroughly consistent with Forrestal's strategy of exploiting the
crisis to obtain rearmament that it would be foolish, in the absence of strong supportive evidence, to take them at face value.
And there is no real supporting evidence that there was concern among military leaders that war was imminent in March
1948. In fact, high-ranking officers were reported to consider
U.M.T. more important than the draft and when specifically
pressed on the likelihood of imminent war, they tended to deny
the possibility. Forrestal's only recorded comment on the question of war was thoroughly circumspect. "It is inconceivable,"
he wrote on March 16, in response to the day's headlines, "that
even the gang who run Russia would be willing to take on war,
but one always has to remember that there seemed to be no
reason for Hitler to start war." However one may weigh political factors in assessing the reactions to Clay's telegram and the
reports of the intelligence services, the basic point is that the
Defense Department had reached the decision that immediate
expansion of the Armed Forces was necessary prior to the
events in Czechoslovakia and Finland, and that developments
there were seen mainly as a promising occasion to wage the
necessary political campaign. At best, the Clay telegram gave
impetus to both the campaign and the sense of urgency with
which it was conducted. It is unlikely that the activities of the
Defense Department—or their impact upon the public mood—
would have been significantly different had the telegram never
been sent.[42]

The President's role in generating the war scare of 1948
was considerably less important than that of Marshall and
Forrestal. The impetus for his decision to address a joint
session of Congress came from Marshall, and the substance of
the President's proposals clearly combined the policies sought
by his two cabinet officers. In terms of impact upon public
opinion, the press build-up given the speech was at least as

important as the speech itself, for the predictions of vast new military initiatives widely reported prior to the address proved unfounded, despite the President's urgent tone. There is no reason to believe that the President was fearful of war in March 1948. Nothing in his memoirs suggests any other conclusion. In speaking of events in eastern Europe he states that "to the people of Europe . . . these communist moves looked like the beginning of a big push," but he does not suggest what the object of a "big push" might have been and seems to be talking about the general increase in tension that produced the Brussels conference, which had been initiated well before February.[43] In any case the President does not suggest that he or anyone else in Washington was seriously concerned about war, and does not even recall the war scare or the Clay telegram.

It seems impossible to avoid the conclusion that the war scare of 1948 was yet another exercise in crisis politics by the Truman administration. This time, however, the impact seems to have been greater than was bargained for, for there were reports that both Truman and Marshall were distressed by the extent of public hysteria that was generated. Marshall regarded the creation of a war mentality as harmful to the campaign for E.R.P., as the likelihood of war made economic aid irrational; there is evidence that he was far from enthusiastic about the Defense Department's decision to push for rearmament beyond U.M.T. in March 1948. His testimony on the revival of Selective Service was notably cool. In May he and the President rather abruptly reined in the Pentagon's campaign to enlarge the military budget and placed a ceiling on the defense program considerably below what the Armed Forces requested. On March 23 *The New York Times* reported that Marshall would personally attend a conference in Latin America, and pointed out that this move seemed intended to calm current fears of war. Two days later General Clay held a press conference in Germany to say that he was "not the least bit apprehensive" and that "much too much is being made of this." [44] During the critical days of House consideration of E.R.P. and prior to the initiation of the Defense Department's campaign for rearmament on March 25, however, the initiatives of both Marshall and Truman tended to heighten rather than calm the crisis atmosphere. By permitting the idea of imminent war to go unrepudiated once it had been introduced, by playing to this fear through the manner in which the President's speech was billed and delivered, both the President and the Secretary of State permitted the speculation in the press to grow steadily more wild and the public mood steadily more agitated. The final battle in the year-long campaign for foreign aid was thus won in the same manner as the first.

4. The Institutionalization of the Truman Doctrine

Passage of E.R.P. was purchased at a price to the Administration's policies. Congress, continuing to take the Truman Doctrine literally and inspired by the war scare, amended the program to include aid to China and to restrict East-West trade.

ALTHOUGH THE ADMINISTRATION SUCCEEDED in winning Congressional approval of its full request for E.R.P. before April 1, 1948, the victory was not total. During debate on Interim Aid there had been indications that on two critical issues—American policy toward China and East-West trade—Congress was inclined to follow the rhetoric of the Truman Doctrine rather than the policy of the Truman administration. Debate on E.R.P. reaffirmed the Congressional attitude on both points.

The Administration's China Aid Program, promised during hearings on Interim Aid, was submitted to Congress on February 20, 1948. It was clear from the draft program that the Administration intended only a minimum effort. Of the 570 million dollars that was requested, almost the entire sum was to be used to finance imports of specific commodities, particularly food and clothing, needed for relief; 60 million dollars was to be available for very limited reconstruction projects, although the State Department made it plain that conditions in China precluded any comprehensive or long-term program of economic recovery. Indeed, nothing was more evident from the State Department's presentation than its reluctance to involve itself in China at all. Marshall described at length the difficulties the Department had experienced in devising ways in which aid could be usefully allocated to China, and indicated that the U.S. could not anticipate much progress from the proposed program or look forward to a time when aid to China would not be necessary. "You will waste a good part of your effort," he told Congress. Moreover, the Secretary was at pains to make it clear that China could be helped only through initiatives of the Nationalist government itself, initiatives that could not reasonably be anticipated in light of that government's past performance, and that the Administration intended to undertake no deep commitment to correcting the situation in China: ". . . the program should not involve the virtual underwriting of the future of the Chinese economy. The United States should not by its actions be put in the position of being charged with a direct responsibility for the conduct of the Chinese government." In executive session Marshall made clear his reason for wishing to avoid such responsibility: the complete defeat of the Nationalist regime, he told the Senate Foreign Relations Committee, was a real and present possibility.[45]

The Administration's program was hardly adequate to satisfy Chiang Kai-shek's advocates in the Congress or elsewhere. While the Administration was willing to make a total effort to save western Europe from communism, it was evidently unwilling, Congressmen suggested during the hearings, to meet the same problem forthrightly in Asia. Administration witnesses were asked, as they had been asked before, to differentiate between the policies for Europe and Asia. Policies same, conditions different, they repeated. They were asked to distinguish between conditions in Greece and China. There were similarities, they admitted, principally that the main threat to both governments was military in nature. Yet the Administration proposed no program of military assistance to China. It quickly became evident that military aid would be the major issue between the Administration and Congress. The House Foreign Affairs Committee heard testimony from William Bullitt and General Wedemeyer insisting that China could be saved only by a substantial investment of military assistance by the U.S. Feeling that no program of military aid that the U.S. could undertake would be effective, the Administration strenuously opposed such proposals. The political lines on the China issue had been drawn months previously, however, and in March the House Republican leadership announced itself in opposition to the Administration on this issue.[46] The bill reported by the House Foreign Affairs Committee and approved by the whole House not only provided a specific grant of military aid to China but included that provision in the section of the omnibus bill covering military assistance to Greece, a procedure that made it clear that America's commitments to the two countries were to be identical.

Although the House version of the China Aid Program was nothing more than a literal implementation of the Truman Doctrine, its implications for American foreign policy could not have been less acceptable to the Truman administration. In presenting its own China Aid Program, the State Department had emphasized its unwillingness to undertake long-term commitments regarding the political and economic future of China. In the end, the Senate saved the Administration from the obvious perils implicit in the House's action by insisting that China aid be provided for in a separate section of the omnibus bill, and by deleting specific mention of military aid to China. The Senate's action drew expressions of praise and relief from many of E.R.P.'s better-informed advocates, and perhaps these were justified in the face of the threat represented by the House bill. But fundamentally it was naïve to expect that the section of the bill in which aid was provided or the specific language by which it was extended would make much difference in the meaning attached to the Administration's action. What would be remembered was that the Administration had undertaken a program of aid to China as part of a global effort to halt the spread of communism. However much the Administration may have hedged its bets in presenting the China Aid Program to Congress, the episode had committed the United States to the defense of China if only by demonstrating the unwillingness of the Administration to repudiate the Truman Doctrine publicly by facing up to the difference between its attitudes toward Europe and Asia. The country witnessed a dramatic example of the Administration's edginess on this point when the President, at his news conference on March 11, denied that the United States had ever sought to include the Communists in a coalition government in China.[47]

Demands for greater restrictions on American exports to communist countries of potential war material had been one of the primary Congressional responses and amendments to the Truman Doctrine. Moreover, many members of Congress had expressed their dismay at the fact that some of the countries of western Europe that were receiving American assistance were trading heavy industrial goods to communist countries. Skirmishes between the Administration and Congress on both issues had occurred during the first session of the Eightieth Congress, but, as in the case of China policy, the showdown came when the Administration sought approval of the European Recovery Program.

Basically, the Administration opposed general prohibitions on American exports of potential war materials to eastern Europe or the Soviet Union. American trade with the Communist world was profitable and necessary to the United States. By one estimate, 40 per cent of America's 432-million-dollar export trade with the communist countries of Europe might come under a general ban on exports of potential war material. Even more importantly, the U.S. was receiving 20 to 25 per cent of its manganese and chrome, both essential to the production of steel, from the Soviet Union. To appease Congressional concern on this issue, however, the Administration did take steps to limit American exports to the U.S.S.R. In

January 1948 the State Department announced limitations on the export of war surplus radar in response to Congressional protests that shipments were being obtained by the Soviet Union. During his testimony on E.R.P., Commerce Secretary Harriman informed Congress that all exports to Europe, east and west, would require export licenses after March 1. These steps were not enough to satisfy Representative Mundt, the most outspoken and tenacious opponent of East-West trade in Congress, who reminded Harriman during the hearings that "we are sort of engaging in economic strife or ideological warfare or something" and indicated that "we are going to have to have some kind of modification to . . . [the] open trade program with the Soviets." Mundt also made it clear that he was dissatisfied with the Administration's attitude toward trade between eastern and western Europe, a trade whose continuation was considered essential to the success of E.R.P. by the American and European governments. Representative Mundt, apparently fearing that western Europe was suicidal, served notice that changes in current policies would have to be made. "If we exercise no control whatsoever," he pointed out, "if western Europe in its natural desire to get wheat and coal, starts trading with the satellite countries, or with the U.S.S.R., freight cars, trucks, implements of war, I cannot see how the E.R.P. can succeed under those conditions." [48]

During House debate on E.R.P., Mundt offered an amendment to the omnibus bill directing the administrator of E.R.P. to refuse deliveries of goods used in the production of war materials to governments that might trade them with Communist countries. The amendment further directed the administrator to halt American exports to the Communist countries of Europe whenever it was in the national interest to do so. How successful Representative Mundt would have been in obtaining approval of this amendment (which the Administration strongly and explicitly opposed) had there been no war scare is impossible to estimate; a poll by the Gallup organization in early February indicated that most Americans felt trade with the U.S.S.R. should be stopped. The war scare, however, made limitations on trade irresistible. The Administration's position was further weakened by the disclosures of a House subcommittee at the height of the war scare concerning American exports of war surplus material, particularly forty-six B-24 engines, from New York to the Soviet Union and Poland in 1947. Despite the hasty imposition by the Administration of new export controls to offset these revelations, the Mundt amendment was adopted by the House with slight modification. Even this, in the circumstances prevailing in the House during the vote on E.R.P., represented a modest victory for the Administration. The enflamed Congressmen came close to imposing an embargo on all American exports to the U.S.S.R. The Mundt amendment was only the beginning of a continuing political battle that would keep the Truman administration on the defensive for the remainder of its tenure. Between 1948 and 1952 Congress would include increasingly serious restrictions on East-West trade in its authorizations of aid to Europe. The Administration, unable to contain this tendency, would be constrained in 1951 to publicly oppose East-West trade while privately assuring European governments that it did not object to this activity.[49]

The attitudes of Congressional majorities on East-West trade and aid to China, and the Administration's inability to resist the inclusion of provisions reflecting them in the E.R.P. legislation, were significant symbols of the basic political reality of the year-long campaign for foreign aid. In March 1948, as in March 1947, it was clear that the Truman administration had failed to inspire broad public understanding and support of its definition of America's international interests. At the end of this year, as at the beginning, Congress affirmed not the strategies of American foreign policy but a rhetoric of anti-communism in the midst of international crisis. Nothing made this latter fact more plain than the insistence of Republican leaders that the European Recovery Program would be endangered if it were offered as a single program rather than as part of a global effort for the containment of communism. The Truman Doctrine, not the Marshall Plan, was approved by Congress in March 1948.

VII

Internal Security, E.R.P., and the Politics of 1948

1. Another Debate on Foreign Aid, Another Drive Against Subversives

The Administration reinforced the anti-communist appeal of its campaign for E.R.P. through a highly publicized series of arrests of alien communist leaders. Its spokesmen also began explicitly to denounce opponents of E.R.P. as communists. These tactics were highly supportive of the President's campaign for nomination and election.

BY THE TIME Congress began considering the European Recovery Program, it was apparent to anyone who had followed developments in Washington since the Truman Doctrine speech that a new campaign against domestic communists could be expected to accompany the new debate on foreign aid. When Congress had been considering Greco-Turkish aid, the Administration had released the report of a presidential commission on subversion in the federal bureaucracy and announced the loyalty program; when it had taken up Interim Aid, it had done so in the midst of a wide-ranging Administration offensive against subversion, effected through educational programs, patriotic rallies, an acceleration of loyalty investigations, and the issuance of the Attorney General's list. Now, in the first months of 1948, as the attention of the country was occupied by the climactic finale of the year-long debate on aid to Europe, a series of aggressive initiatives by the Justice Department once again reminded the American people of the peril to their internal security represented by the international communist movement.

On January 17 newspapers reported that Alexander Bittleman, a prominent official of the American Communist Party, had been arrested on a deportation warrant. An immigrant to the United States from Russia in 1912, Bittleman had joined the American Communist Party upon its founding in 1919, and in ensuing years had become a Communist leader of national reputation, achieving a position on the Party's national committee. Reports of the arrest indicated that action had been taken on specific order from Attorney General Clark acting under the Immigration Act of October 16, 1918, which empowered him to deport "aliens who believe in, advise, advocate, or teach, or who are members of or affiliated with any organization, association, society, or group, that believes in, advises, advocates, or teaches: (1) the overthrow by force or violence of the government of the United States. : . ." The sudden arrest for deportation of a man who had been a resident of the United States for thirty-six years and an avowed Party member for twenty-nine years on the basis of a thirty-year-old law caused some surprise, and the newspaper reports reflected puzzlement over the meaning of the Attorney General's action.[1]

It quickly became clear that Bittleman's arrest was part of a pattern. Less than a week later it was reported that Claudia Jones, an immigrant black writer, secretary of the National Women's Commission of the Communist Party, a prominent figure in the Young Communist League, and a member of the International Committee of the Communist Party, had been arrested by immigration officials on charges similar to those against Bittleman. On February 2 the Justice Department arrested Gerhart Eisler, another immigrant and lately a colorful witness before the House Un-American Activities Committee, on charges of subversion and passport fraud. Eight days later newspapers announced the arrest of John R. Williamson, National Secretary of the Communist Party. The charges against Williamson involved illegal advocacy and making false statements to officials about his birthplace when he emigrated to this country. Six days later Ferdinand C. Smith was arrested. A black immigrant from Jamaica, Secretary of the National Maritime Union, and a member of the National Committee of the Communist Party, Smith was charged with subversive activity and illegal entry. Two days later Mrs. Beatrice Johnson was arrested on a deportation warrant. Also an immigrant, she had been the promotion manager of the *New Masses* and a long-time Party secretary in New York and Chicago. Two days after Mrs. Johnson's arrest, immigration officials announced that Charles Doyle, an immigrant C.I.O. leader, had been taken into custody. Irving Potash, Manager of the Fur and Leather Workers Union, an immigrant and a member of the Central Committee of the Communist Party, was arrested for deportation on order from Attorney General Clark on March 1. It was reported on March 6 that the Justice Department was investigating Harry Bridges, an Australian, and regional director of the C.I.O. on the West Coast, for a possible deportation action. On March 18 Immigration officials arrested eight West Coast aliens for deportation. They were accused of being members of subversive organizations.[2]

These arrests were evidently part of the deportation drive against communist aliens that had been under way since 1946. Nevertheless, the sudden appearance on the front pages of the nation's papers of articles describing deportation actions against major communist figures was a surprising development to most people. Hitherto the Justice Department had not portrayed its deportation activities as directed against communists, and in fact had avoided publicizing its efforts in this area. Now it not only announced that the arrests were part of an anti-communist campaign and openly sought to publicize them, but its method of handling the arrests seemed governed at least as much by a desire to foster public concern over internal security as to execute substantive penalties against specific individuals. The distribution of the arrests at regular intervals over a two-month period, for example, made sense only from a theatrical point of view. Insofar as the complaints against those arrested derived from their connections with the Communist Party (part or all of the charges in every case), the Justice Department had been aware of their activities for years and could have made the arrests at any time. It is more difficult to pinpoint the dates on which the Justice Department became aware that it could bring actions against several of these aliens for passport fraud or illegal entry, but in at least one of the cases, that of Gerhart Eisler, the F.B.I. was fully aware of the relevant incidents by October 1946 and had recommended deportation at that time. The dramatic timing of the arrests seems to have been deliberate and unrelated to the discovery of bases for deportation. In this context the fact that several well-known individuals were arrested in a cluster also suggests a desire by the Justice Department to achieve maximum public effect.[3]

In at least five of the cases, moreover, the arrests amounted to little more than a publicity stunt, for there was no likelihood that deportation actually could or would be effected. Two previous attempts to deport Harry Bridges had failed for lack of evidence of proscribed activity. Bittleman, Johnson, and Potash were all arrested on the sole ground that their membership in the Communist Party in itself exposed them to penalties under laws prohibiting advocacy by aliens of violent revolution. The American Communist Party, of course, did not admit that it advocated violent revolution, and (before 1950) the Justice Department, as Attorney General Clark consistently observed in his elucidations of the futility of the Smith Act, had never persuaded the courts otherwise. Also, because these three cases involved deportations to countries in the Soviet sphere of influence, there was little chance that expulsion could be accomplished even if the courts permitted it; experience had shown that Iron Curtain countries would refuse to receive individuals deported from the United States, and American law held agreement with the receiving country a prerequisite for deportation—a point Clark freely admitted and frequently complained of. While it thus seems clear that deportation was impossible in at least four of the cases, in the instance of Gerhart Eisler it seems unlikely that the Justice Department actually wanted to accomplish expulsion. Eisler's attorney pointed out that Eisler had been trying to get out of the country for years and only a year previously had been arrested for attempting to do so. Clearly this dramatic series of arrests cannot be understood as a simple effort to rid the country of objectionable aliens.[4]

The beginning of a more satisfying explanation appears to lie in the system of political forces that had developed around the campaign for foreign aid. It was obvious to the Administration that the climactic debate on the Marshall Plan would be the occasion for new charges by Congressional Republicans of executive laxity in the field of internal security. This had occurred during every Congressional debate on foreign aid since the Truman Doctrine. Such charges were voiced on schedule, most passionately by Richard Nixon, a young Congressman from California anxious to use his seat on the Un-American Activities Committee to launch a campaign for the Senate. The deportation drive provided the Administration with the defenses it required. Responding to Nixon's charges in an address in Los Angeles in early March, Attorney General Clark was able to point to the recent arrests as evidence that he was working actively against subversion in the United States. But the deportation drive, like the actions against domestic communists during previous debates on foreign aid, had an offensive as well as a defensive aspect. The arrests of Eisler, Smith, and Williamson silenced voices that were actively working against the Administration's foreign policies. At the same time, they contributed to the development of yet another upsurge of popular concern over the internal communist menace that supported the anti-communist appeal of the campaign for E.R.P. It is probably not too much to say that the arrests played a major role in preparing the country psychologically for the war scare of 1948. The arrests also appear to have been an extension of a Justice Department practice of using moments of public concern over communism to press for new authority in the field of internal security. It will be recalled that Clark had attempted to use the popular agitation caused by the Canadian spy disclosures in 1946 to promote the loyalty program, and Hoover had attempted to capitalize on concern over internal security during debate on Greco-Turkish aid to expand his influence over loyalty investigations. In the midst of the popular agitation fostered by the debate on E.R.P. and the alien arrests, Clark submitted to Congress several of the legislative ideas that his staff had developed during 1947. Among these was a proposal that the Attorney General be empowered to detain alien subversives indefinitely without bail until arrangements for deportation could be completed.[5]

While the deportation drive thus reflected several of the same political forces that had surfaced during previous debates on foreign aid, the Administration's use of this issue in early 1948 was unique in its explicit and public combination with the President's campaign for nomination and election. This campaign was going badly at the beginning of 1948. One of the major problems was Henry Wallace: having declared his readiness to lead a third-party movement built around the Progressive Citizen's Association in December 1947, Wallace was campaigning vigorously in early 1948, and his efforts seemed to be having an effect. In February Senator Glen Taylor, one of the Administration's most outspoken critics on foreign policy, announced his decision to join the Wallace ticket as the candidate for the vice-presidency. Simultaneously, the Independent Progressive Party of California achieved a dramatic success in a petition campaign to place the new party and Henry Wallace on the primary ballot in California. Most importantly, in a contest widely regarded as a test of Wallace's strength, a Progressive candidate decisively won a special Congressional election for a traditionally Democratic seat in New York City, despite active campaigning for the Democratic candidate by Mayor O'Dwyer and Eleanor Roosevelt. In combination these developments appeared to indicate substantial strength for Wallace. The press responded by granting him more extensive and serious coverage. The apparent effectiveness of the Wallace campaign had not been expected by the President's political advisers, and began to be a source of serious concern to them.

There were several other signs of the President's political

vulnerability. Southern Democrats, enraged by Truman's civil rights message in early February, were well on the way to forming the Dixiecrat Party that would ultimately split the Democrats on the right and threaten the sweep in the South that Clifford's election strategy had assumed. The Administration's confused handling of the Palestine issue was jeopardizing its support within the Jewish community. Both liberals and labor continued to feel and express alienation from the Administration for a whole list of reasons, and stories of corruption and influence-peddling within the President's circle of advisers damaged his standing with the general electorate. In these circumstances the President's chances for nomination, not to mention election, began to look doubtful. Public opinion polls showed his popularity at a low point and indicated that he would be defeated by Dewey, Stassen, Vandenberg, or MacArthur. Spokesmen for almost every branch of the Democratic Party began to suggest or demand that he step down. A "Draft Eisenhower" movement was launched; it would continue to the eve of the convention.[6]

Since at least November 1947, when Clifford completed his memo on the politics of 1948, the men around the President had seen the anti-communist issue as eminently serviceable in the President's efforts for nomination and election. It was believed that the President could retain the support of urban Catholic voters by emphasizing this issue, and could neutralize Henry Wallace by publicly linking him with the communists. In the political straits in which the President found himself in early 1948, he and his advisers moved to apply this strategy. On February 23 Democratic National Chairman Howard McGrath attacked Wallace for accepting the support of the communists. In one of his speeches of March 17, at the height of the war scare, the President twice rejected the support of "Henry Wallace and his Communists," calling an alliance with the enemies of American security too high a price to pay for election. He repeated the charge that Wallace was an ally of the communists on March 29. The Communist press interpreted the deportation drive completely within the context of this attack on Wallace, an understandable viewpoint inasmuch as the arrests simultaneously crippled a national organization actively working for Wallace and branded as criminal an important part of that organization's leadership. The arrest of Ferdinand Smith the day after he shared a speakers' platform with Wallace seemed a clear effort to associate Wallace with subversive activity.[7]

One of the most interesting examples of the relationship between the President's political efforts and his use of the anti-communist issue involved his attempts to secure the support of organized labor. Clifford considered such support indispensable to the President in 1948, yet labor had been deeply divided in its attitudes toward the Truman administration and its foreign policies. The leadership of the C.I.O. had regarded Truman with suspicion at the beginning of his presidency, had objected strongly to his handling of the wave of strikes in 1946, and had formed an important part of the early resistance to the policy of "firmness" with the Soviet Union. C.I.O. President Philip Murray had been a vigorous critic of the President's loyalty order. Without doubt the major factor shaping the C.I.O.'s positions on these issues was the widely held view that Truman was deserting the liberal, pro-labor policies followed by his predecessor. A secondary but nevertheless significant influence on the C.I.O.'s attitudes came from the communists, who dominated several major industrial unions and held significant power in the national organization. It is a measure of the limiting influence of politics upon the Administration's concern with domestic communism that in 1946 and 1947 neither the President nor the Attorney General attempted publicly to relate communist influence in the C.I.O. to the President's difficulties in winning labor support for his policies. Indeed, the Administration had demonstrated notable sensitivity to the feelings of labor with respect to the issue of communism. When President Truman, in his anger at the threatened railroad strike in 1946, wrote a draft statement condemning communist influences in labor, the speech was discreetly shelved under the gentle prodding of Clifford. When the Attorney General's list was issued in December 1947, it contained not a single labor union or organization.[8]

Even without official condemnation of communist influence in the labor movement, the position of the communists
within the C.I.O. was increasingly compromised during 1946
and 1947 as developing Cold War tensions exposed latent conflicts between liberals and communists. The national leadership moved steadily in an anti-communist direction and into
accord with the Administration's policies; Truman helped this
tendency by vetoing the Taft-Hartley Act and casting the
Marshall Plan in a form that seemed conciliatory to the Soviets.
By October 1947 the national convention of the C.I.O. was
ready to invite Secretary Marshall to address it, to greet him
warmly, and to pass a resolution generally supporting his ideas
on aid to Europe, though the communists retained sufficient
strength to prevent an explicit endorsement of the Marshall Plan.
In the months following the convention, the Communist Party
and communist leaders and sympathizers within the C.I.O. decided to throw their weight against the Marshall Plan and behind a third-party candidacy for Henry Wallace. The stage was
set for an open conflict between these leaders and the national
leadership of the C.I.O. in January 1948 when the National Executive Committee of the labor organization passed resolutions
supporting E.R.P. and opposing Wallace's candidacy. Several
left-wing unions indicated they would not support the national
leadership on either point. Divergence by individual unions
from national policy was not uncommon in the C.I.O., but in
early March the national leadership took the unusual step of insisting that all member unions accept its position on these two
issues or face disciplinary action. Wallace and E.R.P. became
the battlefields on which the internal war between the communists and anti-communists in the labor movement was to be
fought.[9]

It was at this point that the Administration first moved
against union officials it considered communists, and its tar-
gets tended to be the same men who were defying the
national leadership of the C.I.O. Two of those arrested in the
deportation drive of early 1948 were among the small group
of labor leaders responsible for the decision to support Wallace and oppose E.R.P. These were John Williamson, labor

secretary of the Communist Party and the central figure in most accounts of this decision, and Irving Potash, a high official of the Fur and Leather Workers Union and one of the major union leaders to support the dissident move. The appearance of Justice Department officials in San Francisco to consider deportation proceedings against Harry Bridges occurred immediately following his refusal to support the national leadership of the C.I.O. on Wallace and E.R.P. At a minimum, the Administration's actions showed its readiness to attack labor leaders who were opposing both its politics and policies as soon as they had been flushed from the protective shelter of the C.I.O.'s national organization. But the arrests also seemed an attempt to reconstruct the badly damaged alliance between the Democratic administration and the leadership of the C.I.O. that was so important to the President's ambitions. The arrests of several prominent labor leaders who were opposing the policies of the C.I.O. leadership were clear warnings to other union leaders contemplating support of Wallace or opposition to E.R.P. and thus boosted the efforts of the C.I.O.'s National Executive Committee to consolidate the entire organization behind itself. It was being rumored in early 1948 that C.I.O. president Murray was supporting the movement to deny Truman the Democratic nomination. The President's advisers may well have reasoned that by throwing the muscle of the federal government behind Murray in his struggles within the C.I.O., an important step would have been taken toward winning his support for the President's own political efforts.[10]

There is no inconsistency in seeing the deportation drive of early 1948 in relation to both the campaign for the European Recovery Program and the President's campaign for nomination and election. The "neutralization" of Henry Wallace not only weakened the appeal of one of the President's political opponents, but undermined the effectiveness of those who were resisting Cold War foreign policy. By emphasizing the association of Wallace with the communists, whose support Wallace refused to renounce, the implication was made— as Wallace with justice charged in response to the President's

speech of March 17—that only communists supported his
criticism of the Administration's foreign policies. This implication was strongly reinforced by the repeated conjunction of
attacks upon domestic communists with debates on foreign
aid. And such tactics were inevitably generating a public atmosphere in which not only government employees, aliens,
members of dissident organizations, but also individuals in the
general population, were made to feel that public opposition
to the Administration's policies would cause them to be
branded as communists, with all that this was coming to
mean socially and economically. As early as October 1947, a
report in *The New York Times* by William S. White on public
attitudes toward E.R.P. indicated that considerable latent hostility toward foreign aid was being repressed by people fearful
of being considered pro-communist. Now, in the context of a
direct attempt to associate the major national spokesman for
the opposition to E.R.P. with the communists, this fear was inevitably strengthened. These developments prompted Senator
Taylor to tell the Senate of an anti-Administration rally at
which F.B.I. operatives had conspicuously recorded the names
of all present. Taylor commented:

> I think it is getting so that thousands upon thousands
> of loyal Americans are afraid to express any opin-
> ion at variance with the line laid down by the bi-
> partisan moguls for fear of being called red or sub-
> versive.

Taylor's opposition to the Administration's policies makes him
a tainted witness, but the *Washington Post*—whose strong support of the Administration's efforts to promote E.R.P. rendered
its editors reluctant to criticize that campaign directly—took
note of the same mood in commenting upon the reaction of
the White House to criticism of the loyalty program by an
Assistant Secretary of the Interior. "One would think, judging
from the indignation this letter has evoked," the *Post* wrote,
"that criticism of an executive order is tantamount to treason.
. . . This is a very dangerous idea—the idea that dissent is

equivalent to disloyalty." Perhaps the most interesting indication of the political atmosphere that was developing in the United States was a comment by Charles Bohlen, the State Department official directly responsible for the public campaign for E.R.P. and a man who undoubtedly felt great personal responsibility for what was happening. In a remarkable aside inserted in an address on the aims of American foreign policy, Bohlen stated:

> I think is it worthwhile to digress briefly to point out that when we use the term Communism, we need to know just what we mean. . . . Any loose definition of Communism which would embrace progressive or even radical thought of native origin is not only misleading but actually dangerous to the foundations of democratic society. Confusion on this issue and suspicion which can be sown between Americans of different political views but of equally sincere patriotism would be of great advantage to the Communist purpose.[11]

Bohlen's critique of the attempt to associate dissent (note his interesting use of the term "progressive") with communism was, of course, an attempt to quiet the wind by whispering against it, and the political demise of Henry Wallace in 1948 provided a clear indication of the extent to which the association Bohlen feared was taking hold in the United States. In January 1948, before the successes of the Progressives in February and March, a New York *World Telegram* poll showed Wallace getting 7 per cent of the vote in a national election. Following the Administration's efforts to link Wallace with the communists, his popularity showed a steady decline. By June his support had dropped to 6 per cent, by August 5 per cent, and by October 4 per cent. Observers of the campaign agree that it was the association of Wallace with the communists, in the context of the coup in Czechoslovakia and, later, the Berlin blockade, that was responsible for his steady loss of public following. And what happened to the Wallace movement is only partly suggested by public opinion polls:

as the link between Wallace and the communists became established in the popular mind, Wallace and his followers found themselves increasingly subject to every kind of harassment. It became difficult for Wallace to obtain meeting places, and those who made themselves his lieutenants or advocates frequently became the objects of pressure from their employers. The first violent attacks upon those attending a Wallace rally came in April. They continued throughout the campaign.[12]

The primary casualty of this "neutralization" of the Wallace movement was not the Progressive Party or Wallace himself but open public debate about American foreign policy. There are many complaints one might make about Wallace as a spokesman for an alternative to Cold War foreign policy, not the least of which was his failure to understand that the Hullian commercial policies he advocated had been one of the major causes of tension between the American and Soviet governments. And it was true that the Wallace movement depended heavily upon the American Communist Party for its organizational muscle, and Wallace did seem unwilling to face squarely the issues posed by the loyalty of the communists to the Soviet government. But despite all this, Wallace—and Wallace alone among major national figures—did raise questions about American policy, about the official portrayal of the Soviet Union as the aggressive and expansionist force that was causing all the world's troubles, and about the economic motives behind American policies, questions that contained a large part of the truth and bear up at least as well as the official rhetoric of the Administration under the reexamining eye of history. These issues merited full public discussion in 1947–8 by the most responsible and articulate men the country could produce. That, in place of this debate, Wallace's arguments were submerged in a rhetoric of anti-communism and official innuendo about his loyalties, his followers made the subject of harassment and even violence, and members of the general public forced to brave accusations of disloyalty and pro-communism if they listened to the tendency of his thought, deprived the American people of the full public hearing on momentous issues to which they were entitled. More than any other feature of the year-long debate on the foreign aid program, the attack on Wallace symbolized the nature of the methods by which the Administration consolidated public support behind Cold War foreign policy.

Denunciations of Wallace were only part of the Administration's broad campaign against domestic subversion that was an integral part of the overall effort to mobilize support for foreign aid. By March 1948, with the end of the debate on E.R.P., it was possible to develop a sense of the significance of this campaign in the year following the Truman Doctrine speech. Attacks on domestic communism had helped the effort to mobilize support for E.R.P. by strengthening the anti-communist appeal of the Administration's campaign for that program, reinforcing the tactics of crisis politics repeatedly employed in debates on foreign aid, attacking directly opponents of American foreign policies, intimidating potential opponents, and building an association in the popular mind between opposition to communism and support for E.R.P. At the same time, the campaign against subversion had prevented the Republicans from exploiting an issue on which they had scored the Democrats in 1946 and on which they were hoping to capitalize in 1948. Finally, this campaign helped consolidate the Democrats behind the President through its neutralization of Henry Wallace, support of the anti-communist elements in the labor movement, and appeal to Catholic constituencies. Thus, in the year following the Truman Doctrine speech, the attack upon domestic communism, which many believed to have been forced upon the Administration by Republican pressure, had been transformed into one of the most potent political weapons in the Administration's arsenal.

2. The Republicans Try to Recapture the Internal Security Issue

During the spring of 1948 Congressional Republicans made several attempts to regain the initiative in the field of internal security, held by the Administration since early 1947. These failed, but the Administration's use of the subversion issue during the debate on foreign aid helped ensure that it would be a major factor in American politics in 1948 and thereafter.

DESPITE THE USEFULNESS of the anti-communist issue to the Administration in 1947–8, it was by no means clear that in sponsoring such tactics the President was not storing up ills that would affect his political future. The problems of internal security and domestic communism were well established as Republican issues in American politics by reason of that party's long advocacy of stern corrective efforts with regard to them. In promoting public concern over these matters, the President was also inviting Republicans to attempt to turn the issue against his Administration, just as the rhetoric of the Truman Doctrine had invited the Republicans to insist upon an increased American effort in China. The Administration's early success in seizing the initiative on the issue of employee loyalty, and its assiduous efforts to cooperate with and out-flank the Republicans on this issue during the subsequent year, had prevented internal security from becoming an area of major partisan contention during the extended consideration of foreign aid. Nevertheless, partisan conflict over this issue had simmered at the fringes of political debate since the opening of the Eightieth Congress. In early 1948, at the start of an election year that the Republicans believed offered them their best chance to capture the presidency since 1928, and in the anti-communist heat generated by the debate on E.R.P. and the war scare of 1948, it was not possible that they would fail to reassert the traditional leadership in the battle against domestic subversion, which they believed to be one of their most appealing political images. Speaker Martin sounded the call to battle in his Lincoln's Birthday address:

> The New Deal Administration knew full well the intentions of the Kremlin. We Republicans warned of the march of communism for ten or twelve years. We told the nation the communists were sneaking into high government places. Now it is going to take a Republican administration to clear out the fifth columnists and traitors from the government structure. Those who insisted for years on keeping them there will never do the job.[13]

There were two ways in which Congressional Republicans could regain the initiative in the field of internal security. They could take advantage of their control of Congress to enact legislation more impressively anti-communist than the Administration's programs; they could also act upon their announced intention of exposing communist infiltration of the federal bureaucracy, a project that they had deferred in early 1947 owing to the Administration's convention of a federal grand jury to hear evidence on the subject. Both tactics were attempted during the debate on E.R.P.

As might be expected, the House Un-American Activities Committee led the way. Although H.U.A.C. had sponsored no legislation since its creation in 1938, there had been indications in 1947 that its members would attempt to draft a comprehensive set of statutes to cripple the communist movement in the United States. Committee members Mundt and Nixon had worked on anti-communist laws, and Mundt had offered a bill requiring communists to register as foreign agents. These were token gestures, however, and it was not until February 1948 that the committee initiated serious hearings regarding the legislative resources available for the battle against American communists.[14]

Attorney General Clark, H.U.A.C.'s first witness, offered a detailed statement of the legal and practical obstacles to drafting legislation that would effectively curb communist activities in the United States. If certain kinds of activities—such as advocacy of violent overthrow of the government—were proscribed, he stated, communist organizations could escape prosecution by altering their constitutions to comply with the new requirements. It would be extremely difficult to prove them guilty of activities or beliefs that they would be at pains not to endorse and would undoubtedly specifically repudiate, just as they denied any intention of attempting violent overthrow of the government in order to escape existing bans of such advocacy. If, on the other hand, the law specifically named communist organizations as proscribed, it would probably be struck down as being discriminatory, in violation of due process, and possibly a bill of attainder. Moreover, if some constitutional legislation could be drafted that would effectively require communists to acknowledge their subversive intentions, the net effect would be to force them underground, making their activities more difficult to observe. J. Edgar Hoover had opposed bills to outlaw the Communist Party on this practical ground. Although he did not say so explicitly, Clark's testimony strongly implied that he did not believe sweeping new legislation to curb the activities of American communists was desirable. He proposed a few amendments to existing laws and stated that the F.B.I. was making a maximum effort to contain the problem of subversion.[15]

Clark's ill-disguised aversion to efforts to proscribe communist organizations by law obviously offended H.U.A.C.'s own predilections, and Representative Nixon, who conducted the hearings at which Clark appeared, was at pains to extract from the Attorney General some kind of sanction for the committee's intention. He asked Clark if he did not agree that existing legislation was inadequate to deal with the communist problem. Clark implied assent by referring to the fact that he had proposed several legislative ideas himself. Nixon then wondered if the adoption of the Attorney General's proposals would fully curb communist activities. Clark acknowledged that probably they would not do so. Finally Nixon sought the Attorney General's opinion of the general principle of forced disclosure (requiring communist organizations to label them-

selves and their propaganda as communist) as a means of dealing with the problem. Clark replied that if one set aside the
problems of how forced disclosure might be achieved without
driving the Party underground or violating the constitution, he
endorsed the general principle of requiring communist organizations to admit their true nature.[16]

The numerous obstacles to anti-communist legislation
that Clark cited did not discourage H.U.A.C. On March 15, at
the height of the war scare, Representative Mundt introduced
the Communist Control Act of 1948, HR5852; when H.U.A.C.
reported the bill six weeks later it rested its argument for approval squarely upon the rhetoric of the President's foreign
policy:

> On March 17 the President asked the Congress to
> appropriate several billions of dollars to build
> American defenses against the world communist
> conspiracy of which the communist movement in
> the United States is a constituent element. . . . To
> resist communist aggression abroad and ignore it at
> home would be an utterly inconceivable pattern of
> procedure.

The proposed legislation began by defining the communist movement as dominated by a foreign power, determined to establish a communist dictatorship in the United
States, and constituting a clear and present danger to this
country; it then provided severe penalties for participation in
organizations and activities with the purposes it defined communist organizations as pursuing, and, finally, required organizations designated as communist by the Attorney General to
register with the Justice Department. Under the bill, organizations designated communist could register with the Justice
Department and accept the penalties that this admission would
bring upon them, or they could deny that the bill applied to
them and accept prosecution for non-compliance. Quite obviously, the bill did not differ significantly from simple pro-
scription of communist organizations, which Clark opposed
on both constitutional and practical grounds.[17]

House debate on HR5852 demonstrated the political power that the anti-communist issue was developing in the United States. Consider, for example, the manner in which Representative Nixon used Attorney General Clark's testimony before H.U.A.C. on February 5:

> The Attorney General of the United States . . . was asked specifically if he did not like the legislation before the Committee to present his own legislation. He did not do so but he did do this. . . . He did state that a registration statute applicable to such communist organizations would be of assistance to him in meeting this danger. That is one of the principal effects of this legislation. . . . The point I wish to drive home is this: the Attorney General . . . said legislation was necessary to meet the clear and present danger of communism to the United States. On the basis of [his] opinion, the Committee acted. We certainly did not think the Congress, in the face of the Attorney General's own statement that he did not have . . . the legislative power to control this menace, should sit idly by and do nothing. This is why this legislation is before the House today.[18]

It was a remarkable speech. How, in spite of Clark's presentation of a comprehensive list of desirable anti-communist measures, Nixon could assert that the Attorney General had offered no legislation is a mystery. How he could suggest that the Attorney General endorsed the legislation approved by H.U.A.C., indeed that H.U.A.C. was acting at the request of the Attorney General, in the face of Clark's clear statements of opposition to the kind of measure Nixon was presenting, is an even greater mystery. It is difficult to believe that the opponents of HR5852 did not ask Clark to correct Nixon's distorted use of his testimony, and this suggests the greatest mystery of all—Clark made no public comment on HR5852. Clark's silence is understandable only in terms of the political potency that anti-communism had acquired by early 1948. Indeed, this incident deserves attention only because it reveals the extent to which, at this time, a high Administration official with solid anti-communist credentials could be intimidated by the radical anti-communists in Congress. Indeed, Clark's submissive behavior during his interrogation by Nixon during the hearings, when the Congressman tendentiously maneuvered him to obtain an opening for H.U.A.C. action in an area where Clark clearly did not wish the Committee to intrude, was a remarkable illustration of the Administration's unwillingness to place itself in the position of opposing H.U.A.C.'s anti-communist efforts. President Truman, whose record makes it clear that he would have shared Clark's opposition to HR5852, shared also his unwillingness to oppose the measure in public. Asked at a press conference to comment upon the bill, the normally outspoken President remained silent, confining himself to a quotation from J. Edgar Hoover to the effect that it was not a good idea to outlaw the Communist Party. This incident also reveals the limited nature of the Administration's real concern about the Communist Party, for if it regarded the Party as a serious problem it surely would have opposed strenuously legislation that J. Edgar Hoover believed would make the effort to contain communism more difficult.[19]

If neither the President nor the Attorney General felt sufficiently secure politically to denounce a bill they strongly opposed because of the strength of anti-communist sentiment in the country, it was not possible to expect that many members of the House would do so. Indeed, during debate on HR5852, several Congressmen commented on the political difficulty of opposing this legislation, and in the end only fifty-eight Representatives were willing to do so. The bill passed with a bipartisan majority of three hundred and nineteen Representatives supporting it.[20]

If the Communist Control Act of 1948 had ever reached the Senate floor, it is hard to see how it could have been defeated in the atmosphere of an election year in which Congress had just agreed to spend billions of dollars to stop communism in Europe. A veto of this bill at this time in his political career would have earned the President more right to the respect of liberals than his veto of the Internal Security Act of 1950, which incorporated HR5852 and came in time of less political stress.

HR5852, however, was never reported by the Senate Judiciary Committee, which concluded that it was certainly unconstitutional, a result that Attorney General Clark helped promote by sending a letter to the Senate Committee in May specifying legal objections to the measure.[21] Thus was frustrated one significant effort by House Republicans to seize the internal security issue.

The most potent weapon available to House Republicans in their efforts to dramatize simultaneously the strength of their own opposition to communism and the weakness of the Administration's commitment on this issue was the investigation and exposure of what they considered to be the government's continued employment of subversive individuals. This was the issue that the Republicans had expected most hopefully to exploit after the 1946 elections, and the area in which the Administration felt most acutely the need of defending itself. First to raise this issue in 1948, not surprisingly, was House Appropriations Committee Chairman John Taber. Early in February, as the Senate Foreign Relations Committee was debating the role of the State Department in administering E.R.P., Taber informed the *Washington Times Herald* that his committee would soon publish a list of one hundred and eight undesirable State Department employees, some of whom were security risks for reasons of disloyalty. This list was made public on February 27, and less than two weeks later Taber reported that two employees had been fired as a result of his labors. During the second week of March the House Committee on Executive Expenditures held a hearing on Hamilton Robinson, State Department Security Officer, whose loyalty was questioned as a result of the fact that his second cousin was considered a potential security risk. Robinson resigned his position in the Department shortly thereafter.[22]

As predictable as Taber's initiative in first raising the subject of disloyal federal employees was the flamboyance with which the House Un-American Activities Committee involved itself in the issue. On March 1 H.U.A.C. issued a report denouncing Dr. Edward U. Condon, Director of the Bureau of Standards, as "one of the weakest links in American security." This report, which *The New York Times* greeted as a "masterpiece of unfair innuendo," was a collection of Condon's supposed improprieties, supported by distorted, inconclusive, and gossipy documentation. It was pointed out in the press that the report was little more than a warming over of accusations made against Condon by H.U.A.C. Chairman Thomas during 1947, charges that had been so insubstantial that no hearings had been held on them. The only impressive evidence published by the committee was a letter from F.B.I. Director Hoover to the Secretary of Commerce concerning a security investigation of Condon; it referred to Condon's suspicious associations with a Soviet agent. Two days after the committee issued its report, however, the *Washington Post* claimed to have proof that H.U.A.C. had not published Hoover's entire letter, that the committee had, in fact, omitted a final paragraph stating that there was no evidence of misconduct on Condon's part. Subsequently the *Post* reported that the committee also had doctored Hoover's letter to strengthen its case against Condon. In response to H.U.A.C.'s accusations, Condon requested a hearing. Although a date for such a hearing was set by Chairman Thomas, again, as in 1947, the committee failed to follow through. No hearing was held.[23]

Through the entire Condon episode, the House committee, not noted for its strict evidentiary requirements in making charges, provided no reason to believe that its statements were based upon any substantial information. Why the committee placed itself in a position of making accusations it could not support in order to revive a spent controversy has never been conclusively explained. The most reasonable theory is that it was being true to its tradition of doing something spectacular shortly before House consideration of its budget request, scheduled to take place only a week after H.U.A.C. issued its report on Condon.[24] The significance of the "Condon case," however, lies not in the behavior of the House committee, which was only demonstrating yet again its well-proven recklessness, but in the responses to it of the country's leading politicians: the incident demonstrated more clearly than debate on HR5852 the determination of the Republican Party to exploit the internal

security issue and the basic inability of the Democrats to provide effective opposition to their efforts.

The Condon incident was fraught with political implications. Condon had been appointed by Henry Wallace during
the latter's tenure as Secretary of Commerce; H.U.A.C.'s action
in questioning his loyalty placed Truman in the position of defending an official of his Administration who was associated
with a man he was attempting to associate with the communists. Unquestionably the case was well designed to embarrass the President, and it is possibly for this reason that
H.U.A.C. had the full support of the House Republican leadership in its conduct of the case. In May Republican National
Chairman Carroll Reece urged Congressional Republicans to
support H.U.A.C.'s efforts against Condon.[25] The political dimensions of the incident are therefore clear: whatever its
origins, the incident became a partisan effort by House Republicans to harass and embarrass the President. In this context
the response of House Democrats to the situation was particularly revealing.

The House had occasion to vote on two issues involving
H.U.A.C. in the midst of the furor over Condon. The first related
to H.U.A.C.'s budget request for 1949, which came before the
House on March 9, in the midst of the distressing developments in Czechoslovakia and Finland and six days after the
Post had discovered H.U.A.C.'s omission of a key passage from
the Hoover letter. The committee was asking for two hundred
thousand·dollars, twice the amount it had received for 1948
and more than ever had been granted a committee of the
House. H.U.A.C.'s detractors argued that the committee's behavior in the Condon case ought not be rewarded by doubling its
budget. Whatever other Representatives may have felt on the
merits of this question, not many of them were prepared to
vote against the House committee. The requested budget was
passed by an overwhelming bipartisan vote, 337–37, with 1 Republican and 2 American Labor Party Representatives joining
34 Democrats in opposition.[26]

Even more significant was House action on the issue of
access to confidential files that grew out of the Condon case.

In the wake of the *Post*'s claims that H.U.A.C. had published distorted information from Condon's file, the Committee asserted that it had in its possession only those portions of the Hoover letter published in its report, and requested Secretary of Commerce Harriman to settle the questions about the letter by making available to H.U.A.C. the F.B.I.'s file on Condon. Because F.B.I. files contained a potpourri of investigatory material —rumors, reports false and true, miscellaneous accusations that could be, in irresponsible hands, the cause of considerable unjustified political and personal damage to their subjects— the policy of the executive branch had traditionally been to consider them highly confidential documents. Citing this long-standing policy, Secretary Harriman refused to make Condon's file available to H.U.A.C. Committee Chairman Thomas announced that he was prepared for a showdown and submitted to the House a resolution demanding that the President make Condon's file available, thus raising an issue of unlimited implications in terms of the politics of internal security. If H.U.A.C. could demand and receive access to confidential files concerning security investigations of Administration officials, what havoc it could play with the issue of employee loyalty! And there was no reason to doubt—indeed, there was every reason to assume—that H.U.A.C., as the leader of the Republican drive in the field of internal security, would exploit such a precedent to the fullest during the 1948 presidential campaign. Despite these obvious ramifications, the House endorsed H.U.A.C.'s demand for access to the files by an overwhelming bipartisan vote of 399–29, with 104 Democrats joining 196 Republicans in support of the resolution. This vote, together with the vote on H.U.A.C.'s budget, made unmistakably clear the irresistible political power that the internal security issue had assumed by the spring of 1948. With an example of H.U.A.C.'s irresponsibility and partisanship clearly before them, enormous majorities of both parties had voted to double that committee's resources and provide it with access to confidential and explosive information about the Democratic administration. When the issue of Congressional access to confidential information was raised in a second resolution proposed by the House Executive

Expenditures Committee in May, House Democrats, not intimidated by the political consequences of voting against a committee associated with opposition to communism, united in opposition to the measure.[27]

The significance of all this was not lost on President Truman. In the midst of the Condon episode he decided that the time had come to put an end to bipartisan exploitation of the internal security issue, and specifically to the practice of cooperation between his Administration and H.U.A.C. which had obtained since early 1947. As soon as H.U.A.C. made its initial request for access to the Condon file, the President issued a broad directive stating that "any subpoena, or demand, or request for information [concerning F.B.I. loyalty investigations] . . . shall be respectfully declined . . . and shall be referred to the office of the President for such response as the President shall determine to be in the public interest." Attorney General Clark, the architect of the Administration's policy of cooperation with H.U.A.C. in the field of internal security, now dropped the conciliatory tone he had consistently taken toward the committee and publicly accused it of stealing the Hoover letter from Commerce Department files. When H.U.A.C. responded to all this by winning House approval of the resolution demanding that the President open Condon's file, Truman promptly announced his intention to defy the order. After this, the Condon incident petered out. Speaker Martin demonstrated his commitment to the cause by threatening to sponsor a joint resolution insisting that the file be opened, but his effort failed for lack of Senate cooperation.[28]

The Condon incident, like the proposed Communist Control Act of 1948, had little practical result, but together these incidents indicated an important shift of initiative from the Administration to Congressional Republicans in the field of internal security. From early 1947 to early 1948 Congressional Republicans had been forced to accept the cooperation of the Administration with their efforts in this field, and to respond to various Administration actions and initiatives related to internal security. In these circumstances, their carping criticisms of the Administration did little to improve their political grip on

this issue. Driven by the Administration's tactics to demand increasingly stringent action against subversives in order to establish the superiority of their anti-communism, they had
now pushed the issue beyond the point at which the Administration, with the debate on foreign aid completed and Wallace
a diminishing problem, was prepared to match them. They had
defied the Administration by sponsoring legislation that would
effectively outlaw the Communist Party. Even more important, they had resumed the attack upon the Administration's
policies toward employee loyalty. The attack on Dr. Condon
had led to the first clear break between Congressional Republicans and the Administration on an issue of internal security.
In April H.U.A.C. intensified the now open conflict by issuing a
report accusing the Administration of "coddling" American
communists. All these efforts were, of course, inept thrusts,
which the Administration successfully parried, but the efforts
failed for lack of substance, not because the Administration
had political control of the internal security issue. Indeed, even
in failure these initiatives demonstrated conclusively the weakness and vulnerability of the Administration to Republican actions in this area. Both the House and broad public opinion
had shown that they would vote with H.U.A.C. if the Administration attempted to block one of its anti-communist
initiatives. Encouraged by this situation, Congressional Republicans were making clear that they were determined to reassert their traditional dominance in the field of internal security and would make a sustained effort to exploit the public
fear of communist subversion that the Administration's campaign for foreign aid had done so much to encourage. The debate on foreign aid thus ended with the immediate achievement of the Administration shadowed by indications that in
the field of internal security, no less than that of policy toward
China, the full price of success had yet to be reckoned.

VIII
The Legacy of the
Truman Doctrine

1. The Failure of the
Marshall Plan

The political intent of the Marshall Plan to create a Western bloc based upon an American-oriented commercial system was never realized. The cause of this failure was the refusal of the American Congress to reduce barriers to imports, thus preventing the development of balanced trade between Europe and the U.S. Beginning in 1950, the U.S. turned to an integrated, "Atlantic" military organization—N.A.T.O.— for the basis of Western political cohesion.

THE HISTORY of the European Recovery Program between 1948 and 1952, the four years originally projected for its existence, involved the gradual replacement of American economic assistance by military aid and a shift of articulated emphasis from economic and social objectives within a "European" framework to the defense and security of the "Atlantic Community." In retrospect it is possible to see the first indications of these changes as early as the beginning of 1948. At that time Britain, France, and the Benelux federation first suggested a Western defense organization and initiated negotiations with the United States that led, in 1949, to the establishment of both the North Atlantic Treaty Organization (N.A.T.O.) and a modest program of European rearmament financed by the United States. These initiatives, however, were intended not to replace E.R.P. but to support it, and did not imply any alteration of the assumption that economic aid should be the primary tool and economic recovery and reorganization the primary aims of American policy in Europe. N.A.T.O. was to provide an atmosphere of security in which economic recovery could proceed as planned; a basic principle of the rearmament program was that it should not interfere with the economic objectives of E.R.P. "None of us dreamed at that time," George Kennan has written, "that the constructive impulses of this enterprise [E.R.P.] . . . would be swallowed up in the space of two or three years by programs of military assistance." [1] Beginning in 1950, however, the United States assumed the leadership in pressing for greater efforts with respect to the defense and rearmament of western Europe, and persisted in this course at the expense of both economic recovery and economic integration in Europe, two of the major announced objectives of the European Recovery Program.

Obviously something critical to the conception of E.R.P. changed between 1947, when the program was put forward, and 1950, when it was replaced by rearmament. One consideration that had declined in significance during these years involved American exports. In 1947 there had been widespread fear that unless adequate levels of exports could be maintained, the American economy would suffer a serious postwar depression. This fear proved less than fully warranted, however, as it failed to take account of significant changes in the structure of the American economy since 1930. The fear of a postwar depression largely disappeared after the mild recession of 1949, from which the foreign aid program, along with other federal spending programs and monetary devices, helped extricate the economy. By August 1949 the United States had begun a new period of expansion, and, particularly after the outbreak of war in Korea, inflation became a far more important concern than exports for Administration economists.[2]

There were also significant changes in the realm of international politics between 1948 and 1950. Soviet actions in Czechoslovakia and Berlin in 1948–9, whatever they may have meant in fact, impressed many observers in the West with the aggressive character of Soviet policy and provided an initial impetus for a strengthening of Western defenses. The Soviet explosion of an atomic bomb in September 1949 eliminated the American monopoly on atomic energy and with it the deterrent upon which American military policy had relied since the war. The collapse of Nationalist China shifted the balance of power, it seemed, in favor of the Soviets. An analysis of Western defense requirements undertaken by the State and Defense Departments following these latter two developments produced a document, modestly titled NSC–68, calling for massive rearmament of both the United States and western Europe and a quadrupling of the annual American defense budget. Finally, the North Korean attack across the 38th parallel in June 1950 seemed to indicate that the Soviet government was prepared to sponsor military action against areas beyond the line of authority established by its armies during World War II. It also provided the Administration with a political opportunity to ask Congress to approve the rearmament program previously outlined in NSC–68.[3] These developments, particularly the Soviet explosion of an atomic bomb, must be credited with explaining much of the increased emphasis upon Western rearmament beginning in 1950.

There is, however, much about the rearmament program that these developments do not explain. Why, for example, did the United States press for the organization of rearmament on an Atlantic basis, with direct American participation and leadership, rather than—following the model of E.R.P.— on a European basis with American support? Moreover, why did the United States urge the governments of Europe—which were, after all, responsible for the areas endangered by the presumed Soviet threat—to undertake levels of defense expenditure and integrated defense planning significantly greater and more elaborate than what the Europeans themselves felt the situation required, and push this effort to a point that the Europeans eventually rejected large amounts of aid offered by the U.S. to support its defensive plan?[4] The answers to these questions must be found in the relationship between the rearmament program and the broad political policy of the United States with respect to western Europe.

That policy had remained essentially unchanged after 1946, at which time the United States committed itself to organizing a Western bloc of non-communist states under American leadership. A restatement of this policy provided the basic framework of NSC–68. This paper, like Clifford's 1946 memo, saw the world as divided into American and Soviet spheres of influence between which an extended period of tension was to be anticipated, though war was not inevitable. The purpose of Soviet policy—also seen in terms similar to those employed by Clifford in 1946—was described as the extension of Soviet power through the acquisition of new satellites and the weakening of competing systems of power. The appropriate response to this challenge was to construct an opposing and, apparently, equally unified system of power in the West with "the U.S. as its political and material center with other free nations in variable orbits around it." Dean Acheson, the American Secretary of State and one of the architects of NSC–68, accepted the challenge it contained as the guiding purpose of his diplomacy; as an ardent champion of the view that America's most significant interests lay in Europe, he bent his efforts unwaveringly to the organization of the Atlantic community behind American leadership. As a public advocate of the doctrine of NSC–68, Acheson's message was always the same: the United States must create "situations of strength" in the non-communist world; it must promote "strength and unity" in the West; it must "maintain as spacious an environment as possible in which free states might exist and flourish." [5]

This policy, it must be noted, was at least as political as it was military. The construction of an effective defensive system was important, but greater emphasis—in NSC–68 and in the public statements of the Secretary of State—was consistently given to the broader issue of consolidating an American-oriented system of power. On this point the attitude of the Truman administration appears to have been consistent from 1949 to 1952. It originally supported N.A.T.O. not because it would contain an anticipated Soviet offensive—it was acknowledged that no such offensive was likely and that, should one come, the proposed defense arrangements would add little to Western ability to stop it—but because it would promote cohesion within Europe and between Europe and North America. Such cohesion, which inevitably involved American dominance of western Europe, was an essential part of the conception of the Western bloc, for "unity in Europe," Acheson told Congress in 1950, "requires the continuing assistance and support of the United States. Without it free Europe will fall apart." The relative weights attached by Acheson to developing a cohesive organization of the Atlantic community and developing a military defense against Soviet attack was suggested by his response to the defensive arrangements approved at the Lisbon meeting of the N.A.T.O. ministers in 1952. This was a critical meeting, the culmination of two years of American efforts to develop an acceptable basis for integrated Atlantic rearmament. But reviving Franco-German rivalries seemed to be threatening the whole program. The high costs of American defense proposals were causing the European governments to complain that economic recovery was being undermined. At Lisbon a special committee reported on the defense levels that could be attained consistent with the economic capabilities of Europe. Upon hearing the report, Omar Bradley, the American Chief of Staff, insisted that it did not provide for forces adequate to defend Europe against a Soviet attack. The proposals did represent, however, force levels that the N.A.T.O. ministers could and did accept, and Acheson, far from being dejected, was exultant. "We seemed to have broken through a long series of obstacles and to have finally started toward a more united and strengthened Europe and an integrated Atlantic defense system," he later wrote. "The world that lay before us shone with hope." The goal, quite clearly, had been to establish an American-oriented political organization in the West, not to provide protection against a Soviet military thrust.[6]

Although America's basic political policy toward Europe —the organization of the Western bloc or Atlantic community behind American leadership—remained unchanged from 1946 to 1952, the strategy for achieving it altered radically. Clifford's 1946 memo specifically stated that the primary tool for the development of the Western bloc should be economic aid. The assumption of American policy during 1946–8 was that American economic strength, translated into programs of financial aid, could be used to create an American-oriented economic and commercial system upon the basis of which a Western political bloc could be consolidated. During these years American economic power was consistently used to support political elements in Europe friendly to the United States, to undermine those that opposed American leadership, and to commit the countries of Europe to the multilateral commercial practices that would bind them into an American-oriented economic system. As the ineffectiveness of French efforts to promote an independent Europe "between east and west" in 1945–6 indicated, this strategy had been immensely successful. Yet NSC–68 proposed an entirely different method for organizing the Western bloc. What the situation now required, this document held, was "a bold and massive program of rebuilding the west's defensive potential." From 1950 onward, rearmament through N.A.T.O. rather than economic aid through E.R.P. was the mechanism for the organization of the Western bloc.

The issue therefore arises: outside of the positive, strategic considerations urging rearmament upon the United States, was there any compelling reason why the political strategy of economic aid should have been rejected in 1950? The prospect of diminishing American-aid payments after 1952, of course, promised to reduce American leverage on European politics, but this development had always been anticipated, and it had been hoped that, prior to this time, the Western bloc could be firmly established. A more fundamental point was that, despite the success of E.R.P. in rehabilitating the economies of western Europe, the program failed as an instrument for consolidating the Western bloc on a long-term basis. This failure was significantly related to the network of domestic political problems catalyzed by the foreign aid program and by the response of the Truman administration to them.

America's commercial program for the postwar world had always involved one consistently underemphasized contingency: multilateral commercial principles could not be adopted by European states unless the United States accepted significantly increased imports from Europe. There was both a political and an economic basis for this. The political point was that other trading nations were not likely to reduce barriers to American exports unless the United States made reciprocal reductions in its tariffs and quotas. The economic issue, equally important, stemmed from the fact that the main financial problem of European nations after the war was a shortage of dollars; it was to protect dollar reserves that restrictions on imports from America were imposed by the governments of Europe in 1946–7. Only through increased dollar earnings by European countries could this problem be overcome, and an increase in American imports was the most obvious way for this end to be attained. This point, and its relationship to the political goals of the United States, was fully understood by American officials. Acheson stressed it in his Delta Council speech of May 8, 1947, by stating that "we in the United States must take as large a volume of imports as we possibly can. . . . There can be no stability or security in the world for any of us until foreign countries are able to pay in commodities and services for what they need to import." Clayton made the point with equal clarity when he told the Congress that the success of the European Recovery Program depended upon the establishment of the International Trade Organization. The basic vehicle for modifying the American tariff was the Reciprocal Trade Agreements Program, and the members of the Truman administration were explicit about the importance of this legislation to their entire foreign policy. In supporting Reciprocal Trade, for example, Acheson argued that "the preservation and development of sound trading relationships with other countries of the free world is an essential and important element in the task of trying to build unity and strength in the free world." President Truman made the same case. "Unless world trade is increased," he argued in a statement advocating extension of the Trade Agreements

326 THE TRUMAN DOCTRINE AND MCCARTHYISM

Program, "the tremendous investment we are making towards world economic recovery will be largely wasted." [7]

The Truman administration never succeeded in mobilizing strong support for reducing American barriers to imports. Indeed, following the 1946 elections there were several indications that the Eightieth Congress would move American commercial policy in a protectionist direction and the Geneva negotiations on the G.A.T.T. were nearly broken up by Congressional approval of legislation providing for an increase in the American wool tariff. These developments had led the Administration to suppress the entire issue of commercial and import policy during the public campaign for E.R.P. and to place the burden of its advocacy of that program on an anti-communist appeal. During the hearings on E.R.P. in 1948 Congress had been assured by the Administration official in charge of Congressional liaison for the State Department that there was no relationship between E.R.P. and the Reciprocal Trade Agreements Program (see Chapter VI, p. 261). Here was a contradiction of major importance that the Administration would have to resolve if the long-term political and commercial strategy of which E.R.P. was a part was to succeed.

The issue of American import policies was joined very shortly after passage of the E.R.P. In June 1948, the Reciprocal Trade Agreements Program came before the Congress for mandatory reconsideration. The Administration proposed the customary three-year extension and drew attention to the program's importance in its total foreign policy. Congress, still Republican-controlled, brushed the Administration's bill aside, renewed the program for only one year, and added a number of crippling amendments. The most important of these required that the Tariff Commission, generally considered conservative on the issue of tariff reduction, establish with respect to each commodity a "peril point" beyond which tariff concessions would damage a domestic industry, and that the Administration publicly justify any tariff concession beyond this point. In practice, Administration officials were convinced, the findings of the Tariff Commission would establish the limit on which concessions could be granted, with the effect that American tariff negotiations would be limited by an inability to grant concessions that, by a conservative estimate, would cause any damage to a domestic producer. In testimony before Congress Clayton argued that the amended bill "will have the effect of practically scuttling the whole Reciprocal Trade Agreements Program," and he drew attention to the fact that the changes in the 1948 bill were being championed by men who had traditionally opposed the program. In a private appeal to Vandenberg, Clayton argued that "unless the Act is renewed without crippling amendments the United States will be unable to do its part in respect to one of the prime conditions of the E.R.P. legislation . . . the conditions requiring participating countries to cooperate to reduce barriers to trade among themselves and other countries." Such appeals, as we have seen, were of no use. "The 1948 act," according to Assistant Secretary of State for Economic Affairs Willard Thorp, "returns to the old protectionist theory that only the prosperity of an individual industry is affected by a tariff or quota and makes such narrow protectionism the sole criterion for determining the concessions that may be made by the United States." For an Administration that saw the Trade Agreements Program as a tool with which to achieve broad commercial and political objectives, Congressional passage of such a bill was a major defeat.[8]

In retrospect, it is possible to mark 1947 as the beginning of a steady erosion of executive authority to negotiate reductions in the American tariff and a steady increase in protectionist sentiment within the American Congress. This is true despite the fact that following the Democratic victory in the 1948 elections, the Truman administration, as one of its first legislative actions, succeeded in having the 1948 act replaced by a two-year extension of the former program. In practice, even under the new act, the Administration felt sufficiently constrained by the conservative atmosphere that existed with respect to tariff reduction that, between 1949 and 1951, it administered the Trade Agreements Program upon the principle, in Acheson's words, that "no American industry would knowingly be injured by the authority conferred by the

Trade Agreements Act." It is impossible to distinguish this policy from the "narrow protectionism" of which Thorp complained in responding to the 1948 act. Despite this conservative approach to tariff reduction and despite the fact that the Democrats retained control of the Congress after the 1950 elections, the 1951 extension of the act further restricted the Administration's authority to negotiate tariff reduction. It also contained a provision for including in tariff agreements an "escape clause" that the State Department considered inconsistent with the G.A.T.T., and made the general point that the renewal should "not be construed to determine or indicate the approval or disapproval of the Congress for the executive agreement known as the G.A.T.T." [9]

In agricultural policy, as in tariff policy, Congress manifested a tendency toward increasing conservatism and protectionism after 1948. The price-support program was not only renewed but broadened to cover almost all agricultural commodities, which meant that quantitative restrictions were soon being applied to most agricultural products. In 1951 Congress specifically repudiated the restraints concerning imports and controls on agricultural commodities that had been written into the G.A.T.T. [10]

Under these circumstances, the prospects for Congressional approval of the I.T.O. Charter, finally completed at Havana in the spring of 1948, could not be regarded optimistically. In fact, the Administration found itself caught between two schools of commercial thought when it presented the charter to the public and the Congress. The charter had been given advance billing by its champions in the American government as a document that would create vast new commercial opportunities for American business. American negotiators, however, had been unable to surrender many of the commercial restrictions that protected American business and also had been confronted with troubled economic conditions throughout the world. They had been constrained to accept in the charter numerous exceptions to multilateral principles on behalf of various other national interests. The charter finally approved at Havana was so full of limits on the application of multilateralism that domestic groups, particularly business organizations, that had traditionally supported the campaign for multilateralism would not endorse it. At the same time, the increasing power of the protectionists in Congress made the task of winning approval of the charter a much greater challenge than had been faced when the Bretton Woods proposals were submitted in 1944. The combination of these two factors —in the context of an international political situation that had decimated the spirit of internationalism that had rallied support for the U.N. and the Bretton Woods proposals—proved lethal, and despite Clayton's efforts the Administration was unable to mobilize effective Congressional support for the I.T.O. Perceiving the hopelessness of the situation in 1948, the Administration decided not to press the matter in the Eightieth Congress.

Support for commercial internationalism steadily diminished after 1948. In 1950, after the Senate Foreign Relations Committee had failed to hold hearings on the proposed charter, the Administration made a final decision not to seek its approval by Congress. The I.T.O. was thus stillborn, aborted by the same government that had conceived it. Here was a poignant symbol of the retreat of the United States from championship of the Wilsonian principles that had provided the thrust of its wartime program for the peace. Here also was a significant indication that the Administration could not win Congressional support for the critical aspect of the strategy of economic aid that required a liberalization of American import policies.[11]

The implications for the European Recovery Program of America's failure to apply multilateral principles to itself were not long in manifesting themselves. Despite the rapid success of the aid program in inducing the recovery of western Europe's productive capacity, unsatisfactory progress was made with respect to the problem of increasing the dollar earnings of western European economies. In 1949 European exports to both the United States and Latin America actually declined. In this context Britain suffered another economic crisis and in September 1949 was forced to devalue the pound by 30 per cent; in subsequent months almost all other Marshall Plan countries followed suit. While the recession in the United States was a contributing cause of these developments, analysts within the American government were beginning to conclude that more fundamental considerations would prevent European dollar earnings from increasing to a point at which their economies could achieve self-sufficiency. The Council of Economic Advisors first drew attention to this problem in July 1949. By the end of the year both it and other federal agencies came to the conclusion that the C.E.E.C. had asserted in 1948: the E.R.P. offered no prospect for the countries of Europe to balance their payments through exports to the U.S.[12]

A special commission of the Economic Cooperation Administration, the private corporation that was established to administer E.R.P., and the Department of Commerce, appointed in 1949 to analyze this problem, concluded that "the present critical lack of balance in world trade should be corrected primarily by stimulating an expansion of exports of goods and services from other countries to the United States" and that "realization of full import potentials will require the elimination or substantial lowering of existing barriers and other obstacles to the import trade." The E.C.A. itself reported to Congress in December 1949 that "the existence of high tariffs on many items and other restrictive barriers . . . may well make it impossible for Europe to attain the volume of exports necessary to maintain essential imports and bridge the dollar gap." A presidential commission appointed in early 1950 to investigate the same problem reached similar conclusions. Pointing out that "U.S. domestic and commercial policies must be regarded . . . as among the most important factors in determining the volume and character of world trade," the commission stressed the importance of policies that would expand American imports, including an "extension and strengthening" of the Reciprocal Trade Agreements Program, the development of "methods of protecting the price and income position of our farmers which can reduce the necessity and the pressure for import licensing, quotas and embargos," and ratification of the charter of the I.T.O. In the context of Congressional attitudes on these issues, the hopelessness of rehabilitating the economies of Europe on the basis of trade between Europe and the United States was apparent.[13]

Since the countries of Europe could not attain economic self-sufficiency through sales to the dollar area, it was necessary to take steps in other directions to achieve this result. Although several alternative solutions to this problem were put forward in 1949–50, the most significant for the purposes of this study was the attempt to create a "European Market." The basic idea was that western Europe was potentially an immense market capable of supporting a vital industrial economy if only existing barriers to intra-European trade could be eliminated. It was felt that these barriers protected inefficient producers, kept prices high and reduced the volume of trade. The E.C.A. became an aggressive champion of this solution to Europe's economic difficulties and, beginning in late 1949, began to press the countries of western Europe to take drastic steps to reduce obstacles to intra-European trade. At the urging of the E.C.A., the C.E.E.C. countries established, in 1950, a European Payments Union (E.P.U.) to assure that accounts in intra-European trade could be settled on a multilateral basis. At the same time, steps were taken to reduce restrictions on the free movement of goods and services among western European states.[14]

Although these steps seemed to offer at least a partial solution to the economic problems of western Europe, their clear implication of a turning away from participation in an American-oriented commercial system was hardly consistent with the purposes of American foreign economic policy. The movement toward liberalization of intra-European trade was accompanied by increasing discrimination against imports from the dollar area. The E.P.U. threatened to assume, on an exclusively European basis, the function that was to be played by the International Monetary Fund in the global commercial scheme of the United States. In 1947 the State Department had approved the idea of a European Customs Union as a transitional device between the postwar period and the incorporation of western Europe into a global multilateral system centering on the American economy. Now it appeared that this proposal was leading Europe in directions that would weaken the commercial bonds between Europe and the United States and make that area increasingly independent of American economic power. The increase in restrictions on dollar imports permitted the E.R.P. countries, during the fiscal year 1949–50, to build their monetary reserves, whose size the U.S. had always considered an indication of financial independence from the U.S. In short, under the prodding of the E.C.A., E.R.P. was being used to move Europe in economic directions with political implications directly contrary to those for which it had been established. Under these circumstances, a breach developed between the E.C.A. and the State Department, which widened as the latter agency progressively lost interest in the whole concept of liberalizing intra-European commercial arrangements.[15]

This was the status of the European Recovery Program at the time that the decision was made in Washington to shift the emphasis of American assistance from economic aid to the O.E.E.C., the permanent organization of C.E.E.C. countries established under E.R.P., to the development of an Atlantic defense system. The economic significance of this decision was that important elements of the industrial capacity of Europe were shifted away from producing goods for export and domestic consumption and into the production of armaments. The economic result was to reverse the movement toward liberalization of intra-European trade, recreate the dollar gap and extend the period of European dependency upon American assistance, and arrest progress toward the recovery of full economic health before several countries of Europe had achieved pre-war standards of living. On the other hand, given the close relationship of economic organization to defense arrangements, the emphasis on Atlantic rearmament offered the prospect of closer economic integration between Europe and the United States, which might achieve indirectly the American-centered economic and commercial system that E.R.P. had failed to achieve directly.

The institutional changes brought about by rearmament also tended to strengthen the position of the American government vis-à-vis its European counterparts. For example the O.E.E.C. (which, in fact, the U.S. had proposed to join in early 1950, though nothing came of this) was bypassed when the U.S., Britain, and France established a steering committee to deal with the critical economic problem of allocating scarce raw materials under the pressure of rearmament. Although a panic mission to Washington by the O.E.E.C. chairman won for that body a seat on the steering committee, it was clear that the European group was being downgraded and that the geographical context in which such problems were to be considered had been broadened. Also, the E.C.A., which was an independent agency and had taken the leadership in promoting the creation of a "European Market," was abolished and replaced by the Mutual Security Administration, which was under the direct control of the State and Defense Departments. In short, the result of rearmament was to arrest a number of tendencies toward European independence of the United States and to place American assistance to Europe within a framework structurally and administratively subordinate to the American government. Seeing this trend, European leaders began to manifest resentment of and resistance to American purposes. Nevertheless, the mission of NSC–68, to create a Western system of power with the U.S. "as its political and material center and other free nations in variable orbits around it," had been achieved.[16]

The decision to shift the emphasis of American policy toward Europe from economic aid to military aid occurred within the context of the recognized failure of the politico-commercial strategy that was an essential component of the E.R.P. This failure left the kind of rearmament program proposed by NSC–68 as the sole means for building the Atlantic political community to which U.S. policy was consistently committed after 1946. Because American import policies proved to be the weak point in the original strategy of the Marshall Plan, it is not too much to argue that the militarization of diplomatic relations between the U.S. and Europe in the 1950's was at least partially attributable to the Truman administration's failure to build solid political support for its commercial program and its related willingness to rely upon anti-communist propaganda techniques in promoting E.R.P.

2. MacArthur and McCarthy

The Truman administration tried in various ways to quiet the anti-communist emotions that had been aroused by the campaign for E.R.P. But a series of events, most importantly the Soviet atomic explosion, the conquest of China by the Communists, the exposure of Alger Hiss, and the outbreak of war in Korea, intervened to defeat such efforts. These events seemed to confirm the dangers of communism on which the campaign for foreign aid had been based, and Truman now watched helplessly as his political opponents took charge of the anti-communist issue and initiated the period of McCarthyism.

AT THE SAME TIME that the Administration's campaign for E.R.P. was failing to build political support for the commercial elements of the foreign aid program, it was contributing to the development of intense public concern over the issue upon which it had relied, the threat to American security of international communism. During the latter part of 1947 and early 1948 there had been numerous indications of extreme public agitation over this issue, ranging from the passage of anti-communist legislation by state and local governments to outbreaks of violence against communists. The situation was aggravated by the association of opposition to Cold War foreign policy with disloyalty and communism which had been encouraged by the Administration's campaign for E.R.P.: popular hostility toward communists broadened into a distrust of all dissent. Thus, those who supported the political attitudes of Henry Wallace became subject to harassments similar to those directed against members of the American Communist Party.

Numerous voices inside and outside the government warned the country and the Administration of the danger of the growing, wide-ranging, anti-communist emotionalism. The Administration, of course, had ample evidence of the power of this sentiment. It had used this mood effectively to mobilize support for foreign aid, and Republicans in Congress had used it to force the Executive into unwanted commitments to Nationalist China. The House Un-American Activities Committee was using it to advocate legislation that the Administration considered unwise and unconstitutional. The overwhelming support that H.U.A.C. received in the House and in the general population when it proposed legislation to outlaw the Communist Party and demanded access to confidential files on Administration officials were indications of the irresistible political force of the anti-communist issue, and of the Administration's inability to counter it. The latter incident had been so fraught with dangers to the executive branch as well as to Truman's political position that the President had openly defied the will of the House and brought to an abrupt end the cooperative relationship between his administration and H.U.A.C.

In the spring of 1948 the President indicated in various ways his appreciation of the fact that anti-communist sentiment in the country had reached excessive levels and needed to be damped down. He was reported to be surprised and somewhat frightened by the popular response to his speech of March 17 at the climax of debate on E.R.P., and when he sent his defense proposals to Congress the following month he issued no supporting statement in order to avoid further heightening of public agitation. In May he publicly stated, in a reference to the American Communist Party, that he did not believe "the splinter parties do any harm," a type of statement not characteristic of his Administration during the campaign for E.R.P. In a major political address in June he tried to shift the focus of public discussion of communism away from subversive conspiracies and enemy agents to the broader and less sinister issue of social injustice. "As far as the United States is concerned," he told an audience in Chicago, "the menace of communism is not the activities of a few foreign agents or the political activities of a few isolated individuals. The menace of communism lies primarily in the areas of American life where the promise of democracy remains unfulfilled." This was quite a different notion of the communist danger than had been suggested by the loyalty program, the deportation drive, and the Attorney General's list, and seemed very much akin to the ideas associated with the movement for security through education, and particularly the "Zeal for American Democracy" program. Thus, in various public actions and statements during the late spring of 1948, the President appeared anxious to reduce the emotional content of the communist issue and reestablish a sense of proportion in the attitudes of Americans toward this question.[17]

He was at the same time following the course dictated by his instinct for political survival in an election year in which he was given little chance for victory. The President knew that the anti-communist issue was one that could very easily be turned against him. His Republican opponents regarded it as their issue, and during the Eightieth Congress they had repeatedly attempted to exceed the Administration in anti-communist fervor on both international and domestic issues. The President had maintained a tenuous grip on the anti-communist issue only by appearing to apply the Truman Doctrine to Asia and pursuing the "foreign agents" and "isolated individuals" in the Communist Party with an ardor that left little room for the Republicans to urge more energetic initiatives. Even so, during the spring of 1948 Congressional Republicans had tried repeatedly to take the issue away from him and were prevented from doing so only by their failure to discover any serious or apparently serious flaws in the anti-communist programs of the Administration. Looking ahead, however, the President knew that the future would bring developments that would provide more potent ammunition for his opponents than they had had, for example, in the Condon case. Almost certainly, it would bring the defeat of Chiang Kai-shek by the Chinese Communists, a result that inevitably would elicit Republican charges of apostasy to the principles of the

Truman Doctrine. To the extent that the popular agitation over communism continued to grow, the public, retaining the illusions about China that Roosevelt had encouraged and Truman had done nothing to dispel, would be receptive to such charges. And during 1948 the position of the Nationalists was deteriorating rapidly; by October the Administration had given up all hope of preventing a Communist victory and in November the chief American military adviser in China reported the situation to be so hopeless that the American advisory team should be withdrawn lest it be caught in China at the moment of Communist victory.[18]

Another politically volatile issue that the Administration had yet to face was a Republican favorite, the penetration of the New Deal administration of Franklin Roosevelt by communists. Truman and Clark had prevented the public airing of the potentially damaging stories of Elizabeth Bentley and Whittaker Chambers in early 1947 only by convening a federal grand jury to investigate this subject. This stratagem had kept the issue suppressed during debate on E.R.P. and prevented embarrassment to the Administration while it campaigned for Cold War foreign policy. By the spring of 1948 the grand jury was concluding its deliberations and it would be difficult thereafter to keep the stories of Bentley and Chambers from coming to the surface. The Truman administration made a bold effort to solve this problem in June 1948 by quietly altering the nature of the grand jury investigation. The issues of espionage and official subversion were dropped, and in a few quick sessions the Justice Department presented evidence that the American Communist Party advocated violent overthrow of the government. In July the grand jury indicted the leaders of the Communist Party for violations of the Smith Act and adjourned without issuing a single statement about the problem of communism in government. While the grand jury's failure to indict any former or incumbent federal officials for espionage or communist activities may well have reflected the weakness of the evidence presented to it by Bentley, Chambers, and the Justice Department, poor evidence cannot explain its failure even to issue a report on the questions about com-

munist activities considered during twelve months of proceedings. That such a report would have contained information
and allegations embarrassing to the Administration in an election year is obvious, and the total suppression of this subject,
combined with the shift to the Smith Act indictments, is
probably best understood as a political maneuver by the
Truman administration. These moves seemed designed to extricate the Administration from the grand jury without damaging its anti-communist credentials, to outflank Republicans who
were criticizing the Administration's failure to take the communists to court, and to bury in a burst of new anti-communist
activity the whole issue of official subversion. Such a reconstruction of events is, of course, speculative, but Clark's statement to H.U.A.C. in February 1948 that he doubted the
communists could be successfully prosecuted under existing
anti-subversion statutes supports the theory that the Smith Act
prosecutions were viewed by the Administration mainly as a
political device. This view is reinforced by a series of newspaper stories during these spring months indicating that the
White House was pressuring the F.B.I. not to proceed with
investigations of official subversion.

If the President hoped to dispose of the issue of communist penetration of government through the Smith Act
indictments, his strategy did not work, for word was leaked
to H.U.A.C. that the grand jury had suppressed some interesting
information, and in August the committee convened the famous hearings on communist espionage that permitted
Chambers and Bentley to tell the world about Alger Hiss,
Harry Dexter White, and others. The President, in mid-
campaign, was suddenly confronted with an apparently substantial case of Democratic laxity in the field of internal
security. He responded by calling the entire matter a "red
herring" and assuring his countrymen in a major campaign
address that domestic communists posed no real danger to
American security. This was a remarkable performance for a
President who had relied upon frightening the country with
the communist threat during his campaign for foreign aid. Both
Truman and Clark accused H.U.A.C. of irresponsibly attempt-

ing to inflate the communist danger for political purposes. The Attorney General attacked H.U.A.C. in long and detailed statements contrasting the sober anti-communist activities of his department with the reckless ranting of the House committee. He waxed indignant over the fact that all the information disclosed by the committee's investigation was well known to the Justice Department. These were noteworthy charges from an Attorney General who had cooperated fully with H.U.A.C. during the preceding year, had publicly praised the committee for promoting popular concern about domestic communism, and had assisted it on numerous occasions to publicize information well known by the Justice Department.[19]

In retrospect, one of the most interesting features of the 1948 presidential campaign was Truman's success in avoiding serious political damage from Republican exploitation of the communist issue. Post-election analyses would show that despite the deteriorating situation in China and the significant public impact of the Chambers and Bentley allegations, an essential element in the President's victory was the unusually solid support he received from urban Catholic voters who admired his anti-communism. Nevertheless, Truman's escape from political damage on this issue during 1948 did not represent the main current of American politics, for it resulted from circumstances that ceased to exist almost immediately after the election.

The first of these was the campaign strategy of Truman's Republican opponent, Thomas Dewey. Confident of victory, Dewey maintained throughout the campaign a posture of scrupulous bipartisanship with regard to international issues. Although he advocated more vigorous anti-communist measures in Asia than he believed Truman had undertaken, he did not seek to make this a major issue or the basis of a vigorous attack upon the Administration. Circumstances contributed to Truman's good fortune in this regard. The Berlin blockade, instituted by the Soviets in June, not only created a situation in which partisan attacks upon American foreign policy by Dewey would have been irresponsible and politically unwise, but concentrated public attention during the campaign on the Cold

War in Europe, where Truman's policies had been vigorous and apparently effective. Public attention was therefore turned away from Asia, and no dramatic events occurred in China prior to the election to alter this situation.

Dewey also took a relatively high-level approach to the issue of domestic communism and did not attempt to exploit this issue extensively even after the Chambers-Bentley accusations had exposed the Administration's flank. Though Dewey's tactics were not employed by other spokesmen for the party —Republican National Chairman Hugh Scott, for example, made vigorous efforts to exploit the Hiss issue—Dewey's position blunted the effectiveness of the Republican attack. Here, too, circumstances helped Truman, for prior to the election Chambers's accusations remained only accusations and Truman was able to claim that the H.U.A.C. hearings were revealing nothing that the Administration did not know and had not told the grand jury.[20]

Immediately after the election all of the circumstances shielding Truman from political attack on the anti-communist issue disappeared. Truman's upset victory deprived the Republicans of any possible belief in the political value of bipartisanship and discredited the statesmanlike political style that Dewey had employed during the campaign; it set the stage for the resurgence of acrimonious partisanship in the Eighty-first Congress and the downturn of bipartisan cooperation on international issues. Circumstances quickly provided the basis for partisan attack. In November Chambers produced evidence of Alger Hiss's espionage activities that he previously had suppressed, and the following month a New York court indicted Hiss on two counts of perjury for lying in his testimony to H.U.A.C. By January the position of the Nationalists in China had deteriorated so completely that Chiang Kai-shek was constrained to resign as head of state and withdraw to Formosa. Succeeding months brought a steady series of military disasters to the Nationalist armies, making Chiang's doom, anticipated by the Administration since 1946, apparent for all to see. Under these circumstances the Administration felt it necessary to begin clear efforts to extricate itself from

China. It announced the withdrawal of the American military mission and decided that arms shipments to the Nationalists should be suspended. The Hiss indictment and the decision to withdraw from China suddenly opened wide gaps in the Administration's anti-communist program. After almost two years of frustration, during which Republicans had watched Truman develop and manipulate American anti-communism for his own purposes, the Republicans at last were presented with an opportunity to reclaim their traditional control of this issue. Now it would be Truman's turn to watch in frustration as his political opponents attacked him, his administration, and his policies with an issue he had nurtured.[21]

In February 1949, shortly after the convention of the Eighty-first Congress, Republican leaders began to demand a reversal of the announced decision to suspend military aid to Chiang Kai-shek. On February 7 fifty-one Republican Senators sent a letter to the President demanding a complete reexamination of the Chinese situation, and shortly thereafter Styles Bridges proposed a full investigation of the Administration's policies toward China. These attitudes provided a basic and prominent theme of Republican oratory during 1949, as the Nationalist armies steadily lost ground to the Communists. Republican attacks upon the Administration's China policies focused increasingly upon the need to preserve Formosa as an island redoubt for Chiang's forces. In November Senators Taft, Knowland, and Smith urged this policy on the Administration. Taft suggested that the Seventh Fleet be sent into the Formosa Straits to accomplish this. The political potency of this issue was indicated by extensive Democratic support for the Republican position on China. In February 1949, for example, Senator Pat McCarran, an anti-Administration Democrat, introduced a bill to increase military and economic assistance to the Nationalists. Twenty-four Democrats were among the fifty Senators endorsing his proposal.[22]

The Administration exhibited a determination not to be intimidated by these attacks and demands. Its political position in 1949 was firm. It had just won a startling victory in the presidential election and had regained control of Congress.

Public opinion polls indicated the absence of strong support for aggressive action in China. The Administration maintained a course intended to extricate the United States from that country. Early in the year, anticipating the political pressures that disengagement from China would produce, Acheson ordered the preparation of a full account of recent American activities in China, intended to demonstrate that the U.S. had done all it could to prevent the collapse of the Nationalist regime. The Administration strongly opposed McCarran's proposal of increased assistance to the Nationalists on the ground that the situation was beyond help. At the same time, it reaffirmed internally, over the objections of the Defense Department, its determination not to protect Formosa from Communist attack. Indeed, in anticipation of the fall of the island in 1950, the State Department prepared a public information program showing that the U.S. had no significant interests there. When, through an apparent mistake, documents describing this program were obtained by the press, prompting outcries from the Republican leaders who were demanding an American commitment to Formosa, the Administration responded with uncompromising statements of its policy of disengagement.

On January 5, 1950, the President publicly affirmed his unwillingness to "pursue a course which will lead to involvement in the civil conflict in China." The following week, in a major address on China policy, Acheson expressed his opposition to a blanket application of the Truman Doctrine to Asia. He indicated that American aid should be extended only when it could be effective, which required, he believed, both adequate American resources and support of the recipient government by its population. He underlined his view by stating that the western perimeter of America's strategic defenses should be the line of islands beginning with the Aleutians and extending through Japan and the Philippines and that this perimeter should limit American military commitments in the Pacific. (Acheson was referring to a strategic determination that had been made by the Truman administration but not announced.) Speaking of the collapse of the Nationalist regime, he noted the traditional antagonisms between the Soviet and Chinese people, and used this to suggest a policy of accommodation with the Communists. "We must not undertake to deflect from the Russians to ourselves," he said, "the righteous anger, and the wrath, and the hatred of the Chinese people which must develop." The Administration's readiness to follow the course that Acheson's speech implied was indicated by the announcement, concurrent with his speech, that the U.S. considered the question of Chinese Communist admission to the U.N. a procedural matter, not subject to an American veto in the Security Council, and that the U.S. would "accept the decision of the Security Council on this matter when made by an affirmative vote of seven members." [23]

If these statements and actions indicated the Administration's determination to proceed with a policy of disengagement from China and limited commitments in Asia, others suggested that it was not yet ready to rigorously follow the logic of its intentions. It deferred to Republican demands that military aid to Chiang not be suspended. To conciliate those who supported Senator McCarran's proposed aid program, it agreed to permit Chiang to continue drawing on credits previously granted him, despite the expiration of the authorization. In the fall of 1949, to obtain support for the program of European rearmament, it accepted an amendment including arms aid to Chiang, thus reversing in part the decision it had made in opposing McCarran's proposal. In October, when Mao Tse-tung proclaimed the establishment of the Chinese People's Republic and several Western nations announced their intention of recognizing his government, the Administration felt that domestic political considerations prevented it from taking this step. These same considerations undoubtedly figured prominently in Acheson's initiation of a special study in 1949 to "make absolutely certain that we are neglecting no opportunity that would be within our capabilities to achieve the purpose of halting the spread of communism in Asia." Under these pressures the Administration for the first time began to provide major support for the French effort to combat the

Communist-led insurgency in Vietnam. In the spring and summer of 1950 the U.S. initiated modest programs of economic assistance to various countries in Southeast Asia.[24]

The Administration's policies in Asia in 1949 and early 1950 were contradictory on a number of points. It was attempting to withdraw from its commitment to China while taking steps that extended and deepened that commitment. It emphasized the folly of inviting the hostility of the Chinese Communists while implementing what must have appeared to them a policy of encirclement and containment. It spoke of the mistakes of viewing American policy in Asia exclusively in terms of opposing communism and of accepting unlimited American commitments in that region, yet it took a number of actions indicating that it intended to implement just this policy on just this basis. In short, the Administration was attempting to implement policies it thought a rational reflection of real American interests while protecting itself from criticisms of refusing to implement the Truman Doctrine in Asia.

Throughout 1949 a consistent theme of the Republican attack on the Administration's policies toward China was that subversive influences in the State Department were compromising American interests in that country. This notion of course was not new in Republican oratory. Hurley's statement that his efforts in China in 1945 had been undermined by subversive State Department professionals had provided initial impetus to this notion, and similar charges had appeared sporadically in criticisms of the Administration's policy ever since. During the Eightieth Congress Walter Judd had included accusations of communism in the State Department as part of his general attack on the Administration's Asian policies. At the same time, Styles Bridges had fought to remove John Carter Vincent from a position of influence over American policy toward China on grounds of his leftist tendencies, and John Taber had consistently given voice to the view that the State Department was honeycombed with communists. The Hiss revelations gave new life and increased credibility to this school of thought, for Hiss had served in the State Department under Roosevelt and had attended the Yalta Conference, at which, the Republican critique held, Roosevelt had sold out American interests in China and elsewhere to Stalin. Thus, during the hearings to confirm Dean Acheson's appointment as Secretary of State in early 1949, extensive attention was given by Senators to Acheson's acknowledged acquaintance with Hiss, and Bridges was apt to use the word "sabotage" to characterize Acheson's influence on China policy. The charges were revived in August when Hurley denounced the Administration's White Paper on American policy in China as the work of pro-communists in the State Department, and Chiang's supporters in Congress were inspired to new out-pourings of invective against subversives in the diplomatic corps.

Such charges were reflective of the broad public concern with internal security, which had grown steadily in the post-war period and blossomed in the wake of the Hiss indictment. During debate on E.R.P. the Administration actively encour-aged this concern in a manner that reinforced its campaign for foreign aid and Cold War foreign policy, but as the internal security issue increasingly provided a basis for attacking the Administration's foreign policies, the attitude of Truman and his advisers underwent a notable revision. During 1949 the White House began to develop plans for the appointment of a presidential commission on internal security that would re-view the loyalty program, make clear to the public the neg-ligible danger posed by communist infiltration of the federal bureaucracy, and generally defuse public emotion and con-cern over internal security; this was, of course, precisely the opposite of the role played by the President's Temporary Com-mission on Employee Loyalty in 1946–7. A more significant indication of the Administration's new attitude involved its relations with H.U.A.C. Immediately following the 1948 elec-tion, both the President and Attorney General Clark began a determined effort to have H.U.A.C. abolished. When they failed to win enough support in the House to achieve this, they fought to block the reappointment to the Committee of John Rankin and F. Edward Hebert, two anti-Truman Southern

Democrats, and to have them replaced with Truman supporters not inclined to the kind of anti-communist, anti-Administration expositions characteristic of Dies and Thomas. In this they succeeded. During 1949, under the chairmanship of John Wood, the committee was restrained and relatively inconspicuous, and the country was treated to the spectacle of H.U.A.C. refusing T.V. coverage of its hearings.

By 1949 the President and his advisers had developed an acute sense of the dangers of the public concern over internal security, and in fact tended to view the political atmosphere as comparable to that existing in 1798, when the Alien and Sedition Acts were passed. Stephen Spingarn, the member of the White House staff directly responsible for issues related to internal security, stated in a memo to Clifford in April that "with the possible exception of the age of John Adams and A. Mitchell Palmer, it is more dangerous to be a liberal today than at any other period in American history." Such a view of the public mood boded ill for the country and for a Democratic administration that considered itself representative of American liberalism, and the President and his advisers were now as anxious to reduce public concern over internal security as they had been to promote it in 1947–8.[25]

But it was not to be. Early in 1950 the internal security issue received another boost. A week after Acheson's speech on China policy, which had drawn from Republicans demands that the Administration be censured and that Acheson resign, Alger Hiss was convicted of perjury by a New York court. Walter Judd, spokesman for the China bloc in the House, immediately called upon the President to remove his Secretary of State. Two weeks later Klaus Fuchs was arrested in London on charges of high-level espionage in connection with the development of the atomic bomb. Shortly thereafter, two of Fuchs's accomplices, Harry Gold and David Greenglass, were arrested in New York. Now, at the outset of an election year, with China in the hands of Communists while the Administration talked about limiting its commitments in Asia and refused to defend Formosa, with the country's sense of confidence and security badly damaged by reverses in Asia and by the Soviet atomic explosion, with renewed indications of the Administration's alleged laxness on issues of internal security, and events that suggested connections between this laxness and America's international setbacks, the political pot began to boil.[26]

On February 9 Senator Joseph McCarthy delivered his famous speech in Wheeling, West Virginia, accusing the State Department of harboring communists. Though the Senator was merely reiterating familiar charges and employing the inconclusive evidence that John Taber had obtained and publicized in 1947, under the circumstances of 1950 his statements attracted widespread attention. Two weeks after the Wheeling speech he repeated his charges on the floor of the Senate. Early in March, in response to the concern that McCarthy's speeches had generated, the Senate leadership appointed a special committee chaired by Senator Tydings of Maryland to hear his evidence. This committee met continuously during the spring and summer of 1950 and provided McCarthy with a public platform from which to continue his denunciations, which focused increasingly on the Far Eastern Division of the State Department and the influence of the subversives it harbored on China policy. In late March, perceiving the public response that McCarthy's attacks were registering, the Senate Republican Policy Committee announced its support of his efforts. Senator Taft was quoted as advising McCarthy, "if one case doesn't work, try another." Senator Bridges announced that a group of Republicans were going to "go after" Acheson, and he initiated the offensive two days later in a Senate speech. Senator·Wherry announced that Acheson "must go" as a "bad security risk." Taft denounced the "pro-communist group in the State Department who surrendered to every demand at Yalta and Potsdam and promoted at every. opportunity the communist cause in China." Senator McCarran's Judiciary Committee began hearings on internal security legislation, which provided yet another forum for charges against the Administration's laxness in this area. These hearings, like those of the Tydings Committee, continued through the spring and summer.[27]

The public impact of this growing political battle was

evident in the reactions of the Administration. President Truman established a task force within the White House staff to provide rebuttals to McCarthy's charges. In April, when McCarthy announced that he would stand or fall on the case of Owen Lattimore, one-time consultant to the State Department on Asian matters, the President reversed his tenaciously held policy of protecting investigative files from Congressional scrutiny, and permitted the Tydings Committee to inspect Lattimore's file in the hope of silencing McCarthy. In May the President undertook a national tour by train to defend his Administration against Republican attacks. In early June, however, Senator Margaret Chase Smith, a Republican from Maine, was able to win only nine votes in the Senate in support of her "Declaration of Conscience" denouncing McCarthy's attack against the Administration. On June 20 Acheson appeared before a governors' conference and was subjected to four hours of hostile questioning.[28]

Into this ugly and turbulent political storm, only beginning to reveal its force, came the news that war had broken out in Korea. Had a mischievous deity determined to produce an event that would bring to fever pitch the already heated political situation in the United States, he could have succeeded no better than did the North Koreans in their bold attack upon an Asian area that only six months before the American Secretary of State had indicated would not be defended by American arms. That this attack would produce new recriminations against the Administration's policies in Asia, new denunciations of the Secretary of State, new suggestions of subversion in the State Department, could not have been doubted for a moment by any member of the Administration. When the President gathered his advisers about him to develop a response to the crisis, he curtly banned all talk of domestic politics, but there is ample evidence that political considerations pervaded every aspect of the determinations made by the American government in response to the Korean situation.

The Truman administration probably would have decided to commit itself to repelling the North Korean attack even if the issue had not arisen in the midst of a fierce domestic political battle centering on its willingness to fight communism in Asia. Although the Secretary of Defense, Louis Johnson, has cited domestic opinion as one of the factors influencing the Administration to make this decision, it is clear that the major decision-makers—Truman, Acheson, Johnson himself—saw the North Korean attack as a probing action by the Soviets that could not go unanswered without inviting similar initiatives elsewhere and discrediting American commitments all around the world. How strongly the Administration would have felt the latter consideration were it not publicly wedded to the Truman Doctrine is an interesting but unanswerable question. While strategic considerations were undoubtedly sufficient to produce the decision to repel the North Korean attack, the decision not to ask Congress for authority to dispatch troops was primarily political. Both Acheson and Senator Connally, Democratic Chairman of the Senate Foreign Relations Committee, advised Truman that a Congressional debate on this issue could be a disaster. "We were scared of the Hill on this thing," Johnson has recalled. "If we tried to put ground troops in at the beginning there would have been a great deal of trouble." [29] Domestic political considerations also appear to have played a major role in the decisions, taken at this time, to increase American military activities all around the perimeter of China, particularly to intervene in the Chinese civil war by sending the Seventh Fleet into the Formosa Straits and to dispatch a military mission to Indochina.

Certainly, there were strategic arguments in favor of the Formosa action, and the official explanation—that it was a temporary move "without prejudice to political questions affecting that island" to contain the area of fighting and ensure the safety of American troops in Korea—was plausible. But there were equally compelling substantive arguments against this decision, mainly the Administration's desire to extricate itself from China. Though it called the Formosa decision temporary, it must have known that such a step could not easily be undone. The readiness of Truman and Acheson to take an action they had repeatedly resisted in the face of strong advocacy by such Republican leaders as Taft and Hoover has caused most observers of these events to conclude that they were motivated at least in part by the recognition that the political pressures the war was certain to generate left them with no alternative. Without reference to domestic politics, it is difficult to explain the emphasis placed by Acheson on publicly announcing the Formosa intervention when he presented his recommendations to the President; he did not suggest such an announcement with respect to any of his other proposals.[30]

The official explanation of the decision to send a military mission to Indochina—a decision that significantly deepened American involvement in that region—was that the Administration feared the Korean attack to be only the first of a series of military initiatives by the communists. There is no question that this fear existed, but it is unclear why it led to the dispatch of a military mission instead of increased aid to the French, who had already assumed military responsibility for containing communism in Indochina. In this decision, as in the Formosa intervention, it is difficult to avoid the conclusion that the Administration felt the need, at the inception of a potentially difficult and divisive course in Korea and four months before a national election, to establish clearly for a skeptical public and a critical Congress its determination to do everything possible to oppose communism in Asia. The implicit intention of demonstrating this suggests what later events would show, that the Administration had embarked on a course that would take it far beyond its announced determination merely to restore the status quo ante bellum in the Far East.[31]

The modest goals that the U.S. announced when it entered the Korean war reflected the unpromising nature of the military situation then existing. By mid-July 1950, however, the American and South Korean forces had weathered the North Korean offensive, and a build-up of American forces had commenced. Confidence in the military situation appeared in the American government. By July 20, General MacArthur, the American Commander in the Far East, was able to inform the President that the North Koreans had missed their chance for victory. Indeed, as early as July 7 the General had begun to plan a counteroffensive, the first step toward the Inchon landing that he would execute with such spectacular success in September. The prospect of a counterattack by American and South Korean forces confronted the U.S. with the necessity of specifying its military objectives in Korea and raised a number of issues: should American forces be permitted to cross the 38th parallel, which divided North and South Korea, in order to achieve a favorable military result? If not, could they possibly achieve anything like the "peace and security" called for by the U.N. resolution on Korea under which the U.S. was fighting? Indeed, what did "peace and security" mean in the context of Korea: the destruction of the North Korean armies? the unification of the Korean peninsula under U.N. auspices? These issues were debated within the American government during the late summer weeks of 1950. In considering these deliberations, it is essential to keep in mind the domestic political context.

"For two or three weeks after the June 25 attack on South Korea," Acheson has written, "the attack of the primitives quieted down, only to burst into full fury on July 20 when the Tydings subcommittee filed its report." The committee's report, rejecting all of McCarthy's charges as insubstantial and accusing McCarthy of irresponsible behavior, was adopted by the Senate in a party-line vote in late July. Acheson has described his subsequent plight with cryptic sensitivity: "On August 7 Wherry demanded my dismissal; on the fourteenth, my resignation; and on the sixteenth he declared that 'the blood of our boys in Korea is on [Acheson's] shoulders, and no one else.' On the thirteenth four of the five Republican members of the Foreign Relations Committee, followed by Senator Taft, accused President Truman and me of having invited the attack on Korea."

The difficulties of this situation were augmented by early indications that General MacArthur, who enjoyed an immense reputation in the United States, particularly among advocates of an aggressive American policy in Asia, was not averse to publicly assuming political positions that undermined official policy and provided ammunition to the Administration's critics. In early August the General made an unauthorized trip to Formosa that produced newspaper reports that he favored American support of military action by the Nationalists against the mainland—as in fact he did. The Administration attempted to smooth over the incident by sending Averell Harriman to Japan to quietly explain to the Far East Commander "the basic conflict of interest between the U.S. and the Generalissimo's position as to the future of Formosa" and to publicly obtain assurances from MacArthur that he and the President were in accord. Nonetheless, new arguments had been given to those who believed that the U.S. was not doing all it could do to oppose communism in the Far East. A similar result was produced by a message that the General sent to a convention of veterans later in the same month, delineating the strategic importance of Formosa and attacking those who, by opposing the defense of the island, "advocate defeatism and appeasement in the Pacific." The General's officially-induced withdrawal of this statement came too late to prevent the national publication of a statement in opposition to official policy and was certain to make any withdrawal of American support from Formosa more difficult. While these developments were increasing the difficulties of the Administration on Far Eastern policy, Congress was demonstrating the continued political potency of the internal security issue, with which the controversy over Asian policy was inseparably entangled. In early September it passed the Internal Security Act of 1950, produced by McCarran's hearings, with overwhelming bipartisan majorities, many members voting for a bill they opposed but felt politically incapable of resisting.[32]

The Administration made ineffective headway against this steady current of political woe. In September the President appointed George Marshall Secretary of Defense, undoubtedly reasoning—as he had when he appointed the same man Secretary of State in 1947—that the presence of a non-political man of unquestioned integrity and loyalty would defuse partisan attacks upon his foreign policies. This did not occur: instead, General Marshall was subjected to the same bitter denunciations and suggestions of disloyalty that had already been heaped on Acheson. The Administration prepared its own legislative proposals on internal security, in an effort to head off Congressional approval of the McCarran bill, which was modeled in part after the anti-communist legislation developed by Mundt and Nixon in 1948. These proposals were brushed aside, and McCarran's program adopted. On September 20 the President vetoed the McCarran bill, and submitted to each Congressman and Senator a lengthy message covered by a personal letter begging careful consideration of his arguments. This appeal was ignored and the bill reapproved within twenty-four hours. In mid-October, two weeks before the election, the President made an ignominious trip to Wake Island to meet with General MacArthur, and returned to announce that he and his Pacific Commander were in complete agreement on American policy. The public provided its view of all this in November, when the Republicans picked up twenty-eight seats in the House and five in the Senate. In the campaigns of three of the five Republicans whose victories represented gains in the Senate for their party, Senator McCarthy played a crucial role.[33]

It was in this political framework that the Administration, during July and August 1950, decided how to proceed in Korea, now that the military balance had shifted in favor of the American and South Korean forces. Policies of contrary tendencies were suggested. From within the State Department voices were raised to suggest that the U.S. ought not limit its objectives to driving the North Koreans back across the 38th parallel. General MacArthur was asking for authority to cross the parallel and destroy the North Korean armies. The Pentagon indicated that it favored the occupation of the entire peninsula and unification of it under U.N. auspices, upon the assumption that action requisite to achieve these goals did not provoke Chinese or Soviet intervention. At the same time, the British and Indian governments advanced plans, reportedly acceptable in varying degrees to the Soviet and Chinese Communists, looking toward an early peace settlement based upon the status quo ante in Korea. While different in some important respects, both proposals linked a settlement of the war with an alteration in America's position on Formosa and the admission of Communist China to the U.N. The British believed that this latter move would encourage what appeared to be the beginnings of a split between the Soviets and the Chinese.[34]

The British proposal found a sympathetic listener in George Kennan, closing out his career as counselor to the State Department, who advocated it in discussions within the State Department during these summer months. He was motivated by two concerns. First, despite General MacArthur's assurances on this point, he was convinced that the Soviets would not permit the armies of General MacArthur to extend their control over the entire Korean peninsula, which abutted their own territory. Moreover, he shared the British view that Chinese Communist entry into the U.N., while changing no real situation of importance, might provide impetus to a separation of the Chinese and Soviet Communists. According to Kennan's records, his argument was rejected by Acheson (who six months previously had advocated policies tending in this direction) "on the ground," put forward by John Foster Dulles, "that it would confuse American public opinion and weaken support for the President's program looking toward the strengthening of our defenses." Moreover, when Kennan submitted a memo to Acheson asserting that the talk of unifying Korea under U.N. control was ill-considered, that it was not essential to the U.S. to establish an anti-Soviet regime in all Korea, and that, indeed, the U.S. should not exclude the ultimate possibility of Soviet domination of Korea, Acheson did not feel able to consider this a serious policy alternative, despite the fact that Kennan was only reiterating what previously had been the official view of Korea's importance. Acheson has written that Kennan had described "national interest in the abstract" but that "in view of public opinion and political pressure in the concrete, ideas such as these could only be kept as warnings not to get drawn into quicksands."[35]

On the basis of such considerations, the Administration

moved strongly away from any notion of a Korean settlement based upon a repulsion of the North Korean attack. It rejected the British and Indian peace proposals indignantly, informing the Indians on July 11 that it would accept no solution in Korea that left that country in an exposed position. What this implied was obvious, and was given public voice by the President on September 1 when he stated that the Koreans were entitled to a "free, united and independent country." On September 15 the summer-long deliberations of the National Security Council on Korea produced a set of orders to General MacArthur instructing him to either force the North Koreans behind the 38th parallel or destroy their forces, and—provided there was no threat of Soviet or Chinese intervention—to extend his operations north of the parallel and make plans for the occupation of North Korea.[36] Thus, even before the brilliantly successful Inchon landing, the Administration had gone far toward committing itself to asserting military control over all Korea if it could do so.

After Inchon there seemed little doubt that this was possible. MacArthur was sure it could be done and was again providing assurances that the Chinese and Soviets would not come in. Syngman Rhee, the President of South Korea, was saying that he would unite Korea with or without the support of the U.N. Any effort to stem the movement toward an attempt to occupy all Korea would now have to face public statements by MacArthur and his supporters that total victory had been denied the U.N. As Louis Halle, one of the members of Kennan's Policy Planning Staff during this period, has written: "this was a time when the American people were becoming convinced that the foreign policy of the United States had fallen into the hands of communist conspirators. . . . For the government now to order MacArthur to desist from giving the beaten Communists the *coup de grâce* would have appeared to confirm this view. Without the vital test, the people, having MacArthur's word for it, would never have believed that Korea could not have been quickly unified under a friendly democratic regime. . . . Truman's action would have gone down in history as the great betrayal." MacArthur's orders after Inchon instructed him to achieve "the destruction of the North Korean armed forces" and in October the U.S. won U.N. approval of a resolution calling upon MacArthur to achieve the goal, earlier announced by the President, of a "free, united and independent" Korea. The U.S. was now publicly committed to what its orders of September 15 had implied, the occupation of all Korea on behalf of the U.N. Direct and indirect warnings from the Chinese that they would not permit the U.S. to occupy North Korea were labeled blackmail, and whatever fears they prompted in American decision-makers were set aside. On October 1 MacArthur sent the first Korean units under his command across the parallel, to be followed six days later by American troops. On October 14 the Chinese began a build-up of forces in North Korea in anticipation of the massive counterattack, to be launched a month later, that would plunge the United States into war with China.[37]

Just as the initial outbreak of war in Korea had brought the Administration under contradictory pressures from those anxious for a compromise settlement and those eager to pursue a more aggressive policy in Asia, so the outbreak of war between the U.S. and China produced an intensification of these same pressures. Now General MacArthur and his supporters in Congress began to urge the Administration to take action against the Chinese mainland, through strategic bombing and support of an invasion by the Nationalists. Now the British came forward with a new plan for a negotiated peace, again involving a shift in American policy on the issues of Formosa and Chinese Communist admission to the U.N. The Administration was again constrained to plot its course between the conflicting demands of domestic politics and its allies in the U.N. with results not unlike those produced in the summer of 1950. When Prime Minister Attlee came to Washington in December 1950 to plead for his proposed settlement, the President responded by describing the domestic political situation. Truman recalls telling the Prime Minister that "we could not back out in the Far East. The American people would not stand for it. It was impossible." Acheson took a similar view. He told the British officials that "Chiang, rightly or wrongly, had become something of a symbol." The British efforts made no headway.[38]

Although the Administration did not feel it could accept a compromise in Korea, it limited its retaliation against Communist China to the termination of all economic relations with that country. When General MacArthur began to voice publicly his disagreements with official policy, he was relieved of his command. Most observers of these events agree that in the battle for public support on matters related to Asia, Mac-Arthur, basing his appeal upon a literal application of the Truman Doctrine, was doing far better than the Administration at the time he was removed from his command. He returned to a hero's welcome and was invited to address a joint session of Congress. The Administration was summoned before a Senate investigating committee to justify its disagreements with the General. These hearings generally have been considered a victory for the Administration, for in their course public sympathy for MacArthur waned and the recklessness of his proposals became increasingly evident.

Despite these results, the Truman administration, on the extreme political defensive during these hearings, became yet more rigidly entrenched in a China policy that (as it recognized) responded more to the symbols than the realities of the situation. It now denied any thought of recognizing Communist China, though its non-recognition policy had been a temporary political expedient. It now stated that it would not only vote against admission of the Chinese Communists to the U.N. but would consider its vote a veto and attempt to win a judgment to this effect from the World Court, though previously it had indicated that it would consider the matter procedural and accept the vote of a majority. It now expunged all traces of temporariness from its Formosa policy by making it clear that it would not permit the island to be taken by force.[39] These shifts in policy eliminated whatever hopes or illusions of flexibility the Administration had retained in applying the Truman Doctrine to the Far East. It was now fully committed to opposing any further extension of communist power in the Far East as well as refusing to acknowledge the

reality of Communist China. From an initial intention of dis-
engaging the U.S. from China and Korea, reaching an accommodation with the Chinese Communists, limiting military
commitments in the Far East to a defensive perimeter of off-
shore islands, and basing its aid programs on the Asian mainland on pragmatic considerations, the Truman administration
had moved to a position in which its Armed Forces were
deployed to repel almost any extension of communist influence in the Far East. In the short period between the Truman Doctrine speech and early 1951, approximately four years,
the Administration had been led, against its will and policy,
but according to the logic of its rhetoric and politics, to a full
application of the Truman Doctrine in Asia. One legacy of
this remarkable episode was a series of military commitments
to countries around the rim of China, in which American interests were for the most part marginal or even, as in the
case of Formosa, where the U.S. had a recognized conflict of
interest with the regime it was protecting. A second legacy of
these events was the establishment of the principle that to
permit any extension of communist power in Southeast Asia
was to invite political disaster in the United States. Unhappily
conjoined, these elements would shape the course of American
policy in the Far East for the following twenty years.[40]

A third legacy, thoroughly intertwined with the others,
was the period of ascendency that came to Senator McCarthy
and a host of sympathizers and followers in American politics
and American society. The enormous gap between what the
American people had been led to expect in Asia and what
actually occurred there—this ultimate broken hope to cap the
relentless shattering of officially promoted illusions about the
postwar period—probably did more to make McCarthy's
charges credible to Americans than anything else, save the
discovery and conviction of Alger Hiss. And the political impact of the Hiss case, no less than that of the fall of China,
derived in large part from the policies and politics of Truman
and his advisers: an Administration that had assiduously encouraged public concern over internal security in 1947-8
could not credibly argue that domestic communism was not

really a problem after hard evidence of communist activities in the government had been produced. To the average American, who had taken literally and seriously the officially promoted crises over internal security in 1947 and 1948, the efforts of the Truman administration to damp down public agitation over domestic communism in the wake of the Hiss disclosures inevitably seemed less an effort to restore perspective than a blatant attempt to cover up a serious breach in America's internal defenses. McCarthy sensed the depth of public disillusionment with regard to both China and internal security, and much of his initial success stemmed from his effective conjunction of these two issues. His attacks upon State Department policies and personnel in early 1950, upon American policy in Korea, and upon General Marshall following the recall of MacArthur all depended upon a politically lethal marriage of the issues of Asia and internal security. For these attacks and for the manner of his brief career as a national figure, Senator McCarthy has been indignantly reviled by his adversaries in the Truman administration. Their moralism is unbecoming, for it was they who cultivated the public atmosphere in which he thrived. It was the shattering of illusions they had helped to foster and the existence of fears they had promoted that he exploited, and he did so with a rhetoric they had legitimized for their own purposes.

Nor was the debt of McCarthyism to the policies of the Truman administration limited to the promotion of a political atmosphere congenial to the Senator and his adherents. In fact, in 1947–8 Truman and his advisers employed all the political and programmatic techniques that in later years were to become associated with the broad phenomenon of McCarthyism. It was the Truman administration that developed the association of dissent with disloyalty and communism, which became a central element of McCarthyism. It was the Truman administration that adopted the peacetime loyalty program, which provided a model for state and local governments and a wide variety of private institutions. It was the Truman administration, in the criteria for loyalty used in its loyalty program, that legitimized the concept of guilt by association, a favorite tactic of McCarthy. The President saw none of this, of course, and became furious when the integrity of Dean Acheson was questioned because of his association with Alger Hiss. He waxed equally indignant after passage of the Internal Security Act of 1950, calling its registration requirements a violation of free speech; yet in 1947 he had authorized the publication of the Attorney General's list, a far more arbitrary way of limiting political activity than that approved by Congress in 1950. The President vetoed the Immigration Act of 1952 in part because he considered its vaguely defined deportation powers a form of "thought control"; yet he had not objected, in 1947–8, when alien communist activists were being arrested on a variety of technical charges in order to prevent their making non-punishable statements.[41]

President Truman believed himself to be a defender of civil liberties, and wanted to be remembered as such. His resistance to many of the blatant assaults on traditional American freedoms during the early 1950's entitle him to respect in this connection. But in 1947–8, in order to mobilize the country behind his foreign policies, Truman himself employed and permitted his subordinates to employ many of the same means of restricting democratic freedoms that he would later condemn. He legitimized or tried to legitimize for use in peacetime restrictions on traditional freedoms that had previously been limited in application to wartime emergencies. The practices of McCarthyism were Truman's practices in cruder hands, just as the language of McCarthyism was Truman's language, in less well-meaning voices.

Notes
Bibliography
Index

Notes

INTRODUCTION

1. For summaries of events triggering McCarthyism, see Francis Biddle: *The Fear of Freedom* (Garden City, 1951), pp. 5–6; Eric F. Goldman: *The Crucial Decade—And After: America 1945–1960* (New York, 1960), Chapters 5–7.
2. Anthony Eden: *Full Circle* (London, 1960), p. 7. Acheson cited in Harry S. Truman: *Years of Trial and Hope* (Garden City, 1956), p. 254.

I ORIGINS OF THE FOREIGN AID PROGRAM

1. Frances Perkins: *The Roosevelt I Knew* (New York, 1946), p. 381. Robert Sherwood: *Roosevelt and Hopkins* (New York, 1948), p. 227. Cordell Hull: *Memoirs* (New York, 1948), Vol. 2, p. 732.
2. Hull quote from Hull, p. 81. For Clayton, see Ross Pritchard: "Will Clayton: Industrial Statesman," unpublished doctoral dissertation (Fletcher School, Tufts University, 1956), pp. 172, 185–6, 192. For Stimson, see Henry L. Stimson and McGeorge Bundy: *On Active Service in War and Peace* (New York, 1947), pp. 567, 591. For an excellent discussion of the views of various officials on this issue, see Richard Gardner: *Sterling Dollar Diplomacy* (Oxford, 1956), pp. 4–22, 196; see also Sumner Welles: *Where Are We Heading* (New York, 1946), pp. 8–15, 16; Warren Hickman: *Genesis of the European Recovery Program* (Geneva, 1949); Gabriel Kolko: *The Politics of War* (New York, 1968).
3. For growth of U.S. economy during the war, see Council of Economic Advisors: *Annual Economic Review* (USGPO, January 1951), pp. 44–5. For wartime concern with postwar surplus, see Walter Millis and E. S. Duffield, eds.: *The Forrestal Diaries* (New York, 1951), pp. 34, 84; Kolko, pp. 252–4; Gardner, pp. 101–2; Herbert Feis: *Churchill, Roosevelt, Stalin* (Princeton, 1957), p. 641; Harry S. Truman: *Years of Trial and Hope* (Garden City, 1956), pp. 263, 267. Pritchard, pp. 175–6. Clayton quote in Pritchard, p. 269. Acheson quote cited in Kolko, p. 254; Hull quote in Hull, p. 107.

4. For a full treatment of American views on Anglo-American commercial relations, see Gardner and Kolko.

5. Gordon Gray et al: *Report to the President on Foreign Economic Policies* (USGPO, November 1950), pp. 9, 75 ff; see also Raymond F. Mikesell: *United States Economic Policy and International Relations* (New York, 1952).

6. Hull, p. 365.

7. For expectation of U.S. troop withdrawals after the war, see Feis, p. 472; Harry C. Butcher: *My Three Years with Eisenhower* (New York, 1946), p. 492. On the tendency to relate American ideals and self-interest, see the Stimson Diary (Henry L. Stimson Papers, Yale University Library), July 26, 1945, February 15, 1945, May 10, 1945; Kolko, pp. 457 ff.

8. For U.S. awareness of Soviet capabilities in Eastern Europe and the attitude toward this problem, see Sherwood, pp. 311, 708–13; Feis, pp. 23, 26, 27, 31–4, 59, 121, 123, 191, 271–2. For the importance to the U.S. of East-West trade in Europe, see Kolko, pp. 422–8.

9. Sherwood, pp. 372, 396–8; see also Feis, pp. 10, 15.

10. Stimson quote in Stimson and Bundy, p. 592. For Morgenthau, see Gardner, p. 174; E. F. Penrose: *Economic Planning for the Peace* (Princeton, 1953), p. 246. For Hopkins, see Sherwood, p. 817. Roosevelt quote cited in Manuel Gottlieb: *The German Peace Settlement and the Berlin Crisis* (New York, 1960), Chapter 2, note 9. For Quebec discussions, see Gardner, p. 180; Sherwood, p. 813; Herbert Feis: *Between War and Peace* (Princeton, 1960), p. 29. For Stalin's interest in reparations, see Feis: *Churchill, Roosevelt, Stalin*, p. 24. Byrnes quoted in James F. Byrnes: *Speaking Frankly* (New York, 1947), p. 26. For initial plans for World Bank, see Gardner, pp. 74–5. For discussions of underestimation of reconstruction problem, see Penrose, p. 196; Gardner, p. 95.

11. For a discussion of official awareness of the legacy of isolationism at start of World War II, see Dean G. Acheson: *Present at the Creation* (New York, 1969), pp. 3, 21. For Roosevelt, see Welles, p. 15. For Stimson and Hull, see Stimson and Bundy, pp. 591–6, 599. For Forrestal, see Millis and Duffield, p. 9. For Truman, see Harry S. Truman: *Year of Decisions* (Garden City, 1955), p. 97; Truman: *Years of Trial and Hope*, pp. 101–2, 171; Hull, p. 1261.

12. For general discussion of this problem, see H. Bradford Westerfield: *Foreign Policy and Party Politics* (New Haven, 1955), pp. 129–45; Roland Young: *Congressional Politics in the Second World War* (New York, 1956), pp. 178 ff, 231, 236. For UNRRA, see Gardner, pp. 179–80; Penrose, pp. 155–6. For Lend Lease, see Gardner, p. 176; Young, p. 182; Truman: *Year of Decisions*, pp. 231–2.

13. Welles quote in Welles, pp. 18–19. For neglect of the World Bank, see Gardner, pp. 75–7; Penrose, pp. 33–4, 37–8, 55–7, 182–3, 205, 215, 311–12; Westerfield, pp. 139–41; Joseph M. Jones: *The Fifteen Weeks* (New York, 1955), pp. 102–3.

14. For Acheson and Roosevelt, see Acheson, pp. 32–3; see also Gardner, pp. 55–61.
15. Kolko, pp. 283–6; Acheson, p. 28; Gardner.
16. For general reference on the politics of liberation seen from the American perspective, see Harry Coles and Albert Weinberg: *Soldiers Become Governors* (Washington, 1964); Kolko; Hickman. For Italy, see Norman Kogan: *Italy and the Allies* (Cambridge, 1956); Feis, *Churchill, Roosevelt, Stalin*, pp. 172–4, 184–7; Philip E. Mosely, "Hopes and Failures," in Stephen D. Kertesz, ed.: *The Fate of East Central Europe* (Notre Dame, Ind., 1956), p. 61; Butcher, p. 515. For France, see Alfred J. Rieber: *Stalin and the French Communist Party* (New York, 1962), generally and pp. 116–19; Marcel Vigneras: *Rearming the French* (Washington, 1957); Stimson and Bundy, pp. 575–6; *Foreign Relations of the United States (FRUS)*, 1944, Vol. III, pp. 666–7. For the politics of Soviet liberation of eastern Europe, see Feis: *Churchill, Roosevelt, Stalin*, pp. 410, 415–16, 418–19, 475; Rieber, pp. 41–2; Mosely, pp. 51, 57, 58–9; Stephen D. Kertesz in Kertesz, p. 220 and generally; *FRUS*, 1944, III, 720.
17. Sherwood, pp. 748–9; Hull, pp. 1620–1.
18. For Roosevelt see Feis, *Churchill, Roosevelt, Stalin*, p. 174. Harriman in *FRUS*, 1944, IV, 951 (cited in Kolko, p. 259); Stimson, Stimson Diary, May 14, 1945 (cited in Kolko, p. 398). For the views of an official who objected to this strategy, see George F. Kennan: *Memoirs* (New York, 1969), p. 238.
19. Quotation is from Penrose, p. 112. For a discussion of loan negotiations, see Kolko, pp. 333–40.
20. Harriman quote in Kolko, pp. 339–40. Roosevelt quote in John M. Blum: Morgenthau Diaries: *Years of War* (Boston, 1967), pp. 305–6; see also Feis, *Churchill, Roosevelt, Stalin*, pp. 641–7; Kolko, pp. 499–502, 402–3, 410, 424, 425. For the role of the bomb, see Gar Alperovitz: *Atomic Diplomacy* (New York, 1965), especially pp. 203–5; Stimson Diary, February 15, 1945, July 26, 1945, September 4 and 21, 1945.
21. For excellent treatments of the reparations issue, see Bruce R. Kuklick: *Commerce and World Order*, unpublished doctoral dissertation (University of Pennsylvania, 1968); Gottlieb; Kolko, especially pp. 514 ff.
22. For reports on economic conditions in Europe, see Truman, *Year of Decisions*, pp. 45, 102, 105. Harriman quote in Millis and Duffield, pp. 39–40. Stimson in Stimson Diary, letter to Truman of May 16, 1945.
23. Truman, *Year of Decisions*, pp. 227–34; Gardner, pp. 184–7; Kolko, pp. 397–8, 491–3; Acheson, p. 122.
24. Stimson in Stimson and Bundy, pp. 592–3. MacLeish in the Papers of S. I. Rosenman, Box 3, "Report to the Nation on the Potsdam Conference," Letter from MacLeish to Rosenman of July 27, 1945

366 THE TRUMAN DOCTRINE AND MCCARTHYISM

(Truman Library). Wallace in William Clayton Papers, chronological file, memo from Clayton to Benton of October 1, 1945 (Truman Library). Truman in Truman, *Year of Decisions*, p. 262.

25. Gardner, pp. 101–9, 145–52.

26. Gardner, pp. 117–8; see also pp. 71–100, 110–44; see also Kolko, pp. 256–8.

27. Gardner, p. 127.

28. Feis, *Churchill, Roosevelt, Stalin*, p. 174.

29. See Feis, *Churchill, Roosevelt, Stalin*, pp. 23 ff, on the Atlantic Charter; pp. 208–14, on the Moscow Conference.

30. Feis, *Churchill, Roosevelt, Stalin*, pp. 435–6, 550–60; Alperovitz, p. 135; Kolko, pp. 361, 368; Mosely in Kertesz, pp. 62–74.

31. On Dumbarton Oaks, see Feis, *Churchill, Roosevelt, Stalin*, pp. 427 ff. On San Francisco, see the Stimson Diary, memo for the Secretary of State of January 23, 1945, diary entry of April 23, 1945; Stimson and Bundy, p. 604; Millis and Duffield, p. 51; James V. Forrestal Papers, Box 125 (Princeton University Library), excerpt from minutes of White House meeting on April 23, 1945, attached to a letter from Forrestal to Griffis dated August 23, 1947.

32. Sherwood, p. 391; quotation is from Jan Ciechanowski: *Defeat in Victory* (Garden City, 1947), pp. 201–2; see also Arthur Bliss Lane: *I Saw Poland Betrayed* (New York, 1948), p. 312.

33. Hull quote from the *Department of State Bulletin* (*DSB*), Vol. 9, p. 341. Roosevelt quote after Dumbarton Oaks from *DSB*, 11, 365. Roosevelt quote after Yalta from *DSB*, 12, 321. Harriman from Millis and Duffield, p. 40. Stimson in Stimson Diary, April 23, 1945. Leahy from Millis and Duffield, p. 51; see also Westerfield, pp. 143–4.

34. About Potsdam, see Truman, *Year of Decisions*, p. 351; Alperovitz, pp. 84–5, 144–5; Kolko, p. 592. For Truman report to the nation, see *DSB*, 13, 208; Byrnes, p. 104. Byrnes's public information policies in 1945 related in Byrnes, pp. 255–6. For public response to the UN, see Stimson Diary, April 23, 1945; Millis and Duffield, pp. 41, 42; Acheson, p. 111. For the exclusion of the press, see James F. Byrnes Papers (London CFM, [Council of Foreign Ministers], September 1945), September 11, 1945, "Press Arrangements"; Welles, p. 386. For the restraint of dissident officials, see Millis and Duffield, p. 102.

35. For public attitudes about U.S.-Soviet relations, see Hadley Cantril, ed.: *Public Opinion 1935–1946* (Princeton, N.J., 1951), pp. 370–2. For attitudes about the UN, see *Public Opinion Quarterly* (*POQ*), Summer 1945, p. 253.

36. Westerfield, pp. 141–2, 159–62, 168–76; Young, pp. 191–6; Acheson, pp. 72, 81–2, 92–4, 95 ff.

37. Hull comment in *FRUS*, 1944, III, 63–5 (cited in Kolko, p. 290). AIPO poll cited in Raymond A. Bauer: *American Business and Public Policy* (New York, 1963), p. 81. Employment Act of 1946

discussed in Gardner, p. 147. For the campaign for Bretton Woods, see Gardner, pp. 138–41.

38. For commodity controls in GATT, see Gardner, p. 149. For the decision to use reciprocal trade to negotiate GATT, see Pritchard, pp. 315, 317–20; Penrose, pp. 104–15; Gardner, p. 15.

39. For the role of Clayton, see Pritchard, p. 194. On negotiating the loan, see Gardner, pp. 188–223; Kolko, pp. 488–96. Clayton quote in Walter LaFeber: *America, Russia and the Cold War* (New York, 1968), pp. 9, 491–2; Stimson quote from Stimson and Bundy, p. 593. Forrestal quote from Millis and Duffield, p. 246.

40. *FRUS*, 1946, VII, pp. 399–400; *The New York Times* (*TNYT*), March 29, 1946, 11:1; Department of State: *European Recovery Program: Country Studies: France* (1948), p. 31; Rieber, p. 259.

41. Council of Economic Advisors: *Midyear Review* (July 1950), p. 27; *President's Economic Report for 1946*, mimeographed copy in Harry S. Truman Papers, Files of Clark M. Clifford, Box 4, dated January 8, 1947, pp. 33–4.

42. Penrose, "The Gathering Storm."

43. Byrnes quote from Byrnes, p. 99; see also Byrnes Papers, "Private Conferences, Documents," Byrnes-Molotov Conversations at London in August, September 1945, particularly notes for September 16, 1945. In his *Memoirs* Byrnes refers to a comment by John Foster Dulles that "At that moment our postwar policy of 'no appeasement' was born" as a "true appraisal of the London Conference"; see also Byrnes: *All In One Lifetime* (New York, 1958), p. 317.

44. For Soviet strategy, see Rieber, p. 251, also p. 210 note 58. For Byrnes's analysis of Soviet strategy, see Byrnes, *Speaking Frankly*, pp. 70, 105, 160, 163. For Byrnes's rejection of negotiations, see Byrnes, *Speaking Frankly*, p. 255. For Truman's rejection of negotiations, see William Hillman: *Mr. President* (New York, 1952), p. 23. For the impact of demobilization on the U.S. position, see Millis and Duffield, pp. 110, 129; Truman, *Year of Decisions*, pp. 506, 509. For the futility of continuing negotiations, see Byrnes, *All In One Lifetime*, p. 389.

45. For Iran, see Truman, *Years of Trial and Hope*, pp. 94–5, and *Year of Decisions*, pp. 522–23. For Turkey, see Truman, *Year of Decisions*, pp. 522, 551–2, and *Years of Trial and Hope*, p. 95; Stephen Xydis: *Greece and the Great Powers* (Thessalonike, 1963), pp. 83–4, 284–5, 358; Jones, p. 58. For the reallocation of Soviet loan money, see *FRUS*, 1946, VI, pp. 838–9; *FRUS*, 1946, VII, 433.

46. Lucius Clay: *Decision in Germany* (Garden City, 1950), pp. 43, 73–8, 120, 168–9; Gottlieb, 159–63.

47. Alexander Werth: *France: 1940–1955* (New York, 1956), pp. 232 ff, 257–8, 305 ff, 313–16; Rieber, p. 302; *FRUS*, 1946, VII, pp. 412–13, 419–20, 421, 426, 438, 440; *TNYT*, March 22, 1946, 10:6; March 29, 1946, 11:1; June 1, 1946, 7:1; editorial of May 30, 1946, 20:2.

48. For the politics of foreign aid, *FRUS*, 1946, VII, 441, 896; H. Stuart

Hughes: *The United States and Italy* (Cambridge, 1953), p. 156; Xydis, pp. 317–18; Jones, p. 5. For the Western bloc, see Clifford memo in Clifford Papers, Clifford and Miller (Washington, D.C.); Kennan, pp. 285 ff; Byrnes, *Speaking Frankly*, p. 255; Marcus Raskin and Richard Barnett: *After Twenty Years* (New York, 1965), p. 17; Rieber, p. 48; Gottlieb, pp. 245–6.

49. For the absence of fear of war with the U.S.S.R., see transcript of hearings of President's Air Policy Commission, pp. 2266–7 (Truman Library); Clifford memo; Millis and Duffield, p. 195; Kennan, p. 320; *FRUS*, 1946, VII, 472. For popular opposition to rearmament, see Truman, *Years of Trial and Hope*, p. 91; Sidney Warren: *The President as World Leader* (New York, 1964), p. 288. For the policy of the Communist Parties in Europe, see *FRUS*, 1946, VII, 434–5, 446, 459, 468, 471 ff; Kolko, pp. 438–9. For the decision to defer rearmament, see Forrestal Papers, Box 126, memo from Forrestal to Frye of October 19, 1947; Box 74, letter from Forrestal to Gurney of December 8, 1947; Box 126, memo from Forrestal to Truman of December 21, 1947; Millis and Duffield, pp. 350–3; Senate Committee on Foreign Relations: *Hearings on the European Recovery Program*, 80:2, p. 471.

50. Stimson quote in Stimson and Bundy, pp. 593–4. Truman quote in Truman, *Year of Decisions*, p. 308. For France, see *FRUS*, 1946, VII, 415–16, 425, 431–4, 451. For Italy, see *FRUS*, 1946, VII, 894–7, 902–6, 942. For Greece, see Xydis, pp. 443–53. For Britain see the John Snyder Papers, alphabetical file, memo for files by Widman, December 16, 1946 (Truman Library). For the beginnings of the effort to estimate total needs of reconstruction, see Truman, *Years of Trial and Hope*, p. 111; Thomas Blaisdell Papers, *MEA* file, memo on European Reconstruction Survey of December 3, 1946 (Truman Library). State Department quotation from memo by Cleveland, dated November 12, 1946, Blaisdell Papers. Acheson quote from Acheson, p. 201. See also Gardner, p. 294.

51. Byrnes, *Speaking Frankly*, p. 146. See also Acheson, p. 201; Penrose, pp. 328, 336; Kolko, p. 498.

52. For business pressures on Clayton, see Gardner, p. 197. The following discussion of the British loan debate is based upon the accounts in Gardner, pp. 242–7, and Pritchard, pp. 234–53.

53. For Truman's appeals in the name of international responsibility, see his message of January 3, 1946, on reconversion, his radio speech of May 24 regarding the threatened rail strike, his statement of May 21 justifying his seizure of the coal mines, and his veto of the OPA bill on June 29, all in Truman: *Public Papers* (Washington, D.C., 1946), pp. 1, 274, 322, 329.

The following poll of American opinion on foreign policy is cited in Gabriel Almond: *The American People and Foreign Policy* (New York, 1950), p. 73:

(Percentages of Americans naming foreign problems as most vital)

January 1939	14
April 1939	35
December 1939	47
August 1940	48
November 1941	81
(no polls taken during the war years on this issue)	
October 1945	7
February 1946	23
June 1946	11
September 1946	23
December 1946	22
March 1947	54
July 1947	47
September 1947	28
December 1947	30
February 1948	33

For other indications of revived isolationism, see Millis and Duffield, p. 100; *TNYT,* June 16, 1946, Section 4, 7:1. For public reaction to Churchill's speech, see *POQ,* Summer 1946, p. 264. For Vandenberg quote, see Gardner, p. 239.

54. March 1946 poll in *POQ,* Spring 1946, p. 117. Clayton polls cited in Gardner, p. 248. Poll concerning interest in foreign trade cited in Bauer, p. 82.

55. For public attitudes on loan, see *POQ,* Spring 1946, p. 117; Summer 1946, p. 262. For debate on strategy on the loan, see Gardner, p. 249. For attitudes of high officials about public information policy, see Byrnes, *Speaking Frankly,* pp. 255–6; Millis and Duffield, pp. 102, 106–7, 143, 155; Welles, p. 68.

56. On Truman and the liberals, see Westerfield, pp. 212–13; Jonathan Daniels: *The Man of Independence* (Philadelphia, 1950), pp. 312–13. For Truman and labor, see Frank McNaughton: *Harry Truman, President* (New York, 1948), pp. 127–40; Cabell Phillips: *The Truman Presidency* (New York, 1966), pp. 111–26. Truman's reactions to Clifford's memo are from interview of Clifford by the author. For public attitudes on the likelihood of U.S.-Soviet cooperation in 1946, see *POQ,* Spring 1947, p. 150.

57. For the public information policy, see Millis and Duffield, pp. 128–9; Byrnes, *Speaking Frankly,* p. 256. For the handling of the Iran issue, see Welles, pp. 58–9; Trygve Lie: *In the Cause of Peace* (New York, 1954), pp. 75–80; *TNYT,* March 16, 1946, 1:3. For the handling of problem of Turkey, see Millis and Duffield, pp. 192, 211; Xydis, pp. 358, 644 note 76. For the new attitude toward the press, see the Byrnes Papers, "New York CFM," Byrnes-Molotov conversation of December 9, 1946; "Paris CFM, May 1, Force of public information,"

Byrnes-Bidault conversation. For Byrnes's speeches, see Welles, p. 363. For Forrestal's speeches, see Millis and Duffield, p. 211; Forrestal papers, Box 125, letter from Hensel to Forrestal, February 26, 1947. For Kennan's speaking tour, see Kennan, p. 315; Xydis, p. 593 note 104. For the Administration's conciliatory tone prior to elections, see Curtis MacDougall: *Gideon's Army* (New York, 1956), p. 99. For Byrnes's trip to the House of Representatives during the loan debate, see Joseph and Stewart Alsop in the *Washington Post*, January 26, 1948.

58. For the suppression of tariff information, see Pritchard, pp. 326–7. For the proposed Export-Import Bank expansion, see Gardner, p. 291 note 3; *DSB*, Vol. 14, March 10, 1946, p. 382. For the Administration's refusal to go to Congress for loan money, see *FRUS*, 1946, VII, 409–11, 425, 445, 908, 933; Xydis, p. 453. Quotation is from Penrose, p. 334.

II THE TRUMAN DOCTRINE

1. Clayton quote from *Foreign Relations of the United States* (*FRUS*), 1946, VII, 440. For the British economy, see Richard Gardner: *Sterling Dollar Diplomacy* (Oxford, 1956), pp. 308, 310–11, 328; Joseph M. Jones: *The Fifteen Weeks* (New York, 1955), pp. 79–80; Ross Pritchard: "Will Clayton: Industrial Statesman," unpublished doctoral dissertation (Fletcher School, Tufts University, 1956), p. 272; "The British Crisis," *Federal Reserve Bulletin* (September, 1947), XXXIII, 1071 ff. *The New York Times* (*TNYT*) quote is from an editorial of February 14, 1947. The Lippmann quote is from the *Washington Post*, March 1, 1947.

2. For shortages, see United Nations Economic and Social Council (UNESCO): *Report of Temporary Subcommission on Economic Reconstruction of Devastated Areas*, p. 156, September 18, 1946; E. F. Penrose, *Economic Planning for Peace* (Princeton, 1953), pp. 336, 339; William Clayton Papers, Box 42, "Confidential Marshall Plan Memos," memo dated March 5, 1947 (Truman Library); Joseph M. Jones Papers, Abstract of NAC Report (Truman Library).

3. For the British situation, see Jones, pp. 81–2; Great Britain, Parliament, "Papers by Command," Paper 7046 (London, 1947); Marquis Childs in the *Washington Post*, March 13, 1947. For the American perspective, see the Council of Economic Advisors, *Midyear Economic Review* (Washington, 1950), p. 28.

4. For the British situation, see Jones, p. 82. For the Truman speech, see Truman, *Public Papers*, 1947, p. 167. For the relationship of reconstruction to multilateralism, see Pritchard, pp. 269, 284; UNESCO: *Report of the First Session of the Preparatory Committee of the UN Conference on Trade and Employment*, E/PC/T/33 (London, 1946).

5. For Britain's position, see Gardner, pp. 306 ff; Harry S. Truman

Institute: *Conference of Scholars on the European Recovery Program* (Independence, 1964), p. 48. For the problem of communism in Western Europe, see Jones, p. 96. For Mid East Oil, see Walter Millis and E. S. Duffield, eds.: *The Forrestal Diaries* (New York, 1951), pp. 323, 355–8; Harry S. Truman: *Years of Trial and Hope* (Garden City, 1956), p. 95; Senate Foreign Relations Committee: *European Recovery Program* hearings, pp. 378–81; House Committee on Foreign Affairs, 80:1, 2: *United States Foreign Policy for Postwar Recovery*, pp. 242, 479; Clifford memo in Clifford Papers (Washington, D.C.), September 1946, Chapter V; Forrestal Papers, Box 127, letter from Forrestal to Marshall of February 19, 1948. For the November 1946 committee meeting, see Millis and Duffield, pp. 215, 342.

6. For election results see Curtis MacDougall: *Gideon's Army* (New York, 1965), pp. 100–1; *Congressional Quarterly, "Congress and the Nation—1945–64"* (Washington, 1964), p. 3. For Republican record on foreign economic policy, see *TNYT*, November 10, 1946, IV, 1:1, 1:4. For Taber and Bridges, see Cabell Phillips: *The Truman Presidency* (New York, 1966), p. 234.

7. For the Wallace speech, see Harry S. Truman: *Year of Decisions* (Garden City, 1955), pp. 557–8; Byrnes: *Speaking Frankly* (New York, 1947), pp. 239–43; Millis and Duffield, pp. 207–8; *TNYT*, September 14, 1946, 1:2; MacDougall, pp. 63 ff. For Truman's position, see *TNYT*, November 3, 1946, IV, 1:2; November 10, 1946, IV, 1:1–2; Alfred Steinberg: *The Man from Missouri* (New York, 1962), p. 286. The Lippmann quote is from Phillips, p. 161.

8. For Truman's view, see Truman, *Year of Decisions*, p. 505; *Years of Trial and Hope*, pp. 172, 175; Millis and Duffield, p. 218. For Vandenberg's view, see the Arthur Vandenberg Papers, letter from Vandenberg to Tufty of November 11, 1946 (University of Michigan Library). For the Eightieth Congress, see Pritchard, pp. 328–9; *Congressional Record (CR)*, 80:1, p. 37.

9. For Clayton and Acheson, see Dean G. Acheson: *Present at the Creation* (New York, 1969), pp. 200–1. For guarantee about Imperial preference, see Gardner, pp. 349–50.

10. For the State Department quote, see Jones Papers, memo from Jones to Russell of July 18, 1947. For Jones's quote, see Jones, p. 166. For the drafts of Marshall's speech, see the Jones Papers; see also the Clifford memo of September 1946; Jones's memo in Jones Papers, from Jones to Benton of February 26, 1947.

11. For Truman's quote, see Truman, *Years of Trial and Hope*, p. 104. For the initiation of planning, see Jones, p. 199. Acheson quoted in Jones, p. 159.

12. Truman's statement cited by Arthur Krock in *TNYT*, March 23, 1947. For the significance of election for the left, see H. Bradford Westerfield: *Foreign Relations and Party Politics* (New Haven, 1955), p. 219; *TNYT*, November 10, 1946, IV, 3:1; November 24, 1946, 50:4.

13. Truman: *Public Papers* (Washington, D.C., 1947), p. 176.

14. For Vandenberg, see the Vandenberg Papers, letter from Vandenberg to Barton of March 24, 1947. For Case, see the Harry S. Truman Papers, OF426, letter from Case to Truman of May 10, 1947 (Truman Library). See also the transcript of a telephone conversation between Reston and Forrestal on March 13, 1947, in the Clifford Papers (Washington, D.C.).

15. For the Clayton memo, see the William Clayton Papers. For Vandenberg, see the Joseph Davies Papers, Box 25, Chronological File, Diary Entry for March 12, 1947 (Library of Congress); David Watt: "Withdrawal from Greece," in Michael Sissons and Philip French: *Age of Austerity* (London, 1963), p. 106.

16. See, for example, The New York *Herald Tribune,* December 12, 1946. For an example of the Administration's pretense that the British withdrawal was unexpected, see the response of the State Department to question 7 in *DSB Supplement, Aid to Greece and Turkey,* Vol. 16, No. 409A, May 4, 1947, p. 868.

17. See Stephen Xydis: *Greece and the Great Powers* (Thessalonike, 1963), especially pp. 237, 238, 242, 267–8, 286–7, 290, 332, 356, 361, 363, 378, 512–14, 638 note 18; Truman, *Years of Trial and Hope,* p. 99; Millis and Duffield, p. 211; Jones, pp. 5, 58.

18. For a full statement of the Tsaldaris mission, see Xydis, pp. 443–53; Truman Papers, OF206-D, memo from Acheson to the President of December 13, 1946.

19. For the official position, see *DSB Supplement, Aid to Greece and Turkey,* Vol. 16, No. 409A, May 4, 1947, p. 868; Question and Answer No. 7. For the Bevin-Byrnes discussion, see Byrnes, *Speaking Frankly,* p. 300. For comment on actual expectations, see Millis and Duffield, pp. 210, 215–17; Xydis, pp. 363, 430, 432–4, 451, 663 note 81. The interview of Constantine Tsaldaris by Philip C. Brooks of May 4, 1964, is in the files of the Truman Library. The interview of Clark Clifford is by the author. See also Watt, p. 116.

20. House Committee on Foreign Affairs, 80:1, *Assistance to Greece and Turkey* hearings, pp. 2–3, 15–16.

21. Truman Papers, OF426 (1947), letter from Secretary of Agriculture to Steelman of July 16, 1947; *DSB*, 16, June 29, 1947, pp. 1298, 1303; *DSB*, 17, July 13, 1947, p. 96.

22. Senate Committee on Foreign Relations, 80:1, *Assistance to Greece and Turkey* hearings, p. 78.

23. See Westerfield, pp. 206, 209, 215, and especially 273–5; James Reston in *TNYT*, November 10, 1946, IV, 3:3–6; Arthur Krock in *TNYT,* May 2, 1947; article by Thomas L. Stokes in the Jones Papers.

24. For meeting with Congressional leaders, see Acheson, p. 219; Jones, pp. 138–42.

25. For the drafting of the Truman Doctrine, see Jones, pp. 151–2. For Kennan's analysis of this issue, see George F. Kennan: *Memoirs* (New York, 1969), p. 334.

26. The March 6 draft is in the Jones Papers, Box #1, "Drafts of the Truman Doctrine." For Jones on Truman's view of speech, see the Jones Papers, Box #1, "Drafts of the Truman Doctrine," "The drafting of the President's message of March 12, 1947, chronology." For Truman's response, see Truman, *Years of Trial and Hope*, p. 105.

27. For Clifford's suggestions, see Jones, pp. 156–7. Acheson quoted in Jones, p. 162.

28. For Marshall, see Charles Bohlen: *The Transformation of American Foreign Policy* (New York, 1969), pp. 86–7. For Byrnes, see Byrnes, p. 302. For Kennan, see his *Memoirs*, p. 337. For Baruch, see the Davies Papers, Box 25, Chronological File, journal entry for August 9, 1947.

29. See the Jones Papers, letter from Jones to Lippmann of May 7, 1947; Forrestal Papers, Box 76(s), letter from Forrestal to Smith of March 19, 1947. For Childs, Lippmann, and Reston, see Jones, p. 227.

30. House hearings on *Assistance to Greece and Turkey*, pp. 2–3.

31. Senate hearings on *Assistance to Greece and Turkey*, p. 42; House hearings on *Assistance to Greece and Turkey*, p. 43.

32. House hearings on *Assistance to Greece and Turkey*, pp. 91–2.

33. *Ibid.*, pp. 54, 78.

34. *Ibid.*, p. 83; Senate hearings on *Assistance to Greece and Turkey*, p. 7.

35. Senate hearings on *Assistance to Greece and Turkey*, pp. 74–5.

36. House hearings on *Assistance to Greece and Turkey*, pp. 32–3.

37. The following account is drawn primarily from the following works: Tang Tsou: *America's Failure in China* (Chicago, 1963); Herbert Feis: *The China Tangle* (Princeton, 1953); Gabriel Kolko: *The Politics of War* (New York, 1968).

38. For Republican views on China policy, see Tang, pp. 447–8; Truman, *Years of Trial and Hope*, p. 81; the Vandenberg Papers, letter from Vandenberg to Chennault of January 28, 1947; letter from Vandenberg to Montgomery of January 27, 1947; "Marshall and GOP Headed for Clash over China Policy," article in New York *World-Telegram and Sun* reviewing Vandenberg speech, in Vandenberg scrapbook, the Vandenberg Papers.

39. House hearings on *Assistance to Greece and Turkey*, pp. 16–18.

40. For reference to economic issues, see Senate hearings on *Assistance to Greece and Turkey*, p. 81. For poll results on importance of communist issue in public view of Greco-Turkish aid, see the *Washington Post*, March 28, 1947. Roosevelt quote in Jan Ciechanowski: *Defeat in Victory* (Garden City, 1947), pp. 201–2.

III FOREIGN AID AND INTERNAL SECURITY

1. For information on the Dies Committee and the House Un-American Activities Committee (HUAC), as well as the history of Congres-

sional concern with alien and subversive activities, I have relied mainly on three accounts: Robert Carr: *The House Committee on Un-American Activities* (Ithaca, 1952); Walter Goodman: *The Committee* (New York, 1964); August Raymond Ogden: *The Dies Committee* (Washington, 1943).

2. For discussions of the committee's attacks on the New Deal, see especially Goodman, pp. 42, 48–51, 54–5, and Ogden, pp. 48, 62–3, 64, 74, 136.

3. For the committee's attacks on the federal bureaucracy during the war, see Goodman, Chapter 5, especially pp. 125 ff, 135, 142. For Dewey's use of this in 1944, see H. Bradford Westerfield: *Foreign Policy and Party Politics* (New Haven, 1955), pp. 189–90, 195–6.

4. The *Amerasia* case is discussed in Earl Latham: *The Communist Controversy in Washington* (Cambridge, 1966), pp. 203–16. For the Canadian spy disclosures, see Eric F. Goldman: *The Crucial Decade—and After: America 1945–1960* (New York, 1960), pp. 35–6. The public opinion poll is in Bert Andrews: *Washington Witch Hunt* (New York, 1948), pp. 9–12. For the Combs subcommittee report, see House Committee on the Civil Service, 79:2: *Report of Investigation with Respect to Employee Loyalty and Employment Practices in the Government of the U.S.* For the Rees quote, see *ibid.*, p. 9. For an analysis of the significance of Rees's statement, see Latham, p. 365. For Republican use of the issue in 1946, see *U.S. News and World Report*, November 1, 1946, "What U.S. Communists Face"; *The New York Times* (*TNYT*), March 23, 1947, 48:4; T. L. Stokes, "Guilt Complex," in the Washington *Daily News*, March 19, 1947; New York *Post*, April 2, 1947; Westerfield, p. 210.

5. For early predictions of Truman's attitude about subversive employees, see Curtis D. MacDougall: *Gideon's Army* (New York, 1965), p. 131. For the Administration's handling of the Bentley and Chambers stories, see Elizabeth Bentley: *Out of Bondage* (New York, 1951), p. 308; Richard M. Nixon: *Six Crises* (Garden City, 1962), pp. 4–5; Cabell Phillips: *The Truman Presidency* (New York, 1966), pp. 358–9; Benjamin Ginzberg: *Rededication to Freedom* (New York, 1959), p. 111; memo from Elsey to Spingarn of September 10, 1948, White House Assignment, Spingarn Papers (Truman Library); Robert Stripling: *The Red Plot Against America* (Drexel Hill, Pa., 1949); see also Latham, generally.

6. For Clark's advocacy, see the memorandum from Fleming to the Attorney General of July 22, 1946, OF252–1 Truman Papers, Truman Library; memorandum record of a phone call from Steelman to Latta of August 21, 1946, OF252–1, Truman Papers; memorandum from Collet to Steelman of September 18, 1946, OF252–1, Truman Papers. For Clark's action on alien enemies and FBI investigations, see Athan Theoharis: "The Escalation of the Loyalty Program," in Barton J. Bernstein: *Politics and Policies of the Truman Administration* (Chicago, 1970), p. 246. For indications of Hoover's

influence over Clark, see file "E.O.9835 Loyalty-Box" in Vanech Papers, Truman Library.

7. For Truman's orders to Hoover, see Alan D. Harper: *The Politics of Loyalty* (Westport, Conn., 1969), p. 23. For this interpretation of the origins of the loyalty program, see Latham, p. 365; Theoharis; Robert Cushman, "The President's Loyalty Purge," in *Survey Graphic*, May 1947; New York *Post*, April 2, 1947.

8. The best summary of the history of loyalty provisions is in Eleanor Bontecou: *The Federal Loyalty-Security Program* (Ithaca, 1953); see also "The President's Temporary Commission on Employee Loyalty Report," OF252–1, Truman Papers; House Committee on Civil Service, *Report of Investigation With Respect to Employee Loyalty*.

9. For the executive order, see E.O. 9806, *Federal Register*, 1946, p. 13863. For a discussion of the impossibility of the commission's actually conducting an investigation, see the minutes of the commission meeting for December 16, 1946, Spingarn Papers, Treasury Department File, Truman Library. It is interesting to note that the commission justified its failure to investigate the problem by stating that the existence of a problem was to be presumed as a result of the Combs subcommittee hearings and the Presidential order creating the Temporary Commission, yet both of these sources begged ignorance on the subject and indicated only that an investigation should take place. For the commission's attempts to get information from the FBI, see the minutes for January 13 and 17, 1947, in Spingarn Papers. For Clark testimony, see the memo from Clark to Vanech of February 14, 1947, Exhibit 10 in "The President's Temporary Commission on Employee Loyalty."

The totality of the evidence received by the Temporary Commission was as follows: letters from the heads of the various official intelligence services asserting without documentation the seriousness of the problem and describing it not mainly in terms of espionage but in terms of the spread of subversive ideas; the oral testimony of Hoover's assistant Dr. Milton Ladd, who offered no proof of his assertion that the problem of employee loyalty was serious; Clark's testimony, which indicated that the problem was less serious than previously believed; and Herbert Gaston's testimony, which indicated that employee loyalty was not a major problem.

10. The quote from the report of the Interdepartmental Committee is in Bontecou, pp. 17–18. For the discussion of Congressional reaction to this report and the establishment of the second Interdepartmental Committee, see Bontecou, p. 18. For Gaston's testimony, see the minutes of the commission meeting of January 24, Spingarn Papers; see also Gaston's affidavit in "The President's Temporary Commission on Employee Loyalty," Exhibit 11. See this report, pp. 25–6, for the quote regarding counterespionage. The basis for the statement that the Administration did nothing regarding counterespionage is Forrestal's complaint in late 1948 that nothing was being done to

develop the government's counterespionage capabilities: see the memorandum for the President of October 15, 1948, Spingarn Papers, White House Assignment, Internal Security File, Folder 1. For a discussion of the weakness of the federal counterintelligence system, see Hanson Baldwin in *TNYT*, April 10, 1947, p. 13.

Predictions that the new loyalty program would do little to discover espionage agents were amply justified. By 1950 the loyalty program had considered 8,288 cases without discovering a single spy or generating a single indictment. Only 240 individuals were dismissed or refused employment as a result of loyalty investigations, but this included anyone about whom a suspicion of disloyalty could be sustained and did not necessarily involve evidence that disloyal acts had in fact been perpetrated. The head of the loyalty program stated in 1950 that the entire program had not discovered a single case of espionage or a single case "directing toward espionage." See Francis Biddle: *Fear of Freedom* (Garden City, 1951), quoted in Barton J. Bernstein: *The Truman Administration* (New York, 1966), pp. 369–70.

11. For indication that Congress knew about the Bentley-Chambers stories, see Ginzberg, pp. 115–17; also, Stephen Spingarn, a staff member of the President's Temporary Commission, told the author in an interview that this information was known to Congress in 1946. For the President's appointment policy regarding the loyalty program, see Harper, pp. 47–8. Another indication of the influence of Congress over the establishment of the program was the statement of Commissioner Sullivan that "the Congress must be satisfied" in objecting to suggestions that the commission leave open the scope of the proposed program. See the minutes of the commission for January 24, p. 4.

12. The Randolph assertion is based upon a memo for Mr. Connelly of October 1, 1946, OF482, Truman Papers, and Jennings Randolph indicated in an interview with the author that the President had indeed promised him prior to the 1946 elections that a new loyalty program would be forthcoming.

13. For an interesting example of the conjunction of isolationism with opposition to communism, see the speech of Congressman Lemke in House Debate on HR5852, *Congressional Record* (*CR*), 80:2, p. 6114; see also Robert Sherwood: *Roosevelt and Hopkins* (New York, 1948), p. 829.

14. For Byrnes's grilling regarding the loyalty of State Department employees, see Byrnes: *Speaking Frankly* (New York, 1947), pp. 253–4. For Bridges, see the New York *Herald Tribune*, February 17, 1946, article on Canadian Spy Ring. For Taber, see his speech of April 10, 1946, in the *CR*, 79:2, p. 3467. For the quote from the *Christian Science Monitor*, see the issue for March 24, 1947.

15. Martin's speech reported in *TNYT*, January 4, 1947, p. 2. For Jonkman, see the *Washington Post*, January 27, 1947. For Taber, see

the letter from Forrestal to Clifford of January 31, 1947, Forrestal Papers, Box 72(c). For the Lilienthal controversy, see Harper, pp. 67 ff; letter from Forrestal to Hoyt of February 20, 1947, Forrestal Papers, Box 74(H). For the Clapp controversy, see the *Washington Post*, February 7, 1947. For Bridges and Vincent, see the letter from Bridges to Vandenberg of March 24, 1947, Vandenberg Papers. For the Labor Department appropriation, see *CR*, 80:1, March 25, 1947. For the Judiciary Committee, see *TNYT*, March 6, 1947. For the Civil Service Committee, see *TNYT*, January 11, 1947. For the House debate on January 23, see the *CR*, 80:1, pp. 546–51. For a general discussion of Republican readiness to attack U.S. communists, see the *Washington Post*, December 30, 1946, article about Congressmen Brown and Jenkins. An interesting aspect of this impulse relates to the widely voiced opinion among Republican legislators that U.S. communists worked actively and effectively against them during the 1946 campaign; see, for example, the letter from Vandenberg to Toodle of January 29, 1947, Vandenberg Papers.

16. For the HUAC program, see *TNYT*, January 23, 1947. For Martin's commitment, see *TNYT*, February 9, 1947, 42:4. For HUAC's primary interest in disloyal employees, see *TNYT*, January 4, 1947, 14:1, and February 26, 1947, 14:2. For a report of HUAC's preparing to begin investigation, see the *Washington Post*, February 8, 1947.

17. For a discussion of the effect on HUAC of the federal grand jury, see House Committee on Un-American Activities, 80:2: *Interim Report on Hearings Regarding Communist Espionage in the United States Government*, p. 1352. For a discussion of the Administration's strange handling of the Chambers-Bentley stories, see Ralph de Toledano: *Seeds of Treason* (Chicago, 1962), p. 139.

18. For Vandenberg, see his speech to Senate reporting the Greco-Turkish aid bill in *CR*, 80:1. For Thomas, see Harper, p. 46. For Hurley, see Dean G. Acheson: *Present at the Creation* (New York, 1969), pp. 133–5.

19. For Iran, see Trygve Lie: *In the Cause of Peace* (New York, 1954), pp. 75–80. For Greece, see Stephen Xydis: *Greece and the Great Powers* (Thessalonike, 1963), pp. 354–5, 442–3, 540; see also the record of the Byrnes-Molotov conversations, December 9, 1946, Byrnes Papers. For treaties, see Byrnes, *Speaking Frankly*, pp. 152–3; Xydis, pp. 419–20. For public response to the treaties, see *Public Opinion Quarterly* (*POQ*), Spring 1947, p. 150. For the Soviet disarmament campaign, see Walter Millis and E. S. Duffield, eds.: *The Forrestal Diaries* (New York, 1951), pp. 217, 291; letter from Forrestal to Bard of July 11, 1947, Forestal Papers, Box 125; record of telephone conversation between Forrestal and Lippmann of November 29, 1946, Forrestal Papers, Box 70(C).

20. For Truman quotes, see William Hillman: *Mr. President* (New York, 1952), pp. 121–2. For a later statement of the President's fear of

popular susceptibility to Soviet propaganda, see Harry S. Truman: *Years of Trial and Hope* (Garden City, 1956), p. 171. For Clark, see Senate Committee on the Judiciary, 84:2, *Communist Propaganda Activities in the United States*, hearings, pp. v–vi. Forrestal quotes respectively from letter from Forrestal to Brown of October 22, 1946, Forrestal Papers, Box 68(B), and memorandum for the Secretary of State of March 8, 1946, Forrestal Papers, Box 68(B). See also the memorandum from Forrestal to Harriman of October 8, 1946, Forrestal Papers, Box 69(H).

21. See State Department memo on "International Communism," in *Foreign Relations of the United States (FRUS)*, "The Potsdam Conference," I, pp. 267–80. For Hoover, see *FBI Law Enforcement Bulletin*, 1946, I, pp. 2–7. For the shift in Communist tactics see Irving Howe and Lewis Coser: *The American Communist Party* (Boston, 1957), pp. 447 ff. For the Party's reaction to Churchill's speech, see *Political Affairs*, April 1946. For typical communist attacks in 1946, see *Political Affairs* for that year: the editorial in the May issue; "The Anglo-American Bloc" by Alexander Bittleman (July); "The Foreign Ministers' Conference" by Joseph Starobin (August); "American Imperialism, Leader of World Reaction" by William Z. Foster (August); "Defeat the Imperialist Drive Toward Fascism and War" by Eugene Dennis (September). See Dennis's article (September), p. 789, also for the strategy of building bridges to other progressive forces.

22. For Clark on isolationists, see the *CR*, 80:1, p. A815. For Forrestal, see Millis and Duffield, p. 236. Truman quote about propaganda in his *Year of Decisions*, p. 97. For Forrestal about pacifists, see the letter from Forrestal to Marshall of Feb. 6, 1947, Forrestal Papers, Box 125. For Truman quote on liberals, see Hillman, p. 128. For Hoover, see J. Edgar Hoover: *Masters of Deceit* (New York, 1958), p. 228; also "Red Fascism in the United States Today," *American*, February 1947. For Clark, see the *Washington Post*, November 22, 1947. For Forrestal on demobilization, see Arnold A. Rogow: *James Forrestal* (New York, 1963), pp. 126–9, 144. For Cabinet discussions, see Millis and Duffield, pp. 242–3; memo from Forrestal to Connelly of February 11, 1947, Forrestal Papers, Box 125. For the Jones quote, see Joseph M. Jones: *The Fifteen Weeks* (New York, 1955), p. 186; see also Xydis, p. 546.

23. For State Department readiness for the anti-communist campaign, see "International Communism" in *FRUS*, "The Potsdam Conference," I, pp. 267–80. For Grew, see Latham, p. 210.

24. For two characteristic observations on the psychological impact of the loyalty order, see Alistair Cooke: *A Generation On Trial* (New York, 1950): ". . . And if Communism in the United States was an impotent strain of the Russian breed, why had the President set up . . . a permanent loyalty record of the Government's employees?" (p. 48); and Ginzberg: "Once the Commission formulated and Pres-

ident Truman . . . promulgated the loyalty program, the reality of the Communist menace became established by law, so to speak. Instead of questioning the need for a loyalty program . . . the American people concluded that there must be a Communist menace because the government had set up a drastic program to deal with it" (p. 123).

For Clark's role in the campaign for Greco-Turkish aid, see *TNYT*, March 30, 1947, 44:4. For a discussion of the tendency of the manner of the loyalty order's promulgation to stimulate a crisis atmosphere, see Harper, p. 45. The records of the decision to release the Commission's Report can be found in the Spingarn Papers, particularly a memo for the file of February 24, 1947, Treasury Department file; memo of the final meeting of the Temporary Commission of February 20, 1947, Treasury Department file. See also *TNYT* of March 23, 1947, p. 1.

25. Clark's statement that "the disloyalty problem [is] not as serious as it once was" can be found in the notes of commission meeting of February 14, 1947, Springarn Papers, Treasury Department file. The two special assistants were Assistant U.S. Attorneys from Boston and New York, named Duggan and Edelstein. The main instances of distortion in their report were as follows: (1) they relied on the unsupported assertions of FBI officials as to the seriousness of the problem for the summary of the draft report; (2) they made it appear that the Combs subcommittee had held extensive hearings on the problem of employee loyalty rather than the cursory and inconclusive investigation that was conducted; (3) they suppressed Gaston's testimony entirely; (4) in including statistics on numbers of cases of disloyalty in federal bureaucracy, they provided cumulative statistics for a several-year period without indicating that they were cumulative, so that the problem was made to appear growing steadily when in fact it was decreasing; (5) in including information of FBI action in past loyalty cases, they referred to 2,785 cases reviewed by the FBI and stated that in these cases "no action was taken by the employing agency"; this implied that evidence of disloyalty had been found by the FBI but action had not been taken by the agency, whereas agency inaction in fact meant that significant evidence of disloyalty had not been found. General Royall, a commission member, stated that the draft report "greatly exaggerated" the matter, for "certainly nothing had been presented that anybody seriously threatened [American security]." See the commission's minutes for January 30, and Spingarn's notes on the meetings of February 6, February 13, and January 29 in Springarn Papers, Treasury Department file. A copy of Duggan's and Edelstein's draft is also contained in this file.

26. For Budenz's statements about Eisler, see *TNYT*, October 13, 16, 17, 18, 1946. For Thomas's request and Clark's arrest, see *TNYT*, February 5, 1947. The ACLU letter, from Fraenkel and Baldwin to Clark of February 14, 1947, is in the ACLU files, Vol. 9, HUAC #4, 1947

(Princeton University Library). For HUAC and House action regarding contempt citation see *TNYT*, February 7, 18, 1947. For Eisler's indictment by grand jury see Table below:

Disposition by Justice Department of contempt citations voted by HUAC during the period 1940–7.*

Name of Defendant	Date of Citation	Date of Indictment
James H. Dolsen	March 29, 1940	June 30, 1941
George Powers	April 3, 1940	Jan. 30, 1941
Edward K. Barsky	March 29, 1946	March 31, 1947
Helen R. Bryan et al.	April 17, 1946	March 31, 1947
Corliss G. Lamont	June 28, 1946	ignored by jury
George Marshall	August 2, 1946	March 31, 1947
Richard Morford	August 3, 1946	March 31, 1947
Gerhart Eisler	Feb. 19, 1947	Feb. 27, 1947
Eugene Dennis	April 23, 1947	April 30, 1947
Leon Josephson	April 23, 1947	April 30, 1947

* Source: letter from Assistant Attorney General Vinson to author of November 3, 1967.

27. HUAC, 80:1: *Hearings Regarding Gerhart Eisler*, especially pp. 11, 31, 33–4.
28. For the documents, see HUAC, 80:1: *Hearings Regarding Leon Josephson and Samuel Liptzen*, pp. 37–9, 51, 53. For contempt proceedings, see *TNYT*, April 23, 1947, and Table in note 26.
29. For Thomas's statement to Hoover, see the memo from Hoover to Clark of March 14, 1947, Vanech Papers. For Hoover's testimony, see *TNYT*, March 27, 1947, 1:5.
30. For contempt proceeding, see *TNYT*, April 23, 1947, and also Table in note 26.
31. For Roosevelt's attitude about the committee, see Bontecou, p. 9; Stripling, pp: 29, 30, 35; Ogden, pp. 66–7, 85, 86, 115, 142, 161, 208–9, 223–4, 227–8, 245; Goodman, pp. 113–14. For contempt statistics, see the Table in note 26. For the HUAC request of February 1947 for expeditious handling of pending cases, see the Eisler hearings, p. 13.
32. For Hoover's statements on the subject of communism during the war, see *CR*, 80:1, pp. 5218–19. For Hoover's San Francisco speech, see *CR*, pp. A27–A28. For *American* magazine article, see *CR*, pp. A536–A538.
33. Biddle's quote is from David Lilienthal: *The Journals of David Lilienthal: The TVA Years*, p. 429. For Hoover's objection to Clark, see the memo from Hoover to Clark of March 18, 1947, Vanech Papers. For HUAC's request to the President, see Harper, pp. 23–4. A copy of Wilson's article, dated April 6, 1947, is in the ACLU files, Vol. 10, HUAC #1.

34. For Thomas's criticism and Clark's response, see *TNYT*, February 11, 1947, 22:4, and April 23, 1947. Clark quotes in HUAC hearings on HR4422 and HR4581, February 5, 1948.

IV THE MARSHALL PLAN

1. See Joseph M. Jones: *The Fifteen Weeks* (New York, 1955), pp. 199–201; Harry B. Price: *The Marshall Plan and Its Meaning* (Ithaca, 1955), p. 21.
2. For SWNCC, see Jones, pp. 207, 213; for Clayton memo, see Clayton Papers, Box 42, "Confidential Marshall Plan Memos," "The European Crisis."
3. Thomas Blaisdell was appointed Chief of the Mission for Economic Affairs at London in March 1945 and was subsequently designated U.S. representative to the Emergency Economic Committees. His papers, housed in the Truman Library, contain a full record of his conversion to belief in the international organization of the European economy, beginning from a position of skepticism. See, for example: letter to Clayton of November 2, 1945, MEA file; "Draft of Proposed US Plan for a European Settlement," spring 1946; letter from Blaisdell to Hickerson of July 26, 1946; Blaisdell to Clayton, October 1, 1946. For role of young economists who worked on the ECE in developing ERP, see Jones, p. 242; Kennan, *Memoirs*, pp. 356–9. On Germany, see Bruce R. Kuklick: "Commerce and World Order," unpublished doctoral dissertation (University of Pennsylvania, 1968); Dean G. Acheson: *Present at the Creation* (New York, 1969), p. 260. For Kennan's report, see Kennan, *Memoirs*, pp. 353–9; Price, pp. 22–3.
4. For Acheson's speech, see the *Department of State Bulletin* (*DSB*), Vol. 16, p. 991; for Marshall's speech, see *DSB*, Vol. 16, p. 1159. For Clayton's role, see Ross Pritchard: "Will Clayton: Industrial Statesman," unpublished doctoral dissertation (Fletcher School, Tufts University, 1956), pp. 292–5.
5. For the British crisis, see Richard N. Gardner: *Sterling Dollar Diplomacy* (Oxford, 1956), pp. 313–25; *The New York Times* (*TNYT*), June 28, July 9, August 3. For the situation on the continent, see the Committee for European Economic Cooperation (CEEC): *Report: July–September, 1947* (London, 1947), p. 6; *TNYT*, August 4, August 5, 1947.
6. See Pritchard, pp. 305–6.
7. For drafts, see the Senate Committee on Foreign Relations: *European Recovery Program: Basic Documents*, 80:1.
8. For elimination of Imperial preference, see Gardner, pp. 349–50. For Clayton, see Senate Committee on Foreign Relations, hearings on *Assistance to Greece and Turkey*, p. 81; *TNYT*, May 3, 1947, 4:7.

9. For British developments, see Gardner, pp. 356–9; *TNYT*, August 2, August 7, August 8, 1947. For Lovett, see Walter Millis and E. S. Duffield, eds.: *The Forrestal Diaries* (New York, 1951), pp. 304–5. For continental developments, see CEEC *Report*, p. 6.

10. For British views on trade negotiations, see Gardner, pp. 351–5. For wool bill, see William Clayton: "GATT, the Marshall Plan and OECD," *Political Science Quarterly*, Vol. LXXVIII.

11. Pritchard, pp. 196–204; Gardner, pp. 351–4.

12. For the significance of the '48 election, see Acheson, p. 201. For the shift to regional application of multilateralism, see Gardner, p. 304. For the Marshall Plan and the ITO, see *TNYT*, July 3, September 21, 1947; House Committee on Foreign Affairs, *Hearings on Postwar Recovery Policy*, p. 95; *DSB*, Vol. 16, June 22, 1947, p. 1193.

13. For the quote on bilateral contracts, see the House Committee on Foreign Affairs, *Report on S2202* (80:2). For Clayton's quote, see the Senate Committee on Finance, hearings on *Extension of Reciprocal Trade Agreements Act* (80:2), p. 454. See also the Department of State: "Draft Summary of Department's position on ERP," 26 August 1947, Clifford Papers, ERP file (Washington, D.C.); House Committee on Foreign Affairs, *Hearings on Postwar Recovery Policy*, p. 95; Senate Committee on Foreign Relations, 80:2, ERP hearings, pp. 140–1, 209; *TNYT*, September 13, 1947; the *Washington Post*, March 24, 1948; report of the National Advisory Council in June 1947, cited in *TNYT*, June 27, 1947.

14. For confusion about U.S. objectives, see Gardner, p. 304; *TNYT*, July 22, 1947. Interview of Lord Plowden by Philip C. Brooks, June 15, 1964, ERP oral history in files of Truman Library. For resolution, see House Committee on Foreign Affairs, *Hearings on Postwar Recovery Policy*, pp. 332, 337.

15. Acheson quote in Jonathan Daniels: *The Man of Independence* (Philadelphia, 1950), p. 322. For the importance of exports, see *The Economic Report of the President* (Washington, January 1948), pp. 26–7; "Economic Report" dated December 30, 1947, Bureau of Budget Folder, Clifford Papers (Washington, D.C.). For agricultural exports, see the Annual Report of Secretary of Agriculture, January 1948, cited in the *Washington Post*, January 19, 1948; Senate Committee on Foreign Relations, ERP hearings, pp. 312, 319, 322, 323; Raymond F. Mikesell: *United States Economic Policy and International Relations* (New York, 1952), pp. 263–4. For private investment, see Gabriel Kolko: *The Politics of War* (New York, 1968), p. 253. For triangular trade, see the House Committee on Foreign Affairs, *Hearings on Postwar Recovery Policy*, pp. 97, 329; Senate Committee on Foreign Relations, ERP hearings, pp. 50–2, 139, 198–200, 319; see also Mikesell, p. 264; Senate ERP hearings, p. 295. The report of the National Advisory Council is cited in *TNYT*, June 27, 1947.

16. Clayton quoted from the memo on "The European Crisis," Clayton

Papers. Truman quoted in Edwin G. Nourse: *Economics in the Public Service* (New York, 1953), p. 167; see also the Department of State: "Certain Aspects of European Recovery Problem from the U.S. Standpoint," Policy Planning Staff Memo dated July 23, 1947, pp. 3–4, Clifford Papers (Washington, D.C.), ERP file.

17. For the inadequacy of $20 billion, see James Reston in *TNYT*, September 28, 1947; OEEC: *Interim Report on the European Recovery Program* (Paris, 1948). For foreign aid and inflation, see the Senate Committee on Foreign Relations, ERP hearings, p. 296. The speech of William O. Foster is cited in *TNYT*, October 28, 1947, 40:4. Clayton quote from House Committee on Foreign Affairs, *Hearings on Postwar Recovery Policy*, pp. 334–5; see also, *ibid.*, p. 329.

18. For Marshall's speech, see *DSB*, Vol. 16, p. 1159. For Clayton on the Soviet position at Paris, see Clayton, "GATT, the Marshall Plan, and OECD," p. 501.

19. For European reactions to Truman Doctrine, see Jones, pp. 208–9; also memo in the Jones Papers, and David Watt: "Withdrawal from Greece," in Michael Sissons and Philip French: *Age of Austerity* (London, 1963), p. 108. For Clayton's communication of this to the State Department, see Pritchard, p. 292. For the development of Marshall's speech, see George F. Kennan: *Memoirs* (New York, 1969), pp. 359–60; Pritchard, pp. 281, 294–5; Price, p. 24; Jones, p. 253. For Soviet attitudes toward the "E" Committees, see Philip E. Mosely: "Hopes and Failures," in Stephen D. Kertesz, ed.: *The Fate of East Central Europe* (Notre Dame, Ind., 1956), pp. 56–7. For the compatibility of aid to Eastern Europe with American objectives, see the "Economic report" dated December 30, 1947, Bureau of Budget folder, Clifford Papers (Washington, D.C.); Jones, pp. 205, 243; Department of State, "Draft Summary of Department's Position on ERP," August 26, 1947, ERP file, Clifford Papers (Washington, D.C.).

20. For Marshall's conviction that Soviet participation would doom ERP, see Charles Bohlen: *The Transformation of American Foreign Policy* (New York, 1969), pp. 90–7. Kennan quote in Jones, p. 253. For Kennan's strategy, see Price, p. 24.

21. For Clayton and Thorp, see the interview of Stinebower by Garwood, Clayton Papers. For Kennan and Bohlen, see Bohlen, pp. 90–1. For Soviet intentions, see Harry S. Truman: *Years of Trial and Hope* (Garden City, 1956), p. 116. For Forrestal, see Millis and Duffield, p. 279. For official views on the compatibility of the Marshall Plan and the Western bloc, see "Certain Aspects of the ERP from the US Standpoint," Policy Planning Staff Memo, July 23, 1947, Clifford Papers (Washington, D.C.); Millis and Duffield, p. 442.

22. This figure is derived from the fact that aid under ERP amounted to 5 per cent of the GNP of the recipients and had to be matched by contributions of "counterpart funds" by recipients. See Price, p. 259.

23. For Kennan's speech, see Kennan, p. 349. For an analysis of communist strength in European labor, see Alfred J. Rieber: *Stalin and the French Communist Party* (New York, 1962), pp. 214–26, 229; Edouard Dolleans and Gerard Dehore: *Histoire du Travail en France,* Vol. II (Paris, 1955), pp. 150–1.

24. For France, see Rieber, especially "The Dilemma of French Communism," and "The Last Gamble," also pp. 191, 234–5, 310–13; Dolleans and Dehore, pp. 151–5; Alexander Werth: *France, 1940–1955* (New York, 1956), pp. 348–56, 357–8. For Italy, see H. Stuart Hughes: *The United States and Italy* (Cambridge, Mass., 1953), pp. 156, 157.

25. For the shift to oppositionism in communist policy, see Marshall Shulman: *Stalin's Foreign Policy Reappraised* (Cambridge, 1963), p. 16. For strikes and the split in European labor, see Werth, pp. 380–6; Hughes, p. 176; the *Washington Post,* December 20, 1947. For background on the division, see Dolleans and Dehore, pp. 147–8, 164–5. For the U.S. role, see Ronald Radosh: *American Labor and United States Foreign Policy* (New York, 1969), pp. 310–25; Thomas W. Braden, "I'm Glad the CIA is Immoral," *Saturday Evening Post,* May 20, 1967; Forrestal Papers, Box #73, letter from Forrestal to Donovan of 14 August 1947.

26. Werth, pp. 310, 355; Rieber, pp. 246–7, 252, 340–1; the *Washington Post,* December 17 and 24, 1947; *DSB,* Vol. 16, May 4, 1947, p. 822.

27. For the French elections, see Werth, pp. 274, 369. For Lovett, see Millis and Duffield, p. 327; *TNYT,* October 8, 1947. For Marshall, see Millis and Duffield, p. 340. For strikes, see Kennan, pp. 424–5; Millis and Duffield, p. 349; Dolleans and Dehore, p. 163 n; the *Washington Post,* editorials for November 20, 1947, and December 27, 1947. See also Sumner Welles in the *Washington Post,* November 25, 1947, and Walter Lippmann, *ibid.,* November 18, 1947.

28. For Policy Planning Staff comment, see Kennan, p. 359; Price, p. 23. For the strategic importance of western Europe, see Walter LaFeber: *America, Russia and the Cold War* (New York, 1968), p. 48; "Certain Aspects of the ERP from the US Standpoint," Policy Planning Staff memo, Clifford Papers (Washington, D.C.); *DSB,* Vol. 20, March 27, 1949, p. 385.

29. For response to the Truman Doctrine, see Jones, pp. 47, 174–9, 208–9; Arthur Krock in *TNYT,* May 2, 1947; Curtis D. MacDougall: *Gideon's Army* (New York, 1965), pp. 135–6. For the Lippmann quote, see Walter Lippmann: *The Cold War* (New York, 1947), p. 55. On Truman's popularity, see note 5, Chapter VI. For Wallace's speaking tour, see Irwin Ross: *The Loneliest Campaign* (New York, 1968), p. 147; Karl Schmidt: *Quixotic Crusade* (Syracuse, 1960), p. 30.

30. For Acheson's speech, see *DSB,* Vol. 16, p. 991; Acheson, pp. 227–30; Jones, pp. 199 ff. For communications with journalists, see Jones Papers, letter from Jones to Lippmann of May 7, 1947. For

press response, see *TNYT*, editorial and article on May 25, James Reston comment on May 9; the *Washington Post*, editorial on May 9, the Alsops' comment on May 9, Lippmann's comment on May 10.

31. For Vandenberg's quote, see James Reston: *The Artillery of the Press* (New York, 1967), p. 64; Acheson, p. 230; H. Bradford Westerfield: *Foreign Policy and Party Politics* (New Haven, 1955), p. 273.

32. For summary of wool legislation, see *Congressional Quarterly: 1947*, pp. 177–8. For Clayton's letter, see the *Congressional Record* (*CR*), 80:1, pp. 7103–4. For Cooley's advocacy, see *CR*, 80:1, pp. 5752, 7105. For the Hull, Stimson, and Marshall statements, see *CR*, 80:1, p. 7103. See also Clayton, "GATT, The Marshall Plan and OECD," p. 494; *TNYT*, editorial for May 25, 1947.

33. For the direction of the speech to the European audience, see Jones, pp. 244–5; memo about Marshall's speech dated July 2, 1947; Jones Papers; Bohlen, p. 29. For the Administration's efforts to minimize domestic response, see Bohlen, pp. 89–90; James Reston, "The Number One Voice," in Lester Markel et al.: *Public Opinion and Foreign Policy* (New York, 1949), p. 74. For Acheson's meeting with British journalists, see Cabell Phillips: "The Mirror Called Congress," in Markel, p. 182; interview of Miall by Philip C. Brooks, see ERP Oral History (Truman Library). For Truman's support of Marshall, see *TNYT*, June 27, 1947. See also Millis and Duffield, p. 281; memo from Forrestal to Lovett of June 29, 1947, Forrestal Papers, Box 125.

34. For Congressional tours of Europe, see Arthur Krock in *TNYT*, October 31, 1947; the *Washington Post*, editorial for November 9, 1947; John O'Donnell in the *Washington Times Herald*, October 17, 1947; Jerry Greene in *ibid.*, December 2, 1947. For the appointment of special commissions, see Westerfield, pp. 275–6.

35. For the State Department public information program, see W. Phillips Davidson: "More Than Diplomacy," in Markel, p. 139. For public opinion on the Marshall Plan, see the *Public Opinion Quarterly* (*POQ*), Summer 1948, p. 365; survey of opinion in *TNYT*, September 28, 1947.

36. For Vandenberg, see Arthur H. Vandenberg, Jr.: *The Private Papers of Senator Vandenberg* (Boston, 1952), p. 381; the Alsops in the *Washington Post*, July 9, 1947. For Lovett, see Millis and Duffield, p. 296. For Forrestal, see *ibid.*, p. 305. Phillips in *TNYT*, July 20, 1947. For Stassen, see Millis and Duffield, p. 310. Reston in *TNYT*, October 29, 1947; *Washington Post* editorial of November 6, 1947. For Sumner Welles, see *ibid.*, November 11, 1947.

37. See Cripps's speech in *TNYT*, October 9, 1947; also reports in *TNYT*, on October 9 and 10. For discussion of official concern with growth of state trading in Europe in late 1947, see "Economic Report," dated December 30, 1947, Bureau of Budget folder, Clifford Papers, (Washington, D.C.).

38. For discussion of alternative ways to finance Europe, see Arthur

Krock in *TNYT*, September 30, 1947; Gardner, pp. 303–5; James Reston in *TNYT*, October 22, 1947.

39. For Harriman's comment, see Millis and Duffield, p. 302. For anti-communism and relief as the best arguments for foreign aid, see Jones, p. 179; the Alsops in the *Washington Post*, July 9, 1947; William S. White in *TNYT*, October 31, 1947.

40. For early reports of the special session, see James Reston in *TNYT*, May 25, 1947; Cabell Phillips in *TNYT*, July 20, 1947; Millis and Duffield, p. 306. For Truman's meeting with leaders, see Associated Press (AP) story, July 15, in Vandenberg Scrapbook, Vandenberg Papers. See letter from Lovett to Vandenberg of September 21, 1947, Vandenberg Papers. For the calling of the special session, see Westerfield, p. 280.

41. Phillips, "The Mirror Called Congress," pp. 195–9; Ross, pp. 29–54; MacDougall, pp. 154–5, 163, 200–1. Clifford memo discussed in Phillips, 197–9; Ross, p. 21–7; Al Yarnell, "The Impact of the Progressive Party on the Democratic Party in the 1948 Presidential Campaign," unpublished doctoral dissertation, (University of Washington, 1969).

42. Clifford quoted in Yarnell, pp. 26–7, 33–4.

43. Marshall: House Committee on Foreign Affairs, *Interim Aid for Europe* hearings, p. 8. For analyses of the economics of Interim Aid, see *ibid.*, pp. 88, 140, 148, Senate Committee on Foreign Relations, *European Interim Aid Act of 1947* hearings, p. 56.

44. For Truman statements, see his *Public Papers*, 1947, pp. 476, 492. For the report on Greco-Turkish aid, see *TNYT*, November 11, 1947. For the Harriman report, see President's Committee on Foreign Aid: *European Recovery and American Aid* (Washington, 1947), pp. B6–7.

45. See James F. Byrnes: *Speaking Frankly* (New York, 1947), pp. 295, 306 ff; Byrnes does not make clear who were the friends who urged him to write the book, but Forrestal had been suggesting the disclosures made by Byrnes since the summer (see memo from Forrestal to Lovett of 15 July 1947, Forrestal Papers, Box 125), and took a great interest in the book's political impact (see memo from Forrestal to Byrnes of November 1, 1947, Forrestal Papers, Box 126). Clayton's article was "Is The Marshall Plan Operation Rathole?", *Saturday Evening Post*, November 29, 1947. For strikes, see Marquis Childs in the *Washington Post*, March 16, 1948.

46. Vandenberg's comment in his *Private Papers*, p. 380. See also *CR*, 80:1, p. 10702.

47. For Busby, see *CR*, 80:1, p. 11155. Ted Lewis in the *Washington Times Herald*, November 17, 1947. Dirksen quoted in *ibid.*, December 13, 1947.

48. For the AIPO poll, see the *Washington Post*, November 21, 1947. The poll of DC residents is in *ibid.*, November 10, 1947.

49. For Congressional views on East-West trade, see Ted Lewis in the

Washington Times Herald, December 15, 1947. For Knowland's comment, see *CR,* 80:1, p. 10827. For the reduction of the Commerce Department program, see the *Washington Times Herald,* October 17, 1947; editorial in the *Washington Post,* November 25, 1947; article on Thorp testimony before Senate Appropriations Committee in *ibid.,* December 13, 1947; series by Lippmann on East-West trade in the *Washington Post* during November.

50. For China, see Tang Tsou: *America's Failure in China* (Chicago, 1963), pp. 451–64; Westerfield, chapter titled "The Rediscovery of China." For Kennan's efforts, see Kennan, pp. 339, 359, 370–1. For the Nationalist campaign for more U.S. aid, see Millis and Duffield, p. 285. For Vandenberg's comment, see letter from Vandenberg to Marshall of June 24, 1947, Vandenberg Papers.

51. For Vandenberg, see letter from Vandenberg to Webber of October 14, 1947, Vandenberg Papers. For Dewey, see articles in the *Washington Times Herald* on November 21 and 25, 1947. For Administration efforts, see Tang, pp. 464–70; Westerfield, pp. 262–3; Senate Committee on Foreign Relations, Interim Aid hearings, Marshall's opening statement and testimony on p. 43; House Committee on Foreign Affairs, Interim Aid hearings, pp. 2–3, 7. For the Judd-Vorys efforts, see Westerfield, p. 262; editorial in the *Washington Post,* December 11, 1947. For Vandenberg on China as a Republican issue, see letter to Stevenson, April 5, 1948, letter to Knowland, December 11, 1948, letter to McGriff, July 1, 1947, Vandenberg Papers. For comment on the Wedemeyer mission, see Ruth Montgomery in the *Washington Times Herald,* January 8, 1948.

V The Cold War at Home

1. For Congressional inaction on the loyalty-program budget, see memo, Spingarn for file, of April 9, 1947, Spingarn Papers, Internal Security file; memo from Clifford to the President of May 7, 1947, Truman Papers, OF252-K(45–47). For the Rees loyalty bill, see Earl Latham: *The Communist Controversy in Washington* (Cambridge, Mass., 1966), p. 368; *Congressional Record (CR),* 80:1, pp. 8942 ff, 8950 ff. For Bridges and Vincent, see letter from Vandenberg to Peterson of May 27, 1947, Vandenberg Papers.

2. The best account of this incident is in Bert Andrews: *Washington Witch Hunt* (New York, 1948). For the legislative history of the State Department budget in 1947, see *CR,* 80:1, pp. 5187, 7886, 8265. For Marshall's concern with communist propaganda in Europe, see Walter Millis and E. S. Duffield, eds.: *The Forrestal Diaries* (New York, 1951), pp. 242–3; see Marshall's speech of July 1, 1947, in *Department of State Bulletin (DSB),* Vol. 17, p. 83. For Marshall's statement on Taber, see interview of Miall by Brooks in Oral His-

tory Project on ERP at Truman Library. For comment in press suggesting that some of the ten are Communists, see the *Washington Times Herald*, November 3, 1947. *Washington Post* cites from editorial, "Security Resignations," November 19, 1947 and editorial, November 11, 1947.

3. For the FBI-CSC conflict, see memo from Spingarn to Foley of April 9, 1947, Spingarn Papers, Internal Security file. Spingarn quote from memo of Spingarn to Foley of April 4, 1947, Spingarn papers, Treasury Department file; see also the New York *Herald Tribune*, May 12, 1947. For Clark's position, see memo from the Attorney General to the President of May 1, 1947, Truman Papers, OF252-K(45–47). For Clifford's quote on Truman's position, see penciled note dated May 2, 1947, in Elsey Papers, Subject file, Internal Security, Federal Employee Loyalty Program (Truman Library). For Truman's quote, see copy of note from Truman to Clifford in Elsey Papers, Subject file, Internal Security, Federal Employee Loyalty Program. For resolution of conflict, see series of memos by Spingarn in Spingarn Papers. See the same source for final Congressional action.

4. For an excellent statement of the relationship between unity and security, see the President's Advisory Commission on Universal Training, *Report* (Washington, 1947), p. 20.

5. For communist propaganda campaign, see J. Edgar Hoover: *Masters of Deceit* (New York, 1958), p. 75.

6. For a general discussion of the Attorney General's list, see Eleanor Bontecou: *The Federal Loyalty-Security Program* (Ithaca, N. Y., 1953). For the Connecticut State Youth Conference, see the *Washington Post*, December 6, 1947. For the National Council, see "Complaint for Injunction and Declaratory Judgment," filed with the U.S. District Court for the District of Columbia, mimeographed copy in the files of the ACLU, Vol. 9. For a general discussion of the impact of the list on organizations, see Bontecou, pp. 202–3. For discussion of institutions that used the list, see Bontecou, pp. 177–8, 200–1; also the testimony of Ralph S. Brown in Senate Committee on the Judiciary, 84:2, hearings before the Subcommittee on Constitutional Rights, pp. 252–80. For the Supreme Court opinions, see *Joint Anti-Fascist Refugee Committee* v. *McGrath*, 341 U.S. 123, 1950.

7. For the President's Executive Order, see E.O. 9835, quoted in Barton J. Bernstein and A. J. Matusow, eds.: *The Truman Administration* (New York, 1966), pp. 358–63. For the commission's intentions regarding the list, see minutes of the Subcommittee of the President's Temporary Commission on January 14, 1947, Spingarn Papers, President's Temporary Commission, 1946, V.XI; see in the same file the minutes of the commission meeting of January 15, 1947, and memo for the file on the commission meeting of January 15.

8. Letter from Clark to Loeb of May 10, 1949, ACLU files.

9. See Clark testimony before HUAC in House Committee on Un-American Activities, February 5, 1948, hearings on legislation to outlaw the Communist Party, pp. 21-2; also, Clark letter to the Senate Judiciary in Senate Committee on the Judiciary, hearings on HR5852, 80:2, p. 424.

10. For a history of such lists, see August Raymond Ogden: *The Dies Committee* (Washington, D.C., 1943), pp. 17, 25, 35, 157, 178. For Clark on public listings, see HUAC hearings on legislation to outlaw the Communist Party. For Hoover on public listing, see "Red Fascism in the United States Today," *American*, February, 1947. For discussion of the list maintained during World War II, see Bontecou, p. 17. For the lack of relationship between the 1947 list and government employees, see Bontecou, p. 174; also, the opinion of Mr. Justice Burton in 341US128. It should be mentioned, for the record, that Clark was under pressure from various liberal spokesmen to publish the list on the ground that a secret list would be pernicious and create an atmosphere of unresolvable suspicion: see the editorial in the *Washington Post* of November 11, 1947; statement by Eleanor Roosevelt in *The New York Times* (*TNYT*), March 26, 1947; Robert Cushman, "The President's Loyalty Purge," *Survey Graphic*, May, 1947. See also *TNYT* for April 13, 1947, p. 10, April 20, 1947, June 1, 1947, September 12, 1947, December 9, 1947.

11. See Clark's testimony before HUAC on February 5, 1948, in HUAC hearings on legislation to outlaw the Communist Party, pp. 18, 22–4, 32; see also Clark's testimony to the Senate Judiciary in Senate Committee on the Judiciary, 81:1, hearings on S1832, pp. 321–2. For Forrestal's internal advocacy of something like the Attorney General's list, see memo from Forrestal to Clifford of October 16, 1947, Forrestal Papers, Box 126.

12. For Clark's inquiries on legal liability, see memo from Ford to McGregor of April 17, 1947, Vanech Papers, Box 1, file FBI-Loyalty. For Clark's testimony to House Appropriations, see House Committee on Appropriations, hearings on Justice Department budget for 1949, December, 1947, p. 13; see also testimony of T. Vincent Quinn in *ibid.*, p. 67.

13. See the memo dated July 24, 1947, from Edelstein and Duggan to McGregor, Vanech Papers.

14. For Greek-American organizations, see Stephen D. Xydis: *Greece and the Great Powers* (Thessalonike, 1963), p. 546. For the American Slav Congress, see the statement of Dr. Louis L. Gerson regarding opposition of ASC to Marshall Plan in Conference of Scholars on ERP, Truman Library. The *Post* quote is from the editorial of December 6, 1947; for other reactions to the 1947 list, see the *Washington Times Herald*, December 6, 1947 (HUAC); Bontecou, p. 172.

The National Council Case is interesting for showing what an organization had to go through to obtain redress and for how long an unjustified citation could remain in effect. The National Council first sued for redress in D.C. District Court in 1948 and was one of three cases involving the list decided by the Supreme Court in *Joint-Anti-Fascist* v. *McGrath* in 1950. That decision remanded the case to the District Court with instructions that the government show cause for its citation. The Attorney General submitted an affidavit to the court stating, though not documenting, his reasons for considering the Council a communist-front organization. This affidavit asserted that the Council was organized by the Communist Party, that its leaders were appointed by the Party, that the Party took active leadership in the Council's financial affairs and activities, that the Council consistently supported the Communist Party line. The Courts held this information sufficient to justify the Attorney General's listing. Meanwhile, the Internal Security Act of 1950 had been passed, establishing the Subversive Activities Control Board (SACB) and ordering the Attorney General to require subversive organizations to register with the government. The National Council was ordered to register. It disputed the designation and was granted a hearing by SACB. As the charges brought by the government were identical to those upon which the Council's designation on the Attorney General's list was predicated, it is fair to assume that the information presented by the government during this hearing was also that which had led to the original listing. SACB found the order to register justified. The National Council appealed. The Federal Circuit Court of Washington, D.C., ruled in 1964 that the evidence presented by the government was not sufficient to prove that the Council was established by the CP or that its finances or activities were controlled by the Communists. Thus, sixteen years after being cited by the Attorney General, the Council won its reversal; assuming the final decision to be just, the Council had been effectively crippled for sixteen years without cause. See 104F. Supp. 567, pp. 570–1 and 322F.2d375.

15. See the *Washington Post* editorial of December 9, 1947; see also the opinion of Mr. Justice Douglas in 341US123. For Brown's statement, see Brown's testimony before Senate Subcommittee on Constitutional Rights, 84:2, pp. 233–4; for widespread use of the list, see *ibid.*, pp. 252–80. For the relationship between support of the Marshall Plan and anti-communism, see William S. White in *TNYT,* October 31, 1947. For speculation on Wallace, see Frank Waldrop in the *Washington Times Herald,* December 11, 1947; see also numerous speakers in the House debate on HR5852, 80:2. For the FBI attitude toward Wallace, see David Lilienthal: *The Journals of David Lilienthal,* Vol. II (New York, 1964), p. 180. For opposition to the Marshall Plan and loyalty cases, see Alan D. Harper: *The Politics of Loyalty* (Westport, Conn., 1969), p. 49.

16. For the early history of the relationship between opposition to radicalism and immigration laws, see William Preston, Jr.: *Aliens*

and Dissenters (Cambridge, Mass., 1963); John Higham: *Strangers in the Land* (New York, 1965). See also Walter Goodman: *The Committee* (New York, 1968), p. 9; Latham, p. 34.

17. For National Lawyers Guild, see the statement and resolution by it of July 5 and 7, 1946, in Truman Papers, OF10 Misc. (1945–1946). For Clark's statement of February 1947, see House Committee on Appropriations, hearings on Justice Department Appropriation for 1948, p. 17. For the deportation-drive shift into high gear after the Truman Doctrine, see the article in the *Washington Post*, February 22, 1948, "Alien Red Ouster Push Hits Stride." For Clark's statement at the year's end, see House Committee on Appropriations, hearings on Justice Department budget for 1949, p. 39. For Clark and report on ethnicity of communists, see Latham, p. 42; see also Clark's testimony in Senate Committee on the Judiciary, hearings before Subcommittee on Immigration and Naturalization on S1832, 81:1, pp. 318–20. For Lipshitz, see articles by Westbrook Pegler in the *Washington Times Herald* for January 9 and 10, 1948.

18. For Eisler, see the *Washington Times Herald*, February 3, 1948, p. 1; interview in *Daily Worker*, February 1, 1948. For Williamson, see *TNYT*, February 11, 1948. For Smith, see the *Washington Times Herald*, February 17, 1948; Curtis D. MacDougall: *Gideon's Army* (New York, 1965), p. 397. For Clark quote, see his testimony before HUAC on legislation to outlaw the Communist Party, February 5, 1948, p. 31.

19. For Lippmann, see Lippmann's letter to Forrestal of November 11, 1946, Forrestal Papers, Box 70(L). For Forrestal, see Forrestal's letter to Marshall of February 6, 1947, Forrestal Papers, Box 125. For Patterson, see letters Howard to Patterson of August 15 and 16, 1947, and attached response from Patterson to Howard, Papers of Robert Patterson (Library of Congress).

20. The report of October 1947 is in the *Washington Times Herald*, October 18, 1947. For the newsmen's loyalty program, see the letter from Cornish to Foster of October 4, 1948, ACLU files, 1948, Vol. 10; letter from Holmes to Forrestal of October 5, 1948, in *ibid.*; letter from Forrestal to Foster of October 6, 1948, in *ibid.*; letter from Baldwin to Foster of October 13, 1948, in *ibid.*; *TNYT*, October 21, 1948, and December 15, 1948. For Forrestal's censorship plan, see the *Washington Times Herald*, March 5, 1948; the *Washington Post*, March 30, 1948; James R. Wiggins: *Freedom or Secrecy* (New York, 1964) pp. 100–1; Robert Summers: *Federal Information Controls in Peacetime* (New York, 1949); for a related development, see the story on Clay's controls on news reporting in Germany in the *Washington Post* for April 25 and 26, 1948. For the ASNE resolution, see the *Washington Post*, April 18, 1948.

21. For the history of this provision, see minutes of the Subcommittee of the President's Temporary Commission on Employee Loyalty for January 23, 1947, Spingarn Papers, President's Temporary Commis-

sion, V.XI, F1; minutes of the Subcommittee meeting of February 14, 1947, in *ibid.*; letter from Peurifoy to Vanech of February 13, 1947, in *ibid.*; memo from the Justice Department to the President's Temporary Commission of February 18, 1947, in *ibid.*; memo from Spingarn to Foley of February 16, 1947, in *ibid.* See also hearings of the House Committee on Expenditures in the Executive Departments, 80:1, November 14, 1947, pp. 13–14, 21, 27, 32, 34.

22. For Clark's belief in the need for new controls, see his testimony to HUAC hearings on legislation to outlaw Communist Party. For legislation prepared in the Justice Department relative to this, see memo from Spingarn to the President of July 14, 1950, Spingarn Papers. For the quotation from the draft rules, see the Committee on Executive Expenditures, hearings of November 14, 1947, pp. 13–14.

23. For the ASNE resolution, see the *Washington Times Herald,* October 27, 1947. For the investigation by the House Committee on Executive Expenditures, see the hearings of November 14, 1947. For Truman's comment, see Harry S. Truman: *Public Papers* (Washington, D.C., 1947), p. 482. For the press reaction, see the *Washington Times Herald,* editorial of November 10, 1947, article of November 15, 1947; George Sokolsky on November 27, 1947; Frank Holeman on December 30, 1947. For Ferguson, see *CR,* 80:2, p. 10190. For Lovett, see *CR,* 80:2, p. 10190.

24. For the Magil incident, see the *Washington Post,* March 25, 1948, April 2, 1948, April 3, 1948. For Isaacson, see MacDougall, p. 399. For Wallace, see Millis and Duffield, pp. 261–2. For Justice policy on communist visitors, see hearings before Senate Subcommittee on Immigration and Naturalization, July 15, 1949, testimony of Attorney General Clark. For new rules governing alien visitors, see the *Washington Post,* January 17, 1948; see also Title 8, Chapter 1, Code of Federal Regulations, 13 FR296. For an incident arising under these new rules, see stories regarding treatment of Madame Joliot-Curie in the *Washington Times Herald,* March 19, 1948, p. 4; the *Washington Post,* March 20, 1948, April 22, 1948.

25. For Clark's statement, see the *Washington Post,* November 22, 1947; press release of April 11, 1947, Department of Justice, in ACLU files, Vol. 9, Department of Justice, #2; *TNYT,* May 11, 1947, p. 35. For the commission on military training, see the report of the President's Commission on Universal Training, p. 20; Commission on Higher Education: *Report* (Washington, 1947), pp. 2, 7–13. For Forrestal, see letter from Forrestal to Whitney of March 14, 1947, Forrestal Papers, Box 125. For Studebaker, see *TNYT,* December 1, 1947, p. 31.

26. For Stimson, see Henry L. Stimson and McGeorge Bundy: *On Active Service in War and Peace* (New York, 1947), p. 597; Stimson Diary, Stimson Papers, January 9, 1945, p. 2. For Marshall, see Senate Armed Services Committee, 80:2, hearings on Universal Military

Training, p. 5. For Forrestal, see the record of a phone conversation between Forrestal and Hoyt of December 2, 1947, Forrestal Papers, Box 74 (H). For Truman, see Harry S. Truman: *Years of Trial and Hope* (Garden City, 1956), p. 54; also Truman: *Year of Decisions* (Garden City, 1955), pp. 510–12. For Brown, see Millis and Duffield, pp. 243–4.

27. See U.S. Office of Education, Annual Report, 1947. Studebaker's speech reported in *TNYT*, August 31, 1947, E7.

28. For a description of the "Zeal for American Democracy" program, see the Office of Education's Annual Report, 1948, pp. 485–7. For the American Federation of Teachers, see *TNYT*, August 18, 1947, p. 19. For sample bulletins issued under the Zeal for American Democracy Program, see bulletins numbered 10, 11, and 15, issued during 1948.

29. See the Office of Education, Annual Report, 1948; Annual Report of Federal Security Agency, 1949: Office of Education, pp. 10–16.

30. For typical Clark statements on this subject, see his speech in Boston on May 10, reported in *TNYT*, May 11, 1947, p. 35; speech in Danville, Kentucky, reported in *TNYT*, November 16, 1947, 25:2. It is also interesting to note J. Edgar Hoover's preoccupation with the problem of juvenile delinquency during this period. This subject completely dominated featured articles in the *FBI Law Enforcement Bulletin* during 1946–7.

It is interesting to speculate on how the Office of Education could have developed programs that in many ways ran counter to the ideas inherent in other Administration policies. This probably reflects a number of factors, including lack of coordination within the government, the tendency of the Office of Education to take the rhetoric of the Administration's foreign policy literally, and, perhaps most important, the ability of American officials to identify power politics played by themselves with Wilsonian liberalism.

31. For the origins of Freedom Train, see the *Washington Post*, November 22, 1947; "Capital Stuff" in the *Washington Times Herald*, March 4, 1948. For the White House Conference, see *TNYT*, May 16, 1947, 11:4. See also *TNYT*, May 23, 1947, 5:1, and article in the *Magazine*.

32. For Vandenberg, see letter from Vandenberg to Roberts of August 12, 1947, Vandenberg Papers. For references to internal security in the debate on Interim Aid, see *CR*, 80:1, pp. 11064 (Bell), 11099 (Robison), 11095 (Hoffman), 11086 (Rankin), 11110 (Mundt), 11103 (Kersten), 11039 (Rankin). For references to the relationship of internal security to inflation in the debate on Interim Aid, see *CR*, 80:1, pp. 11067 (Landis), 11039 (Buffitt), 11151 (Knutson).

33. For Clifford's memo, see Irwin Ross: *The Loneliest Campaign* (New York, 1968), pp. 23–4; Harper, p. 66. For communist support of Wallace, see MacDougall, pp. 252, 256–7.

34. For the State Department, see *TNYT*, October 8, 1947; ACLU press release, October 13, 1947, ACLU files, Vol. 19, Civil Service #2, 1947. For Fleming, see the *Washington Times Herald*, October 28, 1947, p. 1. For the Loyalty Review Board, see the *Washington Times Herald*, November 9, 1947, p. 1; "The Federal Diary," by Jerry Klutz, in the *Washington Post*, November 14, 1947.

35. *TNYT*, November 11, 1947, p. 29; *TNYT*, November 29, 1947, 15:5; *TNYT*, December 1, 1947.

36. For the patriotic rally, see the *Washington Times Herald*, November 20, 1947. For Clark, see the *Washington Post*, November 27, 1947. For Martin, see the *Washington Post*, November 28, 1947. For Truman, see *TNYT*, November 29, 1947. For Vandenberg, see *CR*, 80:1, Vandenberg's opening speech on Interim Aid.

37. See the *Washington Times Herald*, October 29, December 7, December 9, 1947.

38. See Robert E. Stripling: *The Red Plot Against America* (Drexel Hill, Pa., 1949), pp. 63, 65. For the file on Eisler, see HUAC, 80:1, hearings regarding Hanns Eisler. For the deportation request, see *TNYT*, September 27, 1947. For Justice's compliance and Thomas's quote, see *TNYT*, October 3, 1947.

39. See HUAC, 80:1, hearings regarding Communist Subversion in Hollywood. For a discussion of the registration cards, see Robert K. Carr: *The House Un-American Activities Committee* (Ithaca, N.Y., 1952). For Russell, see HUAC Hollywood hearings, p. 296. For attempts to implicate the Roosevelt administration, see *CR*, 80:1, A2687; Carr, pp. 58, 68–9. For contempt citations, see Table, note 26, Chapter III.

40. For leaks, see the *Washington Times Herald*, October 16, 1947, p. 1, "Capital Stuff" by John O'Donnell; also the *Washington Post*, November 5, 1947, November 11, 1947, p. 1; the *Washington Times Herald*, December 1, December 7, 1947. For a complete list of these leaks, see Volume 17 of *US* v. *Dennis*, pp. 1287–9. For Rogge, see *TNYT*, November 8, 1947; letter to the author of February 7, 1967. For Childs, see the *Washington Post*, November 21, 1947. For the National Guard, see the *Washington Post*, November 10, 1947.

41. For MacLeish, see *TNYT*, May 17, 1947, 17:1. For Kennan, see George F. Kennan: *Memoirs* (New York, 1969), p. 317. For Conant, see *TNYT*, October 18, 1947. For Schlesinger, see *TNYT*, November 2, 1947, VI, p. 7.

42. For the Administration's assurances, see Truman's statement to the Loyalty Review Board, November 14, 1947, in *Public Papers*, 1947, p. 489. For tension in the federal bureaucracy over security, see Lilienthal, who is full of references to the growing paranoia among federal administrators; see especially Vol. II, pp. 189–90. For HUAC's intentions, see the *Washington Post*, December 27, 1947. For public support for HUAC, see the Gallup poll in the *Washington Post*, December 5, 1947. State actions are discussed in Walter Gellhorn: *The*

States and Subversion (Ithaca, 1952), pp. 7–8, 55, 282, and the closing essay, "A General View." For universities, see the *Washington Post* editorial of December 20, 1947. For the Philadelphia incident, see *TNYT*, November 2, 1947. For New York, see *TNYT*, November 17, 1947, 4:5. For Trenton, see MacDougall, p. 215. For other incidents, see MacDougall, pp. 215 ff.

VI The Battle for the European Recovery Program

1. For the Administration's objectives, see the Senate Committee on Foreign Relations, hearings on ERP, pp. 4–6. The Dalton quote is an excerpt from the Dalton Diaries for June 27, 1947, cited in Conference of Scholars on the European Recovery Program, March 20–1, 1964, Harry S. Truman Library, p. 21.
2. See the *Department of State Bulletin (DSB)*, 1948, Vol. 18, p. 451; the Alsops in the *Washington Post,* January 7, 1948.
3. The quotation is from an article, c. the first week in January, 1948, found in the Vandenberg Scrapbooks, Vandenberg Papers. For the Administration's failure to submit breakdown of aid, see the letter from Vandenberg to Snyder of January 24, 1948, Vandenberg Papers. For polls on isolationism, see Chapter I, note 53. For the political impact of inflation, see the Alsops in the *Washington Post,* December 5, 1947.
4. See analyses of Taft's views and their significance in the *Washington Times Herald* for October 29, November 29, and December 1, 1947. For the Wherry group, see the *Washington Post,* January 14, January 31, 1948; the Alsops in the *Post,* January 14, 1948; "Capital Circus" in the *Times Herald,* January 16, 1948. For the Herter proposal, see the *Times Herald,* December 19, 1947.
5. The following poll regarding the President's popularity was published in the *Washington Post,* April 23, 1948.
   Query: Do you approve or disapprove of the way Truman is handling his job as President?

	APPROVE	DISAPPROVE	NO OPINION
Jan. 47	35	47	18
Feb. 47	48	39	13
March 47	60	23	17
July 47	54	33	13
Oct. 47	55	29	16
Today	36	30	14

See also the Alsops in the *Post,* February 4, 1948; Cabell Phillips in *The New York Times (TNYT),* March 7, 1948 (E3); John O'Donnell in the *Times Herald,* March 24, 1948; Marquis Childs in the *Post,* March 26, 1948.

6. The Records of The Committee for the Marshall Plan are housed at the Truman Library; *DSB* is best source for official speeches. Also, for Clayton, see Ross Pritchard: "Will Clayton: Industrial Statesman," unpublished doctoral dissertation (Fletcher School, Tufts University, 1956). For Forrestal, see Walter Millis and E. S. Duffield, eds.: *The Forrestal Diaries* (New York, 1951), p. 367. For Clark, see *TNYT*, January 21, 1948, 13:4.

7. For the emergence of the anti-Soviet theme during summer of 1947, see Acheson's speech of June 15, *DSB*, Vol. 16, 1947, p. 1221. For Marshall's report to nation, see the *Times Herald*, headline articles for December 16 and 19, 1947. For Bohlen's, Marshall's, and Douglas's statements on ERP, see Senate hearings on ERP.

8. For the Policy Planning Staff quote, see Harry Bayard Price: *The Marshall Plan and Its Meaning* (Ithaca, N.Y., 1955), p. 22. For the role of the idea of pastoralizing Germany on U.S. plans, see Manuel Gottlieb: *The German Peace Settlement and the Berlin Crisis* (New York, 1960), pp. 36–9 and generally. For the U.S. attitude toward planning for occupation and its impact on developments in Germany, see Philip E. Mosely, "The Occupation of Germany," *Foreign Affairs*, Vol. 28, No. 4, July 1950. For the U.S. position on level of industry, see Lucius Clay: *Decision in Germany* (Garden City, 1950), p. 109; E. F. Penrose: *Economic Planning for Peace* (Princeton, 1953), p. 295. For U.S. intransigence on Germany, see Bruce R. Kuklick: "Commerce and World Order," unpublished doctoral dissertation (University of Pennsylvania, 1968), generally; Blaisdell letter dated October 1, 1946, in Blaisdell Papers, Box 7, "Miscellaneous Documents from the London Mission: 1945–46."

9. For Marshall's testimony, see Senate Committee on Foreign Relations, hearings on ERP, pp. 2, 4, 10. For the Defense position, see *ibid.*, pp. 444, 478, 485–8. For publication of the documents, see the *Washington Post*, January 22, 1948; the *Washington Times Herald*, January 22, 1948. See Bevin's quote in the *Post*, February 5, 1948; see also Lippmann in the *Post*, February 12, 1948.

10. For the George-Marshall dispute, see the Senate Committee on Foreign Relations hearings on ERP, pp. 159–61. For Marshall's opening statement to the House, see the House Committee on Foreign Affairs, *Hearings on Postwar Recovery Policy*, pp. 29–31.

11. For the first Marshall quote, see the Senate Committee on Foreign Relations, ERP Hearings, p. 4. For the Marshall-Javits dialogue, see the House Committee on Foreign Affairs, *Hearings on Postwar Recovery Policy*, p. 98. For Truman, see *TNYT*, March 26, 1948, p. 8.

12. For Marshall's Pittsburgh speech, see *DSB*, 1948, Vol. 18, p. 108. For Marshall quote, see the House Committee on Foreign Affairs, *Hearings on Postwar Recovery Policy*, p. 31. For Douglas, see pp. 163–4. For Harriman, see the Senate Committee on Foreign Relations, ERP

hearings, p. 249. For Krug, see *ibid.*, p. 355. For Anderson, see pp. 315–16.

13. For Vandenberg, see *ibid.*, p. 325. For Administration arguments on inflation, see pp. 240, 242, 243, 251, 255–6; House Committee on Foreign Affairs, *Hearings on Postwar Recovery Policy*, pp. 329–30. For the self-sacrifice theme, see Bohlen's speech in *DSB*, 1948, Vol. 18, p. 78.

14. For the Clayton-Vandenberg disagreement, see the letter from Dulles to Vandenberg of March 4, 1948, and reply of March 6, 1948, Vandenberg Papers. For Douglas, see the House Committee on Foreign Affairs, *Hearings on Postwar Recovery Policy*, p. 163. For Clayton, see *ibid.*, pp. 322, 324, 325, 377. For Vandenberg's assessment of the rumor that Clayton would be the ERP administrator, see the letter from Vandenberg to Marshall of March 24, 1948, Vandenberg Papers.

15. For ERP and tax reduction and inflation, see the Survey Research Center poll of "better informed citizens" and *Fortune* poll of business executives, summarized in memo from Collisson to Krug, February 5, 1948, subject file, Box 66, Krug Papers (Library of Congress). For the level of public awareness of ERP, see Martin Kreisberg: "Dark Areas of Ignorance," in Lester Markel et al.: *Public Opinion and Foreign Policy* (New York, 1949), p. 52; *Public Opinion Quarterly* (*POQ*), Summer 1948, p. 365. For public conceptions of ERP, see Kriesberg, p. 55.

16. For Vandenberg and Barkley, see the *Washington Post*, January 27, 1948. See the Alsops in the *Post*, January 26, 1948, and Lippmann in *ibid.*, January 20 and February 9, 1948.

17. See the Alsops in the *Washington Post*, January 25 and 26, 1948; Lippmann in the *Post*, February 9, 1948; see also Marquis Childs in the *Post*, February 11, 1948; *Post* editorial, February 11, 1948; *Post* article by Alfred Friendly, January 28, 1948.

18. Lippmann in the *Post*, February 9, 1948; the Alsops in *ibid.*, January 26, 1948.

19. For letters adopting Acheson's line, see Vandenberg's letters to Benscoe of March 4, to Bennett of March 5, to Grace on March 7, 1947, Vandenberg Papers. For the Administration's use of Vandenberg as a speechmaker, see Millis and Duffield, p. 341. Vandenberg's quote is from his *Private Papers of Senator Vandenberg* (Boston, 1956), p. 380. Vandenberg's Scrapbook in the Vandenberg Papers contains an excellent compilation of newspaper articles on his growing role as a presidential candidate.

20. H. Bradford Westerfield: *Foreign Policy and Party Politics* (New Haven, 1955); the Alsops in the *Post*, February 18, 1948.

21. For Eaton, see the *Times Herald*, January 2, 1948, p. 2.

22. For McCormack, see the Papers of the Committee for the Marshall Plan (CMP), minutes of meeting of December 18, 1947. For Com-

mittee for the Marshall Plan, see CMP minutes of December 18, Stein's reports from Washington on February 6, 20 and 26, 1948, in CMP papers; letter from Patterson to Philbin of February 20, 1948, Box 41, Patterson Papers (Library of Congress). For the Alsops, see the *Post*, December 28, 1947, and February 4, 1948. For Lippmann, see the *Post*, December 24, 1947.

23. For Herter, see the *Washington Post*, February 28, 1948. For the House Committee, see *TNYT*, March 2, 1948. For Martin, see *TNYT*, March 8, 1948.

24. *TNYT*, March 9, 10, and 12, 1948; the *Washington Times Herald*, March 10, 1948; the *Washington Post*, March 12, 1948; Marquis Childs in the *Post*, March 10, 1948.

25. Marquis Childs in the *Post*, March 4, 1948; the *Post*, February 27, 1948.

26. *TNYT*, March 11 and 12, 1948; the *Times Herald*, March 14, 1948; Harry S. Truman: *Public Papers* (Washington, D.C., 1948), p. 178.

27. The text of Byrnes's speech is printed in the Senate Committee on Armed Services hearings on *Universal Military Training*, 80:2, pp. 399–403; see also *TNYT*, March 14, 1948; the *Times Herald*, March 12, 1948; the *Post*, March 14, 1948.

28. For Marshall, see the *Washington Post*, March 16, 1948. Headline in the *Times Herald*, March 15, 1948.

29. *TNYT*, March 16, 17, 18, 1948; the *Washington Post*, March 16, 18, 1948; the *Washington Times Herald*, March 16, 17, 18, 1948. Truman's speech in his *Public Papers*, 1948, p. 182.

30. Marshall quote in Senate Armed Services Committee, UMT hearings, p. 4. For headlines, see *TNYT*, March 19, 20 and 21, 1948; the *Washington Times Herald*, March 18, 19, 1948.

31. *TNYT*, March 21 and 24, 1948; the *Washington Times Herald*, March 21 and 24, 1948.

32. For Forrestal, see his opening statement to Senate Committee on Armed Services, UMT hearings on March 25, 1948. For Sullivan, see *ibid.*, p. 365; *TNYT*, March 26 and 28, 1948; the *Washington Post*, March 26, 1948; the *Washington Times Herald*, March 26, 1948.

33. *TNYT*, March 13, 1948; the *Washington Times Herald*, March 13, 1948; the Alsops in the *Washington Post*, March 17, 1948; Jerry Klutz in the *Post*, March 28, 1948; Walter Lippmann in the *Post*, March 30, 1948.

34. For Martin, see *TNYT*, March 17, 1948; the *Washington Post*, March 17, 1948. For the House Committee action, see *TNYT*, March 18, 20, 1948. For the House Committee's report, see the *Congressional Quarterly*, 1948, p. 182. For Hoover, see the *Post*, March 25, 1948. The comment on the role of anti-communism is based upon a reading of the House debate in the *Congressional Record* (*CR*), 80:2. For Kuhn, see the *Post*, April 1, 1948.

35. For appropriation incident, see Westerfield, pp. 289–90.

36. For Czechoslovakia, see Ivo Duchacek: "Czechoslovakia," in Stephen

D. Kertesz, ed.: *The Fate of East Central Europe* (Notre Dame, Ind., 1956), pp. 192–212.

37. See Donald S. Connery: *The Scandanavians* (London, 1966), pp. 496–501.

38. For the President's summary of the origins of the western European pact see Harry S. Truman: *Years of Trial and Hope* (Garden City, 1956), p. 241; also George F. Kennan: *Memoirs* (New York, 1969), pp. 419–21. For the Italian situation, see memo dated September 22, 1947, "Meeting with War and Security Councils," Forrestal Papers, Box 126. For Soviet troop movements, see Conference of Scholars, p. 21. For Clay's telegram, see Millis and Duffield, p. 387.

39. For Kennan's views and his role, see Kennan, *Memoirs*, pp. 422–6. For the Marshall-Bevin conversation, see Charles Bohlen: *The Transformation of American Foreign Policy* (New York, 1969), p. 90. For Marshall's meeting with the Senators, see Millis and Duffield, pp. 384–5; the *Washington Post*, March 3, 1948. For the significance of UMT, see the Senate Committee on Armed Services hearings on UMT, pp. 28, 33, 36; Lippmann in the *Post*, March 22, 1948. For Marshall's comment to the Armed Services, see the Committee's hearings on UMT, p. 20. For Marshall's comment of May 7, see Millis and Duffield, p. 432.

40. For the meeting of February 18, see Millis and Duffield, pp. 375–7. For Forrestal's view, see *ibid.*, p. 378.

41. For the Forrestal-Marshall lunch, see Millis and Duffield, pp. 384–5. For Forrestal's statement about Selective Service, see *ibid.*, p. 386. For the dinner with Byrnes, see James F. Byrnes: *All in One Lifetime* (New York, 1958), pp. 396–7. For the Forrestal-George conversation, see Millis and Duffield, p. 386. For the Key West Meeting, see *ibid.*, p. 390; the *Washington Post*, March 12, 1948.

42. For Clay's telegram and its effect, see Millis and Duffield, pp. 387, 395. For Forrestal's use of it in the campaign for rearmament, see Marquis Childs in the *Washington Post*, April 6, 1948. For the military preference for UMT, see the *Post*, March 19, 1948. For the comment of Army Secretary Royall on the threat of war, see the Senate Armed Services Committee hearings on UMT, p. 339. For the Forrestal quote, see Millis and Duffield, p. 395.

43. For the President's comments on the war scare, see his *Years of Trial and Hope*, p. 241. European press reports from the period do not indicate any general fear of war; in fact they contain consistent repudiations of this rumor. See, for example, report from Norway in the *Washington Post*, April 24, 1948; report from Prague in the *Post*, March 21, 1948; report on the speech of Benjamin Cohen, Assistant Secretary General of the UN, in the *Post*, March 23, 1948; report from the U.S.S.R. in the *Washington Times Herald*, April 8, 1948; report of a speech by Lord Inverchapel, British Ambassador to the U.S., in the *Times Herald*, March 18, 1948.

44. For Truman's concern over the war hysteria, see Millis and Duffield,

p. 408; the *Washington Post*, March 28, 1948. For Marshall's testimony on the Selective Service, see the Senate Committee on Armed Services, UMT hearings, pp. 5, 9. For Marshall's trip, see *TNYT*, March 23, 1948. For Clay's news conference, see *TNYT*, March 26, 1948, p. 13. For Truman's and Marshall's reining in of the Defense Department campaign, see Millis and Duffield, pp. 430–2, 435–40.

45. For the China Aid Program, see Tang Tsou: *America's Failure in China* (Chicago, 1963), p. 472. For Marshall's testimony, see the House Committee on Foreign Affairs, *Hearings on Postwar Recovery Policy*, opening statement on February 20, 1948, and p. 1554. For Marshall's comment on Chiang's collapse, see Tang, p. 356.

46. For House leadership, see statement by Martin in the *Washington Times Herald*, March 8, 1948.

47. For comment by Truman, see Tang, p. 474; see also editorial in the *Washington Post* about House action on China, April 3, 1948.

48. For the economic value of U.S. trade with the U.S.S.R., see James Reston in *TNYT*, March 26, 1948; House Committee on Foreign Affairs, *Hearings on Postwar Recovery Policy*, p. 479. For new limits on U.S. trade with the U.S.S.R., see *ibid.*, p. 487; the *Washington Post*, January 11, 1948. For the first Mundt quote, see House *Hearings on Postwar Recovery Policy*, p. 487. For the Administration's attitude on East-West trade in Europe, see *ibid.*, p. 488; Senate Committee on Foreign Relations hearings on ERP, pp. 113, 304. For Mundt's response, see House *Hearings on Postwar Recovery Policy*, pp. 488–9, 1559–60; see also Wherry speech in the Senate, quoted in *TNYT*, March 5, 1948.

49. For the initial and final versions of the Mundt amendment, see *CR*, 80:2, pp. 3755, 4059. For the Gallup poll, see the *Washington Post*, February 6, 1948. For the March crisis over East-West trade, see *TNYT*, March 24, 1948, p. 1; the *Post*, March 26 and 27, 1948; the *Washington Times Herald*, March 25 and 27, 1948. For consideration of an embargo, see the *Post*, March 31, 1948. For the Administration v. Congress on East-West trade, 1948–52, see Furniss and Snyder: *Introduction to American Foreign Policy* (New York, 1955), p. 13; Dean G. Acheson: *Present at the Creation* (New York, 1969), pp. 559, 634; Price, pp. 168–70, 364; Raymond F. Mikesell: *United States Economic Policy and International Relations* (New York, 1952).

VII INTERNAL SECURITY, ERP, AND THE POLITICS OF 1948

1. For Bittleman's arrest, see the *Washington Times Herald*, January 17, 1948; *Daily Worker*, January 18, 1948. For the Act of October 16, 1918, see 8USC(1946ed) 137.

2. See the *Washington Times Herald* for the following: Jones, January 21, 1948; Eisler, February 3, 1948; Williamson, February 11, 1948; Smith, February 17, 1948; Johnson, February 19, 1948; Doyle, February 21, 1948; Potash, *ibid.*, March 2, 1948; Bridges, March 7, 1948, the *Washington Post*, March 7, 1948. For the West Coast Eight, see the *Post*, March 19, 1948. See also article in the *Daily Worker*, January 26, 1948, for a general discussion of the deportation drive.

3. For the new publicity tactics by the Justice Department, see the *Washington Post*, February 22, 1948, 4M. For evidence about Eisler, see HUAC hearings on Gerhart Eisler, p. 30.

4. For the futility of deportation attempts to eastern Europe, see Clark's testimony in HUAC hearings on legislation to outlaw the Communist Party, p. 23. For the inability to connect communists with advocacy of violent revolt, see *ibid.*, p. 21. This situation was altered by two developments in 1950. First, in *Dennis et al. v. US* (341US494) the Supreme Court held that membership in the Communist Party did involve advocacy of violent revolution. Second, the Internal Security Act of 1950 empowered the Executive to deport aliens with communist connections. Following these developments many of those arrested in 1948 and later freed were rearrested and deported. For Eisler's attorney's statement, see the *Washington Post*, February 3, 1948.

5. For Nixon's charge and Clark's response, see the *Washington Times Herald*, March 10, 1948. For Eisler, Smith, and Williamson, see Chapter V, p. 24. For Justice's legislative proposals, see Clark's opening statement to HUAC hearings on legislation to outlaw the Communist Party.

6. For Taylor's decision, see Curtis D. MacDougall: *Gideon's Army* (New York, 1965), pp. 306–11. For California, see MacDougall, pp. 311–12. For New York election, see MacDougall, pp. 323–5; Irwin Ross: *The Loneliest Campaign* (New York, 1968), p. 66; Al Yarnell, "The Impact of the Progressive Party on the Democratic Party in the 1948 Presidential Campaign," unpublished doctoral dissertation, (University of Washington, 1969). For the press response to Wallace, see MacDougall, p. 306. For more on Truman's political troubles, see Ross, pp. 64, 67–8, 72, 73.

7. For attacks on Wallace, see MacDougall, pp. 325, 337, 341, 363. For the communist interpretation of the deportation drive, see the *Washington Post*, March 7, 1948; the *Washington Times Herald*, February 17, 1948. See also the *Daily Worker* for this period, which consistently expressed this view.

8. For Murray on the loyalty program, see letter from Murray to the President of April 14, 1947, Truman Papers, OF252-K. For the omission of labor from the Attorney General's list, see Eleanor Bontecou: *The Federal Loyalty-Security Program* (Ithaca, 1953), p. 172;

the *Washington Post,* editorial, December 6, 1947. For Truman's statement on communism in labor, see Cabell Phillips: *The Truman Presidency* (New York, 1966), p. 116.

9. For my account of the internal struggles within the CIO, I have relied upon Max M. Kampelman: *The Communist Party vs the CIO* (New York, 1957); Irving Howe and Lewis Coser: *The American Communist Party* (Boston, 1957); MacDougall. For the CIO convention endorsement of the Marshall Plan, see Kampelman, p. 111; for a different version, see Ronald Radosh: *American Labor and U.S. Foreign Policy* (New York, 1969). For the decision of communist unionists to support Wallace and oppose ERP, see Kampelman, pp. 141–4; MacDougall, pp. 262–3. For the decision of the National Executive Committee to enforce its position on Wallace and ERP, see the *Washington Post,* March 11, 1948.

10. For Potash and Williamson, see Kampelman, p. 142. For Bridges, see the *Washington Post,* March 7, 1948; MacDougall, pp. 318–19. For Murray's support of Eisenhower in early 1948, see MacDougall, p. 473.

11. For Wallace's critique of Truman's charges, see the *Washington Post,* March 20, 1948. For White, see *The New York Times* (*TNYT*), October 31, 1947. For Taylor, see the *Washington Post,* March 10, 1948. For the *Post* editorial, see edition of January 10, 1948. For Bohlen, see the *Department of State Bulletin* (*DSB*), Vol. 18, No. 46, p. 79.

12. The *Telegram* poll is cited in Ross, p. 149; for subsequent polls, see pp. 157, 166, 228. For harassment of Wallace supporters, see MacDougall, pp. 340, 361–3, 366, 369, 374, 375, 396 ff; for earlier manifestations, see pp. 150, 158–9, 167. For the influence of international events, see MacDougall, p. 343. For the decisive nature of the communist issue in Wallace's demise, see Ross, p. 224; MacDougall, p. 435.

13. For Martin's speech, see the Popular Government League *Bulletin* No. 230, March 12, 1948, in ACLU files, Vol. 10, Loyalty Probes and Seditious Speech. Cooperation between Congress and the Administration did not entirely disappear in early 1948, though it became such a minor theme of American politics that its manifestations are not worth detailed discussion. Nevertheless, for some examples see articles on Justice Department response to complaints by Senator Ball about tax status of subversive organizations, in the *Washington Times Herald,* February 3, 5, 1948. See also Clark's promise to assist Mundt in drawing up anti-communist legislation in HUAC hearings on legislation to outlaw the Communist Party, p. 31.

14. Mundt stated in a letter to the author that he and Nixon worked on anti-communist legislation in early 1947, and reports of this activity were carried in the *Washington Post* on December 7, 21, and 27, 1947. Mundt's 1947 bill was HR4422, 80:1.

15. See HUAC hearings on legislation to outlaw the Communist Party.

16. *Ibid.*, pp. 33–4.
17. Quotation from HUAC report on HR5852, April 30, 1948, 80:2.
18. For Nixon's statement, see the *Congressional Record* (*CR*), 80:2, p. 6047.
19. The statement about the President is based upon the fact that he tended to follow the advice of Clark on issues like this and in 1950 used the arguments Clark made to HUAC in 1948 in his veto of the Internal Security Act. Moreover, he frequently quoted Hoover on the inadvisability of outlawing the Communist Party.
20. For statements in Congress about the political difficulty of opposing HR5852, see *CR*, 80:2, pp. 5866 (Javits), 5873 (Holifield), 5853 (Lynch), 5864 (Miller), 5868 (Carroll).
21. For Clark's letter, see the Senate Committee on the Judiciary, 80:2, hearings on HR5852, pp. 422–5.
22. For Taber, see the *Washington Times Herald*, February 10 and 28, 1948; *CR*, 80:2, p. 2585. For Executive expenditures, see *TNYT*, March 13 and May 22, 1948.
23. For a detailed study of the Condon report, see Robert K. Carr: *The House Un-American Activities Committee* (Ithaca, 1952), pp. 131–53. For the 1947 charges against Condon, see Marquis Childs in the *Washington Post*, March 12, 1948. For *Post* disclosures on Hoover letter, see issues of March 3 and 25, 1948.
24. For the relation of the Condon case to the HUAC budget debate, see Carr, pp. 132–3.
25. For Condon and Wallace, see Marquis Childs in the *Washington Post*, March 12, 1948. For Reece's statement, see *TNYT*, May 2, 1948. For Martin, see p. 317.
26. See *CR*, 80:2, pp. 2405, 2407, 2409 (Busbey), 2412 (Blatnik).
27. For the vote on the HUAC resolution, see the *Washington Post*, April 23, 1948. For an earlier debate over Congressional access to files, see dispute between Hoffman and the Administration, October, 1947. Hoffman, the Chairman of the House Executive Expenditures Committee, requested access to certain files in October 1947 and was refused on grounds similar to those given in the Condon case. (See the letter from Truman to Hoffman of October 8, 1947, Truman Papers, OF2 [1947].) The President had made one exception to this rule when the State Department gave Taber information on security checks of its employees. Taber, as the case of the dismissal of ten State Department employees in June 1947 indicates, was in a special position and used the information to launch a public attack on the Department in early 1948. For House action on the resolution of the Executive Expenditures Committee, see the *Congressional Quarterly*, 1948, p. 277.
28. For Truman's directive, see his *Public Papers*, 1948, p. 181; the *Washington Post*, March 16, 1948; Harry S. Truman: *Years of Trial and Hope* (Garden City, 1956), p. 282. For Clark's statement, see *TNYT*, May 14, 1948.

VIII THE LEGACY OF THE TRUMAN DOCTRINE

1. For the relationship of rearmament to recovery in 1948–9, see Dean
G. Acheson: *Present at the Creation* (New York, 1969), p. 309;
Harry S. Truman: *Years of Trial and Hope* (Garden City, 1956),
p. 24; letter from Vandenberg to Sheppard of January 27, 1949,
Vandenberg Papers; Louis Halle: *The Cold War As History* (Lon-
don, 1967), p. 189. For the Kennan quote, see George F. Kennan:
Russia, the Atom, and the West (New York, 1957), p. 9.
2. See the Council of Economic Advisors: *Midyear Economic Review*
(Washington, July 1950), pp. 27–37, 47; Gordon Gray et al.: *Report
to the President on Foreign Economic Policies* (Washington, D.C.,
November 1950), pp. 70–1.
3. For Soviet policies, see Truman: *Years of Trial and Hope*, pp. 240–1.
For impact of bomb and China, see Acheson, p. 345. For Korea as
opportunity for rearmament, see Marcus Raskin and Richard Barnett:
After Twenty Years (New York, 1966), p. 29.
4. The question of European *v.* Atlantic rearmament is raised and dis-
cussed in Ben T. Moore: *NATO and the Future of Europe* (New
York, 1958), pp. 1, 24–7. For European rejection of U.S. military
aid, see Acheson, p. 709.
5. The quoted passage from NSC–68 is taken from Cabell Phillips:
The Truman Presidency (New York, 1966), pp. 303–6; see also
Paul Y. Hammond: "NSC–68: Prologue to Rearmament," in Warner
R. Schilling et al.: *Strategy, Politics and Defense Budgets* (New
York, 1962), pp. 307–18. For Acheson quotes, see *Department of
State Bulletin (DSB)*, March 20, 1950; House Ways and Means Committee, 82:1, hearings on *Extension of Reciprocal Trade Agreements
Act*, p. 7; see also Kennan, Chapters 18 and 19, especially p. 488.
6. For political significance of rearmament, see Walter LaFeber: *Amer-
ica, Russia, and the Cold War* (New York, 1968), pp. 77–8; Truman,
Years of Trial and Hope, p. 248; Barnett and Raskin, pp. 18, 22, 23,
27. For Lisbon meeting, see Acheson, p. 623.
7. For the first Acheson quote, see *DSB*, Vol. 16, p. 991. For Clayton,
see above, Chapter VI, p. 261. For the second Acheson quote, see the
Senate Committee on Finance, 82:1, hearings on *Extension of Reciprocal Trade Agreements Act*, p. 4. For Truman, see the House
Committee on Ways and Means, 81:1, hearings on *Extension of Reciprocal Trade Agreements Act*, pp. 2, 6–7; Senate Committee on
Finance, 80:2, hearings on *Extension of Reciprocal Trade Agreements Act*, 80:2, pp. 483–5; George McGhee, "Economics of Peace,"
DSB, Vol. 16, June 22, 1947, p. 1196.
8. For a summary of the 1948 Act, see the House Ways and Means
Committee, 81:1, hearings on RTA extension, p. 4; Raymond F.
Mikesell: *United States Economic Policy and International Relations*

(New York, 1952), p. 307. For Clayton, see the Senate Committee on Finance, 80:2, hearings on RTA extension, p. 464. For the Clayton-Vandenberg exchange, see the letters from Clayton to Vandenberg of April 21, June 8, and June 12, 1948, and Vandenberg replies of April 22 and June 9, 1948, Vandenberg Papers. For Thorp, see the State Department press release cited in Mikesell, p. 307.

9. For movement toward protectionism after 1947, see William Y. Elliot et al.: *The Political Economy of American Foreign Policy* (New York, 1955), p. 299, note 3; Richard N. Gardner: *Sterling Dollar Diplomacy* (Oxford, 1956), p. 373; Acheson, p. 634. For the Acheson quote, see the Senate Committee on Finance, 82:1, hearings on RTA extension, pp. 6–7. For inconsistencies with GATT in the 1951 Act, see *ibid.*, p. 11; Gardner, p. 375.

10. For agricultural policy, see Gardner, pp. 374–5. For repudiation of GATT, see Senate Committee on Finance, 82:1, hearings on RTA extension, p. 11.

11. For demise of ITO, see Gardner, pp. 361–78; Ross Pritchard: "Will Clayton: Industrial Statesman," unpublished doctoral dissertation (Fletcher School, Tufts University, 1956), pp. 385, 392, 393. For Administration's rejection of Hullianism, see Acheson, p. 727.

12. For the import decline, see Harry Bayard Price: *The Marshall Plan and Its Meaning* (Ithaca, 1955), p. 102. For devaluations, see Price, p. 130. For conclusions about ERP, see the Council of Economic Advisors: *Midyear Economic Review* (Washington, D.C., July 1949), p. 41; Council of Economic Advisors: *Annual Economic Review* (Washington, D.C., January 1950), p. 123; Council of Economic Advisors: *Midyear Economic Review* (Washington, D.C., July 1950), p. 88; *Report of the ECA-Commerce Mission* (Washington, D.C., 1949), p. 4; Price, p. 129; Acheson, p. 325.

13. See the *Report of the ECA-Commerce Mission*, pp. 8, 11; Economic Cooperation Administration: *Seventh Report to Congress* (for the quarter ended December 31, 1949); Gray et al., pp. 76, 79, 87, 94; Elliot et al., pp. 290–305.

14. See Price, pp. 100, 101, 121–7, 134–5.

15. For the impact of European integration on trade with the dollar area, see Price, p. 284; Gray, et al., p. 26; William Diebold: *Trade and Payments in Western Europe* (New York, 1952), pp. 13, 233. For the building of reserves, see Gray et al., p. 32. For the U.S. loss of interest in the liberalization of intra-European trade, see Price, p. 324; Ernst H. Van Der Beugel: *From Marshall Aid to Atlantic Partnership* (Amsterdam, 1966), p. 264.

16. For the economic result of rearmament, see Mikesell, p. 331; Diebold, pp. 420, 427; Gray et al., pp. 7, 33, 37; Price, pp. 156–7, 363; Committee for Economic Development: *Economic Aspects of North Atlantic Security* (1951), pp. 10–11, 13, 15–16, 31–2. For rearmament and the Atlantic economic integration, see Mikesell, pp. 283–4. For the U.S. attempt to join the OEEC, see Acheson, p. 395. For

institutional changes, see Price, p. 165; Diebold, p. 424. For European resentment of U.S. policies, see Price, pp. 324, 359; Acheson, pp. 560, 569.

17. For Truman's fear of public response to the special message on defense proposals, see the *Washington Post*, March 28, 1948. For the statement on splinter parties, see Truman, *Public Papers*, 1948, Press Conference of May 13. The June speech is cited in Irwin Ross: *The Loneliest Campaign* (New York, 1968), p. 82.

18. For the Administration's loss of hope on China in October 1948, see Tang Tsou: *America's Failure in China* (Chicago, 1963), p. 495. For the report of the military adviser, see Acheson, p. 305.

19. For the change in the nature of the grand jury proceeding, see "Affidavit of John FX McGohey," filed in opposition to motion to dismiss indictments in *U.S.* v. *Dennis*, Vol. 17. For Republican calls for prosecution of American Communists, see J. Parnell Thomas, cited in *The New York Times* (*TNYT*), April 2, 1947, 32:1. For Vandenberg and Ferguson, see Vandenberg speech of April 26, 1948, cited in *TNYT*, April 29, 1948. For the dispute between the White House and the FBI on the grand jury, see George Sokolsky in the *Washington Times Herald*, March 10, 1948; see also Sokolsky article in *ibid.*, March 8, 1948. For the tip to HUAC on grand jury proceedings, see Robert E. Stripling: *The Red Plot Against America* (Drexel Hill, Pa., 1949), pp. 95–6. For Truman's "red herring" comment, see *TNYT*, September 3, 1948, 1:1. For Truman's campaign address about domestic communism, see his Oklahoma City speech of September 28, 1948, in Truman's *Public Papers*, 1948; Ross, pp. 203–4. For background of drafts of the speech, see the Spingarn Papers, White House Assignment. For Truman's denunciation of HUAC, see *TNYT*, August 20, 1948. For Clark's denunciation of HUAC, see *TNYT*, August 16, 1948; "Monthly Bulletin" #80 of ACLU, November 1948, in ACLU files. Vol. II, HUAC #9, 1948. For a general discussion of these events, see Alan D. Harper: *The Politics of Loyalty* (Westport, Conn., 1969), pp. 69 ff.

20. For the view that the communist issue helped Truman in 1948, see Ross, pp. 253–4. For public support for HUAC hearings, see the Washington *Star*, September 7, 1948. For Dewey's campaign tactics, see Ross, pp. 197 ff; H. Bradford Westerfield: *Foreign Policy and Party Politics* (New Haven, 1955), pp. 296 ff.

21. For the Hiss indictment, see Walter Goodman: *The Committee* (New York, 1968), pp. 265–6. For China, see Acheson, pp. 305–7; K. S. Latourette: *America's Record in the Far East* (New York, 1950), p. 105; Senate Armed Services Committee, 82:1, *Hearings on the Military Situation in the Far East*, pp. 1855–6; Tang, pp. 498–9.

22. For Congress, see Tang, pp. 499–501, 518, 529, 534; Acheson, pp. 302–7, 349–52, 354, 370.

23. For public opinion about China, see Gabriel Almond: *The American*

People and Foreign Policy (New York, 1950), p. 105; Tang Tsou, p. 538. For the preparation of the China White Paper, see Acheson, p. 302. For Formosa, see the Senate Armed Services Committee, *Hearings on the Military Situation in the Far East*, pp. 1667–9, 1672–5, 1681; Acheson, p. 350. For Truman's statement, see Acheson, p. 351. For Acheson's speech, see Acheson, pp. 357–8; Tang Tsou, p. 535; Latourette, p. 58; *DSB*, January 13, 1950, pp. 116–17. For the announcement on the UN, see Tang, pp. 523, 526.

24. For U.S. policy on recognition, see Tang, pp. 513, 514–16. For the Acheson quote, see *TNYT*, October 5, 1951, p. 1; Tang, pp. 506, 547. For the impact of the fall of China on U.S. policy in Southeast Asia, see Latourette, pp. 57, 66–7; Harold M. Vinacke: *The United States and the Far East* (London, 1952), pp. 96–7; *The Role of ECA in Southeast Asia* (Washington, 1951), pp. 2–3. For China and European rearmament, see Tang, pp. 502–3, 511 ff; Alfred Steinberg: *The Man from Missouri* (New York, 1962), p. 360. For Vietnam, see George Kahin and John W. Lewis: *The United States in Vietnam* (New York, 1969), pp. 30–1.

25. For Acheson and the confirmation hearings, see Acheson, pp. 250–3. For Bridges, see Tang, p. 501. For Hurley's response to the White Paper, see Tang, p. 509. For Congressional response to the White Paper, see Acheson, p. 307. For the presidential commission on loyalty, see the memo by Stephen Spingarn in Spingarn Papers, White House Assignment—Internal Security File, folder on "National Defense—Internal Security and Individual Rights," Vol. I, Folder 1, Box 30. For the attempt to abolish HUAC, see Goodman, pp. 272 ff; memo from Clark to the President of December 21, 1948, Clifford Papers, folder on Committee on Un-American Activities. For the Administration's assessment of the public mood, see memo from Spingarn to Clifford of April 6, 1949, Spingarn Papers, White House Assignment, "Internal Security File—National Defense and General Loyalties," folder on "National Defense—Loyalty Legislation," Box 33. For Truman's articulation of this analysis, see editorial in the *Washington Post*, January 19, 1949.

26. See Acheson, pp. 321, 360–1; Tang, p. 509; Phillips, p. 373.

27. See Phillips, pp. 384–5; Tang, pp. 540–4; Acheson, pp. 364–5.

28. For McCarthy *vs.* Administration, see Phillips, pp. 385–6, 392; for Truman tour, see Steinberg, pp. 371–2.

29. For complete accounts of the decision to intervene, see Truman, *Years of Trial and Hope*, pp. 331–9; Acheson, pp. 401–13; Glenn D. Paige: *The Korean Decision* (New York, 1968), pp. 79–272; Tang, p. 558. For the first Johnson quote, see Paige, p. 177. For the decision regarding troops, see Paige, pp. 149, 187. For the second Johnson quote, see Paige, p. 264. For Truman's refusal to discuss domestic politics, see Paige, p. 141.

30. For discussions of Formosa decision, see Paige, pp. 125–6, 133, 244; Tang, pp. 558–61; Louis Halle: *The Cold War as History* (London,

1967), pp. 206–10; Kennan, *Memoirs,* p. 513; Truman, *Years of Trial and Hope,* p. 334.

31. For the announced U.S. goal in Korea, see Paige, p. 205; Tang, p. 569.

32. For the Acheson quote, see Acheson, p. 365. For the MacArthur incidents, see Acheson, pp. 422, 425; Truman, *Years of Trial and Hope,* pp. 349–58.

33. For Marshall's appointment, see Acheson, p. 365. For the veto, see Truman, *Years of Trial and Hope,* p. 284. For the Wake Island trip, see *ibid.,* pp. 363–70; Halle, p. 223. For the election, see LaFeber, pp. 107–8.

34. For debate on military goals in Korea, see Acheson, pp. 445–52; Kennan, *Memoirs,* pp. 514–15; Matthew Ridgway: *Soldier* (New York, 1956), p. 43.

35. See Kennan, *Memoirs,* pp. 517–23; Acheson, p. 446.

36. For the rejection of the peace plans, see Acheson, p. 419. For Truman's statement, see Truman, *Years of Trial and Hope,* p. 359. For MacArthur's instruction, see *ibid.,* p. 359. See also Tang, p. 569 ff.

37. For the Halle quote, see Halle, pp. 219–20. For MacArthur's orders and the UN resolution, see Acheson, pp. 452–3. For the U.S. response to Chinese warnings, see Halle, pp. 213–25; Acheson, p. 452; Truman, *Years of Trial and Hope,* pp. 361–2. For Chinese intervention, see Allen Whiting: *China Crosses the Yalu* (New York, 1960), pp. 92–116; Tang, pp. 580–6.

38. For the Truman quote, see Truman, *Years of Trial and Hope,* pp. 403–4. For the Acheson quote, see Acheson, pp. 478–85.

39. For the termination of trade with China, see Latourette, p. 134; Senate Armed Services Committee, *Hearings on the Military Situation in Far East,* p. 1725. For Formosa, see *ibid.,* p. 1755. For the recognition of China, see *ibid.,* p. 1820. For Chinese Communist admission to the UN, see *ibid.,* pp. 1935, 2024. For MacArthur's use of the Truman Doctrine, see Truman, *Years of Trial and Hope,* pp. 353–4.

40. For a statement of the difference in attitude toward communism in Southeast Asia in the late 1940's and the 1960's, see Kennan, *Memoirs,* p. 339.

41. For Truman's attitude toward the Internal Security Act of 1950, see the veto message in Truman, *Public Papers,* 1950 p. 254. For Truman's attitude toward the Immigration Act of 1952, see the veto message in *Public Papers,* 1952–3, p. 445.

Bibliography

INTERVIEWS WITH THE AUTHOR

Clark Clifford (1966)
Jennings Randolph (1967)
James Reston (1966)
Stephen J. Spingarn (1966)

UNPUBLISHED SOURCES

American Civil Liberties Union, files. Princeton University Library, Princeton, New Jersey.
Thomas Blaisdell Papers. Truman Library, Independence, Missouri.
Philip C. Brooks: "Oral History of the European Recovery Program," Truman Library, Independence, Missouri.
James F. Byrnes Papers. Clemson University Library, Clemson, South Carolina.
William Clayton Papers. Truman Library, Independence, Missouri.
Clark Clifford Papers. Law offices of Clifford and Miller, Washington, D.C.
Clark Clifford Papers. Truman Library, Independence, Missouri.
Committee for the Marshall Plan, files. Truman Library, Independence, Missouri.
Tom Connelly Papers. Library of Congress, Washington, D.C.
Joseph Davies Papers. Library of Congress, Washington, D.C.
George Elsey Papers. Truman Library, Independence, Missouri.
James V. Forrestal Papers. Princeton University Library, Princeton, New Jersey.
Joseph M. Jones Papers. Truman Library, Independence, Missouri.
Kuklick, Bruce R.: "Commerce and World Order," unpublished doctoral dissertation. University of Pennsylvania, 1968.
Robert Patterson Papers. Library of Congress, Washington, D.C.

Pritchard, Ross: "Will Clayton: Industrial Statesman," unpublished doctoral dissertation. Fletcher School of Law and Diplomacy, Tufts University, 1956.

Samuel I. Rosenman Papers. Truman Library, Independence, Missouri.

John Snyder Papers. Truman Library, Independence, Missouri.

Stephen J. Spingarn Papers. Truman Library, Independence, Missouri.

State Department Files. Historical Division of the State Department, Washington, D.C.

Henry L. Stimson Papers. Yale University Library, New Haven, Connecticut.

Harry S. Truman Papers. Truman Library, Independence, Missouri.

Arthur H. Vandenberg Papers. Clement Library, University of Michigan, Ann Arbor, Michigan.

A. Devitt Vanech Papers. Truman Library, Independence, Missouri.

Yarnell, Al: "The Impact of the Progressive Party on the Democratic Party in the 1948 Presidential Campaign," unpublished doctoral dissertation, University of Washington, 1969.

NEWSPAPERS AND PERIODICALS

The following publications were systematically screened for the periods indicated.

The Daily Worker   February 1947–April 1948
Department of State Bulletin (DSB)   1943–8
FBI Law Enforcement Bulletin   1946–9
The New York Times (TNYT)   February 1947–April 1948
Political Affairs   1945–6
Public Opinion Quarterly (POQ)   1945–8
The Washington Post   February 1947–April 1948
The Washington Times Herald   February 1947–April 1948

PUBLISHED SOURCES

Acheson, Dean G.: *Present at the Creation*. New York: Norton; 1969.

Almond, Gabriel: *The American People and Foreign Policy*. New York: Praeger; 1950.

Alperovitz, Gar: *Atomic Diplomacy: Hiroshima and Potsdam*. New York: Simon & Schuster; 1965.

Andrews, Bert: *Washington Witch Hunt.* New York: Random House; 1948.

Bauer, Raymond A.: *American Business and Public Policy.* New York: Atherton; 1963.

Bentley, Elizabeth: *Out of Bondage.* New York: Devin-Adair Co.; 1951.

Bernstein, Barton J., and A. J. Matusow: *The Truman Administration.* New York: Harper & Row; 1966.

Biddle, Francis: *The Fear of Freedom.* Garden City, N.Y.: Doubleday; 1951.

Blum, John M.: *From the Diaries of Henry Morgenthau, Jr.: Years of War.* Boston: Houghton Mifflin; 1967.

Bohlen, Charles: *The Transformation of American Foreign Policy.* New York: Norton; 1969.

Bontecou, Eleanor: *The Federal Loyalty-Security Program.* Ithaca: Cornell University Press; 1953.

Braden, Thomas W.: "I'm Glad the CIA is Immoral," *The Saturday Evening Post,* May 20, 1967.

Brown, Ralph S., Jr.: *Loyalty and Security.* New Haven: Yale University Press; 1958.

Butcher, Harry C.: *My Three Years with Eisenhower.* New York: Simon & Schuster; 1946.

Byrnes, James F.: *All In One Lifetime.* New York: Harper & Brothers; 1958.

————: *Speaking Frankly.* New York: Harper & Brothers; 1947.

Cantril, Hadley, ed.: *Public Opinion 1935–1946.* Princeton, N.J.: Princeton University Press; 1951.

Carr, Albert Z.: *Truman, Stalin and Peace.* Garden City, N.Y.: Doubleday; 1950.

Carr, Robert K.: *The House Un-American Activities Committee.* Ithaca: Cornell University Press; 1952.

Ciechanowski, Jan: *Defeat in Victory.* Garden City, N.Y.: Doubleday; 1947.

Clay, Lucius: *Decision in Germany.* Garden City, N.Y.: Doubleday; 1950.

Clayton, William: "GATT, The Marshall Plan and OECD," *Political Science Quarterly,* Vol. LXXVIII.

Coles, Harry, and Albert Weinberg: *Civil Affairs: Soldiers Become Governors,* Department of the Army. Washington, D.C.: USGPO; 1964.

Committee for Economic Development: *Economic Aspects of North Atlantic Security;* 1951.

Committee of European Economic Cooperation: *Report: July–September, 1947*. London: HRM Stationary Office; 1947.

Congressional Quarterly Service: *Congress and the Nation: 1945–1964*. Washington, D.C.: Congressional Quarterly Service; 1964.

Connery, Donald S.: *The Scandanavians*. London: Eyre and Spottiswoode; 1966.

Cooke, Alistair: *A Generation on Trial*. New York: Knopf; 1950.

Cooper, Kent: *The Right To Know*. New York: Farrar, Straus & Cudahy; 1956.

Cross, Harold L.: *The People's Right To Know*. New York: Columbia University Press; 1953.

Cushman, Robert: "The President's Loyalty Purge," *Survey Graphic*, May 1947.

Daniels, Jonathan: *The Man of Independence*, Philadelphia: Lippincott; 1950.

Davidson, W. Phillips: "More than Diplomacy," in Lester Markel et al.: *Public Relations and Foreign Policy*. New York: Council on Foreign Relations; 1949.

De Toledano, Ralph: *Seeds of Treason*. Chicago: Henry Regnery; 1962.

Diebold, William: *Trade and Payments in Western Europe*. New York: Harper & Brothers; 1952.

Djilas, Milovan: *Conversations With Stalin*. Translated by Michael B. Petrovich. New York: Harcourt, Brace & World; 1962.

Dolleans, Edouard, and Gerard Dehore: *Histoire du Travail en France*, Vol. II. Paris: Editions Domat Montchrestien; 1955.

Duchacek, Ivo: "Czechoslovakia," in Stephen D. Kertesz, ed.: *The Fate of East Central Europe*. Notre Dame, Ind.: University of Notre Dame Press; 1956.

Eden, Anthony: *Full Circle*. London: Cassell; 1960.

Elliot, William Y., et al.: *The Political Economy of American Foreign Policy*. New York: Holt; 1955.

Feis, Herbert: *Between War and Peace*. Princeton: Princeton University Press; 1960.

———: *The China Tangle*. Princeton: Princeton University Press; 1953.

———: *Churchill, Roosevelt, Stalin*. Princeton: Princeton University Press; 1957.

Forrestal, James V., Millis, Walter, and E. S. Duffield, eds. *The Forrestal Diaries*. New York: Viking; 1951.

Gardner, Richard N.: *Sterling Dollar Diplomacy*. Oxford at the Clarendon Press; 1956.

Gellhorn, Walter: *The States and Subversion*. Ithaca: Cornell University Press; 1952.

Ginzberg, Benjamin: *Rededication to Freedom*. New York: Simon & Schuster; 1959.

Goldman, Eric F.: *The Crucial Decade—and After: America 1945-1960*. New York: Vintage; 1960.

Goodman, Walter: *The Committee*. New York: Farrar, Straus & Giroux; 1968.

Gottlieb, Manuel: *The German Peace Settlement and the Berlin Crisis*. New York: Paine-Whitman; 1960.

Gray, Gordon, et al.: *Report to the President on Foreign Economic Policies*. Washington, D.C.: USGPO; November 1950.

Great Britain, Parliament, "Papers by Command," Paper 7046. London: HRM Stationery Office; 1947.

Halle, Louis: *The Cold War as History*. London: Chatto and Windus; 1967.

Harper, Alan D.: *The Politics of Loyalty*. Westport, Conn.: Greenwood Publishing Co.; 1969.

Hickman, Warren: *Genesis of the European Recovery Program*. Geneva: Popular Printers; 1949.

Higham, John: *Strangers In the Land*. New York: Atheneum; 1965.

Hillman, William: *Mr. President*. New York: Farrar, Straus & Young; 1952.

Hoover, J. Edgar: *Masters of Deceit*. New York: Henry Holt; 1958.
———: "Red Fascism in the United States Today," *American*, February, 1947.

Horowitz, David: *The Free World Colossus*. New York: Hill & Wang; 1965.

Howe, Irving, and Lewis Coser: *The American Communist Party*. Boston: Beacon Press; 1957.

Hughes, H. Stuart: *The United States and Italy*. Cambridge, Mass.: Harvard University Press; 1953.

Hull, Cordell: *Memoirs*, Vol. 2. New York: Macmillan; 1948.

Jones, Joseph M.: *The Fifteen Weeks*. New York: Viking; 1955.

Kahin, George M., and John W. Lewis: *The United States in Vietnam*. New York: Delta; 1969.

Kampelman, Max: *The Communist Party vs. The CIO*. New York: Praeger; 1957.

Kennan, George F.: *Memoirs*. New York: Bantam; 1969.
———: *Russia, the Atom, and the West*. New York: Harper; 1957.

Kertesz, Stephen D., ed.: *The Fate of East Central Europe*. Notre Dame, Ind.: University of Notre Dame Press; 1956.

Kogan, Norman: *Italy and the Allies*. Cambridge, Mass.: Harvard University Press; 1956.

Kolko, Gabriel: *The Politics of War*. New York: Random House; 1968.

Kreisberg, Martin: "Dark Areas of Ignorance," in Lester Markel et al.: *Public Opinion and Foreign Policy*. New York: Council on Foreign Relations; 1949.

LaFeber, Walter: *America, Russia, and the Cold War*. New York: Wiley; 1968.

Lane, Arthur Bliss: *I Saw Poland Betrayed*. New York: Bobbs-Merrill; 1948.

Latham, Earl: *The Communist Controversy in Washington*. Cambridge, Mass.: Harvard University Press; 1966.

Latourette, K. S.: *America's Record in the Far East*. New York: Macmillan; 1950.

Lie, Trygve: *In the Cause of Peace*. New York: Macmillan; 1954.

Lilienthal, David: *The Journals of David Lilienthal: The Atomic Energy Years and The TVA Years*. New York: Harper & Row; 1964.

Lippmann, Walter: *The Cold War*. New York: Harper & Brothers; 1947.

MacDougall, Curtis D.: *Gideon's Army*. New York: Mazzani & Munsell; 1965.

McNaughton, Frank: *Harry Truman, President*. New York: Whittlesee House, McGraw-Hill; 1948.

Markel, Lester, et al.: *Public Opinion and Foreign Policy*. New York: Council on Foreign Relations; 1949.

Mikesell, Raymond F.: *United States Economic Policy and International Relations*. New York: McGraw-Hill; 1952.

Millis, Walter, and E. S. Duffield, eds.: *The Forrestal Diaries*. New York: Viking; 1951.

Moore, Ben. T.: *NATO and the Future of Europe*. New York: Council on Foreign Relations; 1958.

Mosely, Philip E.: "Dismemberment of Germany: The Allied Negotiations from Yalta to Potsdam." *Foreign Affairs*, Vol. 28, No. 3, April 1950.

——: "Hopes and Failures," in Stephen D. Kertesz, ed.: *The Fate of East Central Europe*. Notre Dame, Ind.: University of Notre Dame Press; 1956.

——: "The Occupation of Germany," in *Foreign Affairs*, Vol. 28, No. 4, July 1950.

National Foreign Trade Council, Inc.: *Franco-American Economic Relations*. New York, 1947.

Nixon, Richard M.: *Six Crises.* Garden City, N.Y.: Doubleday; 1962.

Nourse, Edwin G.: *Economics in the Public Service.* New York: Harcourt; 1953.

Ogden, August Raymond: *The Dies Committee.* Washington, D.C.: The Catholic University of America Press; 1943.

Organization of European Economic Cooperation: *Report on the European Recovery Program.* Paris, 1948.

Paige, Glen D.: *The Korean Decision.* New York: Free Press; 1968.

Penrose, E. F.: *Economic Planning for the Peace.* Princeton: Princeton University Press; 1953.

Perkins, Frances: *The Roosevelt I Knew.* New York: Viking; 1946.

Phillips, Cabell: *The Truman Presidency.* New York: Macmillan; 1966.

————: "The Mirror Called Congress," in Lester Markel et al.: *Public Opinion and Foreign Policy.* New York: Council on Foreign Relations; 1949.

President's Advisory Commission on Universal Training: *Report.* Washington, D.C.: USGPO; 1947.

President's Commission on Higher Education: *Report.* Washington, D.C.: USGPO; 1947.

President's Committee on Foreign Aid: *European Recovery and American Aid.* Washington, D.C.: USGPO; 1947.

Preston, William, Jr.: *Aliens and Dissenters.* Cambridge, Mass.: Harvard University Press; 1963.

Price, Harry Bayard: *The Marshall Plan and Its Meaning.* Ithaca: Cornell University Press; 1955.

Radosh, Ronald: *American Labor and U.S. Foreign Policy.* New York: Random House; 1969.

Raskin, Marcus, and Richard Barnett: *After Twenty Years.* New York: Vintage; 1966.

Reston, James: *The Artillery of the Press.* New York: Harper & Row; 1967.

————: "The Number One Voice," in Lester Markel et al.: *Public Opinion and Foreign Policy.* New York: Council on Foreign Relations; 1949.

Ridgway, Matthew: *Soldier.* New York: Harper & Brothers; 1956.

Rieber, Alfred J.: *Stalin and the French Communist Party.* New York: Columbia University Press; 1962.

Rogow, Arnold A.: *James Forrestal.* New York: Macmillan; 1963.

Ross, Irwin: *The Loneliest Campaign.* New York: New American Library; 1968.

Schilling, Warner R., et al.: *Strategy, Politics, and Defense Budgets.* New York: Columbia University Press; 1962.

Schmidt, Karl: *Henry Wallace: Quixotic Crusade 1948.* Syracuse: Syracuse University Press; 1960.

Sherwood, Robert: *Roosevelt and Hopkins.* New York: Harper & Brothers; 1948.

Shulman, Marshall: *Stalin's Foreign Policy Reappraised.* Cambridge, Mass.: Harvard University Press; 1963.

Steinberg, Alfred: *The Man from Missouri.* New York: Putnam; 1962.

Stimson, Henry L., and McGeorge Bundy: *On Active Service in War and Peace.* New York: Harper & Brothers; 1948.

Stripling, Robert E.: *The Red Plot Against America.* Drexel Hill, Pa.: Bell Publishing Co.; 1949.

Summers, Robert: *Federal Information Controls in Peacetime.* New York: H. W. Wilson; 1949.

Tang Tsou: *America's Failure in China,* 2 Vols. Chicago: University of Chicago Press; 1963.

Theoharis, Athan: "The Escalation of the Loyalty Program," in Barton J. Bernstein: *Politics and Policies of the Truman Administration.* Chicago: Quadrangle; 1970.

Truman, Harry S.: *Economic Report of the President.* Washington, D.C.: USGPO; 1948.

————: *Memoirs.* 2 Vols.: *Year of Decisions* (1955) and *Years of Trial and Hope* (1956). Garden City, N.Y.: Doubleday; 1956.

————: *Public Papers.* Washington, D.C.: USGPO; 1945–51.

United Nations Economic and Social Council: *Report of the First Session of the Preparatory Committee of the UN Conference on Trade and Employment,* E/PC/T/33. London, 1946.

————: *Report of the Temporary Subcommission on Economic Reconstruction of Devastated Areas,* E/156. September 18, 1946.

United States v. *Dennis et al.,* U.S. Court of Appeals, Second Circuit, Vol. 17. New York: Adams Press; 1949.

U.S. Attorney General: *Annual Report: 1948.* Washington, D.C.: USGPO; 1949.

————: *Annual Report: 1949.* Washington, D.C.: USGPO; 1950.

U.S. Congress, hearings of the House Committee on Appropriations: *Third Supplemental Appropriation for 1948.* 80:2.

————: *Justice Department Budget for 1948.* 80:1.

————: *Justice Department Budget for 1949.* 80:1.

U.S. Congress, hearings of the House Committee on the Civil Service: *Report of Investigation with Respect to Employee Loy-*

alty and Employment Practices in the Government of the United States. 79:2.

U.S. Congress, hearings of the House Committee on Foreign Affairs: *Assistance to Greece and Turkey*. 80:1.

———: *United States Foreign Policy for Postwar Recovery*. 80:1 and 2.

———: *Report on S2202*. 80:2.

U.S. Congress, hearings of the House Committee on Un-American Activities: *HR4422 and HR4581*. 80:2. Proposed legislation to curb or control the Communist Party of the United States.

———: *Regarding Communist Subversion in Hollywood*. 80:1.

———: *Regarding Hanns Eisler*. 80:1.

———: *Regarding Leon Josephson and Samuel Liptzen*. 80:1.

———: *Interim Report on Hearings Regarding Communist Espionage in the United States Government*. 80:2.

———: *Report on HR5852*. 80:2.

———: *Transcript of Proceedings: February 6, 1947*. 80:1.

U.S. Congress, hearings of the House Committee on Ways and Means: *Extension of Reciprocal Trade Agreements Act*. 81:1.

U.S. Congress, hearings of the Senate Committee on Armed Services: *Military Situation in the Far East*. 82:1.

———: *Universal Military Training*. 80:2.

U.S. Congress, hearings of the Senate Committee on Finance: *Extension of Reciprocal Trade Agreements Act*. 80:2.

———: *Extension of Reciprocal Trade Agreements Act*. 82:1.

U.S. Congress, hearings of the Senate Committee on Foreign Relations: *European Recovery Program: Basic Documents*. 80:1.

———: *Assistance to Greece and Turkey*. 80:1.

———: *European Interim Aid Act of 1947*. 80:1.

———: *European Recovery Program*. 80:2.

U.S. Congress, Senate Committee on the Judiciary: *Hearings before the Subcommittee on Constitutional Rights*. 84:2.

———: *Hearings before the Subcommittee on Immigration and Naturalization, July 15, 1949*. 81:1.

———: *Hearings on HR5852*. 80:2.

———: *Hearings on S1832*. 81:1.

U.S. Council of Economic Advisers: *Annual Economic Review*. Washington, D.C.: USGPO; 1950.

———: *Annual Economic Review*. Washington, D.C.: USGPO; 1951.

———: *Midyear Economic Review*. Washington, D.C.: USGPO; July, 1949.

U.S. Council of Economic Advisers: *Midyear Economic Review,* Washington, D.C.: USGPO; July, 1950.

U.S. Department of Justice: *Press Releases 1948.* Washington, D.C., 1948.

U.S. Department of State: *Foreign Relations of the United States (FRUS).* Vol. 3, 1944: *The British Commonwealth and Europe.* Washington, D.C.: USGPO; 1965.

————: *FRUS.* Vol. 6, 1946: *Eastern Europe: The Soviet Union.* Washington, D.C.: USGPO; 1969.

————: *FRUS.* Vol. 7, 1946: *The Near East and Africa.* Washington, D.C.: USGPO; 1969.

————: *FRUS.* Vol. 1: *The Potsdam Conference.* Washington, D.C.: USGPO; 1960.

————: European Recovery Program/Economic Cooperation Administration: *Country Studies,* 16 Volumes. Washington, D.C.: USGPO; 1949.

U.S. Economic Cooperation Administration: *Report of the ECA-Commerce Mission.* Washington, D.C.: USGPO; 1949.

————: *Role of the ECA in Southeast Asia.* Washington, D.C.: USGPO; 1951.

————: *Seventh Report to Congress.* Washington, D.C.: USGPO; 1950.

U.S. Federal Reserve: "The British Crisis," *Federal Reserve Bulletin,* Vol. 33, No. 9, September 1947.

U.S. Federal Security Agency: *Annual Report.* Washington, D.C.: USGPO; 1949.

U.S. Office of Education: *Annual Report.* Washington, D.C.: USGPO; 1948.

Van Der Beugel, Ernest H.: *From Marshall Aid to Atlantic Partnership.* Amsterdam: Elsevier Publishing Co.; 1966.

Vandenberg, Arthur H., Jr.: *The Private Papers of Senator Vandenberg.* Boston: Houghton Mifflin; 1952.

Vigneras, Marcel: *Rearming the French.* Department of the Army. Washington, D.C.: USGPO; 1957.

Vinacke, Harold M.: *The United States and the Far East.* New York: Knopf; 1952.

Warren, Sidney: *The President as World Leader.* Philadelphia: Lippincott; 1964.

Watt, David: "Withdrawal from Greece," in Michael Sissons and Philip French: *Age of Austerity.* London: Hodder and Stoughton; 1963.

Wedemeyer, Albert C.: *Wedemeyer Reports.* New York: Henry Holt; 1958.

Welles, Sumner: *Where Are We Heading*. New York: Harper & Brothers; 1946.

Werth, Alexander: *France, 1940–1955*. New York: Henry Holt; 1956.

Westerfield, H. Bradford: *Foreign Policy and Party Politics*. New Haven: Yale University Press; 1955.

Whiting, Allen: *China Crosses the Yalu*. New York: Macmillan; 1960.

Wiggins, James R.: *Freedom or Secrecy*. New York: Oxford University Press; 1964.

Xydis, Stephen D.: *Greece and the Great Powers*. Thessalonike: Institute for Balkan Studies; 1963.

Young, Roland: *Congressional Politics in the Second World War*. New York: Columbia University Press; 1956.

Index

Index

vii